THE WOMAN QUESTION

THE WOMAN QUESTION

SECOND EDITION

EDITED BY
MARY EVANS

SAGE Publications
London • Thousand Oaks • New Delhi

Second edition published 1994

The first edition of *The Woman Question*, containing a different
selection of readings, was published in 1982 by Fontana Paperbacks.

SAGE Publications Ltd
6 Bonhill Street
London EC2A 4PU

SAGE Publications Inc
2455 Teller Road
Thousand Oaks, California 91320

SAGE Publications India Pvt Ltd
32, M-Block Market
Greater Kailash – I
New Delhi 110 048

British Library Cataloguing in Publication data

Woman Question. - 2Rev.ed
  I. Evans, Mary
  305.42

  ISBN 0–8039–8747–1
  ISBN 0–8039–8748–X Pbk

Library of Congress catalog card number 93–87757

Typeset by Photoprint, Torquay, Devon
Printed in Great Britain by The Cromwell Press Ltd,
Broughton Gifford, Melksham, Wiltshire

Contents

Acknowledgements

The idea for a new edition of *The Woman Question* came from Karen Phillips and I would like to thank her, and Louise Murray, at Sage Publications for their help and assistance in completing this volume. Louise Murray read the manuscript with great zeal and I am most grateful to her.

I would also like to thank Carole Davies, Hilary Joce and Rebecca Edwards of Darwin College secretarial office at the University of Kent who patiently typed and retyped my copy. My thanks also go to the students on the MA in Women's Studies, whose reading of many of the items included here helped to maintain my interest and excitement in the issues raised.

The editor and publishers wish to thank the following for permission to use copyright material: Mary Louise Adams for 'There's No Place Like Home: On the Place of Identity in Feminist Politics', *Feminist Review*, 31, 1989, pp. 23–33; Kum-Kum Bhavnani and Margaret Coulson for 'Transforming Socialist-Feminism: The Challenge of Racism', *Feminist Review*, 20, 1986, pp. 81–92; Blackwell Publishers for Jennifer Temkin, 'Women, Rape and Law Reform', in Sylvana Tomaselli and Roy Porter (eds), *Rape: A Historical and Social Enquiry*, 1986, pp. 16–40; and material from Carole Pateman, *The Sexual Contract*, 1988, pp. 219–34, Polity Press; Irene Bruegel for 'Sex and Race in the Labour Market', *Feminist Review*, 32, 1989, pp. 50–68; Jayne Egerton for 'Out But Not Down: Lesbians' Experience of Housing', *Feminist Review*, 36, 1990, pp. 75–88; Harvard University Press for material from Catharine A. MacKinnon, *Toward a Feminist Theory of the State*, 1989, copyright © 1989 by Catharine A. MacKinnon; Madhu Kishwar for 'A Horror of Isms', abridged from 'Why I do Not Call Myself a Feminist', *Manushi*, 61, 1990, Nov.–Dec., pp. 2–8; Elaine Markson Literary Agency Inc. on behalf of the author for material from Andrea Dworkin, *Pornography: Men Possessing Women*, Dutton, New York, 1989, copyright © 1989, 1994 by Andrea Dworkin, all rights reserved; The Merlin Press Ltd for Lynne Segal, 'False Promises – Anti-Pornography Feminism', in Ralph Miliband and Leo Penitch (eds), *The Socialist Register*, 1993; Oxford University Press for Marie Lauret, 'Feminism and Culture – the Movie: A Critical Overview of Writing on Women and Cinema', *Women: A Cultural Review*, 2 (1), 1991, pp. 52–69; Donna Haraway, 'Reading Buchi Emecheta: Contests for Women's Experience in Women's Studies', *Women: A Cultural Review*, 1 (3), 1990, pp. 240–55; Sandra Harding, 'Feminism and Theories of Scientific Knowledge', *Women: A Cultural Review*, 1 (1), 1990, pp. 87–98; and Selma James, 'Woman's Unwaged Work – the Heart of the Informal

Sector', *Women: A Cultural Review*, 2 (3), 1991, pp. 267–71; Pergamon Press Ltd for Liz Stanley, 'Recovering *Women* in History from Feminist Deconstructionism', *Women's Studies International*, 13 (1/2), 1990, pp. 151–7; Radical Philosophy for Kate Soper, 'Feminism, Humanism and Postmodernism', *Radical Philosophy*, 55 (Summer), 1990, pp. 11–17; Routledge for Ann Phoenix, 'Narrow Definitions of Culture: the Case of Early Motherhood', in S. Westwood and P. Bhachu (eds), *Enterprising Women*, 1988, pp. 153–75; and material from Carol Smart, *Feminism and the Power of Law*, 1989, pp. 114–37; Charlotte Sheedy Literary Agency on behalf of the author's Estate for material from Audre Lorde, *Sister Outsider*, The Crossing Press, 1984, pp. 114–23; Felly Nkweto Simmonds for '*She's Gotta Have It*: The Representation of Black Female Sexuality on Film', *Feminist Review*, 29, 1988, pp. 10–22; The University of Chicago Press for Carol Cohn, 'Sex and Death in the Rational World of Defense Intellectuals', *Signs*, 12 (4), 1987, pp. 687–712; and Patricia Hill Collins, 'The Social Construction of Black Feminist Thought', *Signs*, 14 (4), 1989, pp. 745–73; Verso for Jacqueline Rose, *Sexuality in the Field of Vision*, Verso, 1986, pp. 83–103; and Maxine Molyneux, 'The "Woman Question" in the Age of Perestroika', *New Left Review*, 183, 1990, pp. 23–49; The Women's Press for material from Sheila Jeffreys, *Anticlimax*, 1990, pp. 287–16.

Every effort has been made to trace all the copyright holders, but if any have been inadvertently overlooked the publishers will be pleased to make the necessary arrangement at the first opportunity.

Introduction

Since the publication of *The Woman Question* in 1982 feminism and feminist politics have undergone a transformation. The issue of race has become central to feminist politics, the privacy of the household (always questionable to feminists) has been further breached by the continued public discussion of domestic violence and the physical and emotional abuse of children, and theoretical discussions about women have become informed by innovations in the use of psychoanalysis and in social theory. Equally important, the political context in which we all live has changed dramatically; the Cold War has ended and the national and ideological map of Europe has been remade. Apparent certainties about national boundaries and international alliances have disappeared, and what has emerged in their place is a set of shifting coalitions – some of which, as in the case of the disintegration of Yugoslavia, have given rise to bloody and bitter civil wars. To assume, as was possible in 1982, the continuity of West/East divisions, is now impossible.

Nevertheless, despite all these radical changes, many of which are still entirely unresolved, there has been relatively little change in two important social relationships which are of central concern here. The first is that of the continuing social inequality between women and men. The second sex is still precisely that: throughout the West women have a lower level of higher and professional education than men, they are paid less, have less social power and are still assumed to have the primary, if not exclusive, responsibility for the care of children and dependent relatives. The 'new' woman remains just as much a fiction (or no doubt in some quarters a spectre) as the 'new' man. Women in some Western societies may have made some inroads in some portions of junior/middle management, but to all effects and purposes the public world, of institutional power, remains dominated by men. Feminists have come to question why this should be,[1] but in theoretical terms the answers still remain much the same as they have always been: the various pressures of motherhood make participation in public life impossible for women. For women without children, the 'fact' of women's domestic responsibilities then becomes an ideology which marginalizes those women who remain outside this pattern.

It is thus largely mistaken to assume that the battles of feminism in 1982 have been fought and won. Some aspects of the social construction of gender which were deeply oppressive to women have started to shift (for example changes in the way in which victims of rape are treated and legal perceptions of the sexual relationship between husband and wife) but the organization of the institutional world remains one which is congruent only with traditionally male patterns of social life. Despite the continuing collapse – at least in Britain and the United States – of the 'traditional' nuclear family, in which the man was the breadwinner, the rise in the number of divorces (most of which are initiated by women) and the numbers of children brought up in female-headed households, the Western state remains consistently unable to abandon its fantasies of family life in favour of a recognition of both historical and contemporary reality.

Whilst many Western governments continue to ignore the changed experiences and choices of their populations, a second social relationship (which affects both women and men) remains, that between countries of the 'North' and the 'South'. Development agencies (and indeed the World Bank) have recently publicly recognized, and stated, that the key to population control (and to a certain extent rural and urban poverty) is the education of women. What this statement formally acknowledges is a fact long known to feminists – that while much of the world's population is, by Western standards, poor, the poorest of the poor are women. A famous feminist postcard points out that:

> Women
> constitute *half* the world's
> population,
> perform nearly *two-thirds*
> of its work hours,
> receive *one-tenth* of the world's income
> and own less than *one-hundredth*
> of the world's property.[2]

The information on which this text is based is taken from a 1980 United Nations report. Little has changed since that date, although in the crucial area of public debates and discussions about development the issue of gender has become central. The poor, it is acknowledged, are particularly women, and just as social and material inequalities exist between the sexes in the 'North' so they exist, and are magnified tenfold, in countries of the South.

So in discussing women, and gender relations, in 1992 we do so in a context which assumes an unequal and exploitative relationship between North and South and distinct inequalities between the women and the men in different countries. But what has also followed from an acknowledgement of the diverse inequalities between women and men is the difficulty in developing a single feminist politics. Let us take just one example of the problems implicit in this issue. In Western societies an almost taken-for-granted tenet of feminism has been a critique of the family, since it is seen as the site of patriarchal control and power. For many feminists, the current instability in 'family' membership in the West is symptomatic of women's increasing resistance to a social form which does not meet their needs. Why, and whether, this is the case is a matter for debate. What is assumed, however, by women outside the West is that feminism is in some fundamental sense 'against' the family. The Western 'export' of feminism, whilst acceptable in terms of such issues as the access of women to education, autonomous contraception and political rights, founders on the question of the extent to which feminism is actually incompatible with deeply held and regarded ties of family and kin. As the article by Madhu Kishwar suggests, resistance to the label 'feminist' is extremely important for women outside the West, since the label carries with it a set of assumptions that many women would wish to reject.

That reaction to feminism is not dissimilar to a tradition of dissent from feminism in the West. The great nineteenth-century campaigns in the West for suffrage, education and contraception all met resistance, not just from men but often from women. Several famous, and influential, nineteenth-century women (for example George Eliot, Florence Nightingale and Queen Victoria) went on record as condemning the 'madness' of women's rights. For George Eliot, changes in suffrage threatened the very nature of women's being and were such as to endanger the particular character of femininity. Although she did not express her opposition in the terms of the battle over the control of the construction of the feminine, this reaction was symptomatic of later, fierce debates about the nature of the 'feminine' and the 'masculine'. Whilst George Eliot maintained the right of women to determine many aspects of their situation, she remained implacable on the issue of absolute, and natural, differences between the sexes.

The issue of the construction of gender identity which was first raised in the nineteenth century shows no sign of disappearing. The impact of biological difference on behaviour, understanding and interest remains crucial, and central, to feminism. It is difficult to contest the statement that 'biology is destiny' since the evidence to demonstrate the case is so compelling. At the same time it is equally difficult to ignore the many ways in which a fixed gender identity has, for centuries, been contested. The rediscovery of the history of both female and male homosexuality demonstrates that the biological differences between women and men have been interpreted in a number of distinct ways. The history of sexuality (post-Foucault) has been organized in terms of a theory of shifting 'discourses', in which a multiplicity of sexualities is deemed to have existed, with constantly changing norms and codes of behaviour. So a consensus has emerged in which it is agreed that there have always been social meanings attached to biological difference, but these meanings have been the site of fierce battles and diverse interpretations.

Within this history of the battlegrounds and skirmishes of the war, not just between the sexes, but of control of sexed identity, feminism has made a substantial, but varied, contribution. For feminists, the fact of biological difference (particularly post-Freud) was deeply problematic, since as long as difference existed, so (apparently) would the congruence of female biology and female inferiority. The very body in which feminists themselves lived was one labelled by men as 'feeble' and 'unstable'. A considerable tradition read difference as inferiority/superiority. Men, for example, were the sex capable of advanced moral reasoning whilst women had innate qualities of nurturance and care for others. Within this context, it was inevitable that women would wish to demonstrate that they were in every way the equal of men, and that the impact of biological difference was much exaggerated.

The problem of reading 'equality' in a way which does not automatically imply 'the same' is one which has consistently dogged feminists, and indeed all students of gender. The case for demonstrating that women have the same competences as men is overwhelming in a society where measured and assessed abilities constitute the basis of entry into paid labour. But asking (indeed, in the case of some state socialist societies actually demanding) that women play an 'equal' role in the workforce entirely ignores the domestic responsibilities of women and leaves exploitative gender relations and ideologies largely untouched. The long battles fought by feminists for civil rights and 'equality' in public life have, in fact, come to appear misconceived in the light of feminism's own attempt to end the division between the public and the private and to demonstrate the impact of the latter on the former. Equality, in the light of what feminists now assume about the gendered construction of apparently gender-neutral terms, is one in the considerable line of concepts which are regarded with some suspicion.

Thus, in the last twenty years Western feminism has been increasingly preoccupied with the demonstration that all social life is gendered. The political fury and intense passion of works of the early 1970s (such as *The Female Eunuch* and *Sexual Politics*) in which it was argued that a powerful misogyny dominated Western culture has given way to more detailed studies of the ways in which culture and knowledge have been formed in gendered ways. The very values on which Western intellectual life prides itself – reason, rationality, objective knowledge – have come to be regarded, by authors such as Sandra Harding, as masculinist constructions. The original radical feminist thesis – most vividly argued by Mary Daly and Adrienne Rich – that women are absolutely different from men, is now being developed in terms of discussions of the distinctions between women and men in the ways in which both sexes construct knowledge. The impetus to do this has in the past come from a reacceptance by feminism of Freud and psychoanalysis. No longer regarded as a woman-hater, Freud (and a long tradition of later analysts) has been brought in from the theoretical cold and extensively used in feminist literary criticisms and epistemology. The different accommo- dations that women and men have to make with their biology have come to be perceived as a rich source of the explanation of perceptual differences. In a sense, the political confidence given to women by feminism has made possible the intellectual confidence to examine theories and ideas which were previously assumed to be merely derogatory to women.

From this integration of psychoanalysis into feminism (and particularly feminist literary criticism) has come feminist work of great sophistication and complexity, which is reflected in the following pages. What this volume also attempts to do is provide a documentation of the inequalities and injustices which the majority of the world's women face. Just as there is a place within feminism for sophisticated analysis (derived from and relevant to the particular concerns of the highly educated) so there is a place for statements about the material reality in which most women live. 'Crude materialism' has often been attacked by feminists who wish to distance themselves from simple-minded theories. Unfortunately, materialism – crude and frequently cruel – is precisely the condition in which many women live, and making links with, and space for the expression of, that experience is an essential part of the organization of the following pages.

Notes

1. In particular, feminists have come to see the world of paid work as deeply gendered. See, for example, the discussion in Sylvia Walby, *Theorizing Patriarchy: Unsettling Relations* (Blackwell, Oxford, 1990), pp. 150–201.

2. The Rio de Janeiro conference (the 'Global Forum') adopted as a major principle the following statement: 'Women have a vital role in environmental management and development. Their full participation is therefore essential to achieve sustainable development.'

SECTION I

THE CONTEXT OF CONTEMPORARY FEMINISM

It is now two hundred years since the publication of Mary Wollstonecraft's *A Vindication of the Rights of Woman*,[1] and in those years the world has undergone numerous social transformations. Wollstonecraft, writing at the crest of the wave of Enlightenment optimism, was innocent of the experience of living in an imperial industrial society or within the shadow of world wars and the Holocaust. Her conceptual world knew nothing of the transformations of understanding which would result from these experiences, or the interpretations by Marx and Freud which would radically shift understanding of both the social and the emotional world.

But for all the distance which now separates feminists from Mary Wollstonecraft much remains which unites the present with the past. As suggested in the Introduction, despite the changes which have occurred as a result of industrialization, the nature of the relationship of women to both men and the social world has remained in many ways the same. Women in the West are now able to control their fertility in ways unknown to Mary Wollstonecraft, and all women, like all men, receive – at least in Western societies – a minimum of ten years' free state education. Women (again – and emphatically – in the West rather than universally) have far more extensive formal and civil freedoms (to travel, vote, own property and so on) than was the case in 1792. At the same time, and as numerous feminists have pointed out, women remain primarily responsible for the care and nurturance of children and frequently of other kin. Freud's assertion that 'biology is destiny' still largely holds true for the majority of women in the world, even though the nature and condition of that destiny differs widely.

The first wave of feminism, which has been so admirably discussed and represented in Maggie Humm's reader, *Feminisms*,[2] is usually dated, in both Britain and the United States, from the middle of the nineteenth century. The concerns of this period in feminism's history are generally assumed to be the emancipation of women from a dependent, and subordinate, civil status and their incorporation into the modern industrial state as citizens on the same terms as men. That statement, however, whilst accurate as a description of some of the campaigns of some women has now come to be seen as a partial and oversimplistic account of the history of women, and women's struggles. The problem is, of course, that the assumption of a 'core' canon of feminism – derived largely from the West, and from particular countries in the West at that – is as fraught with difficulties, contradictions and inadequacies as is the acceptance of *any* canon. In feminism, as in any other contexts, the canon has been deconstructed, and what was once seen as 'the' tradition of feminism has now come to be seen as nothing more than (or as much as) a tradition representing the values, interests and concerns of white, middle-class Western women. If we take just one classic feminist text, Virginia Woolf's *A Room of One's Own*,[3] the problems of the classic canon becomes clear. The text assumes both literacy and individual aspiration; moreover, it says nothing about the source of that much-quoted £500 a year or the relationship of the woman with £500 a year to women with no pounds a year. Passionately and elegantly Woolf makes the case for the equality of bourgeois women with bourgeois men, but at no point is there a suggestion that the wealth and privilege of some women is related to the deprivation of others – both within and outside a specific culture.

The recognition of the relations implicit in imperialism and the global economy, and the gradual acceptance by many people in the West that the wealth of 'the North' is dependent on the poverty of 'the South' has now made it more difficult for feminists to read Woolf, De Beauvoir and other great names of the first wave of feminism in the same way. The achievements of these women are still widely respected and recognized, but now the context in which they wrote, and the issues to which they chose to give priority, are part of the discussion. The reappraisal of other strands in feminist history is equally well advanced. The famous bestselling texts of the 'second wave' of feminism (such as Germaine Greer's *The Female Eunuch* and Kate Millett's *Sexual Politics*) were primarily concerned with the experiences of white, university-educated women.[4] But at the same time as these and other works were receiving considerable attention another, and equally important, development was taking place in feminism which chronicled the concerns of women outside the charmed Western circle of higher education and professional life. These books – about the experiences of working-class women, women of colour and women of ethnic minorities – spoke of a way of life of struggle and marginality. Sheila Rowbotham's *Hidden from History*, and the early work of bell hooks, Audre Lorde and Alice Walker, all helped to establish the diversity of women's lives.[5]

Thus the history and 'the canon' of feminism is as problematic as that of any other traditional academic discipline or social movement. Whilst the well-known figures of the canon attract public attention and establish the issue of sexual difference and sexual inequality on the social agenda they do so in ways which for many women are as suspect (or almost as suspect) as the traditional forms of the patriarchal and dominant culture. One theme in particular which has always run through mainstream, bourgeois feminism is that of autonomy and independence. From Wollstonecraft onwards, middle-class feminists (and men such as John Stuart Mill and Engels who have been associated, in one way or another, with the feminist project) have argued for the right of women to be 'free' and 'independent'.[6] De Beauvoir's *The*

Second Sex concludes with passages invoking the ideal life for women as that of the single, urban woman with a professional job.[7] As various critics have pointed out, this version of a feminist heaven is for many women entirely irrelevant or unacceptable.[8] It is, whatever we may conclude about it as a model of the good life, a blueprint for reality which is constructed out of white, middle-class Western life. For women with children, for women in other cultures, for women whose concerns are not those of the professional middle class, this view of the perfect existence is unacceptable.

So as much as writers like De Beauvoir have demonstrated the force of sexual inequality (as they see it) other equally feminist writers have deconstructed the values and aspirations of particular feminist analyses and solutions. Feminism as a whole is therefore placed in a situation in which there is no doubt that the word 'woman' is of crucial organizing significance, but is equally beset with complex issues of difference. Many of these issues relating to 'difference' are explored in the following section, but in so far as the readings here are concerned what remains important is the assertion by women of different cultures of their different interests. Equally, and no less important, is the discussion by Kate Soper of the impact of post-modernism on feminism.[9]

When Millett et al. wrote, in the late 1960s and early 1970s, their passionate critiques of Western culture largely assumed a set of fixed assumptions about the world. But even as they wrote, the very world which they were so critical of was rapidly changing. Feminism's central argument in the early 1970s was to attack the universality of the central ideas of post-Enlightenment thinking. Yet this attack can now be seen as part of the more general project which has now become known as postmodernism, and which, as Sabina Lovibond points out, 'refuses to conceive of humanity as a unitary subject striving towards the goal of perfect coherence (in its common stock of beliefs) or of perfect cohesion and stability (in its political practice)'.[10] The disappearance of the coherent, single subject was, of course, entirely attuned to feminism's own attack on masculinity and men, as the norm, and the normal, of human history and understanding. However, whilst that much of postmodernism was coincident with feminism's agenda, the issue of a multiplicity of political projects raised more difficult questions, and questions which still remain problematic for feminism.

The complexity of constructing a feminist agenda has become one which is central to feminist politics. Few people today would have the confidence to embark upon a definitive statement of feminist politics; for women in the West, the impact of postmodernism has disrupted absolute certainties about definitions of feminism. However, outside the West – in the 'South' and in the once Soviet-dominated states of Eastern Europe – it is possible to see, in the very absence of feminism, the meaning of feminism. This paradox, of revelation through absence, is part of contemporary feminism. While feminists in the West wrestle with questions arising from 'multiple realities' and 'identity politics' feminists in other countries are attempting to construct a feminist agenda in cultures where the rights of the individual had always been seen as subordinate to those of the state, or the collectivity. In this difference we can see clearly how much of the organizing force of Western feminism came, in the nineteenth and twentieth centuries from the tradition of individual rights and liberty. This tradition brought to people the possibilities of political and civil liberty, but at the same time it contributed towards the construction of a culture which minimized the interdependence of individuals. The feminist ideal of sisterhood provided a vision of the collective ideal in politics and personal life, but the fragility and instability of the concept – when challenged by differences of class and race – still makes it of considerable political and intellectual difficulty. The following readings outline some of the difficulties in the context of changed, and changing, perceptions and understandings of the world.

Notes

1. Mary Wollstonecraft's *A Vindication of the Rights of Woman* was published in 1792. For secondary material see Jennifer Lorch, *Mary Wollstonecraft: The Making of a Radical Feminist* (Berg, Oxford, 1990) and Virginia Sapiro, *A Vindication of Political Virtue: The Political Theory of Mary Wollstonecraft* (University of Chicago Press, London, 1992).

2. Maggie Humm, *Feminisms* (Harvester Wheatsheaf, Hemel Hempstead, 1992).

3. Virginia Woolf, *A Room of One's Own* (Penguin, Harmondsworth, 1984).

4. Germaine Greer, *The Female Eunuch* (Grafton Books, London, 1970); Kate Millett, *Sexual Politics* (Virago, London, 1977).

5. Sheila Rowbotham, *Hidden from History* (Pluto, London, 1973).

6. See the discussion on Engels in J. Sayers, M. Evans and N. Redclift (eds), *Engels Revisited* (Tavistock, London, 1987).

7. The implications of this have been discussed by Margaret Walters in 'The rights and wrongs of women', in Ann Oakley and J. Mitchell (eds), *The Rights and Wrongs of Women* (Penguin, Harmondsworth, 1976), pp. 304–76.

8. Recent 'readings' of De Beauvoir include Jane Heath, *Simone de Beauvoir* (Harvester Wheatsheaf, Hemel Hempstead, 1989) and Sonia Kruks, 'Gender and subjectivity: Simone de Beauvoir and contemporary feminism', *Signs*, 18, 1 (1992), pp. 89–110.

9. For further general reading on postmodernism see David Harvey, *The Condition of Postmodernity* (Blackwell, Oxford, 1990). For a discussion of feminism and postmodernism see Linda Nicholson (ed.), *Feminism/Postmodernism* (Routledge, London, 1990). Central to discussions of women and modernity is *Gynesis* by Alice Jardine (Cornell, London, 1985).

10. Sabina Lovibond, 'Feminism and postmodernism', *New Left Review*, 178 (1989), p. 6.

Feminism, Humanism and Postmodernism

Kate Soper

I shall not begin, as I probably should, by offering to define my terms. Instead, I shall acknowledge that I have brought together three concepts admitted on all sides to be well-nigh indefinable. Or, if they are definable, they are so only by reference to a particular thinker's usage (Lyotard's or Huyssens' or Baudrillard's of 'postmodernism', Heidegger's or Wolf's or Foucault's of 'humanism', De Beauvoir's or Kristeva's or Wittig's of 'feminism', etc. – and this is to speak only in the French or German of the last fifty years . . .). Yet we know, too, even as we recognize our reliance on this more specific anchorage of terms, that the concepts of 'postmodernism', 'humanism' and 'feminism' also embrace the sum of these more particular discourses – and that a large part of their usefulness lies in this generality of reference. So I shall not begin with further definitions, but with an appeal to intuition: an appeal to that vague sense which I am assuming anyone at all interested in reading a piece such as this will already have of these terms.

For the point of their conjunction, really, is to signal a problem, and a problem which I *shall* here attempt to make as explicit as possible. Postmodernist argument (or the argument of 'modernity', as others have wanted to call it)[1] has issued a number of challenges: to the idea that we can continue to think, write and speak of our culture as representing a continuous development and progress; to the idea that humanity is proceeding towards a telos of 'emancipation' and 'self-realization'; to the idea that we can invoke any universal subjectivity in speaking about the human condition. Lyotard has argued, for example, that neither of the two major forms of *grands récits* ('grand narratives') by which in the past we have legitimized the quest for knowledge can any longer perform that function. Neither the instrumental narrative of emancipation which justifies science and technology by reference to the poverty and injustice they must eventually eliminate, nor the purist defence of knowledge accumulation as something inherently beneficial, can any longer command the belief essential to warding off scepticism about the purpose and value of the

From *Radical Philosophy*, 55 (Summer), 1990, pp. 11–17.

techno-sciences. With this scepticism has gone a loss of confidence in the whole idea of human 'progress' viewed as a process more or less contemporaneous with Western-style 'civilization', and a calling into question of the emancipatory themes so central to the liberal, scientific and Marxist/socialist discourses of the nineteenth century.

This loss of credulity is in turn associated with the collapse of 'humanism'. There are two aspects to this collapse, both of them registered in much of the writing, theoretical and literary, of recent times. Firstly (though this aspect of the critique of humanism was launched by the humanist Karl Marx, and continued within a tradition of socialist-humanist thinking), there is an acknowledgement of the partial and excluding quality of the supposedly universal 'we' of much humanist discourse. Secondly, and partly as a consequence of this exposure of liberal hypocrisies and the ethnocentricity of Western humanism, there has been a refusal of the 'we' which lurks in the unifying discourse of the dialectic: a rejection of all attempts to find a sameness in otherness. Instead, we have been witness to a theoretical celebration of difference, a resistance to all synthesizing discourse, an assertion of an indefinite and multiplying plurality of particulars and specificities.

Insistence on the specificity of 'woman' or the 'feminine' has by no means been confined to the latter wave of criticism. An initial feminist 'deconstruction' of the humanist subject was made as long ago as 1792 by Mary Wollstonecraft in her demand for women to be included within the entitlements claimed by the 'rights of Man'. But it is only in comparatively recent times that feminists have gone beyond an exposure of the maleness of the supposedly universal subject invoked by humanist rhetoric, to denounce the 'masculinism' of humanism as such. Whereas, in the past, the call of feminist critiques of liberal humanism was for women to be recognized as 'equal' subjects of that discourse, equally entitled to the 'rights' which were claimed for 'all men',[2] today what is more at issue is the maleness of the subject place to which these earlier feminists were staking their claim. Today, there is a whole body of feminist writing which would shy away from an 'equality' which welcomed women (at last) as human subjects on a par with men. For this 'human' subject, it is argued, must always bear the traces of the patriarchal ordering which has been more or less coextensive with the 'human' condition as such: a patriarchal culture in the light of whose biased and supposedly 'masculine' values (of rationality, symbolic capacity, control over nature) the 'human' is at the 'beginning' of 'culture' defined in opposition to the 'animal' and the discourse of 'humanism' itself first given currency. And so conceived, 'feminism' and 'humanism' would appear to aspire to incompatible goals, for 'feminism' is the quest for the registration and realization (though quite in what language and cultural modes it is difficult to say . . .) of feminine 'difference': of that ineffable 'otherness' or negation of human culture and its symbolic order (and gender system) *which is not the human* as this human is spoken to in humanism. Humanism, inversely, according to this way of thinking, is the discourse which believes or wishes or pretends that there is no such difference.

But humanism is also, we might note in passing, the discourse which likes to think it can take back into the fold of the human all those who conceive of themselves as excluded. Or perhaps it would be better to describe it as the discourse which would say to all those who feel themselves excluded, or who prefer to exempt themselves from its sentimentality, that even in their exclusion or exemption they are within the fold; for resistance or indignation, they too are human, and humanism can embrace all opposition, difference and disdain for it. To say this is only to point out that there are *many* humanist discourses contesting each other's collectivities and claiming that theirs alone is truly universal. Thus it is in the name of a more universal humanism that Sartre delivers his 'anti-humanist' fulminations against bourgeois humanism. And thus it is, more generally, that religious conflicts, political battles, such as those between liberals and socialists, or even the philosophical oppositions between dialectic and anti-dialectic, can be viewed as 'humanist' sparrings for the right to represent the human race, its meaning and destiny.

I shall return to these points at a later stage, particularly as they affect the ultimate incompatibility of a feminist and a humanist outlook. Here, for the time being, let us stay with the arguments of the so-called 'difference' feminists: with those who, in varying ways, have questioned any ultimate compatibility. Two of the more prominent voices here are those of Hélène Cixous and Luce Irigaray. To these one might very tentatively add the name of Julia Kristeva: very tentatively, because she herself has forcefully criticized 'difference' feminisms, and is opposed to all theoretical moves which tend to an essentialism of 'femininity', and hence to a 'denegation of the symbolic' and removal of the 'feminine' from the order of language.[3] On the other hand, her own position is very equivocal. For, insofar as she is concerned to forestall any discourse on femininity which implies the 'ineffability' of the 'feminine' at the level of the symbolic, and to remind us that if the 'feminine' exists it does so only within the order of meaning and signification, she is herself implicitly invoking a feminine 'otherness'. The anxiety to check this 'silencing' of the 'feminine' is itself premised on a notion of the latter as a transgression and disrupting element within the prevailing code of the Symbolic. The 'existential crisis' of the 'feminine' as so conceived lies in the fact that it can only be spoken to within the existing order of language but is also that whose existence is denied or occluded by the very terms of that language. In other words, insofar as Kristeva relies on a Lacanian framework, her argument is constantly pulled towards acceptance of an equivalence between the 'masculine' and the Symbolic, whose effect, willy-nilly, is to cast the 'feminine' in the role of 'otherness' or 'difference' to the cultural order.

The resulting tensions have if anything been made more acute by recent developments in Kristeva's arguments wherein she has associated this feminine 'negativity' with a more positively accented pre-linguistic sensuality which she refers to as the 'semiotic', and that in turn with the 'maternal'. It is true that this 'semiotic' is not theorized literally as 'outside language' or inevitably deprived of cultural expression. For Kristeva finds it manifest not only in women's writing, but in the works of Joyce, Lautréamont, Mallarmé and a number of other male modernist writers. (Indeed, she has suggested that modernism should be viewed as a cultural movement of restitution or realization of the feminine semiotic, though this is certainly a controversial interpretation).[4] But the association of the feminine semiotic with a pre-Oedipal eroticism characteristic of the mother–infant relationship, and the suggestion that the maternal activities of gestation and nurturance break with conceptions of self and other, subject and object, which are of the essence of masculine logic, surely comes dangerously close to a differentiation of the feminine in terms of maternal function – precisely the essentialism which Kristeva has warned feminism against espousing and professes herself to wish to avoid.[5]

Irigaray and Cixous, on the other hand, have rejected the Lacanian eternalization of the cultural 'negativity' of women; but their challenge, nonetheless, to the supposed inevitability of masculine pre-eminence relies on an invocation of feminine difference which would seem to offer no better outlet from a phallocentric universe. For the difference in question refers us to the difference in the female body and body experience in a manner which arguably reintroduces the masculine Symbolic identification of sexuality with genitality,[6] and essentializes the maternal function (particularly so in the case of Cixous' inflated celebrations of the plenitude, richness and fecundity of the feminine body). As has been pointed out in respect of Kristeva's appeal to the maternal,[7] this tends to an elision of symbolic and empirical features which is theoretically confusing: after all, if feminine difference is being defined in terms of maternal function, then many actual, empirical, women are going to find themselves cast out from femininity insofar as they are not mothers nor intending to become so. At the same time, the association of the feminine with the maternal or with the feminine body is deeply problematic for many feminists who see in this precisely the male cultural signification which they are attempting to contest, and which, they would argue, has been the justification for a quite unreasonable and unfair domestication of women and a very damaging social and economic division of labour from the point of view of female self-fulfilment and self-expression.

In a more general way, we must surely also contest the reductionism of the argument found in different forms in both Irigaray's and Cixous' theories of the feminine (in Irigaray's advocacy of *parler femme* and Cixous' notion of *écriture féminine* as speaking to a kind of feminine unconscious) that language, whether spoken or written, directly mirrors physical morphology. It is a radical misunderstanding of the nature of signs to suppose that the two lips of the vulva or breast milk or menstrual blood are 'represented' in contiguous statements or in the unencodable libidinal gushings of a feminine prose *in any but a purely metaphorical sense*. But if we treat the supposed representation as purely metaphorical, then 'feminine writing' is being defined in terms of a certain image or metaphor of itself, and we end up with a purely tautological argument.

Again, the whole association within the writings of Cixous and Irigaray of feminine subjectivity with the pre-linguistic and pre-conceptual, with that which has no meaning and cannot be spoken in (male) culture, comes very close to reproducing the male–female dichotomies of traditional epistemology and moral argument – for which woman is 'intuitive', 'natural', 'immanent' – and 'silent' – and man is 'rational', 'cultural', 'transcendent' – and 'vocal'. The only difference is that the supposedly feminine characteristics will have been accorded a positive charge – and given the recurrent romanticization and idolization of the feminine within the masculine cultural order itself, even that may not prove a very major shift.

At any rate, the important point would seem to be that where the appeal to difference is made, it tends to an essentialism of the female physique and function which reproduces rather than surpasses the traditional male–female divide and leaves 'woman' once again reduced to her body – and to silence – rather than figuring as a culturally shaped, culturally complex, evolving, rational, engaged and noisy opposition. The total disengagement of the feminine in the position of Cixous and Irigaray,[8] the complete severance of any masculine–feminine cultural intercourse, removes this opposition to the point where one might say there was no longer any feminist critique of patriarchy but only a self-absorption in the feminine.

On the other hand, if difference is not given this kind of anchorage in the feminine body and function, it is not clear why there is any reason, once set on the path of difference, for feminism to call a halt. In other words, if one disallows the feminine universal of a common bodily essence, then the commitment to difference ought to move into a deconstruction of feminine difference itself. Having exposed the 'masculinism' of humanism in the name of feminine difference, one must surely go on, by the same logic, to expose the generalizing and abstract (and quasi-humanist) appeal to feminine difference in the name of the plurality of concrete differences between women (in their nationality, race, class, age, occupation, sexuality, parenthood status, health, and so on.) For on this argument 'woman' can no more be allowed to stand for all women than can 'man' be allowed to stand for all members of the human species. The way then, of course, lies open to an extreme particularism in which all pretensions to speak (quasi-humanistically) in general for this or that grouping, or to offer an abstract and representative discourse on behalf of such putative groups, must give way to a hyper-individualism.[9] From this standpoint, any appeal to a collectivity would appear to be illegitimate – yet another case of 'logocentric imperialism', to use the inflated rhetoric of poststructuralism.

But at this point, one is bound to feel that feminism as theory has pulled the rug from under feminism as politics. For politics is essentially a group affair, based on the idea of making 'common cause', and feminism, like any other politics, has always implied a banding together, a movement based on the solidarity and sisterhood of women, who are linked by perhaps very little

else than their *sameness* and 'common cause' as women. If this sameness itself is challenged on the grounds that there is no 'presence' of
womanhood, nothing that the term 'woman' immediately expresses, and
nothing instantiated concretely except particular women in particular
situations, then the idea of a political community build around women – the
central aspiration of the early feminist movement – collapses. I say the 'idea',
for women do still come together in all sorts of groups for feminist purposes,
and will doubtless continue to do so for a good while to come even if their
doing so transgresses some Derridean conceptual rulings. But *theoretically*,
the logic of difference tends to subvert the concept of a feminine political
community of 'women' as it does of the more traditional political communities of class, party, trade union, etc. And theory does, of course, in the
end get into practice, and maybe has already begun to do so; one already
senses that feminism as a campaigning movement is yielding to feminism as
discourse (and to discourse of an increasingly heterogeneous kind).

In the face of this dispersion, with its return from solidarity to individualism, it is difficult not to feel that feminism itself has lost its hold, or at
any rate that much contemporary theory of the feminine is returning us full
circle to those many isolated, and 'silent', women from which it started – and
for whom it came to represent, precisely, a 'common voice'. It is a
renversement, moreover, which leaves feminism exposed to the temptations
of what are arguably deeply nostalgic and conservative currents of
postmodernist thinking. It would seem quite complicit, for example, with the
distaste for anything smacking of a militant feminist politics implicit in
Baudrillard's suggestion that it is our very resistance to reactivating
traditional feminine charms which is pre-empting cultural renewal. 'Only by
the power of seduction does woman master the symbolic universe,' he tells
us,[10] in a piece of rhetorical blandishment redolent with nostalgia for the
good old days when men ruled and women cajoled. It is true that it is not
officially as an ideologue of patriarchal culture that Baudrillard offers this
Rousseauian advice. On the contrary, he would seduce us back into
seduction with the altogether more respectable end, so he claims, of taking
us beyond all sociality, sentimentality and sexuality.[11] But it is interesting, all
the same, that it remains out of place for woman directly to contest the
father's authority, and that our cultural duty requires us still to have recourse
to the subtler arts of cajolery: to beguile the phallus round. By such means,
so Baudrillard tempts us to think, women will readily contrive to wrap the
symbolic order around her charming little finger.[12]

This kind of sophistry, in truth, is not very tempting and probably
unimportant. But I think in a general way it is fair to claim that the same logic
of 'difference' which ends up subverting the project of feminine emancipation by denying the validity of any political community in whose name it
could be pursued also deprives feminist argument of recourse against such
retrograde poststructuralist idealism.

In introducing the term 'emancipation', one opens the way to consideration of another aspect of the problem of the relations between feminism,

humanism and postmodernism. For if the building of political collectivities becomes problematic in the light of anti-humanist critique, this also reflects a reluctance of these critiques 'to speak on behalf of' others: to say, in short, what others – in this case women – want. In other words, the observance of the logic of difference has also made feminist theorists reluctant utopians. This caution in speaking for others' desires is understandable against a background of so much claimed knowledge of the 'alienation' and 'true needs' of others (especially of that notorious 'universal subject' of humanity, the proletariat). It is a needed corrective to the enforced collectivizations of interests and needs which have been given theoretical legitimation in the past. But again, the thinking which motivated this healthy resistance to glib pronouncements of solidarity and struggle has also in recent argument developed a momentum which begins to undermine the possibility of speaking of any kind of political collective and agreement at all. Foucault, for example, has denounced any totalizing attempt in theory (any attempt, that is, to offer general diagnoses and general remedies for the ills of society) as 'totalitarian'. Even Habermas, who is hardly a Stalinist in theory, and who argues no more than that people should be allowed to discover the truth of their interests in the free discussions of his 'ideal communication situation', has been denounced by Lyotard for aspiring to a consensus.[13]

In other words, the drift of such arguments would seem to rule out any holistic analysis of societies (any analysis of the kind that allows us to define them as 'capitalist' or 'patriarchal' or 'totalitarian'), together with the radically transformative projects which such analyses tend to recommend. Indeed, as Isaac Balbus has argued in his defence of object-relations feminism against Foucauldian logic, if we accept the claim that any continuous history or *longue durée* accounting is posturing as 'True' (and therefore dominating) discourse, then feminism itself becomes a form of totalitarianism. The very idea of a centuries-old subordination of women explicable by reference to transhistorical patriarchal structures becomes deeply problematic from the standpoint of the 'postmodernist' rejection of truth and scientific knowledge and of the continuities they posit. If all that we once called knowledge or theory is now mythopoeic 'narrative', then the narrative of male oppression is itself but one more myth of Knowledge generated in response to a 'Will to Power'. And, by the same token, 'progress' out of oppression becomes a meaningless aspiration.[14]

My primary aim in this survey has been to diagnose a problem rather than prescribe its remedy. It is true, however, that, insofar as I have presented both the 'maternal' feminism of Kristeva, Irigaray and Cixous, and the more radical deconstruction of the 'feminine' invited by the logic of difference, as 'problematic' for the project of female emancipation, I have implied the need for some alternative course. Indeed, at times I have gone much further, suggesting that both positions are inherently conservative: either difference is essentialized in a way which simply celebrates the 'feminine' other of dominant culture without disturbing the hold of the latter; or the critique is taken to a point where the 'feminine' and its political and cultural agents in the women's movement and feminist art and literature no longer exist in the sense of having any recognizable common content and set of aspirations. These implications of my argument, however, stand in need of more elaboration than I have given them and admit of certain qualifications which I have not yet considered. In conclusion, then, I would pursue the charge of political conservatism a little further, offering some arguments both in defence but also in mitigation of it.

I have already indicated my main reason for thinking that 'maternal' feminism and *écriture féminine* are open to this charge. But my objection is not only to the fact that the emphasis on the distinctiveness of the female body and its reproductive and erotic experience comes so close to reinforcing patriarchal conceptions of gender difference. I would also argue that, despite its avant-gardist pretensions, the style in which this feminism is couched is disquietingly confirming of traditional assumptions about the 'nature' of feminine thought and writing. The dearth of irony; the fulsome self-congratulation; the resistance to objectivity; the sentimentalization of love and friendship and the tendency always to reduce these relations to their sexual aspect: to focus on the 'erotic' conceived as an amorphous, all-engulfing, tactile, radically unintellectual form of experience; the overblown poetics and arbitrary recourse to metaphor (which so often lack the hardness of crystalline meaning as if exactitude itself must be avoided as inherently 'male'): all this, which is offered in the name of allowing 'woman' to discover her 'voice', itself voices those very conceptions of female selfhood and self-affection which I believe are obstacles to cultural liberation. And the reason I find them obstacles is not simply because they so directly lend themselves to a patriarchically constructed ideology of femininity and its modes of self-expression, but because the ideology is, like all ideologies, at best partial in its representation and therefore illegitimately generalizing of a certain specific form of understanding. Moreover, when this understanding relates so directly to images of selfhood and subjectivity, it is peculiarly offensive and arrogant – to the point, in fact, of operating a kind of theft of subjectivity or betrayal of all those who fail to recognize themselves in the mirror it offers. At the same time, because ideologies of their nature are always fractured reflections of society, exploded in the very moment which reveals their ideological status, those who cling to them and reinforce their decaying hold are also always marginalizing their own discourse: ensuring that it cannot be taken seriously in the world at large.

In response to this it will be said, perhaps, that the neutrality of my own presentation of the issue is misleading since 'the world at large' is essentially a 'male' world, and for women to reject eulogies of the 'feminine' on the grounds that this guarantees a shrugging off of their importance, is itself to be complicit with a culture which has consistently treated reproduction and nurturing activities as of secondary importance to traditional 'male' pursuits. If to be 'taken seriously' women must speak and act 'like men', are not those who do so lending themselves to these standard cultural norms and thus equally open to the charge of quietism?

The premise of all such objections, however, is a simplistic acceptance of the equation between masculinity and culture (or the 'Symbolic'); and this premise is itself conservative because it rules out the identification of 'masculine' with 'maternal' activity which I would argue must be an important part of the aspiration of all those wanting a revaluation of cultural norms. To put the point crudely, and more empirically, it is only when men are enabled to identify themselves as nurturers (among other things) and women as other things (as well as nurturers) that nurturing will cease to be signified as 'feminine'. But it is precisely this transformability of cultural codings and norms which is ruled out by a theory premised upon the permanence of their existing meanings. What is wrong with 'maternal' feminism is not that it celebrates a hitherto derided femininity, but that it seems to rule out aforehand as 'masculinist recuperation' any general cultural revaluation of it.

Associated with this pre-empting of any confusion of traditional cultural gender codings is an overly rigid and stereotypic conception of what it is to act and speak 'like a man'. For, in the last analysis, it is only if we assume that 'acting like a man' is of its nature to act in a conservative and self-defensive manner that the admonition not to do so retains its critical force. But the self-defeating nature of this assumption is revealed rather clearly if we consider that the very designation of the 'cultural' or 'symbolic' as patriarchal implicitly admits that subversion, disruption, the continual challenging of received wisdoms (for that is what culture is, or at any rate includes) is the outcome of 'male' speech and action. In other words, if everything that is 'cultural' is 'masculine' then 'masculinity' itself ceases to retain any distinctive meaning, and we are deprived of any means of discriminating between cultural modes which serve the maintenance of patriarchy and cultural modes which tend to subvert it.

These points bear on the lesser confidence I feel in pressing the charge of 'conservatism' against the other direction of poststructuralist feminism: against the position which would pursue the logic of difference to its ultimate conclusion in the dispersion of any essential conception of the 'feminine'. For it might seem to follow from this that we should welcome this collapse of 'femininity' as a progressive rather than a retrograde development. Ought we not to approve it as a break from feminist theories and strategies which, in focusing always on feminine gender and the distinctive experiences of women, have helped to reconfirm the binary system? Such a feminism, if it can be called such, would be directed towards the realization of the 'in-difference' advocated by Derrida, who has been suggesting that feminists should give up 'feminine difference' as the first strategic move in the dissolution of the 'phallologocentric'.

This definitely seems a more attractive and progressive policy. But it, too, is not without its problems and particular tendencies to conservatism. In the first place, Derrida's recommendation to give up describing the specifically female subject in favour of 'in-differentiation' is inherently self-subverting since it must invoke the gender difference it invites us to ignore. In this sense, as Linda Kintz has argued, it is 'posed from the very terrain of the binary oppositions he warns against'.[15] The injunction, in other words, for women to be 'in-different': neither to speak 'as a woman' nor to speak 'like a man' (for both in their differing ways reinforce phallocracy, or at any rate do not disturb it) can arguably only be offered from a male subject place since it depends on presenting women as 'other': it depends on the assumption, for example, that woman is 'imitating' even if she speaks 'like a man'. You have not to be a man in order to do it, just as in nineteenth-century India you had not to be English in order to be Anglicized.[16] The issues are complex and I shall not pursue them further here. Suffice it to say that there is indeed a distinction to be drawn between gender-blind and gender-indifferent positions, and that Derrida's advice may be delivered from a position which has not sufficiently discriminated between the two. (I acknowledge, however, that a 'Derridean' response to these kinds of objection might simply be to point out that any 'Derridean' strategy will of its nature contain these elements of self-subversion.)

In any case, a more important difficulty with the strategy of 'in-difference' is that it recommends changes at the level of discourse and consciousness rather than at the level of material – economic and social – circumstance, and like all such recommendations is open to the charge that it is politically conservative because it is too little dialectical. Because it refuses to discriminate between 'world' and 'text', between the 'material' and the 'discursive', it follows that it has no theoretical purchase on the interdependence and mutual conditioning of the two. Of course, these arguments themselves can have no purchase on a position which eschews the metaphysical vocabulary of materialism and idealism. There is simply here no common discourse, and all that one can do is to charge poststructuralist 'idealism' with lacking the conceptual apparatus for making important distinctions between different areas or modalities of social life. Adopting this critical position, however, I would argue that there are many material circumstances firmly in place which tend to the disadvantaging of women and whose correction is not obviously going to be achieved simply by a revaluation of theory on the part of a poststructuralizing feminist elite. In fact there are some concrete and universal dimensions of women's lives which seem relatively unaffected by the transformation of consciousness already achieved by the women's movement. To give one example: despite the indisputable gains of feminist theory and action, the fact remains that women live in fear of men, and men do not live in fear of women. When I say 'live in fear' of men, I do not mean that we live our lives in a continual and conscious anxiety, or that we think an attack on our persons is very likely (it isn't statistically and we are rational enough to accept it). I mean that women live in a kind of alertness to the possibility of attack and must to some degree organize their lives in order to minimize its threat. In particular, I think, this has constraints from which men are free on our capacity to enjoy solitude. As a woman, one's reaction to the sight of a male stranger approaching on a lonely road or country walk is utterly different from one's reaction to the approach of a female stranger. In the former case there is a frisson of anxiety quite absent in the latter. This anxiety, of course, is almost always confounded by the man's perfectly friendly behaviour, but the damage to the relations between the sexes has already been done – and done not by the individual man and woman but by their culture. This female fear and the constraints it places on what women can do – particularly in the way of spending time on their own – has, of course, its negative consequences for men too, most of whom doubtless deplore its impact on their own capacities for spontaneous relations with women. (Thus, for example, the male stranger has to think twice about smiling at the passing woman, exchanging the time of day with her, etc. for fear he will either alarm her or be misinterpreted in his intentions.) But the situation all the same is not symmetrical: resentment or regret is not as disabling as fear; and importantly it does not affect the man's capacity to go about on his own.

This, then, is one example of the kind of thing I have in mind in speaking of 'material circumstances' which have been relatively unaffected by changes at a discursive and 'Symbolic' level. They are circumstances which relate to conditions which are experienced by both sexes, and in the most general sense therefore culturally universal. But they are conditions which are differently experienced simply by virtue of which sex you happen to be, and in that sense they are universally differentiated between the sexes: *all* men and *all* women are subject to them *differently*. It is this sex-specific but universal quality of certain conditions of general experience which justifies and gives meaning to collective gender categories. To put the point in specifically feminist terms, there are conditions of existence common to all women which the policy of in-difference – with its recommendation not to focus on *female* experience – is resistant to registering in theory and therefore unlikely to correct in practice.

The implication of these rather open-ended remarks, I think, is that feminism should proceed on two rather contrary lines: it should be constantly moving towards 'in-difference' in its critique of essentializing and ghettoizing modes of feminist argument; but at the same time it should also insist on retaining the gender-specific but universal categories of 'woman' or 'female experience' on the grounds that this is essential to identifying and transforming all those circumstances of women's lives which the pervasion of a more feminist consciousness has left relatively unaffected. In short, feminism should be both 'humanist' and 'feminist' – for the paradox of poststructuralizing collapse of the 'feminine' and the move to 'in-difference' is that it reintroduces – though in the disguised form of an aspiration to no-gender – something not entirely dissimilar from the old humanistic goal of sexual parity and reconciliation. And, while one can welcome the reintroduction of the goal, it may still require some of the scepticism which inspired its original deconstruction.

Notes

1. Thus Alice Jardine, *Gynesis: Configurations of Women and Modernity* (Ithaca and London, 1985), see especially pp. 22–4: cf. Barbara Creed, 'From here to modernity: feminism and postmodernism', *Screen*, 28, 2 (Spring 1987).

2. Though there was a definite class bias in much of the early liberal discussion of such rights: 'all men' being conceived often enough as having practical extension only to all males in possession of a certain property and concomitant social status.

3. See J. Kristeva, 'Women's time' (first published as 'Le Temps des femmes' in 33/44: *Cahiers de recherche de sciences des textes et documents*, 5 (Winter, 1979)) in Toril Moi (ed.), *The Kristeva Reader* (Blackwell, Oxford, 1986), pp. 187–213: cf. 'Il n'y a pas de maître à langage', *Nouvelle Revue de Psychanalyse* (1979) cited in Moi, *Kristeva*, p. 11.

4. See the discussion by Andreas Huyssen, *After the Great Divide: Modernism, Mass Culture and Postmodernism* (London, 1986), pp. 44–62.

5. For a sense of this development in Kristeva's thinking, see the excerpts from *About Chinese Women* (1974): 'Stabat mater' (1977); 'The true-real' (1979); and 'Women's time' (1979), included in Moi, *Kristeva*. Cf. also the discussions of Kristeva in Toril Moi, *Sexual/Textual Politics* (London, Methuen, 1985), and in Jacqueline Rose, *Sexuality in the Field of Vision* (London, Verso, 1986). For a critique of Kristeva's 'ethic' of feminine negativity, see Drucilla Cornell and Adam Thurschwell, 'Feminism, negativity, subjectivity', in Drucilla Cornell and Seyla Benhabib, *Feminism as Critique* (Oxford, 1987), pp. 151–6.

6. Irigaray, for example, has treated *parler femme* as an analogue of female genitalia, in which the continuous, non-adversarial and elliptical quality of the statement of feminine writing is a reflection of the two lips of the vulva.

7. Cornell and Thurschwell, in *Feminism as Critique*, pp. 150–1.

8. A disengagement reflected in Kristeva's Lacanian presentation of the feminine as semiotic 'other' of the Symbolic even as it is criticized by Kristeva herself.

9. Recent feminist self-criticism regarding the 'white middle-class' outlook of feminist politics reflects this anxiety about conceptual conflations, even if it does not collapse into the extreme particularism which would seem to be its ultimate logic.

10. Jean Baudrillard, *De la séduction* (Paris, 1979), p. 208; cf. Jardine, *Gynesis*, p. 67.

11. Jean Baudrillard, interview in *Marxism Today*, January 1989, p. 54.

12. There will be some, no doubt, who will come to Baudrillard's defence. They argue, perhaps, that he is in fact repaying the debt of patriarchy with a clear and self-confessed vagina envy. Or they may point out that Baudrillard is simply saying that the means must match the end, and that for women to use 'male' methods is to give themselves over to the masculine forms of power they wish to contest. Very well, then, let him for his part, show his good faith by yielding up the language of 'female sacrifice' and 'female seduction'. And let him ask men, too, to put a hand in the churn of cultural revolution. Or is the subversion of the Symbolic to be wholly women's work?

13. François Lyotard, *The Postmodern Condition* (Manchester, 1986), p. 66; cf. pp. 10–16; 25; 57–9; 63–5.

14. Isaac Balbus, 'Disciplining women', in Cornell and Benhabib, *Feminism as Critique*, pp. 110–27.

15. Linda Kintz, 'In-different criticism', in Jeffner Allen and Irish Marion Young, *The Thinking Muse: Feminism and Modern French Philosophy* (Indiana, 1989), p. 113.

16. Ibid., pp. 130–3.

A Horror of Isms

Madhu Kishwar

At the time we launched *Manushi* in 1978, though I did not then openly challenge being labelled a feminist, I resisted pressure that *Manushi* be called a feminist magazine. Some of us felt that if the magazine proclaimed that as its identification, large sections of potential readers would be alienated, since the term was alien to the vocabulary of women in India and inadequate to *Manushi*'s purposes. It would inevitably evoke associations with the women's movement in the West, which was known in India mostly through simplistic stereotypes.

We deliberately chose the subtitle 'a journal about women and society', which, along with the word *Manushi*, with its emphasis on the word 'humane', we felt would indicate that *Manushi* is concerned not just with women's equality, as the term 'feminist' would imply, but with the protection of the human rights of all the disadvantaged or discriminated groups in our society, while having a special emphasis on women's rights.

The avoidance of the label was not restricted to the title or subtitle of the magazine. The term 'feminism' almost never appeared in any of my writings even in the early days of *Manushi*.

Time-specific isms

A distinction must first be made between two different kinds of isms that are operative in political theory and practice. The first kind is that which emanates from a specific situation and often finds expression in one specific movement in a particular time and place. This kind of ideology evolves under the pressure of the specific challenges of its time. Often, it comes to be identified with the name of a particular thinker or political leader. Some examples include Marxism, Leninism, Maoism, and Gandhism. However, when the movement dies down, or after it achieves some of its immediate aims, and usually after the leader's death, the ism reifies. It is then used more as a ritual chant and reduced to a set of deadening formulae by its votaries to

From 'Why I do not call myself a feminist', *Manushi: A Journal about Women and Society* (New Delhi), 61, 1990, Nov.–Dec., pp. 2–8, abridged.

justify their own actions, though these may or may not be a logical outcome of the original ideology. My problem with this kind of ism is that while in its original version it may play an important role in a creative upsurge of ideas and action in its own time, it becomes moribund when sought to be institutionalized at a later point as the final truth and applied in changed circumstances, even when it is appropriate in its original context.

Culture-specific isms

The second kind of ism does not arise from one movement or one individual leader or thinker, but often pervades many different movements in the form of an idea or tendency. Some examples of this second kind of ism are anarchism, humanism and feminism. Feminism was an outgrowth of eighteenth-century humanist thought in Europe and the USA, reinforced by thinkers from many other schools of thought, such as utilitarianism and Marxism. This second type of ism may not be more time-specific but is as culture-specific.

As I mentioned at the start, while I stand committed to pro-women politics, I resist the label of feminism because of its overclose association with the Western women's movement. I have no quarrel with Western feminist movements in their own context, and feel strengthened by the existence of women's movements in Western as in Eastern countries. We have received a lot of love and support from all over the world from women who take pride in their feminist ideology and solidarity and there are many feminists in India whose work and ideas I respect.

However, given our situation today, where the general flow of ideas and of labels is one way – from West to East, in the overall context of a highly imbalanced power relation – feminism, as appropriated and defined by the West, has too often become a tool of cultural imperialism. The definitions, the terminology, the assumptions, even the issues, the forms of struggle and institutions are exported from West to East, and too often we are expected to be the echo of what are assumed to be more advanced women's movements in the West.

Importance of an independent self-view

For instance, anyone working for women's rights in India is automatically assumed to be a feminist, no matter how different a form their work takes. Yet people working for peace and disarmament in the West are not assumed to be Gandhians, even though Gandhi is the most outstanding leader of modern times to have provided a philosophy and politics of non-violence and led the most noteworthy mass movement based on non-violent principles. We are labelled 'feminists' without so much as a by-your-leave, not only by Western feminists but also by their counterparts in India. Many view our refusal to accept the label either as an act of betrayal or as a sign of insufficient ideological growth. However, I believe that accepting or rejecting labels is not a meaningless much ado about nothing. Being able to choose an appropriate name and definition for one's politics is an important aspect of evolving an independent self-view, provided the exercise is not merely restricted to ritual debates about words.

Imported labels

Sections of the women's movement in India have picked up not just the term 'feminist' from the West but all the norms, assumptions and debates that emerged from the women's movement in the West, and to some extent from the polemics of the Russian revolutionaries. The most blatant example of the movement here being compelled to act as an echo of the supposedly more advanced movements in the West is the way divisions were assumed to exist before they had taken shape. When, in the late 1970s, *Manushi* and a number of new women's groups began to emerge, certain self-appointed theoreticians immediately went about labelling different groups and individuals as belonging to one of three trends – bourgeois feminist, socialist feminist and radical feminist. Some of these self-appointed certificate givers descended directly from the West; others, although 'natives' like us, were better grounded in the Western women's movement debates than in the reality of women's lives here. I remember my bewilderment at that time at the ferocity of the label warfare. Where did it descend from? Certainly not from any split in India on ideological lines. There were less than a handful of groups and individuals at that time working on women's issues. Most of the groups had not crystallized organizationally or theoretically. No political action on any significant scale had yet been undertaken, therefore hardly any meaningful dialogue over strategy and tactics had taken place. Yet those mesmerized by the rhetoric of other movements tried to force us to assume the existence at that time not only of a major women's movement here, but also of divides within it. We were supposed to have split even before we had a real opportunity to get together, see or hear one another, let alone carry out a debate among ourselves.

These labels were not used as descriptions of the positions taken by individuals or groups or the work being done by them, but as epithets to condemn people you did not like, that is, as good or bad character certificates. Label givers assumed that the most respectable term was 'socialist feminist'. This was usually reserved for oneself and one's friends, as proof of one's correct political credentials. Those one did not like were sought to be condemned as 'bourgeois feminists' or 'radical feminists'. The utter absurdity of these ism labels was evident. These versions of available isms have been used as sticks with which to beat up people, to stifle intellectual growth and enquiry, to frighten people from thinking things out for themselves, to bully them into blindly accepting formula-ridden politics and repeating meaningless mantras, and to subject them to slander if they resist. Therefore, I found it difficult to identify with them emotionally or intellectually.

Interestingly, *Manushi* was honoured often, at one and the same time, with all three epithets. We were called everything from radical feminist men-haters to bourgeois feminists to leftist extremists, even though we steadfastly refused to adhere to any of the labels. Those using these labels to describe *Manushi* were clearly not describing our politics. Those who imagined themselves socialists called us bourgeois, those who were anti-Marxist called us Naxalites and radicals. Realizing that this ideological ism warfare was an unreal one, we chose not to enter into it. Instead, whenever accused of being bourgeois feminists or whatever else, we would ask the persons concerned to define the term and then to point out what in the magazine conformed to their definition. Not one of the label givers we spoke to actually ended up completing the exercise.

The labelling requirement distorts not only the present but even the past. I remember being attacked at a seminar organized by a group of feminists at a women's college in Delhi University for presenting in a positive light the protest poetry of women like Mahadeviakka or Mirabai. Their argument was that these women did not talk of women's independence and equality as they ought to have; that they merely chose to substitute slavery to a husband for slavery to a god. In short, that they were inadequate as historical sources of inspiration for women because they could not be called feminist. Expecting Mirabai to be a feminist is as inappropriate as calling Gautam Buddha a Gandhian or Jesus Christ a civil libertarian.

Expected to be a mirror image

The use of the term 'feminism' and the resultant ism warfare brought with it a host of other problems. Even in forms of organization, we were expected to live up to the standards, patterns or mythologies evolved by Western feminists, and to mimic all the stances taken within the movement there. You had to pre-decide, for instance, whether you were going to walk hand in hand with, ahead of, or behind men. We were bullied to take a position on separatism simply because the issue had been the cause of a major controversy in the West and in certain left movements in other countries.

In the early years, there were occasions when certain feminists from the West who believed in totally excluding men from participating in women's movements threatened to launch a boycott of *Manushi* since it included a few articles and letters by men. At the other end of the spectrum, a section of those who considered themselves socialist feminists in India accused *Manushi* of being anti-men and also attempted to organize a boycott against it. During all these years, despite these pressures and attacks on us, we studiously avoided duplicating the postures and responses of factions within the Western feminist movement on the issue of men's participation in the women's movement. It seemed as foolish to take an *a priori* position of confrontation against men, as some separatist feminists insisted on doing, as it would be to insist, as a cardinal principle, on an unconditional alliance with men, as those who called themselves socialist feminists required of everyone. It made no sense to expect an undifferentiated response from all men – or from women for that matter. I felt that the actual responses of people, men and women, to the issues we advocated would provide a better indicator on who to build meaningful alliances with. Thus neither did we woo men, nor did we shun them on the basis of a theoretically postulated confrontation or alliance. Partly as a consequence, *Manushi* has over the years received an unusual amount of support from numerous men owing allegiance to a variety of ideological orientations.

An example of the importation of institutional forms from the West in the name of feminism is that of battered women's homes. Over the last decade, innumerable Western feminists have asked us: 'Do you have battered women's homes in India?' The assumption is that not to have such homes is to be at a lower stage of development in the struggle against violence on women, and that such homes will be one inevitable outcome of the movement's development. The psychological pressure exerted on us when the question is repeatedly asked should not be underestimated. The tendency inevitably grows to wonder whether all organizations in any way related to women should in fact be creating battered women's homes. Some may ask what is wrong with having a common response to a common problem of wife-battering. My answer would be that the completely different socioeconomic and cultural contexts should be studied before we accept a predetermined response.

Battered women's homes in the West for a while seemed to act as a useful type of short-term intervention because of (a) the existence of a welfare system which includes some, even though inadequate, provisions for public assistance, unemployment benefits, subsidized housing and free schooling for children; (b) the overall employment situation being very different from that in India; (c) the lower stigma on women living on their own and moving around on their own; and (d) the existence of certain avenues of employment that are not considered permissible for a middle-class woman here, for instance domestic service. Feminist groups in the West who run battered women's homes aim to offer moral support required by a woman making the transition from dependence on husband to self-dependence, in a context where natal families are not usually available to offer this support. In India, hardly any woman requires just moral support – they are in more dire need of economic and social support. So a battered women's home, like a widows' home, inevitably turns into a few token charitable establishments for providing a subsistence standard of living; charity, by itself, cannot be said to further women's equality. The battered women's homes run by women's organizations most often end up trying to persuade the marital families of these women to accept them back on slightly improved terms. Only rarely have we been able to help women carve out independent lives.

Yet, such is the hypnotic power of feminist ideology that comes from the

West that, despite our different experience of dealing with women in distress, setting up refuges and shelters continues to be presented as one of the key components in resolving problems of battering and maltreatment. This is so even though the movement in the West for setting up shelters and refuges has lost much of its steam because even there it is not proving to be an effective remedy against domestic violence. It is unfortunate that the import of ideology follows a pattern similar to that of other imports, for example that of certain technologies and drugs. Many things known to be obsolete or unworkable and therefore discarded in the West continue to be dumped in Third World countries. Likewise, ideas and institutions which have been discarded by major elements in the feminist movement in the West continue to be advocated here as appropriate feminist responses.

It is not just that issues and campaigns have been imported. There has also been an attempt to emotionally live through the responses of the women's movement in the West, even though the situation women face has been different in India. For example, while the feminist movement in the West did experience ridicule, and even outright hostility, especially in the mass media, feminists in India (as distinguished from the oppressed women they try to represent) have, by and large, not been rudely treated. Sometimes they even get disproportionate attention. The mainstream mass media have gone out of their way to offer rhetorical support to feminists and their work. The media created space for feminists without resistance. The support has been fairly uncritical on the whole. Yet the vocabulary used by feminists in India is nevertheless often one that is used by a persecuted movement, and India's mass media are often portrayed as though they have responded as critically towards Indian feminists as have many sections of the Western media.

All these factors seriously inhibit and stunt the process of understanding the reality of women's lives in India. Women's struggles in India have followed quite a different course. However, feminist scholarship has often failed to provide an appropriate means of analysis. Its literature is subject to wide swings with every change in fashion in the West, structuralism yesterday, deconstructionism today.

Agreements and differences

Apart from serious ideological reservations, there are practical reasons for refusing to call *Manushi* a feminist magazine.

One may be a feminist and a militarist, another may be a feminist and a pacifist. Yet, the common or shared use of the term 'feminist' creates a misleading assumption of consensus. It is wrong to assume that all those calling themselves feminists ought to be able to act together on most issues related to women and if they fail to do so it is due to personal rivalry.

I have often been asked reproachfully by feminists: 'How can you not join the campaign on such and such issues if you are a feminist?' But, on many important issues concerning women, I often find myself differing more from current feminist opinion than from other political groups not claiming to be feminist. One way of resisting being dragged into issues taken up by some feminists on which I hold differing positions, was to learn to say: 'I do not call myself a feminist, though I am committed to the struggle for women's rights. Let us discuss the concrete facts of the case and consider the pros and cons of the approach being proposed and find out if we share any common ground, instead of starting out by assuming an overall solidarity or agreement just because we all state we are committed to women's equality.'

Let me illustrate the point. Some feminists have campaigned and lobbied for more stringent legislation and tougher implementation of laws to deal with obscenity or the degrading portrayal of women. I have had serious reservations regarding their approach and could not make common cause with it, despite my abhorrence of insulting images of women. My reservations were not related to a lack of commitment to women's equality but to my mistrust of the state machinery and of attempts to arm the state with even more repressive powers than it already has in the name of the curbing pornography. I find this a risk and unacceptable way of fighting for women's dignity. In this case, my commitment to freedom of expression assumed primacy.

Similarly, a number of feminists welcomed the death penalty for wife-murderers, as they did in the Sudha Goel murder case or when it was included as part of the anti-sati law after the protests about the killing of Roop Kanwar. I continue to demand an end to capital punishment, no matter what the crime. Many do not. But I believe that their not doing so is based not on their feminism or lack of feminism but on an objection to legitimizing killing by the state machinery, even when the pretext may be protection of women. A similar conflict arose over the Muslim Women's Bill, where a supposedly feminist position became the pretext for a large section of opinion to stir up anti-Muslim hysteria. This could only work to the detriment of Muslim women, as was recognized by many Muslim women in their refusal to see the bill as benefiting them. Even Shah Bano decided to withdraw her case.

Over the last ten years of editing *Manushi*, we have often received articles from women who called themselves feminist. Often, the writers assumed that merely by labelling their articles 'feminist' they were guaranteed not only ideological correctness but also superior grasp of the issues. However, in judging the worth of a piece of writing we have never tried to ascertain whether or not the writer is a feminist or an adherent of any other ism. When judging the worth of our own writing or that of others, we find it more useful to ask: does it make sense? Has it got the facts of the situation right? Does it take into account the many-sided versions of a situation or does it oversimplify reality to fit it into a preconceived notion of what the situation ought to be? Will the solution proposed lead society towards more humane and egalitarian norms and expand the horizons of people's freedom rather than further restricting them? Does it aid oppressed people to survive and make greater efforts to throw off their oppression?

An important reason for *Manushi*'s survival has been its ability to keep a deliberate distance from many of the preoccupations of Western feminists as well as from the wars between various isms in India. Paradoxically, it has enabled us to have a genuine, mutually beneficial interaction with many Western feminists and believers in other isms. It enabled us to reach a much wider cross-section of concerned people as well as to keep our minds less fettered.

Finally, all this does not mean that I do not have an ideology. I do, although it does not have a name – I would like to see a world in which the means for a dignified life are available to all human beings equally, where the polity and economy are decentralized so that people have greater control over their own lives, where the diversity of groups and individuals is respected, and nondiscrimination and equality are institutionalized at all levels.

I believe in a non-authoritarian politics of consensus and non-violence and my immediate political goals include: working to ensure survival needs of all, especially of vulnerable groups; working for the accountability of governments, for the provision of basic amenities to all with a minimizing of state control over people's lives; ensuring of social and political space to minority groups for the evolution of their identities; and moving towards the lessening of economic disparities. A primary motive in my life is working for women's equality and freedom in all areas of life.

I do not rule out the possibility that if in the future any ism arises that seems to me to be sufficiently specific to our culture and our times in a way that it can creatively further the goals listed above, among others, I may choose to accept it. However, I do not feel any sense of loss or disadvantage in working without the support of an ism. In fact, it gives me a much greater sense of freedom in trying to work out meaningful responses to our specific social situation, for I have to assume full responsibility for my political ideas. I cannot blame any ism or others for the mistakes I make.

SECTION II

THE CONCEPT AND IMPACT OF SEXUAL 'DIFFERENCE'

In one of his more plaintive and self-doubting moments Freud asked the question 'What do women want?'[1] The question assumed that what women wanted was in some sense different from the wants, and needs, of men. Women, it was implicitly suggested, constituted a completely different world. Not only was their biology different from that of men, but so was the way in which they perceived the world. Freud was not, of course, the first person to voice the question. A long tradition in all societies has taken the view that the sexes are absolutely different; biological differences are nothing compared to the differences in assumption and interpretation between the sexes. Indeed, Freud was only one of many people to suggest that physical differences between women and men are only an indication (indeed, as Lacan was to describe it, a 'sign') of the much more significant differences in the emotions and the intellect.[2] The more vulgar forms of Western culture assume that the body is the basis, and the essential nature of difference, between women and men, but other voices within the culture also suggest that whilst the body, and bodily differences, are important, it is only one part of the way in which sexual difference is constructed. Freud's theory of the unconscious, and the polymorphous sexuality of the human infant of both sexes, at least gave some common ground to women and men.

But in recent years the shift in Western thought from modernism to postmodernism has brought with it a rethinking of our ideas about the body. Freud was a central thinker of modernism, and as such his work has had a profound impact on our culture; indeed, his work has in a way become part of our culture. Equally, his work was never without its critics, and amongst those critics have been many feminists.[3] Nevertheless, notwithstanding feminist critiques of Freud, psychoanalysis has become part of Western feminism and is now deeply integrated into its practice. The impact of psychoanalytic theory on feminist literacy theory is widely acknowledged, and few works of feminist theory do not, in one way or another, include psychoanalysis, or psychoanalytical insights.

However, just as the method and theory of psychoanalysis have become a standard part of feminist theory, so the transformations that postmodernism has imposed have brought with them a reinterpretation and a redefining of the body, and with that – inevitably – a redefinition of sexual difference. When Freud outlined his theory of sexual and emotional development he did so assuming a fixed, 'normal', mode of social masculinity and femininity in which 'normal' masculinity and 'normal' femininity had predictable social paths. For example, in an age where contraception was unreliable it was entirely reasonable to suppose that 'normal' heterosexual intercourse led to 'normal' motherhood and fatherhood. Whether individuals wished for this or not, such was the direct impact of biology on destiny.

Yet once this link between sexual intercourse and reproduction was broken, it became possible to reconsider the nature of this impact of biology. As endless feminists have pointed out, biology still determines destiny in social expectations about mothering, but this pragmatic reality is only part of the possibilities of sexuality within a postmodernist age. Whereas being male or female was once what has been described as a 'meta-narrative', being male and female in the postmodernist West becomes only part of an individual identity, and the very categories male and female permeable and diverse.

It is this quality of the increasing diversity of the category of woman (or man) which makes sexual difference so complex an idea for feminism in a postmodern age. On the one hand, feminists welcome the greater possibilities that postmodernity gives to women. The shift from a construction of gender in terms of absence/presence to a construction around the sexually neutral concepts of 'need' and 'desire' seems to promise more negotiating space for women, particularly for women who wish to move between sexual identities. In *Gender Trouble* Judith Butler has argued persuasively for this idea:

> Gender ought not to be construed as a stable identity or locus of agency from which various acts follow; rather, gender is an identity tenuously constituted in time, instituted in an exterior space through a stylized repetition of acts. . . . That gender reality is created through sustained social performances means that the very notions of an essential sex and a true or abiding masculinity or femininity are also constituted as part of the strategy that conceals gender's performative character and the performative possibilities for proliferating gender configurations outside the restricting frames of masculinist domination and compulsory heterosexuality.[4]

What is crucial about this argument is the idea that women (and indeed men) can escape from a single, fixed, sexual identity. In Judith Butler's book, and in other works on the same subject (for example Stephen Heath's *Sexual Fix*)[5] what is questioned, challenged and rejected is the norm of a stable sexual identity. For generations all cultures have known, and tolerated to a greater or lesser extent, sexual diversity. But, the argument goes – particularly about the West and post-Foucault – in the nineteenth century sexual 'regulation' imposed on the world a rigid orthodoxy about sexual behaviour.[6] Evidence for this argument is plentiful: the social marginalization and criminalization of male homosexuality in England in the nineteenth century is just one example of the way in which a sexual plurality was abandoned in favour of prescriptive sexual codes. Jeffrey Weeks and others have illustrated and developed this shift with special emphasis on the consequences for gay men; feminist writers – for example Sheila Jeffreys – have also articulated and challenged the apparently general, and remorseless, growth of a culture of conformity to a model of sexual 'normality'.[7] For both Jeffreys and Weeks the focus of the attack is the idea of 'compulsory heterosexuality', a theme explored persuasively by Adrienne Rich in a famous essay in 1980.[8] All these writers, and many others, challenge what they see as the dominance of the ideology which equates sexual 'normality' with heterosexuality. Freud, inevitably, is part of their target, since his work provides a theoretical underpinning for the view that homosexuality – whether male or female – is 'immature' and 'perverse'.[9] Developing his view of homosexuality, Freud unfortunately wrote about it as 'inversion' and 'aberration', a description which has led many critics to condemn his views as hopelessly prejudiced in favour of a norm of heterosexuality.[10]

Whatever Freud's views on homosexuals, the case made by Weeks, Jeffreys et al. remains a central part of contemporary theory about sexual practice. The reasons for the social prescription of heterosexuality inevitably remain a matter of contention. For Weeks, and many other gay writers, the real explanations lie in the homophobia of the culture whilst for Jeffreys, Rich and others the cause of the marginalization of lesbianism is patriarchy, and men's fear of the loss of the sexual and social control of women. The argument about the relationship between sexual orthodoxy and social control has now come to form the basis of feminist accounts of other aspects of social life, such as the debate around pornography.[11]

In these controversies and discussions about sexuality, the body is inevitably a central theme, and all debates return to the issue – indicated earlier – of the body as a determining factor in human behaviour. Feminism has woven (to use an explicitly feminist term) a fascinating, if at times contradictory, path through these debates. For nineteenth-century Western feminists the body, whether male or female, was as problematic as it ever is today. Feminists denied the body, made the body central and reinforced cultural stereotypes about the nature of the body. Sexual pleasure (as Linda Gordon and Ellen du Bois have pointed out) was the theme around which many of these debates were organized.[12] The question, in 1860 as much as in the 1990s, was that of how sexual pleasure and desire were constructed, how both were controlled, and by whom. For many feminists, a rejection of heterosexual activity *per se* offered the only way to personal autonomy, a theme in the sexual politics of England in the late nineteenth century encapsulated in the literary representation of the 'new woman' of Arnold Bennett, H.G. Wells and Bernard Shaw. All these – male – writers (articulated a powerful social concern (described by Sheila Jeffreys in *The Spinster and her Enemies*) about the nature of the emancipation of women.[13]

The eventual extension of citizenship to women, as well as improved contraception, established the female person and the female body as formally 'free'. However, once mechanical and structural impediments to women's freedom were improved, the body, paradoxically, became even more important. Since feminists could no longer argue that inadequate contraception, formal barriers to education and so on limited the activities of women, the debate shifted to biological difference. As biology was not affected by social change, it was appropriate to reconsider – as Freud had done – the difference that biology makes.

In the 'second wave' of feminism (of the 1960s and the 1970s) the body becomes central. What makes it so important is the issue of essentialism, which becomes for feminism a major point of contention both within its own parameters and externally. In rejecting social and sexual definition by physical biology, feminists had argued that biology was not, and should not be, destiny. In debates against patriarchal orthodoxy, feminists had asserted their right not to be defined by a female biology. The argument was, in essence, an argument for androgyny. The traditions which were established within feminism by this view are represented in the denial of femininity in works such as De Beauvoir's *The Second Sex* and much of the organization of the late nineteenth- and early twentieth-century higher education for women.[14] Traditional femininity became, for feminists, deeply suspect.

It was to remain so throughout most of the first half of the twentieth century, and feminist critics of the domestic culture of the West continued to reject and condemn the social equation of being biologically female and being a wife and mother. But just as this argument was becoming widely discussed (through books such as Betty Friedan's *The Feminine Mystique*) a group of French writers – collectively known as 'the new French feminists' – began to suggest alternative understandings of the female body and femininity.[15] This work – the writing by Cixous, Wittig and Irigaray – became widely influential[16] and turned feminist debate away from arguments about the social construction of gender to a theory (or theories) which suggested an essential, biologically derived, female identity. In her widely read book, *The Sex Which Is Not One*, Luce Irigaray argued that women do not constitute a sex in the same way as men.[17] What she does in this book is to suggest that the perception of women as castrated men puts women not in the category of 'imperfect' men, as traditionally supposed, but outside the symbolic order which is constructed from male sexuality. The absence of the penis, seen from Freud onwards as the absence which limits and constrains women, is interpreted by Irigaray as the means of liberation. For Irigaray women are not just a female version of human sexuality, but a completely different sex.

The radicalism of this idea has made Irigaray – and in different ways Cixous and Wittig – particularly important in the context of theories of representation. All three women share, in different ways, a concern with challenging Freud's castration theory, and for them the female body has an integrity, and completeness, which markedly separates them from Freudian, or neo-Freudian, analysis. Woman, and women, gain through this perception an obvious sense that the feminine is derived from a female body which has its own order and definition. Women, in short, are not defined by men.

In this interpretation of the impact of the body, and sexual difference, on the construction of female and male, women are given an enhanced sense of being, since they are no longer perceived in terms of being different from men. The liberation from that idea is part of the major contribution of Irigaray, Cixous and Wittig. On the other hand, as some critics have pointed out, the idea contains its own version of essentialism, and its own ethnocentric assumption that all cultures are both phallocentric and uniformly negative in their perceptions of women.[18] For many non-white women, as Patricia Hill Collins argues in this section, the post-Enlightenment European tradition with which Irigaray et al. engage is both masculinist (as Irigaray would no doubt concede) and also Eurocentric.[19] This Eurocentric tradition places reason – as defined by white men – at the centre of its project, and is radically different from the Afrocentrist way of knowing in which, Collins argues, 'Neither emotion nor ethics is subordinated to reason. Instead, emotion, ethics, and reason are used as interconnected, essential components in assessing knowledge claims.'[20]

In this assertion of another form of radical difference, no longer that between the sexes but between cultures, the debate about sexual difference enters a new form. What now becomes contentious is the impact on thinking of both gender *and* race. Patricia Hill Collins and Audre Lorde make the case for the part which race plays in thinking about sexual difference; in terms of 'white' culture Sandra Harding has become widely known as one of the major critics of the norms of Western science and rationality. All these writers extend the context in which debates about sexual difference take place; the body becomes, in this developed debate, a matter of contention not just in itself, but in terms of the way in which it has been described and discussed. Inevitably, the debate turns to questions about nature, reason and the sexual neutrality of the mind. Sexual difference, it would appear, is much more than skin deep.

Notes

1. See 'Woman, the dark continent', in Peter Gay, *Freud* (Macmillan, London, 1989), pp. 501–22.

2. See Jacques Lacan, 'The signification of the phallus', in *Ecrits*, translated Alan Sheridan (Tavistock, London, 1977) and the discussion in Janet Sayers, *Sexual Contradictions* (Tavistock, London, 1986), pp. 79–96.

3. Juliet Mitchell's *Psychoanalysis and Feminism* (Penguin, Harmondsworth, 1975) has been central in the feminist discussion of Freud. For more critical discussions see Elizabeth Wilson, 'Psychoanalysis: psychic law and order', *Feminist Review*, 9 (1981), and the reply by Janet Sayers in *Feminist Review*, 10 (1981), pp. 91–5.

4. Judith Butler, *Gender Trouble* (Routledge, London, 1990), pp. 140–1.

5. Stephen Heath, *Sexual Fix* (Macmillan, London, 1982).

6. Michel Foucault, *The History of Sexuality*, Vol. I (Allen Lane, London, 1979).

7. Jeffrey Weeks, *Sexuality and its Discontents* (Routledge, London, 1985), and Sheila Jeffreys, *The Spinster and her Enemies* (Pandora, London, 1975) and *AntiClimax* (Women's Press, London, 1990).

8. Adrienne Rich, 'Compulsory heterosexuality and lesbian experience', *Signs*, 5, 4 (1980), pp. 631–60.

9. Sigmund Freud, *On Sexuality* (Penguin, Harmondsworth, 1986), p. 46.

10. See Andrea Dworkin, *Pornography: Men Possessing Women* (Women's Press, London, 1981).

11. Linda Gordon and Ellen du Bois, 'Seeking ecstasy on the battlefield', *Feminist Review*, 13 (1983), pp. 42–54.

12. See Sheila Rowbotham and Jeffrey Weeks, *Socialism and the New Life* (Pluto, London, 1977) and Weeks, *Sexuality and its Discontents*.

13. Jeffreys, *Spinster and her Enemies*, Chapter 7.

14. See Jane Heath, *Simone de Beauvoir* (Harvester, Hemel Hempstead, 1989).

15. Betty Friedan, *The Feminine Mystique* (Penguin, Harmondsworth, 1983); first published 1963.

16. See Elaine Marks and Isabelle de Courtivron (eds), *New French Feminisms* (Harvester, Brighton, 1981).

17. Luce Irigaray, *Ce Sexe qui n'en est pas un* (Minuit, Paris, 1977).

18. See Alison Jaggar, *Feminist Politics and Human Nature* (Rowman & Allanheld, Totowa, NJ, 1983) and Nancy Hartsock, 'The feminist standpoint', in Sandra Harding and Merrill Hintikka (eds), *Discovering Reality* (Reide, Boston, 1983).

19. Patricia Hill Collins, 'The social construction of black feminist thought', *Signs*, 14, 4 (1989), pp. 745–73, reprinted in abridged form in this volume.

20. Ibid., p. 754.

Age, Race, Class and Sex:
Women Redefining Difference

Audre Lorde

As a forty-nine-year-old Black lesbian feminist socialist mother of two, including one boy, and a member of an inter-racial couple, I usually find myself a part of some group defined as other, deviant, inferior, or just plain wrong. Traditionally, in American society, it is the members of oppressed, objectified groups who are expected to stretch out and bridge the gap between the actualities of our lives and the consciousness of our oppressor. For in order to survive, those of us for whom oppression is as American as apple pie have always had to be watchers, to become familiar with the language and manners of the oppressor, even sometimes adopting them for some illusion of protection. Whenever the need for some pretense of communication arises, those who profit from our oppression call upon us to share our knowledge with them. In other words, it is the responsibility of the oppressed to teach the oppressors their mistakes. I am responsible for educating teachers who dismiss my children's culture in school. Black and Third World people are expected to educate white people as to our humanity. Women are expected to educate men. Lesbians and gay men are expected to educate the heterosexual world. The oppressors maintain their position and evade responsibility for their own actions. There is a constant drain of energy which might be better used in redefining ourselves and devising realistic scenarios for altering the present and constructing the future.

Somewhere, on the edge of consciousness, there is what I call a *mythical norm*, which each one of us within our hearts knows 'that is not me'. In America, this norm is usually defined as white, thin, male, young, heterosexual, Christian, and financially secure. It is with this mythical norm that the trappings of power reside within this society. Those of us who stand outside that power often identify one way in which we are different, and we assume that to be the primary cause of all oppression, forgetting other distortions around difference, some of which we ourselves may be practicing. By and large within the women's movement today, white women

---

Extract from *Sister Outsider*, Crossing Press, Trumansburg, 1984, pp. 114–23.

focus upon their oppression as women and ignore differences of race, sexual preference, class, and age. There is a pretense to a homogeneity of experience covered by the word *sisterhood* that does not in fact exist.

Unacknowledged class differences rob women of each other's energy and creative insight. Recently a women's magazine collective made the decision for one issue to print only prose, saying poetry was a less 'rigorous' or 'serious' art form. Yet even the form our creativity takes is often a class issue. Of all the art forms, poetry is the most economical. It is the one which is the most secret, which requires the least physical labor, the least material, and the one which can be done between shifts, in the hospital pantry, on the subway, and on scraps of surplus paper. Over the last few years, writing a novel on tight finances, I came to appreciate the enormous differences in the material demands between poetry and prose. As we reclaim our literature, poetry has been the major voice of poor, working-class, and Colored women. A room of one's own may be a necessity for writing prose, but so are reams of paper, a typewriter, and plenty of time. The actual requirements to produce the visual arts also help determine, along class lines, whose art is whose. In this day of inflated prices for material, who are our sculptors, our painters, our photographers? When we speak of a broadly based women's culture, we need to be aware of the effect of class and economic differences on the supplies available for producing art.

As we move toward creating a society within which we can each flourish, ageism is another distortion of relationship which interferes with our vision. By ignoring the past we are encouraged to repeat its mistakes. The 'generation gap' is an important social tool for any repressive society. If the younger members of a community view the older members as contemptible or suspect or excess, they will never be able to join hands and examine the living memories of the community, nor ask the all-important question, 'Why?' This gives rise to a historical amnesia that keeps us working to invent the wheel every time we have to go to the store for bread.

We find ourselves having to repeat and relearn the same old lessons over and over that our mothers did because we do not pass on what we have learned, or because we are unable to listen. For instance, how many times has this all been said before? For another, who would have believed that once again our daughters are allowing their bodies to be hampered and purgatoried by girdles and high heels and hobble skirts?

Ignoring the differences of race between women and the implications of those differences presents the most serious threat to the mobilization of women's joint power.

As white women ignore their built-in privilege of whiteness and define *woman* in terms of their own experience alone, then women of Color become 'other', the outsider whose experience and tradition is too 'alien' to comprehend. An example of this is the signal absence of the experience of women of Color as a resource for women's studies courses. The literature of women of Color is seldom included in women's literature courses and almost never in other literature courses, nor in women's studies as a whole.

All too often, the excuse given is that the literatures of women of Color can only be taught by Colored women, or that they are too difficult to understand, or that classes cannot 'get into' them because they come out of experiences that are 'too different'. I have heard this argument presented by white women of otherwise quite clear intelligence, women who seem to have no trouble at all teaching and reviewing work that comes out of the vastly different experiences of Shakespeare, Molière, Dostoevsky, and Aristophanes. Surely there must be some other explanation.

This is a very complex question, but I believe one of the reasons white women have such difficulty reading Black women's work is because of their reluctance to see Black women as women and different from themselves. To examine Black women's literature effectively requires that we be seen as whole people in our actual complexities – as individuals, as women, as human – rather than as one of those problematic but familiar stereotypes provided in this society in place of genuine images of Black women. And I believe this holds true for the literatures of other women of Color who are not Black.

The literatures of all women of Color recreate the textures of our lives, and many white women are heavily invested in ignoring the real differences. For as long as any difference between us means one of us must be inferior, then the recognition of any difference must be fraught with guilt. To allow women of Color to step out of stereotypes is too guilt provoking, for it threatens the complacency of those women who view oppression only in terms of sex.

Refusing to recognize difference makes it impossible to see the different problems and pitfalls facing us as women.

Thus, in a patriarchal power system where whiteskin privilege is a major prop, the entrapments used to neutralize Black women and white women are not the same. For example, it is easy for Black women to be used by the power structure against Black men, not because they are men, but because they are Black. Therefore, for Black women, it is necessary at all times to separate the needs of the oppressor from our own legitimate conflicts within our communities. This same problem does not exist for white women. Black women and men have shared racist oppression and still share it, although in different ways. Out of that shared oppression we have developed joint defenses and joint vulnerabilities to each other that are not duplicated in the white community, with the exception of the relationship between Jewish women and Jewish men.

On the other hand, white women face the pitfall of being seduced into joining the oppressor under the pretense of sharing power. This possibility does not exist in the same way for women of Color. The tokenism that is sometimes extended to us is not an invitation to join power; our racial 'otherness' is a visible reality that makes that quite clear. For white women there is a wider range of pretended choices and rewards for identifying with patriarchal power and its tools.

Today, with the defeat of Equal Rights Amendment, the tightening economy, and increased conservatism, it is easier once again for white women to believe the dangerous fantasy that if you are good enough, pretty enough, sweet enough, quiet enough, teach the children to behave, hate the right people, and marry the right men, then you will be allowed to co-exist with patriarchy in relative peace, at least until a man needs your job or the neighborhood rapist happens along. And true, unless one lives and loves in the trenches it is difficult to remember that the war against dehumanization is ceaseless.

But Black women and our children know the fabric of our lives is stitched with violence and with hatred, that there is no rest. We do not deal with it only on the picket lines, or in dark midnight alleys, or in the places where we dare to verbalize our resistance. For us, increasingly, violence weaves through the daily tissues of our living – in the supermarket, in the classroom, in the elevator, in the clinic and the schoolyard, from the plumber, the baker, the saleswoman, the bus driver, the bank teller, the waitress who does not serve us.

Some problems we share as women, some we do not. You fear your children will grow up to join the patriarchy and testify against you, we fear our children will be dragged from a car and shot down in the street, and you will turn your backs upon the reasons they are dying.

The threat of difference has been no less blinding to people of Color. Those of us who are Black must see that the reality of our lives and our struggle does not make us immune to the errors of ignoring and misnaming difference. Within Black communities where racism is a living reality, differences among us often seem dangerous and suspect. The need for unity is often misnamed as a need for homogeneity, and a Black feminist vision mistaken for betrayal of our common interests as a people. Because of the continuous battle against racial erasure that Black women and Black men share, some Black women still refuse to recognize that we are also oppressed as women, and that sexual hostility against Black women is practiced not only by the white racist society, but implemented within our Black communities as well. It is a disease striking the heart of Black nationhood, and silence will not make it disappear. Exacerbated by racism and the pressures of powerlessness, violence against Black women and children often becomes a standard within our communities, one by which manliness can be measured. But these woman-hating acts are rarely discussed as crimes against Black women.

As a group, women of Color are the lowest-paid wage earners in America. We are the primary targets of abortion and sterilization abuse, here and abroad. In certain parts of Africa, small girls are still being sewed shut between their legs to keep them docile and for men's pleasure. This is known as female circumcision, and it is not a cultural affair as the late Jomo Kenyatta insisted, it is a crime against Black women.

Black women's literature is full of the pain of frequent assault, not only by a racist patriarchy, but also by Black men. Yet the necessity for and history of shared battle have made us, Black women, particularly vulnerable to the false accusation that anti-sexist is anti-Black. Meanwhile, womanhating as a recourse of the powerless is sapping strength from Black communities, and our very lives. Rape is on the increase, reported and unreported, and rape is not aggressive sexuality, it is sexualized aggression. As Kalamu ya Salaam, a Black male writer points out, 'As long as male domination exists, rape will exist. Only women revolting and men made conscious of their responsibility to fight sexism can collectively stop rape.'[1]

Differences between ourselves as Black women are also being misnamed and used to separate us from one another. As a Black lesbian feminist comfortable with the many different ingredients of my identity, and a woman committed to racial and sexual freedom from oppression, I find I am constantly being encouraged to pluck out some one aspect of myself and present this as the meaningful whole, eclipsing or denying the other parts of self. But this is a destructive and fragmenting way to live. My fullest concentration of energy is available to me only when I integrate all the parts of who I am, openly, allowing power from particular sources of my living to flow back and forth freely through all my different selves, without the restrictions of externally imposed definition. Only then can I bring myself and my energies as a whole to the service of those struggles which I embrace as part of my living.

A fear of lesbians, or of being accused of being a lesbian, has led many Black women into testifying against themselves. It has led some of us into destructive alliances, and others into despair and isolation. In the white women's communities, heterosexism is sometimes a result of identifying with the white patriarchy, a rejection of that interdependence between women-identified women which allows the self to be, rather than to be used in the service of men. Sometimes it reflects a die-hard belief in the protective coloration of heterosexual relationships, sometimes a self-hate which all women have to fight against, taught us from birth.

Although elements of these attitudes exist for all women, there are particular resonances of heterosexism and homophobia among Black women. Despite the fact that woman-bonding has a long and honorable history in the African and African-American communities, and despite the knowledge and accomplishments of many strong and creative women-identified Black women in the political, social and cultural fields, hetero-sexual Black women often tend to ignore or discount the existence and work of Black lesbians. Part of this attitude has come from an understandable terror of Black male attack within the close confines of Black society, where the punishment for any female self-assertion is still to be accused of being a lesbian and therefore unworthy of the attention or support of the scarce Black male. But part of this need to misname and ignore Black lesbians comes from a very real fear that openly women-identified Black women who are no longer dependent upon men for their self-definition may well reorder our whole concept of social relationships.

Black women who once insisted that lesbianism was a white woman's problem now insist that Black lesbians are a threat to Black nationhood, are consorting with the enemy, are basically un-Black. These accusations, coming from the very women to whom we look for deep and real understanding, have served to keep many Black lesbians in hiding, caught between the racism of white women and the homophobia of their sisters. Often, their work has been ignored, trivialized or misnamed, as with the work of Angelina Grimke, Alice Dunbar-Nelson and Lorraine Hansberry. Yet women-bonded women have always been some part of the power of Black communities, from our unmarried aunts to the amazons of Dahomey.

As Paulo Freire shows so well in *The Pedagogy of the Oppressed*,[2] the true focus of revolutionary change is never merely the oppressive situations which we seek to escape, but that piece of the oppressor which is planted deep within each of us, and which knows only the oppressors' tactics, the oppressors' relationships.

Change means growth, and growth can be painful. But we sharpen self-definition by exposing the self in work and struggle together with those whom we define as different from ourselves, although sharing the same goals. For Black and white, old and young, lesbian and heterosexual women alike, this can mean new paths to our survival.

We have chosen each other
and the edge of each others battles
the war is the same
if we lose
someday women's blood will congeal
upon a dead planet
if we win
there is no telling
we seek beyond history
for a new and more possible meeting.[3]

Notes

1. From 'Rape: a radical analysis, an African-American perspective', by Kalamu ya Salaam in *Black Books Bulletin*, 6, 4 (1980).
2. Seabury Press, New York, 1970.
3. From 'Outlines', unpublished poem.

Femininity and its Discontents

Jacqueline Rose

Psychoanalysis has often been accused of 'functionalism'. It is accepted as a theory of how women are psychically 'induced' into femininity by a patriarchal culture, but is then accused of perpetuating that process, either through a practice assumed to be *prescriptive* about women's role (this is what women *should* do), or because the very effectiveness of the account as a *description* (this is what is demanded of women, what they are *expected* to do) leaves no possibility of change.

It is this aspect of Juliet Mitchell's pioneering book *Psychoanalysis and Feminism* which seems to have been taken up most strongly by feminists who have attempted to follow through the political implications of psychoanalysis as a critique of patriarchy.[1]

Thus Gayle Rubin, following Mitchell, uses psychoanalysis for a general critique of a patriarchal culture which is predicated on the exchange of women by men.[2] Nancy Chodorow shifts from Freud to later object relations theory to explain how women's childcaring role is perpetuated through the earliest relationship between a mother and her child, which leads in her case to a demand for a fundamental change in how childcare is organized between women and men in our culture.[3] Although there are obvious differences between these two readings of psychoanalysis, they nonetheless share an emphasis on the social exchange of women, or the distribution of roles for women, across cultures: 'Women's mothering is one of the few universal and enduring elements of the sexual division of labour'.[4]

The force of psychoanalysis is therefore (as Janet Sayers points out)[5] precisely that it gives an account of patriarchal culture as a trans-historical and cross-cultural force. It therefore conforms to the feminist demand for a theory which can explain women's subordination across specific cultures and different historical moments. Summing this up crudely, we could say that psychoanalysis adds sexuality to Marxism, where sexuality is felt to be lacking, and extends beyond Marxism where the attention to specific historical instances, changes in modes of production etc., is felt to leave something unexplained.

Extract from *Sexuality in the Field of Vision*, Verso, London, 1986, pp. 83–103, abridged.

But all this happens at a cost, and that cost is the concept of the unconscious. What distinguishes psychoanalysis from sociological accounts of gender (hence for me the fundamental impasse of Nancy Chodorow's work) is that whereas for the latter, the internalization of norms is assumed roughly to work, the basic premise and indeed starting-point of psychoanalysis is that it does not. The unconscious constantly reveals the 'failure' of identity. Because there is no continuity of psychic life, so there is no stability of sexual identity, no position for women (or for men) which is ever simply achieved. Nor does psychoanalysis see such 'failure' as a special-case inability or an individual deviancy from the norm. 'Failure' is not a moment to be regretted in a process of adaptation, or development into normality, which ideally takes its course (some of the earliest critics of Freud, such as Ernest Jones, did, however, give an account of development in just these terms). Instead 'failure' is something endlessly repeated and relived moment by moment throughout our individual histories. It appears not only in the symptom, but also in dreams, in slips of the tongue and in forms of sexual pleasure which are pushed to the sidelines of the norm. Feminism's affinity with psychoanalysis rests above all, I would argue, with this recognition that there is a resistance to identity at the very heart of psychic life. Viewed in this way, psychoanalysis is no longer best understood as an account of how women are fitted into place (even this, note, is the charitable reading of Freud). Instead psychoanalysis becomes one of the few places in our culture where it is recognized as more than a fact of individual pathology that most women do not painlessly slip into their roles as women, if indeed they do at all. Freud himself recognized this increasingly in his work. In the articles which run from 1924 to 1931,[6] he moves from that famous, or rather infamous, description of the little girl struck with her 'inferiority' or 'injury' in the face of the anatomy of the little boy and wisely accepting her fate ('injury' as the *fact* of being feminine), to an account which quite explicitly describes the process of becoming 'feminine' as an 'injury' or 'catastrophe' for the complexity of her earlier psychic and sexual life ('injury' as its *price*).

Elizabeth Wilson and Janet Sayers are, therefore, in a sense correct to criticize psychoanalysis when it is taken as a general theory of patriarchy or of gender identity, that is, as a theory which explains how women wholly internalize the very mode of being which is feminism's specific target of attack; but they have missed out half the (psychoanalytic) story. In fact the argument seems to be circular. Psychoanalysis is drawn in the direction of a general theory of culture or a sociological account of gender because these seem to lay greater emphasis on the pressures of the 'outside' world, but it is this very pulling away from the psychoanalytic stress on the 'internal' complexity and difficulty of psychic life which produces the functionalism which is then critized.

The argument about whether Freud is being 'prescriptive' or 'descriptive' about women (with its associated stress on the motives and morals of Freud himself) is fated to the extent that it is locked into this model. Many of us will be familiar with Freud's famous pronouncement that a woman who does not succeed in transforming activity to passivity, clitoris to vagina, mother for father, will fall ill. Yet psychoanalysis testifies to the fact that psychic illness or distress is in no sense the prerogative of women who 'fail' in this task. One of my students recently made the obvious but important point that we would be foolish to deduce from the external trappings of normality or conformity in a woman that all is in fact well. And Freud himself always stressed the psychic cost of the civilizing process for all (we can presumably include women in that 'all' even if at times he did not seem to do so).

All these aspects of Freud's work are subject to varying interpretation by analysts themselves. The first criticism of Freud's 'phallocentrism' came from inside psychoanalysis, from analysts such as Melanie Klein, Ernest Jones and Karen Horney who felt, contrary to Freud, that 'femininity' was a quality with its own impetus, subject to checks and internal conflict, but tending ultimately to fulfilment. For Jones, the little girl was 'typically receptive and acquisitive' from the outset; for Horney, there was from the beginning a 'wholly womanly' attachment to the father.[7] For these analysts, this development might come to grief, but for the most part a gradual strengthening of the child's ego and her increasing adaptation to reality, should guarantee its course. Aspects of the little girl's psychic life which were resistant to this process (the famous 'active' or 'masculine' drives) were defensive. The importance of concepts such as the 'phallic phase' in Freud's description of infantile sexuality is not, therefore, that such concepts can be taken as the point of insertion of patriarchy (assimilation to the norm). Rather their importance lies in the way that they indicate, through their very artificiality, that something was being *forced*, and in the concept of psychic life with which they were accompanied. In Freud's work they went hand in hand with an increasing awareness of the difficulty, not to say impossibility of the path to normality for the girl, and an increasing stress on the fundamental divisions, or splitting, of psychic life. It was those who challenged these concepts in the 1920s and 1930s who introduced the more normative stress on a sequence of development, and coherent ego, back into the account.

I think we go wrong again, therefore, if we conduct the debate about whether Freud's account was developmental or not entirely in terms of his own writing. Certainly the idea of development is present at moments in his work. But it was not present *enough* for many of his contemporaries, who took up the issue and reinstated the idea of development precisely in relation to the sexual progress of the girl (her passage into womanhood).

'Psychoanalysis' is not, therefore, a single entity. Institutional divisions within psychoanalysis have turned on the very questions about the phallocentrism of analysts, the meaning of femininity, the sequence of psychic development and its norms, which have been the concern of feminists. The accusations came from analysts themselves. In the earlier debates, however, the reproach against Freud produced an account of femininity which was more, rather than less, normative than his own.

The politics of Lacanian psychoanalysis begin here. From the 1930s,

Lacan saw his intervention as a return to the concepts of psychic division, splitting of the ego, and an endless (he called it 'insistent') pressure of the unconscious against any individual's pretension to a smooth and coherent psychic and sexual identity. Lacan's specific target was 'ego-psychology' in America, and what he saw as the dilution of psychoanalysis into a tool of social adaptation and control (hence the central emphasis on the concepts of the ego and identification which are often overlooked in discussions of his ideas). For Lacan, psychoanalysis does not offer an account of a developing ego which is 'not *necessarily* coherent',[8] but of an ego which is 'necessarily *not* coherent', that is, which is always and persistently divided against itself.

Lacan could therefore be picked up by a Marxist like Althusser not because he offered a theory of adaptation to reality or of the individual's insertion into culture (Althusser added a note to the English translation of his paper on Lacan criticizing it for having implied such a reading),[9] but because the force of the unconscious in Lacan's interpretation of Freud was felt to undermine the mystifications of a bourgeois culture proclaiming its identity, and that of its subjects, to the world. The political use of Lacan's theory therefore stemmed from its assault on what English Marxists would call bourgeois 'individualism'. What the theory offered was a divided subject out of 'synch' with bourgeois myth. Feminists could legitimately object that the notion of psychic fragmentation was of little immediate political advantage to women struggling for the first time to find a voice, and trying to bring together the dissociated components of their life into a political programme. But this is a very different criticism of the political implications of psychoanalysis than the one which accuses it of forcing women into bland conformity with their expected role.

Psychoanalysis and history: the history of psychoanalysis

What, therefore, is the political purchase of the concept of the unconscious on women's lived experience? And what can it say to the specific histories of which we form a part?

One of the objections which is often made against psychoanalysis is that it has no sense of history, and an inadequate grasp of its relationship to the concrete institutions which frame and determine our lives. For even if we allow for a moment the radical force of the psychoanalytic insight, the exclusiveness or limited availability of that insight tends to be turned, not against the culture or state which mostly resists its general (and publicly funded) dissemination,[10] but against psychoanalysis itself. The 'privatization' of psychoanalysis comes to mean that it only refers to the individual as private, and the concentration on the individual as private is then seen as reinforcing a theory which places itself above history and change.

Again I think that this question is posed back to front, and that we need to ask, not what psychoanalysis has to say about history, but rather what is the history of psychoanalysis, that is, what was the intervention of psycho-analysis into the institutions which, at the time of its emergence, were controlling women's lives? And what was the place of the unconscious, historically, in that? Paradoxically, the claim that psychoanalysis is a-historical dehistoricizes it. If we go back to the beginnings of psychoanalysis, it is clear that the concept of the unconscious was radical at exactly that level of social 'reality' with which it is so often assumed to have nothing whatsoever to do.

Recent work by feminist historians is of particular importance in this context. Judith Walkowitz, in her study of the Contagious Diseases Acts of the 1860s, shows how state policy on public hygiene and the state's increasing control over casual labour, relied on a category of women as diseased (the suspected prostitute subjected to forcible examination and internment in response to the spread of venereal disease in the port towns).[11] Carol Dyhouse has described how debates about educational opportunity for women constantly returned to the evidence of the female body (either the energy expended in their development towards sexual reproduction meant that women could not be educated, or education and the overtaxing of the brain would damage their reproductive capacity).[12] In the birth control controversy, the Malthusian idea of controlling the reproduction, and by implication the sexuality, of the working class served to counter the idea that poverty could be reduced by the redistribution of wealth.[13] Recurrently in the second half of the nineteenth century, in the period immediately prior to Freud, female sexuality became the focus of a panic about the effects of industrialization on the cohesion of the social body and its ability to reproduce itself comfortably. The importance of all this work (Judith Walkowitz makes this quite explicit) is that 'attitudes' towards women cannot be consigned to the sphere of ideology, assumed to have no purchase on material life, so deeply implicated was the concept of female sexuality in the legislative advancement of the state.[14]

Central to all of this was the idea that the woman was wholly responsible for the social well-being of the nation (questions of social division transmuted directly into the moral and sexual responsibility of subjects), or where she failed in this task, that she was disordered or diseased. The hysteric was either the overeducated woman, or else the woman indulging in non-procreative or uncontrolled sexuality (conjugal onanism), or again the woman in the lock hospitals which, since the eighteenth century, had been receiving categories refused by the general hospitals ('infectious diseases, "fever", children, maternity cases, mental disorders, as well as venereal diseases').[15] It was these hospitals which, at the time of the Contagious Diseases Acts, became the place of confinement for the diseased prostitute in a new form of collaborative relationship with the state.

This is where psychoanalysis begins. Although the situation was not identical in France, there are important links. Freud's earliest work was under Charcot at the Salpêtrière Clinic in Paris, a hospital for women: 'five thousand neurotic indigents, epileptics, and insane patients, many of whom were deemed incurable'.[16] The 'dregs' of society comprised the inmates of the Salpêtrière (psychoanalysis does not start in the Viennese parlour). Freud was working under Charcot, whose first contribution to the study of hysteria was to move it out of the category of sexual malingering and into that of a specific and accredited neurological disease. The problem with Charcot's work is that while he was constructing the symptomatology of the disease (turning it into a respected object of the medical institution), he was reinforcing it as a special category of behaviour, visible to the eye, and the result of a degenerate hereditary disposition.

Freud's intervention here was twofold. Firstly, he questioned the visible evidence of the disease – the idea that you could know a hysteric by looking at her body, that is, by reading off the symptoms of nervous disability or susceptibility to trauma. Secondly (and this second move depended on the first), he rejected the idea that hysteria was an 'independent' clinical entity, by using what he uncovered in the treatment of the hysterical patient as the basis of his account of the unconscious and its universal presence in adult life.

The 'universalism' of Freud was not, therefore, an attempt to remove the subject from history; it stemmed from his challenge to the category of hysteria as a principle of classification for certain socially isolated and confined individuals, and his shifting of this category into the centre of everybody's psychic experience: 'Her hysteria can therefore be described as an acquired one, and it presupposed nothing more than the possession of what is probably a very wide-spread proclivity – the proclivity to acquire hysteria'.[17] The reason why the two moves are interdependent is because it was only by penetrating behind the visible symptoms of disorder and asking what it was that the symptom was trying to *say*, that Freud could uncover those unconscious desires and motives which he went on to expose in the slips, dreams and jokes of individuals paraded as normal. Thus the challenge to the entity 'hysteria', that is, to hysteria *as* an entity available for quite specific forms of social control, relied on the concept of the unconscious. 'I have attempted,' wrote Freud, 'to meet the problem of hysterical attacks along a line other than *descriptive*.'[18] Hence Freud's challenge to the visible, to the empirically self-evident, to the 'blindness of the seeing eye'.[19] (Compare this with Charcot's photographs offered as the evidence of the disease.) It is perhaps this early and now mostly forgotten moment which can give us the strongest sense of the force of the unconscious as a concept against a fully social classification relying on empirical evidence as its rationale.

The challenge of psychoanalysis to empiricist forms of reasoning was therefore the very axis on which the fully historical intervention of psychoanalysis into late nineteenth-century medicine turned. The theories of sexuality came after this first intervention (in *Studies on Hysteria*, Freud's remarks on sexuality are mostly given in awkward footnotes suggesting the importance of sexual abstinence for women as a causal factor in the etiology of hysteria). But when Freud did start to investigate the complexity of sexual

life in response to what he uncovered in hysterical patients, his first step was
a similar questioning of social definitions, this time of sexual perversion as
'innate' or 'degenerate', that is, as the special property of a malfunctioning
type.[20] In fact, if we take dreams and slips of the tongue (both considered
before Freud to result from lowered mental capacity), sexuality and hysteria,
the same movement operates each time. A discredited, pathological, or
irrational form of behaviour is given its psychic value by psychoanalysis.
What this meant for the hysterical woman is that instead of just being looked
at or examined, she was allowed to *speak*.

Some of the criticisms which are made by feminists of Freudian psychoanalysis, especially when it is filtered through the work of Lacan, can
perhaps be answered with reference to this moment. Most often the
emphasis is laid either on Lacan's statement that 'the unconscious is
structured like a language', or on his concentration on mental representation
and the ideational contents of the mind. The feeling seems to be that the
stress on ideas and language cuts psychoanalysis off from the materiality of
being, whether that materiality is defined as the biological aspects of our
subjectivity, or as the economic factors determining our lives (one or the
other and at times both).

Once it is put like this, the argument becomes a version of the debate
within Marxism over the different instances of social determination and their
hierarchy ('ideology' versus the 'economic') or else it becomes an accusation
of idealism (Lacan) against materialism (Marx). I think this argument
completely misses the importance of the emphasis on language in Lacan
and of mental representation in Freud. The statement that 'the unconscious
is structured like a language' was above all part of Lacan's attempt to
establish a continuity between the seeming disorder of the symptom or
dream and the normal language through which we recognize each other and
speak. And the importance of the linguistic sign (Saussure's distinction
between the signifier and the signified)[21] was that it provided a model
internal to language itself of that form of indirect representation (the body
speaking because there is something which cannot be said) which
psychoanalysis uncovered in the symptomatology of its patients. Only if one
thing can stand for another is the hysterical symptom something more than
the logical and direct manifestation of physical or psychic (and social)
degeneracy.

This is why the concept of the unconscious – as indicating an irreducible
discontinuity of psychic life – is so important. Recognition of that discontinuity in us all is in a sense the price we have to pay for that earlier
historical displacement.

Feminism and the unconscious

It is, however, this concept which seems to be lost whenever Freud has been
challenged on those ideas which have been most problematic for feminism,

in so far as the critique of Freudian phallocentrism so often relies on a return to empiricism, on an appeal to 'what actually happens' or what can be *seen* to be the case. Much of Ernest Jones's criticism of Freud, for example, stemmed from his conviction that girls and boys could not conceivably be ignorant of so elementary a fact as that of sexual difference and procreation.[22] And Karen Horney, in her similar but distinct critique, referred to 'the manifestations of so elementary a principle of nature as that of the mutual attraction of the sexes'.[23] We can compare this with Freud: 'from the point of view of psycho-analysis the exclusive sexual interest felt by men for women is also a problem that needs elucidating and is not a self-evident fact based upon an attraction that is ultimately of a chemical nature'.[24] The point is not that one side is appealing to 'biology' (or 'nature') and the other to 'ideas', but that Freud's opening premise is to challenge the self-evidence of both.

The feminist criticism of Freud has of course been very different since it has specifically involved a rejection of the evidence of this particular norm: the normal femininity which, in the earlier quarrel, Freud himself was considered to have questioned. But at this one crucial level – the idea of an unconscious which points to a fundamental division of psychic life and which therefore challenges any form of empiricism based on what is there to be observed (even when scientifically tested and tried) – the very different critiques are related. In *Psychoanalysis and Feminism*, Juliet Mitchell based at least half her argument on this point but it has been lost. Thus Shulamith Firestone, arguing in *The Dialectic of Sex* that the girl's alleged sense of inferiority in relation to the boy was the logical outcome of the observable facts of the child's experience, had to assume an unproblematic and one-to-one causality between psychic life and social reality with no possibility of dislocation or error.[25] The result is that the concept of the unconscious is lost (the little girl rationally recognizes and decides her fate) and mothering is deprived of its active components (the mother is seen to be only subordinate and in no sense powerful for the child).[26] For all its more obvious political appeal, the idea that psychic life is the unmediated reflection of social relations locks the mother and child into a closed subordination which can then only be broken by the advances of empiricism itself:

> Full mastery of the reproductive process is in sight, and there has been significant advance in understanding the basic life and death process. The nature of ageing and growth, sleep and hibernation, the chemical functioning of the brain and the development of consciousness and memory are all beginning to be understood in their entirety. This acceleration promises to continue for another century, or however long it takes to achieve the goal of Empiricism: total understanding of the laws of nature.[27]

Shulamith Firestone's argument has been criticized by feminists who would not wish to question, any more than I would, the importance of her intervention for feminism.[28] But I think it is important that the part of her programme which is now criticized (the idea that women must rely on scientific progress to achieve any change) is so directly related to the empiricist concept of social reality (what can be *seen* to happen) which she offers. The empiricism of the goal is the outcome of the empiricism at the level of social reality and psychic life. I have gone back to this moment because, even though it is posed in different terms, something similar seems to be going on in the recent Marxist repudiation of Freud. Janet Sayers's critique of Juliet Mitchell, for example, is quite explicitly based on the concept of 'what actually and specifically happens' ('in the child's environment' and 'in the child's physical and biological development').[29]

Utopianism of the psyche

Something else happens in all of this which is probably the most central issue for me: the discarding of the concept of the unconscious seems to leave us with a type of utopianism of psychic life. In this context it is interesting to note just how close the appeal to biology and the appeal to culture as the determinants of psychic experience can be. Karen Horney switched from one to the other, moving from the idea that femininity was a natural quality, subject to checks, but tending on its course, to the idea that these same checks, and indeed most forms of psychic conflict, were the outcome of an oppressive social world. The second position is closer to that of feminism, but something is nonetheless missing from both sides of the divide. For what has happened to the unconscious, to that divided and disordered subjectivity which, I have argued, had to be recognized in us all if the category of hysteria as a peculiar property of one class of women was to be disbanded? Do not both of these movements make psychic conflict either an accident or an obstacle on the path to psychic and sexual continuity – a continuity which, as feminists, we recognize as a myth of our culture – only to reinscribe it in a different form on the agenda for a future (post-revolutionary) date?

Every time Freud is challenged, this concept of psychic cohesion as the ultimate object of our political desires seems to return. Thus the French feminist and analyst, Luce Irigaray, challenges Lacan not just for the phallocentrism of his arguments, but because the Freudian account is seen to cut women off from an early and untroubled psychic unity (the primordial state of fusion with the mother) which feminists should seek to restore. Irigaray calls this the 'imaginary' of women (a reference to Lacan's idea of a primitive narcissism which was for him only ever a fantasy). In a world felt to be especially alienating for women, this idea of psychic oneness or primary narcissism has its own peculiar force. It appears in a different form in Michèle Barrett's and Mary McIntosh's excellent reply to Christopher Lasch's thesis that we are witnessing a regrettable decline in the patriarchal family.[30] Responding to his accusation that culture is losing its super-ego edge and descending into narcissism, they offer the particularly female qualities of mothering (Chodorow) and a defence of this very 'primary narcissism' in the name of women against Lasch's undoubtedly reactionary lament. The problem remains, however, that whenever the 'feminine' comes into the argument as a quality in this way we seem to lose the basic insight of psychoanalysis – the failure or difficulty of femininity for women, and that fundamental psychic division which in Freud's work was its accompanying and increasingly insistent discovery. If I question the idea that psychoanalysis is the 'new orthodoxy' for feminists, it is at least partly because of the strong political counterweight of this idea of femininity which appears to repudiate both these Freudian insights together.

To return to the relationship between Marxism and psychoanalysis with which I started, I think it is relevant that the most systematic attack we have had on the hierarchies and organization of the male Left[31] gives to women the privilege of the personal in a way which divests it (*has* to divest it) of complexity at exactly this level of the conflicts and discontinuities of psychic life. Like many feminists, the slogan 'the personal is political' has been central to my own political development; just as I see the question of sexuality, as a political issue which *exceeds* the province of Marxism ('economic', 'ideological' or whatever), as one of the most important defining characteristics of feminism itself. But the dialogue between feminism and psychoanalysis, which is for me the arena in which the full complexity of that 'personal' and that 'sexuality' can be grasped, constantly seems to fail.

In this article I have not answered all the criticisms of psychoanalysis. It is certainly the case that psychoanalysis does not give us a blueprint for political action, or allow us to deduce political conservatism or radicalism directly from the vicissitudes of psychic experience. Nor does the concept of the unconscious sit comfortably with the necessary attempt by feminism to claim a new sureness of identity for women, or with the idea of always conscious and deliberate political decision-making and control (psycho-analysis is *not* a voluntarism).[32] But its challenge to the concept of psychic identity is important for feminism in that it allows into the political arena problems of subjectivity (subjectivity *as* a problem) which tend to be suppressed from other forms of political debate. It may also help us to open up the space between different notions of political identity – between the idea of a political identity for feminism (what women require) and that of a feminine identity for women (what women are or should be), expecially given the problems constantly encountered by the latter and by the sometimes too easy celebration of an identity amongst women which glosses over the differences between us.

Psychoanalysis finally remains one of the few places in our culture where our experience of femininity can be spoken as a problem that is something other than the problem which the protests of women are posing for an increasingly conservative political world. I would argue that this is one of the reasons why it has not been released into the public domain. The fact that psychoanalysis cannot be assimilated directly into a political programme as such does not mean, therefore, that it should be discarded, and thrown back into the outer reaches of a culture which has never yet been fully able to heed its voice.

Notes

First published in *Feminist Review*, 14 (Summer 1983), pp. 5–21, this essay was originally requested by the editors of *Feminist Review* to counter the largely negative representation of psychoanalysis which had appeared in the journal, and as a specific response to Elizabeth Wilson's 'Psychoanalysis: psychic law and order', *Feminist Review*, 8 (Summer 1981). (See also Janet Sayers, 'Psychoanalysis and personal politics: a response to Elizabeth Wilson', *Feminist Review*, 10 (1982).) As I was writing the piece, however, it soon became clear that Elizabeth Wilson's article and the question of *Feminist Review*'s own relationship to psychoanalysis could not be understood independently of what has been – outside the work of Juliet Mitchell for feminism – a fairly consistent repudiation of Freud within the British Left. In this context, the feminist debate over Freud becomes part of a larger question about the importance of subjectivity to our understanding of political and social life. That this was in fact the issue became even clearer when Elizabeth Wilson and Angie Weir published an article 'The British women's movement' in *New Left Review*, 148 (November–December 1984), which dismissed the whole area of subjectivity and psychoanalysis from feminist politics together with any work by feminists (historians and writers on contemporary politics) who, while defining themselves as socialist feminists, nonetheless query the traditional terms of an exclusively class-based analysis of power.

1. Juliet Mitchell, *Psychoanalysis and Feminism* (Allen Lane, London, 1974).
2. See Gayle Rubin, 'The traffic in women'; and for a critique of the use of Lévi-Strauss on which this reading is based, Elizabeth Cowie, 'Woman as sign', *m/f*, 1978, pp. 49–63.
3. Nancy Chodorow, *The Reproduction of Mothering* (University of California Press, Berkeley, 1978).
4. Ibid., p. 3.
5. Janet Sayers, 'A response to Elizabeth Wilson', *Feminist Review*, 10 (1981), pp. 91–5.
6. Sigmund Freud, 'The dissolution of the Oedipus complex' (1924); 'Some psychical consequences of the anatomical distinction between the sexes' (1925); 'Female sexuality' (1931), *Standard Edition of Complete Psychological Works* (Hogarth, London, 1955–74), vol. 19.
7. Ernest Jones, 'The phallic phase', *International Journal of Psycho-Analysis*, 14 (1933), p. 265; Karen Horney, 'On the genesis of the castration complex in women' (1924), in *Feminine Psychology* (London, 1967), p. 53.
8. Elizabeth Wilson, 'Reopening the case – feminism and psychoanalysis', opening seminar presentation in discussion with Jacqueline Rose, London 1982. This was the first of a series of seminars on the subject of feminism and psychoanalysis which ran into 1983; see articles by Parveen Adams, Nancy Wood and Claire Buck, *m/f*, 8 (1983).
9. Louis Althusser, 'Freud and Lacan', see publisher's note in *Lenin and Philosophy and Other Essays* (London, 1971), pp. 189–90.
10. For a more detailed discussion of the relative assimilation of Kleinianism through social work in relation to children in this country, especially through the Tavistock Clinic in London, see Michael Rustin, 'A socialist consideration of Kleinian psychoanalysis', *New Left Review*, 131 (1982), p. 85 and note. As Rustin points out, the state is willing to fund psychoanalysis when it is a question of helping children to adapt, but less so when it is a case of helping adults to remember.
11. Judith Walkowitz, *Prostitution and Victorian Society – Women, Class and the State* (London and New York, 1980).
12. Carol Dyhouse, *Girls Growing Up in Late Victorian and Edwardian England* (London, 1981).

13. Angus McLaren, *Birth Control in Nineteenth Century England* (London, 1978).

14. Walkowitz, *Prostitution*, p. 69.

15. Ibid., p. 59.

16. Ilza Veith, *Hysteria: the History of a Disease* (London, 1975), p. 229.

17. Freud, *Studies on Hysteria*, Pelican Freud Library, vol. 3 (Penguin, Harmondsworth, 1976), pp. 122, 187.

18. Freud, 'Preface and footnotes to Charcot's Tuesday lectures' (1892–4), *Standard Edition*, vol. 1, p. 137.

19. *Studies on Hysteria*, pp. 117, 181.

20. Freud, *Three Essays on the Theory of Sexuality*, Pelican Freud, vol. 1, part I.

21. Ferdinand de Saussure, *Cours de linguistique générale* (1915), Paris, 1972; trans. Roy Harris, *Course in General Linguistics* (London, 1983), pp. 65–70.

22. Jones, 'The phallic phase', p. 15.

23. Horney, 'The flight from womanhood' (1926), in *Feminine Psychology*, p. 68.

24. *Three Essays*, pp. 146n, 57n.

25. Shulamith Firestone, *The Dialectic of Sex* (Women's Press, London, 1979).

26. See Mitchell, 'Shulamith Firestone: Freud feminised', *Psychoanalysis and Feminism*, Part 2, Section 2, chapter 5.

27. Firestone, *Dialectic*, p. 170.

28. Ibid., introduction by Rosalind Delmar.

29. Sayers quoted by Wilson in 'Reopening the case'.

30. Michèle Barrett and Mary McIntosh, 'Narcissism and the family: a critique of Lasch', *New Left Review*, 135 (September–October 1982).

31. Sheila Rowbotham, Lynne Segal and Hilary Wainright, *Beyond the Fragments – Feminism and the Making of Socialism* (London, 1979).

32. Sayers, 'Response to Elizabeth Wilson', pp. 92–3.

Creating the Sexual Future

Sheila Jeffreys

Heterosexuality as an Institution

To many people the word 'heterosexual' would be obscure in meaning. The fact that the social relationships in Western male supremacy are organized on a heterosexual principle, i.e. based on the act of sexual intercourse, would seem as little worth comment as the fact that rain falls from the skies. The heterosexual principle is seen as part of nature, requiring neither a particular word to describe it nor, most particularly, an explanation. It was the late nineteenth-century sexologists who, in the course of stigmatizing homosexuality, popularized the word they needed for its opposite. Heterosexuality was named. It was presented as the normal and desirable form for the expression of sexual emotion. The current *Oxford Dictionary* definition derives from this coining. 'Hetero' is defined by the *Oxford Dictionary* as meaning 'other, different'. 'Heterosexual' is defined as 'relating to or characterized by the normal relation of the sexes.[1]

The sexologists propagated the idea that it was deviant and sick or hereditarily flawed for members of the same sex class to relate to each other. They limited their definition of this deviance to sexual acts and feelings. They did not portray heterosexuality as a political institution. Their limited definition is the one that has been in use until the current wave of feminism. In the last wave of feminism the term was not used in political discussion. Sexological language had not yet become the common parlance save for those women who became followers of the sexologists.

This does not mean that our foresisters were not aware of the political implications of heterosexuality. They criticized marriage vigorously and, indeed, all forms of sexual and love relations with men. Many chose to be spinsters or lesbians for political reasons. But the language they used was different from that of today.

In the current wave of feminism, feminist and lesbian theorists have seen heterosexuality as a political institution. They have rejected utterly the idea that it is 'normal' or 'natural' for women to relate sexually to men. They have used the term 'heterosexuality' not just to mean sexual feelings, but to

From *Anticlimax*, Women's Press, London, 1990, pp. 287–316.

describe a political system. Similarly lesbianism has been defined by feminists not just as a form of sexual attraction, but as a politics, and a strategy for revolution.

In the 1960s and 1970s a new approach to sexuality by psychologists took over from the pathologizing of sexual deviation which had dominated the rest of the century. This was the sexual preference model, or what Celia Kitzinger, in her book *The Social Construction of Lesbianism*, calls liberal humanism. Humanistic psychologists challenged the disease model of homosexuality. The humanistic model sees homosexuality and hetero-sexuality as equally valid and seeks to counter what is seen as irrational prejudice or homophobia towards homosexuals. Kitzinger explains:

> The 'pathological' model has already been widely criticised in the professional literature for its methodological and theoretical inadequacies and its ideological biases, and it no longer represents the dominant psychological approach to lesbianism. In its place is a model of lesbianism (and male homosexuality) as a normal, natural and healthy sexual preference or lifestyle, and the issue of pathology has shifted to the diagnosis and cure of the new disease of 'homophobia' (fear of homosexuals).[2]

Acceptance of this model depends upon accepting that heterosexuality, if not 'natural', is at least inevitable for the vast majority of people. Homosexuals are seen as a harmless minority who should be tolerated and indeed assimilated into main stream heterosexual culture. There is no challenge to heterosexuality in this approach. Heterosexuality is certainly not seen as a political institution. Heterosexuality and homosexuality are seen as sexual preferences or choices, defined by sexual activities and feelings or even 'lifestyles', but having no more to do with politics than a preference for peas over cabbage. The majority of those involved in the feminist and gay movements have adopted this approach and determinedly resisted a political analysis of heterosexuality. As Kitzinger points out, liberal humanistic research is 'cited enthusiastically by many gay people and, especially in the anti-gay climate encouraged by the AIDS scare, liberal humanistic beliefs about homosexual normality and mental health are often experienced as reinforcing and affirming gay and lesbian culture'.[3] The sexual libertarians take this perspective. The politics of sexuality for them is restricted to combating the ways in which the free expression of the preference is restricted by repressive agencies. There is no political critique of heterosexuality here.

Why is this depoliticized approach taken by so many feminists, lesbians and gay men? Kitzinger points out that liberalism is the answer of the ruling class to finding its hegemony threatened. It is designed to damp down any serious challenge and smooth out conflict. She quotes Kathie Sarachild on the political role of liberalism:

> Liberal leadership emerges whenever an oppressed group begins to move against the oppressor. It works to preserve the oppressor's power by avoiding and preventing exposure and confrontation. The oppressed is always resisting the

oppressor in some way, but when rebellion begins to be public knowledge and the movement becomes a powerful force, liberalism becomes necessary for the oppressor to stop the radical upsurge.[4]

Thus does liberal humanism work to remove any threat to the heterosexual system. Political lesbians and gays are forced into the use of liberal concepts such as sexual preference because such arguments can appeal to the liberal establishment. In an increasingly hostile climate demonstrated by the 1988 anti-gay legislation in Britain, lesbians are forced to conceal the radicalism of their politics in order to gain credibility.

The radical or revolutionary feminist challenge to heterosexuality as a political institution has encountered a hostile response from feminists and lesbians who take a liberal humanistic approach. From the birth of lesbian feminism lesbians have asserted that lesbianism is a fundamental threat to male supremacy. We have asserted that lesbianism is a crucial strategy for women to undertake if they wish to end their subordination. This lesbian radicalism has been carefully tidied away by the new wave of assimilationist, designer dykes but it cannot be expunged from the record entirely. The most famous of lesbian feminist manifestos, the 'Woman-identified woman' paper by Radicalesbians, written in 1970, gives an uncompromisingly political definition of lesbianism:

> A lesbian is the rage of all women condensed to the point of explosion. She is the woman who, often beginning at an extremely early age, acts in accordance with her inner compulsion to be a more complete and freer human being than her society . . . cares to allow her.[5]

The Radicalesbian paper asserts that it is necessary for women to become lesbians if they are to develop self-love and work effectively for their own liberation. They explain:

> Our energies must flow toward our sisters, not backwards toward our oppressors. As long as women's liberation tries to free women without facing the basic heterosexual structure that binds us in one-to-one relationships with our own oppressors, tremendous energies will continue to flow into trying to straighten up each particular relationship with a man, how to get better sex, how to turn his head around – into trying to make the 'new man' out of him, in the delusion that this will allow us to be the 'new woman'.[6]

In the early 1970s many radical lesbians all over the Western world were stating in various ways that lesbianism was the political strategy necessary for the liberation of women and that heterosexual practice was not consonant with feminism. Jill Johnston stated this particularly clearly in her 1973 collection, *Lesbian Nation*:

> Feminism at heart is a massive complaint. Lesbianism is the solution. Which is another way of putting what Ti-Grace Atkinson once described as feminism being a theory and lesbianism the practice. When theory and practice come together we'll have the revolution. Until all women are lesbians there will be no true political revolution. No feminist *per se* has advanced a solution outside of accommodation to the man . . . Feminists who still sleep with the man are delivering their most vital energies to the oppressor.[7]

Within the lesbian feminist community in Britain this idea was quite widely accepted in the 1970s but was not written down until 1979 by the Leeds Revolutionary Feminist Group, of which I was a member, in the 'Political lesbian' paper. This was written for the Revolutionary Feminist conference held in September of that year. It was a brief conference paper intended to stimulate discussion rather than to attempt a detailed analysis.

The paper explains that the writers were often asked by heterosexual feminists when they were explaining their political position, whether they thought all feminists should be lesbians. The answer was: 'We do think that all feminists can and should be political lesbians.' A political lesbian is defined as 'a woman-identified woman who does not fuck men'.[8] Up until the time of writing the paper we had felt under pressure to dissemble in order not to cause offence. Now we wanted to set out the politics behind saying that all feminists should be lesbians. The paper explains that sexuality is important because 'it is specifically through sexuality that the fundamental oppression, that of men over women, is maintained'. It states that as the form of the oppression of women changed and 'more women are able to earn a little more money and the pressures of reproduction are relieved so the hold of individual men and men as a class over women is being strengthened through sexual control'.[9]

The role of heterosexuality as a political institution in the oppression of women is described:

> The heterosexual couple is the basic unit of the political structure of male supremacy. In it each individual woman comes under the control of an individual man. It is more efficient by far than keeping women in ghettoes, camps, or even sheds at the bottom of the garden. In the couple, love and sex are used to obscure the realities of oppression, to prevent women identifying with each other in order to revolt, and from identifying 'their' man as part of the enemy. Any woman who takes part in a heterosexual couple helps to shore up male supremacy by making its foundations stronger.[10]

The paper went down well at the conference and only became a *cause célèbre* when it was printed, on request, in the national feminist newsletter *WIRES* some months later. Angry letters flooded in. There were also some in support, but at the time when we were trying to cope with the ferocity of the personal attacks we were receiving, they were not the ones we noticed most clearly. Responses to the paper generally ignored what was being said about the political role of sexuality and heterosexuality and concentrated on the fact that the paper was telling feminists that they should be lesbians. This selection from correspondence indicates the tenor of the hostile response:

> one might think that these women were automatons. Or more exactly one would think that they were trying to be 'cadres' (professional revolutionaries) in the vanguardist Marxist tradition; shining eyes fixed on the glorious future after the revolution, jumpers covered in badges and hearts beating to the rhythm of the right-on line.[11]

> It is . . . the most patronising, arrogant piece of rubbish I have ever read, including orthodox psychology etc. about women.[12]

Sheila Rowbotham wrote . . . about the Leninist 'vanguard' of the left. It is to get away from this kind of politics that many of us came to the WLM in the first place. Do we really want it here?[13]

The paper and some of the responses were later published by Only-women Press and the paper by itself was included in other collections. It was responsible for many women beginning to think about leaving men. But the analysis of the politics of heterosexuality which we had hoped would develop went no further. It was the style of the paper that was attacked, and the personalities of the writers. The ideas about sexuality were ignored. The Leeds group broke up under the strain of being under such serious outside attack.

At the time we were not able to understand why the paper had provoked such a virulent attack. The protesters accused us of 'telling women what to do' as if we were a powerful authority. But we were a group of five women who wrote a brief conference paper which was published in a very small-circulation feminist newsletter. The characterization of us as 'cadres', as authoritarian and so on, seemed wholly inappropriate. We had no power and were able only to express an opinion. It was the power of the idea that feminists were reacting to, though they experienced this as the power of the writers.

Respondents did not seek to counter the basic arguments behind political lesbianism. For women serious about working for a feminist revolution they were unimpeachable. It did not make much sense to place women first in your life, to love women and proclaim sisterhood and then to commit all the most important emotional and sexual energies to men. Pouring energy into men when men were the problem and women the solution did look unreasonable. Heterosexual feminists who decried the paper therefore employed liberal humanistic arguments. They spoke of choice. They would not approach the argument that heterosexuality was a political system and that their 'choices' could uphold or threaten that system. They simply spoke of loving or being sexually attracted to men as if these things were given and unchangeable despite years of feminist analysis of the social construction of both romance and sexuality.

The scale of adverse reaction to the 'Political lesbian' paper taught us how fundamental and sacred an institution heterosexuality is to male supremacy. Women who had been very brave in many other respects could not bear even to hear a serious critique of heterosexuality and their own sexual choices.

The tension between the liberal humanistic approach to heterosexuality and the lesbian feminist challenge was starkly revealed. So long as lesbians asked for toleration as a persecuted minority, and the right to exercise their sexual preference, they could receive a hearing within the women's liberation movement, even if no active support. If lesbians challenged heterosexuality, then they would be anathematized.

The most hostile reactions to the paper came from socialist feminists. Anna Coote and Beatrix Campbell are dismissive in their account of the history of women's liberation in Britain. They write: 'Leeds Revolutionary Feminists confounded an already depressed movement with a paper published in 1979' and are congratulatory towards the critics who rejected the 'doctrinaire approach of the Leeds group'.[14] Lynne Segal in her book *Is the Future Female? Troubled Thoughts on Contemporary Feminism* writes of the paper, 'How could such concrete reductionism, such phallic obsession, have got such a hold on feminism?'[15]

Adrienne Rich's article 'Compulsory heterosexuality and lesbian existence' was published in the American women's studies journal *Signs* in 1980. Unlike the 'Political lesbian' paper it did not ask heterosexual women to make a choice to become lesbian and thus avoided an intensely hostile reaction. The article gives a cogent analysis of the forces employed to conscript women into heterosexuality. It would be difficult for heterosexual readers to claim that they had chosen a 'sexual preference' when faced with this evidence. Rich states:

> Feminist theory can no longer afford merely to voice a toleration of 'lesbianism' as an 'alternative life-style', or make token allusion to lesbians. A feminist critique of compulsory heterosexual orientation for women is long overdue.[16]

Rich shows how most literature seen as feminist portrays heterosexuality as a sexual preference and inevitable for most women. This she describes as 'heterocentric'. Rich explains that heterosexuality is enforced on women 'as a means of assuring male right of physical, economical, and emotional access'.[17] She lists the forces which she sees as enforcing heterosexuality as including: 'The chastity belt; child marriage; erasure of lesbian existence (except as erotic or perverse) in art, literature, film; idealization of heterosexual romance and marriage'.[18]

She throws light on the reasons for heterosexual feminists' fierceness in resisting criticism of heterosexuality.

> What deserves further exploration is the double-think many women engage in and from which no woman is permanently and utterly free: however much woman-to-woman relationships, female support networks, a female and feminist value system, are relied on and cherished, indoctrination in male credibility and status can still create synapses in thought, denials of feeling, wishful thinking, a profound sexual and intellectual confusion.[19]

What they are resisting is the idea that 'for women heterosexuality may not be a "preference" at all but something that has had to be imposed, managed, organized, propagandized, and maintained by force'.[20] She describes heterosexuality as being a political system of oppression like capitalism or the caste system designed to produce a class of inferior status which can be exploited for the benefit of the ruler class and maintained 'by a variety of forces, including both physical violence and false consciousness'.[21] Rich's paper was dynamic in its effect on theorizing around heterosexuality. Widely used on women's studies courses it has led to the concept of 'compulsory heterosexuality' coming into general usage in feminist theory.

But Rich's paper did not encapsulate radical lesbian theorizing on heterosexuality. One criticism of her paper is that by concentrating on a critique of 'compulsory heterosexuality' rather than on heterosexuality *per se*, she has managed to validate 'optional heterosexuality'. If it is only the compulsory nature of heterosexuality that is a problem, then feminists can say they have seen through all the pressures forcing them towards heterosexuality and have still, in the end, chosen it. Ariane Brunet and Louise Turcotte explain:

> Once one has recognised the obligatory character of heterosexuality, she's rid of this same obligation to conform. She can now, voluntarily, take a new direction, a new understanding of heterosexuality – consensual or optional heterosexuality. Thusly one can move from obligatory heterosexuality to an 'optional' hetero-sexuality, reducing heterosexuality and lesbianism to a simple sexual choice . . . How can one speak of choosing between the political institution of the dominators and the power of revolt of the dominated? How can one compare the enforced accessibility of women with the sexual autonomy of lesbians?[22]

By writing about compulsory heterosexuality rather than heterosexuality, it is argued, Rich has reinforced the very sexual preference model she was determined to expose.

Janice Raymond criticizes Rich for her concept of the lesbian continuum. Rich put women who loved, had friendships with, and worked politically alongside women, on the lesbian continuum, even though they might relate emotionally and sexually to men. Rich defines the lesbian continuum thus:

> I mean the term lesbian continuum to include a range – through each woman's life and throughout history – of woman-identified experience; not simply the fact that a woman has had or consciously desired genital sexual experience with another woman. If we expand it to embrace many more forms of primary intensity between and among women, including the sharing of a rich inner life, the bond-ing against male tyranny, the giving and receiving of practical and political support . . .[23]

Raymond comments that she has a 'gnawing intuition that this affirmation is logically incorrect, morally shortchanging to women who are Lesbians, and patronizing to women who are not Lesbians'.[24] Raymond points out that there is a difference between being woman-identified and being a lesbian and that becoming a lesbian involves a change of consciousness and an acceptance of the risks involved, risks which woman-identified women do not share. 'Woman-identified women who are not Lesbians, while showing courage in the midst of a woman-hating society and taking other risks, have not taken the specific risk of choosing and acknowledging Lesbian Be-ing.'[25]

The Rich paper is seen as much less offensive to heterosexual women than the 'Political lesbian' paper. It seems to allow heterosexual women to continue their relationships with men while feeling politically validated by sharing in a lesbian continuum. Heterosexuality is not indicted, only the force necessary to get women to participate. Neither paper has managed to spark off a debate which asks what role heterosexuality plays in the oppression of women. Radical lesbians in Montreal are asking this question. Brunet and Turcotte define the political role of heterosexuality thus:

Heterosexuality is the institution that creates, maintains, supports, and nourishes men's power. Without woman's subjugation to heterosexuality, man could not survive on his own, or so he thinks. Women's maintenance of men voluntary or forced, paid or unpaid, is what generates men's power and enables them to continue living on women's energy.[26]

They go further than simply identifying heterosexuality as the structural support of male supremacy. They identify heterosexuality as the root of all other oppressions that exist under male supremacy. Heterosexuality is based on and justified by the concept of difference. Without this concept, rooted in heterosexuality, other systems of oppression could not function.

From heterosexuality flow all other oppressions. Heterosexuality is the corner-stone on which men have grounded the norm, located the source and the standard for defining all relationships. The concept of difference is inherent to heterosexuality. That concept, as explained by Monique Wittig in *La Pensée Straight*, makes us view the other as different. But to view the other as different one has to consider one's own difference as the norm, for the norm confers power and control . . . The concept of difference, institutionalised as heterosexuality, rests on a value system where one is superior and the other inferior, one is dominant and the other dominated.[27]

It is the system of heterosexuality that characterizes the oppression of women and gives it a different shape from other forms of exploitative oppression. The extraction of unpaid women's labour for men in the workplace of the home, whether that labour is domestic, sexual, emotional or reproductive, depends on the heterosexual system. This exploitative relationship is justified by and predicated upon the practice of the act of sexual intercourse. Around the practice of this act family relationships are constructed. The work relationship is disguised under notions of love and family.

From the heterosexual basis of the 'family' a system of what Janice Raymond calls hetero-relations then organizes the social relations of the whole of the rest of male-supremacist society. Sex roles originate from heterosexuality. Raymond explains that women and men are constructed so as to necessitate heterosexual union. Sex roles must be created so that no human being of either gender is fully capable of independent functioning and heterosexual coupling then seems natural and inevitable.

hetero-reality and hetero-relations are built on the myth of androgyny. 'Thou as a woman must bond with a man' to fulfill the supposed cosmic purpose of reunifying that which was mythically separated into male and female. Arguments supporting the primacy and prevalence of hetero-relations are in some way based on a cosmic male–female polarity in which the so-called lost halves seek to be rejoined. In a hetero-relational world view, the overcoming of such polarity requires the infusion of all of life with the comings-together of the separated halves. All of life's relations are then imbued with an androgynous energy and attraction that seeks to reunite the selves divided from each other, forever paired in cosmic complementarity. All of life becomes a metaphor for marriage. Every social relation demands its other half, its cosmic complement. The two – female and male – must become one, whether in the bedroom or the board room. Hetero-relational complementarity becomes the 'stuff of the cosmos'.[28]

Raymond's book shows the ways in which men have sought to prevent women from bonding together not just in lesbianism but in any form of friendship, the ways in which women have been prevented from valuing each other and themselves.

According to a radical lesbian analysis, heterosexuality is constructed by various means, including force, and relies upon the prevention of the bonding of women. This is the missing link in feminist theory. Feminist analyses of love, sex, domestic labour, male violence, sex roles and the division of labour all fall into place coherently when heterosexuality is understood as the system that organizes male supremacy. Brunet and Turcotte, like other radical lesbians, call any version of feminist or lesbian theory which does not focus on heterosexuality, 'heterofeminism', i.e. a kind of trade unionism of the oppressed in which the workers get together to improve the conditions of labour with no real attempt to change the system altogether.

The aim of women's liberation and most particularly of lesbian liberation must be the destruction of heterosexuality as a system. It is time we started to envisage how to organize a society that is not structured by heterosexuality. Lesbian separatists are creating such a society and showing that a world beyond heterosexuality is possible.

Heterosexual desire

Heterosexual desire is eroticized power difference. Heterosexual desire originates in the power relationship between men and women, but it can also be experienced in same-sex relationships. Heterosexuality as an institution is founded upon the ideology of 'difference'. Though the difference is seen as natural, it is in fact a difference of power. When men marry women they carry into the relationship considerable social and political power. The organizations of state will back their power through religion, the courts, the social services. Their use of battering and rape within marriage will be condoned through these institutions. The women they marry will generally have less earning power since women's wages are lower than men's. The women will be trained not to use physical strength or be aggressive. They will have been inculcated with social expectations of service, obedience and self-sacrifice. But this is not enough to ensure male power. Means of reinforcing the power differences are employed when men choose partners. They are encouraged to seek in marriage women who are smaller in stature and younger in age. The serious taboos that exist against men marrying women who are taller or older are too well known to need emphasis.

But there are taboos also against men marrying women with the slightest possible advantage in terms of education or earning power. To show the extent to which the ruling male establishment accepts and supports male power in marriage, we need only look at the way that criminologists explain crimes of violence against women. A 1975 study interviewed the wives of rapists and incest offenders to understand why the husbands committed the offences. The authors, Garrett and Wright, found that the wives had, on average, about one year more schooling than their husbands. They suggest that these 'powerful' wives deliberately married men to whom they could feel superior. The men were then driven to their assaults by a feeling of inferiority. The authors conclude that 'for this sample, rape and incest by husbands served as a particularly useful lever by which the wives can further build positions of moral and social dominance'.[29] Male power is so normal to these men that women who happen to be married to less-educated men are credited with a power complex and responsibility for their husbands' sexually abusive behaviour. Presumably the fact that men routinely select less-educated women to marry is seen as unquestionably appropriate behaviour. In support of their conclusions, Garrett and Wright use a study in which educational advantage in wives is said to explain wife battering. The power that men have in marriage, both that which is given them by the sex-role training of a male-supremacist society and that which they individually seek out, is so much part of the fabric of life that it is invisible to male academics. They only notice and object when such male power is not total.

It would be a matter for some astonishment, surely, if, in this carefully engineered situation of inequality, men's sexual desire for women turned out to be egalitarian. It is not of course. Men need to be able to desire the powerless creatures they marry. So heterosexual desire for men is based upon eroticizing the otherness of women, an otherness which is based upon a difference of power. Similarly, in the twentieth century, when women have been required to show sexual enthusiasm for men, they have been trained to eroticize the otherness of men, i.e. men's power and their own subordination. The avalanche of sexual advice and 'scientific' sexological literature testifies to the efforts required to construct heterosexual desire. Sexologists over the last hundred years have argued that male sexuality is inevitably aggressive, active and delights in inflicting pain. Female sexuality has been seen as its opposite: inevitably submissive, passive and delighting in the receiving of pain. Sexologists have differed in the form of explanation they have offered for this phenomenon. Havelock Ellis used an evolutionary explanation, Freud used childhood influences in the family but resorted to biology in the final analysis. But they have been united in seeing this system as inflexible.

Feminists in both waves of feminism in this century have opposed this sexological prescription. They have demanded that men change their sexual behaviour and they have opposed the sexological version of women's sexuality. Recently, libertarian gay men and lesbians have proclaimed sadomasochism to be a revolutionary sexuality and have stated that 'power' is inherent in sexuality.

Once the eroticizing of otherness and power difference is learned, then in a same-sex relationship, where another gender is absent, otherness can be reintroduced through differences of age, race, class, the practice of sadomasochism or role playing. So it is possible to construct heterosexual desire within lesbianism and heterosexual desire is plentifully evident in the practice of gay men. The opposite of heterosexual desire is the eroticizing of sameness, a sameness of power, equality and mutuality. It is homosexual desire.

Sexual pleasure

Under male supremacy, sex consists of the eroticizing of women's subordination. Women's subordination is sexy for men and for women too. For years this was a secret within women's liberation. In order to challenge men's pornography which reiterated that women enjoyed pain and humiliation, and to campaign against sexual violence in a culture which asserted that women enjoyed sexual abuse, feminists denied that women were masochists. Feminist theorists of male violence would acknowledge that women had sadomasochistic fantasies but assert that there was a huge difference between the fantasy and the reality. No women, they said, wanted abuse. The existence of s/m fantasies was not really dealt with as an issue because of its explosive potential. This left the women's liberation movement wide open to attack when a sadomasochist lobby developed.

It should not be a surprise to find that s/m fantasy is significant in women's sex lives. Women may be born free but they are born into a system of subordination. We are not born into equality and do not have equality to eroticize. We are not born into power and do not have power to eroticize. We are born into subordination and it is in subordination that we learn our sexual and emotional responses. It would be surprising indeed if any woman reared under male supremacy was able to escape the forces constructing her into a member of an inferior slave class.

From the discriminating behaviour of her mother while she is still in the cradle, through a training in how to sit and move without taking up space or showing her knickers, how to speak when spoken to and avert her gaze from men, a girl learns subordination. She is very likely to experience overt sexual harassment from men. She will experience unwanted overtures from males and will have to learn to respond positively or negatively. Training of this kind is not geared to creating a strong and positive emotional and sexual personality in any woman. Within women's liberation negative self-image, lack of confidence, worries about appearance, negative emotional patterns in relationships, have all received attention from consciousness-raising groups. The burgeoning of feminist therapy in place of consciousness-raising as the movement has lost its radical edge testifies to the urgency with which women are seeking to overcome our conditioning. But the negative effects of this training on our sexual feelings have scarcely been explored.

Sex has been seen as different. Feminists accepted the basic idea of the sexual revolution that sexual response was an ultimate good. According to sexual revolutionary ideology, how sexual response was achieved was of little or no importance so long as it was achieved. Sex, we were led to understand, was somehow disconnected with the rest of life. It was a pleasurable garden of delights which was unaffected by the outside real world and certainly had no effect on the workings of the real world. Therefore, the fact that women might have sexual feelings which mirrored the undesirable emotional responses they were trying to change was seen as no problem. A sexual problem for a feminist was understood to be lack of orgasm or the correct number of orgasms. Masochism was not on the agenda. The fact that for many women orgasm and masochism, especially in masturbation, were apparently inextricably connected was avoided or positively affirmed.

The construction of women's sexual pleasure only became a subject for serious debate with the development of the feminist challenge to pornography. Campaigners who had sexual responses to the materials they were opposing found themselves in a dilemma. There was a pressure to conceal such responses for fear of disapproval. Campaigners who claimed never to have experienced any kind of response to sadomasochistic material appeared scandalized at those who did. How was it possible, after all, to campaign against something which turned you on? Speakers against pornography would receive hostility from women who felt guilty about their response to pornographic material and turned their anger on to the messengers rather than the material. It became necessary to explain that a sexual response to pornography was not at all unusual, was not a reason for guilt or shame and did not preclude our anger at pornography. It was possible to be even more angry at pornography because it revealed the extent to which our subordination had affected those feelings we had been encouraged to feel were most our own.

To deal with the problem of the eroticizing of our subordination we really need a new language, and a new way of categorizing our sexual feelings. There is a cultural assumption in a post-sexual-revolution society that sexual arousal is 'pleasure'. This makes it particularly painful to experience pornography, which clearly shows the humiliation of women, as sexually arousing. We feel guilt at having taken pleasure in or 'enjoyed' the oppression of women. The literature of the libertarians has no word or category for sexual response that is not positive, no word that would allow us to describe the complexity of our feelings in such a situation. This is not an accident. Part of the repertoire of techniques for political control is the control of language. It is hard to 'think' about things for which no word is available. Women are not supposed to think in a way which is not positive about sex. In the absence of a word which could distinguish negative sexual feelings or experience the libertarians are able to label feminists as 'anti-sex'. They have a one-dimensional view of sex as inevitably good. Thus only two positions on sexuality are acknowledged: pro- and anti-sex. A feminist approach to the question of desire requires the invention of a new language. We need to be able to describe sexual response which is incontrovertibly negative.

Linda Gordon and Ellen Dubois give us an example of the confusion felt by some feminists about women's sexual response. They are libertarians and see sexual response as positive and even revolutionary for women. They include women's capacity for orgasm in their description of how nineteenth-century middle-class women engaged in 'resistance that actually challenged' the 'sexual system', i.e. the supposedly repressive morality of the nineteenth century.[30] These women apparently had orgasms, according to a survey of the time. Forty per cent reported orgasms occasionally, 20 per cent frequently, and 40 per cent never. Since we can assume that these women were in unregenerately oppressive relationships it is difficult to see how their orgasms were 'resistance'. Their orgasms indicate a remarkable ability to accommodate themselves to their oppression so that they can find in it a source of satisfaction, but that is very different from resistance. The absence of orgasm might more appropriately be seen as a form of resistance in such a situation. It is, after all, lack of orgasm which the sexologists have treated as resistance to male power all this century.

The libertarian feminists, as well as the sexologists from whom they take their inspiration, have seen sexual response as inevitably positive and generally revolutionary, but when we look at the situations in which men and women can experience orgasm, this approach has to be questioned. Men experience orgasms whilst killing women. Girls and women can have orgasms during rape and sexual abuse and then spend years in guilt and shame for 'enjoying' what happened to them. In fact the body is capable of physiological responses quite unconnected with an emotional state of 'pleasure'. Similarly the mind can cause a sexual response in situations where words like 'enjoy' or 'pleasure' are entirely inappropriate. Most women probably have experience of waking from sexual dreams involving rape or abuse, feeling uncomfortable or distressed. This is quite different from the feelings of well-being that can be associated with a positive sexual experience. The sexologists and their libertarian heirs have mandated that women distrust their feelings. In *The ABZ of Love* and *The Joy of Sex*, women are required to overcome their 'inhibitions' and rename their discomfort 'pleasure'. But if we listen to our feelings about sex sensitively instead of riding roughshod over them through guilt or anxiety about being prudes, we can work out what is positive and what is negative. The negative feelings are about eroticized subordination or heterosexual desire.

The resurgence of heterosexual desire

In the early years of this wave of feminism there was criticism of the dominance and submission roles of heterosexuality. As well as a dominant concern with the possibilities for women's sexual pleasure and how these had been limited in relationships with men, there was a real desire for equality. In the 1980s, in a feminist community which has accepted use of the term 'postfeminism', this search for equality in sex is being vigorously challenged both by some heterosexual women and by some lesbians. The British heterosexual feminist theorist Sheila Rowbotham explained in 1984 why she and some other feminists had given up the attempt to 'democratize' desire. She says that 'moral earnestness' came to grief when confronted with 'lust, romantic fantasy, fear of ageing, sado-masochism'. The most serious reason for abandoning the attempt to democratize desire was the fact that such equality was not sexy. She recounts the experience of an American therapist who encouraged her clients to democratize their relationships. The couples kept returning to her with a new problem: they were 'unable to summon up desire. Love yes, but not desire.'[31]

Feminists have always been uncomfortably aware that men's sexual passion was likely to fade if relationships were democratized. Rowbotham tells us that this is a problem for women too. The sociologist Jessie Bernard's 1972 book *The Future of Marriage* dealt at length with the issue of men's difficulties with democratic desire. She explains that research as long ago as the 1950s had suggested that the search for companionate marriage was destroying marital sex life. Companionate marriages were to be based upon equality.

> Veroff and Feld were beginning to raise disturbing questions about the way an ideology oriented toward egalitarian companionship might affect the sexual component of marriage . . . they were speculating that the conception of the 'traditional marital relationship [as] a friendship relationship may play havoc with the potential that the marital role has to permit sexual and interpersonal activity.' In other words, can you mix companionship and sex? The future of marriage rides on the answer.[32]

In tune with the hopefulness of the early 1970s Bernard answers: 'Can you mix companionship and sex? My own answer, is, Yes, you can.'[33] Bernard did not see men's linking of power and aggression with sex as biological or innate. She saw this linkage as being about status and she was optimistic about change. Women's refusal to accept inferior status was bound to cause men to transform their sexual responses in their own interests.

But Rowbotham's answer is very different. She concludes that the feminists like herself who tried to change had:

> too great a confidence that in altering the outward manifestation, the pattern of relationships in which we experienced desire, our inner feelings would fall automatically into place. There was an incongruity between overt democracy and hidden yearnings.[34]

She recommends the abandonment of the task of democratizing desire in favour of recognizing 'its capacity to surprise, to take us unawares'. She then embarks upon a lyrical description of what she sees as the characteristics of 'desire'.

> Desire has the capacity to shift us beyond commonsense. It is our peep at the extraordinary. It is the chink beyond the material world.
> The glimpse we still have in common. And in its daftness desire is thus a democrat, not the solemn, public face of democracy, but the inward openness which is prepared like the fool to step over the cliff.
> True it can land us down with a bump. Folly, fear, embarrassment, humiliation, violence, tumble about with ecstasy and bliss. Desire is a risk, but so is freedom.[35]

As feminists we might have to ask, as Rowbotham does not, who profits from the undemocratic nature of desire under male supremacy. We might find it worrying that there should be such an asymmetry in the ways that male and female desire are constructed. For all her attempts to provide a metaphysical status for desire, not to be questioned by ordinary mortals, feminists find that desire does not exist beyond the material world but in it, and is formed out of the material inequalities between men and women. What Rowbotham tries to disguise is that the 'risk' of desire lies in the fact that it is based upon the eroticizing of women's subordination. To equate the 'risk' of desire with the 'risk' of freedom is a shoddy and quite prestidigitational trick. It may well be that some women, as well as plenty of men, will choose their ability to experience a particular form of sexual passion over the desire to be free, but they are not the same thing. Indeed a feminist approach to sex would suggest that women's freedom cannot be achieved whilst some people who see themselves as radical and progressive place their right to take pleasure from women's lack of freedom before the task of creating freedom.

The defence of heterosexual desire within feminism is associated with a tendency to promote the validity of heterosexuality as a sexual choice and to attack lesbians for questioning it. A spate of writers in the mid-1980s started to talk about the necessity for heterosexuality to 'come out of the closet' on the grounds that lesbians had forced heterosexual women to feel embarrassed about their preferences. It is an astonishingly insensitive choice of term comparing as it does the real oppression of lesbians with the discomfort some heterosexual women who are aware of the incongruity of their 'desire' might feel within women's liberation. Rowbotham uses the phrase and it seems clear from the rest of the article that she defines heterosexuality as eroticized power difference. The resurgence of hetero-sexual desire, or eroticized power difference, is seen by such women as emerging bravely from a closet that it was never in. In a sado-society heterosexual desire is very 'out' indeed.[36]

Eileen Phillips is another heterosexual socialist feminist who validates the conflict and fear involved in heterosexual desire. She describes 'desire' as:

> unnecessary, irrational, an excess – and also compelling. When going to meet the desired one, we can be sweating, our legs trembling, our heart beating fast – in fact behaviourally we can be exhibiting all the symptoms of fear. Yet it feels exciting as well as scary, the very strangeness producing a peculiar sort of clarity which often eludes us in many other activities of daily life.[37]

It looks as if desire is not being very democratic here either. Phillips provides this description of desire in combination with an attack on lesbian feminism as a 'politics of voluntarism and male banishment' and disparages attempts by both lesbians and heterosexual women to challenge the centrality of sexual intercourse. It seems that Phillips, Rowbotham and other such feminists understand very well that the sexual attraction involved in heterosexuality is eroticized power difference. Since they have rejected the lesbian alternative they have no choice but to attack lesbian feminists who offer a cogent critique of their sexual choice. Lesbian feminists are a problem because they question the necessity for any woman to organize her life around the eroticizing of her own subordination.

Rowbotham's retreat from the pursuit of sexual equality is not taking place in a vacuum. Mainstream heterosexual feminism in America gives evidence of a similar phenomenon. In May 1986 *Ms* magazine produced a health issue called 'The Beauty of Health'. The only article on sex in the magazine was an interview with a husband and wife sex advice team called the Mershorers. Entitled 'Going for the Big "O" ', the article advised women how to have multiple orgasms through masochism. It might have been expected that a feminist health magazine dealing with sex would touch on some of those problems that really interfere with sexual well-being for women, such as sexual abuse, pornography and sadomasochism. In fact, far from recognizing sadomasochism as a health problem, the sexologists see it as a way to achieve sexual health.

The goal of the Mershorers' advice is how to get not just one orgasm but up to a hundred. The Mershorers' book recounts the ways in which some multi-orgasmic women achieve their success. These ways include various forms of eroticized subordination such as the wearing of gender-fetishized clothing and 'the minister's sister who craves bondage and group sex'.[38] But what they have in common is the ability to 'completely let go'. It turns out that this requires surrender. Here we are back in the 1950s. Marc Mershorer explains:

> The woman is out there competing with men, used to guarding her vulnerabilities – she has to. But the requirements out there in the world are much different from the requirements for deriving pleasure from making love. And that's a real contradiction today for many women.
>
> But – and this is a very important concept for a woman to understand – when a woman lets go, gives up, she is surrendering herself, not to her partner, but to Nature. She's giving herself to herself.[39]

The Mershorers seem to have been aware that they were being interviewed for a feminist magazine. So though the woman still surrenders in strict conformity with sexological prescriptions she no longer surrenders to the man but to 'Nature' and 'herself'. This slight change does not alter the construction of male and female sexuality though it might disinfect it a little. Men are not being advised to 'surrender'. It is difficult to see how sex as it is constructed under male supremacy could survive if men went in for surrendering. The Mershorers tell us that no matter what changes feminism and changing social realities have wrought in woman's role outside the bedroom, inside it she must continue as before.

An article in *Cosmopolitan* magazine in 1985 has the same themes but pays even less lip service to feminism, though *Cosmopolitan* has a reputation for being sexually progressive. The article, 'Sexual surrender', seeks to instruct women how to achieve 'satisfying sexual surrender'. This is defined as 'when we accept – or surrender to – our deep psychological needs for connection, intimacy, and the full expression of our sexuality'.[40]

According to the writer men can and should surrender in sex too, but men's and women's sexuality is different, so obviously they won't be doing so as often or in the same way. She explains:

> In their sincere attempts not to be sexist, both men and women risk overlooking the real differences between them. As George Gilder writes in *Sexual Suicide*, 'There are no human beings; there are just men and women, and when they deny their divergent sexuality, they reject the deepest sources of identity and love. They commit sexual suicide.'[41]

The differences that women should acknowledge are the old-fashioned ones of male aggression and female submission. Men's aggression is largely socially constructed, the article tells us, but none the less unchangeable, because 'centuries of biological and cultural reinforcement have taught men to forge ahead, making, doing, conquering and controlling' with the result that men 'feel aggressive during sexual intercourse'.[42] So women must accept traditional gender roles in sexual behaviour although these may be more apparent than real since in sexual intercourse the man 'appears to control' and the woman 'appears to surrender'.

Like the Mershorers, the writer of this article shows an awareness that such a prescription might seem incongruous to women reared in a world of feminism and greater opportunities. Woman is assured that she can be liberated in the public sphere as long as she remains a traditional passive woman in the bedroom. Considering that sexologists throughout the twentieth century have been convinced that 'surrender' in the bedroom did not stop at the bedroom door but spilt over into the whole relationship with a man and other areas of life, then the surrender that is being vaunted must actually be the antidote to feminism. Women may have greater opportunities but while they surrender in bed they will become no real threat to male privilege. Accordingly the *Cosmopolitan* article admonishes women that though 'the freedom to earn equal pay and satisfaction through a career' have been a 'tremendous breakthrough' women should not 'throw out the old-fashioned joys of womanhood in the bargain'. The old-fashioned joys turn out to consist of being the object of male sexual attention in the form of being 'pursued, chosen and adored'. The *Cosmopolitan* article concludes with a warning that is clearly anti-feminist. Women must not try to be too equal.

> Part of those old-fashioned joys is being pursued, chosen, and adored. It's hard to pursue someone who is already pursuing. Although contemporary women are still developing their ability to take charge, being cast in the role of the one who surrenders is potentially a woman's greatest asset.[43]

The resurgence of heterosexual desire within feminism after a brief period in which it was questioned fits into the increasingly sadistic tenor of male-supremacist society. Women Against Pornography in New York point out that men's pornography has become more and more violent and sadistic in the late 1970s and early 1980s. The androgyny and unisex of the late 1960s and early 1970s has given way to a pronounced gender fetishism in fashion and in the entertainments industry. This new gender fetishism focuses much more obviously than that of the 1950s on violence. The language of fashion in the early 1980s has been heavily reliant on black leather, chains and handcuffs. There is a much more prominent sexual aggression in fashion. The miniskirt of the 1960s looks tame and domesticated compared with the tiny clinging, black, late-1980s variety.

How can the increasingly sadistic tone of male-supremacist culture be explained? It cannot simply reflect the right-wing turn of politics and the move towards nuclear confrontation of Reaganism and Thatcherism. Certainly masculine values dominate the enterprise culture of the 1980s, but the 1950s too were a time of cold war and McCarthyism, and such overt sadism did not infuse the culture then. This new aggressive masculinity can be explained as an answer to the threat of women's liberation, an answer made possible by the sexual revolution which normalized male sexual aggression. It certainly seems effective, particularly inasmuch as it has percolated through into the women's liberation movement itself.

Homosexual desire

The demolition of heterosexual desire is a necessary step on the route to women's liberation. Freedom is indivisible. It is not possible to keep little bits of unfreedom, such as in the area of sexuality, because they give some people pleasure, if we are serious about wanting women's liberation. Male-supremacist sexuality is constructed from the subordination of women. If women were not subordinate then sex as the eroticized subordination of women would not be thinkable. Those who wish to fight feminists in order to retain dominance and submission sex are standing in the path of a feminist revolution. Feminist revolution is not 'sexy' because it would remove those material power differences between the sexes on which eroticized power difference is based. To retain sadomasochism it is necessary to prevent the progress of women's liberation. It should not surprise us, therefore, to discover the libertarians launching vigorous attacks on feminism, lesbian feminism, and lesbian separatism. It should not surprise us that the libertarians have achieved a serious slowing down and in some cases destruction of feminist initiatives against violence against women. The feminist challenge to male violence cannot thrive in harmony with the promotion of sadomasochistic values by women who in some cases call themselves feminists and in others escape challenge through the wearing of a radical veneer.

The feminist fight against male violence requires the reconstruction of male sexuality. The abuse and murder of women and girls cannot be separated from sexual 'fantasy' and pornography. The relationships of power that exist in the world do not exist as a result of nature but as a result of being imagined and created by those who benefit from them. The subordination of women is 'thought' in the fantasy and the practice of sex.

The 'thought' of women's sexual subordination delivers powerful reinforcement to men's feelings of dominance and superiority. The liberation of women is unimaginable in this situation since it would disrupt the possibilities of pleasure. But even if men cannot imagine it, it is necessary that we should. If we cannot imagine our liberation then we cannot achieve it.

Male sexuality must be reconstructed to sever the link between power and aggression and sexual pleasure. Only then can women be relieved of the restrictions placed upon their lives and opportunities by male sexual objectification and aggression. Men's pleasure in women's subordination is a powerful bulwark of their resistance to women's liberation. The reconstruction of male sexuality must extend to gay men too. While they vigorously promote eroticized dominance and submission as sex they constitute a serious obstacle to women's liberation. It is not to be expected that men, gay or straight, will voluntarily choose to relinquish the pleasure and privilege they derive from the eroticized subordination of women. Though some are capable of political integrity and of working against their own interests as a class, we cannot expect this to take place on any mass scale.

As women and as lesbians our hope lies only in other women. We must work towards the construction of homosexual desire and practice as a most important part of our struggle for liberation. However important heterosexual desire has been in our lives we will all have some experience of its opposite. We will have experience of sexual desire and practice which does not leave us feeling betrayed, a sexual desire and practice which eroticizes mutuality and equality. It is this avenue that we should seek to open up while gradually shutting down those responses and practices which are not about sexual 'pleasure' but the eroticizing of our subordination. We need to develop sensitive antennae for evaluating our sexual experience. None of this will be easy. It will take some effort, but then nobody said that the journey to our liberation would be an easy ride. The question we have to ask ourselves is whether we want our freedom or whether we want to retain heterosexual desire. Feminists will choose freedom.

The libertarians are trying to turn feminism into a movement for sexual liberation. Ti-Grace Atkinson described the problem clearly as long ago as 1975 in a speech to the Masochists' Liberation Front, a precursor of the s/m lesbians of the 1980s. She explained:

> Feminists are on the fence, at the moment, on the issue of sex. But I do not know any feminist worthy of that name who, if forced to choose between freedom and sex, would choose sex. She'd choose freedom every time.[44]

She contrasts this with the stated choice of a masochist in an s/m publication: 'if an M has to choose between oppression and chastity, the M considers chastity the worse alternative'.[45] She asserts that 'By no stretch of imagination is the Women's Movement a movement for sexual liberation' and explains that 'That used to be an old Left-Establishment joke on feminism: that feminists were just women who needed to get properly laid.'

It is in the interests of the male ruling class that some women are now asserting that sexual liberation and women's liberation are analogous. This should be particularly clear from the fact that the sexual liberation that such women are pursuing replicates the hopes and dreams of our oppressors. It is the liberation not of 'sex' but of sadomasochism. They are seeking to gain more satisfaction from their oppression in a way which a century of sexological literature has confidently predicted would subordinate women. Masochism, the sexologists believed, would disempower women and render us quiescent. It would cause us to embrace our oppression and cease to struggle against it. The last laugh over the sadomasochism of lesbian or pre-lesbian women must go to the male establishment. Women have been lured into accepting a substitute for their liberation which is designed to ensure that they cannot achieve liberation. The aim of the sexological industry over the last century was that women would be trained to eroticize their subordination. The result they hoped for was that women would then have a stake in prolonging their own oppression and resist any attempt to end it. The resurgence of heterosexual desire among some ex-feminists shows how successful the sexologists have been. They have been successful in a period of backlash against feminism but feminism has not yet completely died out. If we are to revive the movement for our liberation then we must start working towards the construction of an egalitarian sexuality.

Our struggle for liberation does not necessarily require chastity, though many women do choose this path and it is an honourable choice. Such a strategy could only cause disbelief in a male-supremacist society in which sex has been made holy. Sex is holy because of its role as a sacred ritual in the dominant/submissive relationship between men and women. The importance attached to sex defies rationality and can only be explained in this political way. But we can also choose, as many of us have done, to work towards homosexual desire if that suits our lives and relationships. We must remember that homosexual desire will not be recognized as 'sex'. We do not even possess suitable words to describe it. The course of eroticizing equality and mutuality has received no prizes from male supremacy or its agents but it is time we shared our wisdom and experience, learned from feminists and lesbians in our history and became proud of what distinguishes lesbian experience from male-supremacist culture.

Psychoanalysts have described lesbianism pejoratively as 'narcissistic regression'.[46] This means that in loving their own sex lesbians are in fact loving themselves and need to mature into loving the other, i.e. men. Narcissism is seen as negative and dangerous. In fact, the psychoanalysts have spotted the basis of homosexual desire. It is heretical in this culture deliberately to avoid the rituals of sadomasochistic sex and to choose to eroticize sameness and equality. Differences of race and class can provide power differences to eroticize even in same-sex relationships. Lesbians committed to the creation of an egalitarian sexuality must be prepared to challenge this too, since same-sex relationships do not automatically ensure a symmetry of power and privilege. It is not surprising that sexologists who have been dedicated to the construction of heterosexual desire and are enthusiastic about lesbian sadomasochism have derided lesbian love. We should value what our enemies find most threatening.

Readers who consider themselves to be heterosexual will probably be wondering whether homosexual desire can fit into an opposite-sex relationship. In a society which was not founded upon the subordination of women there would be no reason why it should not. But we do not live in such a society. We live in a society organized around heterosexual desire, around otherness and power difference. It is difficult to imagine what shape a woman's desire for a man would take in the absence of eroticized power difference since it is precisely this which provides the excitement of heterosexuality today.

Heterosexuality is the institution through which male-supremacist society is organized and as such it must cease to function. It is difficult to imagine at this point what shape any relationship between different sexes would take when such a relationship was a free choice, when it was not privileged in any way over same-sex relationships and when it played no part in organizing women's oppression and male power. In such a situation, when heterosexuality was no longer an institution, we cannot yet be sure what women would choose.

Notes

1. *Concise Oxford Dictionary* (Oxford University Press, 1964), p. 573.
2. Celia Kitzinger, *The Social Construction of Lesbianism* (Sage Publications, London, 1987), p. 33.
3. Ibid.
4. Kathie Sarachild, 'Psychological terrorism', in Redstockings (ed.), *Feminist Revolution* (Random House, New York, 1975), p. 57.
5. Radicalesbians, 'The woman-identified woman', in Phil Brown (ed.), *Radical Psychology* (Tavistock, London, 1973), p. 471.
6. Ibid., p. 479.
7. Jill Johnson, *Lesbian Nation* (Simon & Schuster, New York, 1973), pp. 166–7.
8. Leeds Revolutionary Feminist Group, 'Political lesbianism: the case against heterosexuality', in Onlywomen Press (Onlywomen Press, London, 1981), p. 60.
9. Ibid.
10. Ibid.
11. Ibid., p. 12.
12. Ibid., p. 14.
13. Ibid., p. 16.
14. Anna Coote and Beatrix Campbell, *Sweet Freedom: The Struggle for Women's Liberation* (Picador, London, 1982), p. 225.
15. Lynne Segal, *Is The Future Female? Troubled Thoughts on Contemporary Feminism* (Virago, London, 1987), p. 97.
16. Adrienne Rich, 'Compulsory heterosexuality and lesbian existence', in Snitow et al. (eds), *Desire: The Politics of Sexuality* (Virago, London, 1984), p. 212.
17. Ibid., p. 226.
18. Ibid., p. 220.
19. Ibid., p. 225.
20. Ibid., p. 226.

21. Ibid., p. 227.

22. Ariane Brunet and Louise Turcotte, 'Separatism and radicalism', *Lesbian Ethics*, 2, 1, p. 47. This article is reprinted in Sarah Lucia Hoagland and Julia Penelope, *For Lesbians Only: A Separatist Anthology* (Onlywomen Press, London, 1988), which is an excellent resource for separatist theory on heterosexuality.

23. Rich, 'Compulsory heterosexuality', p. 227.

24. Janice G. Raymond, *A Passion for Friends* (Women's Press, London, 1986), p. 16.

25. Ibid., p. 18.

26. Brunet and Turcotte, 'Separatism', p. 46.

27. Ibid.

28. Raymond, *Passion*, p. 12.

29. Sheila Jeffreys, 'The sexual abuse of children in the home', in Friedman and Sarah (eds), *On the Problem of Men* (Women's Press, London, 1982), p. 61.

30. Linda Gordon and Ellen Dubois, 'Seeking ecstasy on the battlefield: danger and pleasure in nineteenth-century feminist sexual thought', in Carole S. Vance (ed.), *Pleasure and Danger: Exploring Female Sexuality* (Routledge and Kegan Paul, London, 1984), p. 36.

31. Sheila Rowbotham, 'Passion off the pedestal', *City Limits*, 126 (2–8 March 1984), p. 21.

32. Jessie Bernard, *The Future of Marriage* (Yale University Press, New Haven, CT, 1982), p. 140; first published 1972.

33. Ibid., p. 155.

34. Rowbotham, 'Passion', p. 21.

35. Ibid.

36. See Mary Daly and Jane Caputi, *Webster's First New Intergalactic Wickedary* (Women's Press, London, 1987), p. 94. Daly and Caputi define the 'sadosociety' as: 'society spawned by phallic lust: the sum of places/times where the beliefs and practices of sadomasochism are The Rule'.

37. Eileen Phillips, *The Left and the Erotic* (Lawrence & Wishart, London, 1983), p. 34.

38. Sarah Crichton, 'Going for the big "O" ', *Ms*, New York (May 1986), p. 86.

39. Ibid.

40. Elizabeth Brenner, 'Sexual surrender', *Cosmopolitan*, 19, 4 (October 1985), p. 106.

41. Ibid.

42. Ibid.

43. Ibid.

44. Ti-Grace Atkinson, 'Why I'm against s/m liberation', in Robin Ruth Linden et al. (eds), *Against Sadomasochism* (Frog in the Well Press, San Francisco, 1982), p. 91.

45. Ibid.

46. See the section on 'Sex and psychology' in Dolores Klaich, *Woman plus Woman: Attitudes toward Lesbianism* (New English Library, London, 1975).

Recovering *Women* in History from Feminist Deconstructionism

Liz Stanley

Although welcoming difference, feminist deconstructionist argument implicitly portrays as essentialism the differing and sometimes multiple identities painstakingly *constructed* in the very recent past, by lesbians, older women, women of colour, disabled women, and working-class women (to name only some). What must it be like to be a black woman, having gone through much to have named oneself thus and to have recovered something of the history of one's foremothers, to have it implied that this is not only not enough but an intellectual error, an ontological oversimplification to have done so? As a working-class lesbian (for so I continue to name myself this different kind of woman), and thus having gone through comparable, if not similar, struggles to name, I sigh another bitter sigh at yet another, although surely unintended, theoretical centrism: the resurgence of Theory from those who were once the certificated namers of other women's experiences and who are now likely to become the certificated deconstructors of the same.

What is needed – and indeed must be insisted upon by those of us who are black, lesbian, aged, disabled, working class – is that *all* difference must be attended to *equally*. In particular, there must be an end to the now ritual invocation of 'and black women' as the only such difference seen but which actually goes no further than a formula of words that leaves untouched actual relations of power between differently situated groups of black and white women, and which also masks a refusal to see that *black women* is itself no unitary category, but one internally differentiated on grounds of age, class, able-bodiedness, and sexuality.

And yet there is much in Denise Riley (1988) and other feminist deconstructionists' arguments about the ontological experience of *women* as shaky, as something we inhabit or are forced into only periodically, as it were at the points, the disjunctures, the fracturings, of ordinary being introduced by actual oppressions in our lives. Nonetheless, oppression and its struggles should be neither denied nor silenced, nor explained away as a

From *Women's Studies International*, 13 (1/2), 1990, pp. 151–7, abridged.

momentary and passing necessity transcended by the supposed greater intellectual rigour of deconstructionism. And my view is that there are other alternative routes out of the political oscillations described by Riley than those she suggests.

What has come to be described as the feminist standpoint epistemology – feminist social science research should start from the material experience of actual women and theorize from out of this – is itself a fractured position. Sandra Harding (1987) suggests that once one feminist standpoint, as a materially experientially grounded epistemology, is admitted to exist, then we need to consider two related possibilities. One is that other standpoints, as women of colour, of age, of class, lesbian women, disabled women, and so on, exist. The other is that there are no *a priori* epistemological grounds for deciding a hierarchy of standpoints – of the superordinate right or correct one over and against subordinate standpoints. Oppressions cannot be weighted against each other; those feminists who do attempt to put oppressions into a hierarchy against each other need to have the moral and political, as well as intellectual, dubiousness of this pointed out to them.

This opens up possibilities (and closes down dubious assumptions) for feminism. No longer claiming 'I am right, you are wrong,' we necessarily move into the realm of the ethically/morally/politically *preferable*, into the realm of minded choice. It simultaneously enables us to reject the role of anyone – theorists of grand feminist theory, poets of feminist common language, feminist deconstructors of the category *women* – to name and not to name on our behalf. This is not to dismiss, nor even to deconstruct, feminist deconstructionism. Rather, it is to welcome its strengths but also to recognize that, as Sandra Harding says in the discussion referred to above, although feminist standpoint approaches and feminist deconstructionism may be contradictory and even work towards somewhat different feminist ends, nonetheless we need them both.

Women in one history: drawing some conclusions

I now want briefly to situate some of the points introduced above in relation to a discussion of some features of the particular history outside of my own that I know best. This is that contained in the unedited original Hannah Cullwick (1833–1909) diaries, as well as the edited published volume of these (Stanley, 1984).

One implication of the essentialist vs. deconstructionist debate within feminism is that a deconstructionist postmodern and non-essentialist view of the category *women* is both new, and also provided by feminists and/or academics. I suggest that the first is a dubious assumption and can be easily shown to be so by looking closely at appropriate historical materials; and that the second is the equally dubious product of a traditional and actually elitist view of the researcher/researched and theory/experience relation-ship, which locates the researcher on a different critical plane and assigns theory to her (the researched experience, and the researcher theorizes that experience).

Hannah Cullwick was a thoroughly working-class woman who worked for most of her life from a very young age in a succession of domestic service places. Also, she wrote diaries over a period of time (1854–73) in which few other working-class women spoke in their own words and on paper, or at least in a form which has survived for us now to read and think about. Obviously I cannot describe in any detail the features of Hannah Cullwick's working life, which anyway are better read in her own words (I refer readers to Stanley, 1984 for this). However, it seems to me not inappropriate to characterize Hannah Cullwick as a mid-nineteenth-century deconstructionist. She was as well aware as any contemporary feminist deconstructionist of the non-essentialist and internally fractured nature of the category *women*. Repeatedly, she makes distinctions concerning these various fractures in detail in her diaries. I discuss four of them here, although she herself deals with more.

First, over and over there are detailed – and differing – accounts of the distinctions that Hannah drew between herself and other labouring women on the one hand, and her upper-class mistresses in her domestic service places on the other. For Hannah Cullwick, it is these upper-class women who are *women*. She notes, in a myriad of concrete instances, their physical incompetence in domestic labour and other household tasks, but also their often dithery and feminine minds, moods and behaviours. She drew her distance from them as surely as any man convinced of his own superiority, for she was certainly (although cross-cut by other factors) sure of hers.

Second and relatedly, the kind of labouring women that Hannah identified with were not just working-class women; no such simplicities of class identification informed her estimation of others. Rather, she was aware of internal distinctions to be made between groups of working-class women: her own identifications were strongly with the old-fashioned countrywomen in the lower and less fine ranks of female domestic service, who retained more traditional ways of dress, of conduct, of speech, and of self-estimation and self-presentation. These rough but also thoroughly respectable working women were freer than most by virtue of their dress, demeanour and conduct: Hannah and her friends could frequent public houses and walk back home late at night without heed or molestation. Both her physical strength and her unwomanly (defined in terms of current fashion and self-presentation) appearance and conduct meant that few men saw Hannah in sexed terms.

This may seem mere romanticism on my part. However, unless readers totally disbelieve the Cullwick diaries, it is clear that she did indeed go into men's places and roam at night at will and without interference, or, if it was intended, headed it off in a variety of ways. I think it is difficult for us now to appreciate two important factors. One is that working-class people were seen in mid-nineteenth-century England as a different species, almost not human at all, by their betters – much as the most imperious of colonialists treated black peoples at this time and later. The other is that it seems to have been comparatively easy for women across the classes to unsex themselves, signal themselves as undesirable in conventional heterosexual terms.

Third, an attempt to understand difference in race terms is no late twentieth-century monopoly. For Hannah Cullwick, race difference loomed large in her life in one way, and had secondary reverberations in another as well. In more personal terms, Hannah struggled both to live and to understand her relationship (which resulted in marriage in 1873, following their meeting in 1854), with decidedly upper-class Arthur Munby (Hudson, 1972). Class was then a matter of a divide, a chasm, so wide as to be comprehensible only in race terms for those who attempted to cross it. It was certainly so for Munby and Hannah, given his oddities concerning working women and her feelings about working men who tried to dominate and render subservient working women. It is also important to remember that the concept or category *race* was then not defined in solely colour terms: the Irish loomed large in considerations of race; so too did the feckless working class.

Hannah Cullwick and Munby set up their own relationship terms around complex dominances and subserviences; the longer the relationship persisted, the more the dependence was Munby upon Hannah. The cross-cutting of power in their relationship is not my concern here (although it is discussed in detail in Stanley, 1987); however, the terms in which it was conducted is. The language, and indeed on occasion the appearance, of race formed the language in which they communicated, with black/white serving as a complicated metaphor for class differences, but with interesting complexities in that the white and ladylike Munby and the black and unsexed or even manly Hannah crossed and recrossed conventional (then and now) power divides. Invariably, Hannah addressed Munby as 'Massa' (which they took to be the form of address used by black slaves towards those who owned them) and on occasion she used soot and black-lead to actually black up, then wrote in her diary (which was sent to him) about such occasions. But then, Munby in a sense depended upon such external displays to enable him to have any basis at all on which to communicate with Hannah; and, more particularly, as he was at least as – and indeed more so – incompetent in the ordinary activities that compose looking after yourself as any of the mistresses that Hannah half-despised and half-admired, it seems likely that Hannah constructed Munby in similarly complex political and emotional terms. And of course, just as black people cannot help dealing with white, nor lesbians and gay men with heterosexual people, nor working-class people with the middle classes: we know too much about our betters, and they very little about us.

Additionally, black people in person, and also representations of black people, were an actual presence in the lives of Hannah and Munby both and from which the relationship terms alluded to above were derived. I mention here one example of this: the minstrel troupes that were such a feature of London street life in the 1850s and 1860s. These minstrels were sometimes black people, but more often were composed of white men, then some white women as well, who blacked up to sing supposed minstrel songs in the streets. Hannah as much as Munby sees these white women as having unsexed themselves: clearly white women can be respectably sexed only by maintaining some reserve in public places, some gendered distinctions in their public presence as compared with men. What remains unclear is whether and to what extent it is blackness that unsexes such women and how much their unusual public self-displays; I would suggest that the two cannot be distinguished in this instance.

Fourth, it is very clear indeed that Hannah saw relationships with men which entail some degree of publicly legitimized control over her as most definitely to be eschewed. Early on in her diary writing she says that the source of her relationship with Munby was that he didn't try to dominate her in the way that working-class men did. On a number of other occasions she notes the problems that threatened men presented when confronted with her height and physical strength (sweeping them off their feet into her arms was one means she used of dealing with them!). Perhaps most poignantly, Hannah notes in the 1870s that although she felt that Munby should offer to marry her, for this was her due, she felt this came as an imposition from outside, in the form of social opprobrium for unconventional relationships (she was faced with losing her character, the written recommendation that was her only means to future employment) which pushed them in the direction of a more conventional one. She is also very insistent that marriage was 'too much like being a woman', in her words.

At least as I read her diaries, then, Hannah Cullwick was to a remarkable degree an unsexed woman, one who was loosened if not freed from the fetters of middle-class and dependent helpless womanly womanhood, but also one who had determined upon not entering working-class married womanhood and control over her person by an individual man. She struggled to piece together a language – in her case not only conceptual but also literal, in terms of the practical difficulties of communicating at a basic level with Munby as the denizen of a different although contiguous world – in which to speak and write of this. And the metaphor she most often used for doing so revolved around race and its divisions and hierarchies.

In doing this Hannah Cullwick was as proficient a theorizer of her experience and that of others as any contemporary feminist theoretician. Indeed, I would say a jolly sight more so, for she took as axiomatic a number of things which white heterosexual feminists have been dragged to in effect kicking and screaming after prolonged protest from black and lesbian women. As I hope my brief account will have indicated, for Hannah Cullwick *women* was a structural category to which she had necessarily to relate and respond, but in complex ways related to her class position, her rural background, and also her particular and unique biographical gathering together of experiences and understandings. We have much to learn from her and from other women whose lives admit rumpled complexities, rather than these being removed under the heavy iron of Theory.

In summary, it seems to me if we leave on one side the ridiculous assumption of positivist deductionist theoreticians, which people merely experience while theorizing is the prerogative of a special class or group, we can begin to recognize things that education regressively strips from us. One is that the complexities of the categories *women* and *men* are not reserved knowledge for theoreticians/researchers; any detailed examination of historical or contemporary people's lives conducted in a spirit of humility and a genuine desire to understand would yield similar findings as I have outlined with regard to Hannah Cullwick. Another is that for as far back as we have sufficient biographical information we can discern such complexities in understandings of *women* and *men*. And yet another is that it thereby becomes patently obvious that theorizing is the stuff of everyday life and understanding and that attempts by feminist and other traditionalists to insist that experience is theoretically denuded (and see here the review of such debates in Stanley and Wise, 1990) is actually elitist and blinkered.

References

Bauman, Zigmunt (1988) 'Is there a postmodern sociology?', *Theory, Culture and Society*, 5: 217–37.

Daniels, Kay (1985) 'Feminism and social history', *Australian Feminist Studies*, 1: 27–40.

Davidoff, Leonore and Hall, Catherine (1987) *Family Fortunes: Men and Women of the English Middle Class 1780–1850*. London: Hutchinson.

Foucault, Michel (1976) *The History of Sexuality, Part 1*. Harmondsworth: Penguin.

Genovese, Elizabeth Fox (1982) 'Placing women's history in history', *New Left Review*, 133: 5–29.

Harding, Sandra (ed.) (1987) *Feminism and Methodology*. Milton Keynes: Open University Press.

Hudson, Derek (1972) *Munby: Man of Two Worlds*. London: John Murray.

Riley, Denise (1988) '*Am I That Name?' Feminism and the Category of 'Women' in History*. London: Macmillan.

Stanley, Liz (ed.) (1984) *The Diaries of Hannah Cullwick*. London: Virago Press.

Stanley, Liz (1987) 'Biography as microscope or kaleidoscope? The case of "power" in Hannah Cullwick's relationship with Arthur Munby', *Women's Studies International Forum*, 10: 19–31.

Stanley, Liz and Wise, Sue (1979) 'Feminist theory, feminist research and experiences of sexism', *Women's Studies International Quarterly*, 2: 359–74.

Stanley, Liz and Wise, Sue (1990) 'Method, methodology and epistemology in feminist research processes', in Liz Stanley (ed.), *Feminist Praxis: Research, Theory, and Epistemology in Feminist Sociology*. London: Routledge.

Wittig, Monique (1980) 'The straight mind', *Feminist Issues*, 1(1): 103–11.

Wittig, Monique (1981) 'One is not born a woman', *Feminist Issues*, 1(2): 47–54.

The Social Construction of Black Feminist Thought

Patricia Hill Collins

Sojourner Truth, Anna Julia Cooper, Ida Wells Barnett and Fannie Lou Hamer are but a few names from a growing list of distinguished African-American women activists. Although their sustained resistance to Black women's victimization within interlocking systems of race, gender and class oppression is well known, these women did not act alone.[1] Their actions were nurtured by the support of countless, ordinary African-American women who, through strategies of everyday resistance, created a powerful foundation for this more visible Black feminist activist tradition.[2] Such support has been essential to the shape and goals of Black feminist thought.

The long-term and widely shared resistance among African-American women can only have been sustained by an enduring and shared standpoint among Black women about the meaning of oppression and the actions that Black women can and should take to resist it. Efforts to identify the central concepts of this Black women's standpoint figure prominently in the works of contemporary Black feminist intellectuals.[3] Moreover, political and epistemological issues influence the social construction of Black feminist thought. Like other subordinate groups, African-American women not only have developed distinctive interpretations of Black women's oppression but have done so by using alternative ways of producing and validating knowledge itself.

A Black women's standpoint

The foundation of Black feminist thought

Black women's everyday acts of resistance challenge two prevailing approaches to studying the consciousness of oppressed groups.[4] One approach claims that subordinate groups identify with the powerful and have no valid independent interpretation of their own oppression.[5] The second approach assumes that the oppressed are less human than their

From *Signs*, 14 (4), 1989, pp. 745–73, abridged.

rulers and, therefore, are less capable of articulating their own standpoint.[6] Both approaches see any independent consciousness expressed by an oppressed group as being not of the group's own making and/or inferior to the perspective of the dominant group.[7] More important, both interpretations suggest that oppressed groups lack the motivation for political activism because of their flawed consciousness of their own subordination.

Yet African-American women have been neither passive victims of nor willing accomplices to their own domination. As a result, emerging work in Black women's studies contends that Black women have a self-defined standpoint on their own oppression.[8] Two interlocking components characterize this standpoint. First, Black women's political and economic status provides them with a distinctive set of experiences that offers a different view of material reality than that available to other groups. The unpaid and paid work that Black women perform, the types of communities in which they live, and the kinds of relationships they have with others suggest that African-American women, as a group, experience a different world than those who are not Black and female.[9] Second, these experiences stimulate a distinctive Black feminist consciousness concerning that material reality.[10] In brief, a subordinate group not only experiences a different reality than a group that rules, but a subordinate group may interpret that reality differently than a dominant group.

Many ordinary African-American women have grasped this connection between what one does and how one thinks. Hannah Nelson, an elderly Black domestic worker, discusses how work shapes the standpoints of African-American and white women: 'Since I have to work, I don't really have to worry about most of the things that most of the white women I have worked for are worrying about. And if these women did their own work, they would think just like I do – about this, anyway.'[11] Ruth Shays, a Black inner-city resident, points out how variations in men's and women's experiences lead to differences in perspective: 'The mind of the man and the mind of the woman is the same. But this business of living makes women use their minds in ways that men don't even have to think about.'[12] Finally, elderly domestic worker Rosa Wakefield assesses how the standpoints of the powerful and those who serve them diverge: 'If you eats these dinners and don't cook 'em, if you wears these clothes and don't buy or iron them, then you might start thinking that the good fairy or some spirit did all that. . . . Blackfolks don't have no time to be thinking like that. . . . But when you don't have anything else to do, you can think like that. It's bad for your mind, though.'[13]

While African-American women may occupy material positions that stimulate a unique standpoint, expressing an independent Black feminist consciousness is problematic precisely because more powerful groups have a vested interest in suppressing such thought. As Hannah Nelson notes, 'I have grown to womanhood in a world where the saner you are, the madder you are made to appear.'[14] Nelson realizes that those who control the schools, the media and other cultural institutions are generally skilled in establishing their view of reality as superior to alternative interpretations.

While an oppressed group's experiences may put them in a position to see things differently, their lack of control over the apparatuses of society that sustain ideological hegemony makes the articulation of their self-defined standpoint difficult. Groups unequal in power are correspondingly unequal in their access to the resources necessary to implement their perspectives outside their particular group.

One key reason that standpoints of oppressed groups are discredited and suppressed by the more powerful is that self-defined standpoints can stimulate oppressed groups to resist their domination. For instance, Annie Adams, a southern Black woman, describes how she became involved in civil rights activities:

> When I first went into the mill we had segregated water fountains. . . . Same thing about the toilets. I had to clean the toilets for the inspection room and then, when I got ready to go to the bathroom, I had to go all the way to the bottom of the stairs to the cellar. So I asked my boss man, 'What's the difference? If I can go in there and clean them toilets, why can't I use them?' Finally, I started to use that toilet. I decided I wasn't going to walk a mile to go to the bathroom.[15]

In this case, Adams found the standpoint of the 'boss man' inadequate, developed one of her own, and acted upon it. In doing so, her actions exemplify the connections between experiencing oppression, developing a self-defined standpoint on that experience, and resistance.

The significance of Black feminist thought

The existence of a distinctive Black women's standpoint does not mean that it has been adequately articulated in Black feminist thought. Peter Berger and Thomas Luckmann provide a useful approach to clarifying the relationship between a Black women's standpoint and Black feminist thought with the contention that knowledge exists on two levels.[16] The first level includes the everyday, taken-for-granted knowledge shared by members of a given group, such as the ideas expressed by Ruth Shays and Annie Adams. Black feminist thought, by extension, represents a second level of knowledge, the more specialized knowledge furnished by experts who are part of a group and who express the group's standpoint. The two levels of knowledge are interdependent; while Black feminist thought articulates the taken-for-granted knowledge of African-American women, it also encourages all Black women to create new self-definitions that validate a Black women's standpoint.

Black feminist thought's potential significance goes far beyond demonstrating that Black women can produce independent, specialized knowledge. Such thought can encourage collective identity by offering Black women a different view of themselves and their world than that offered by the established social order. This different view encourages African-American women to value their own subjective knowledge base.[17] By taking elements and themes of Black women's culture and traditions and infusing them with new meaning, Black feminist thought rearticulates a consciousness that already exists.[18] More important, this rearticulated consciousness gives African-American women another tool of resistance to all forms of their subordination.[19]

Black feminist thought, then, specializes in formulating and rearticulating the distinctive, self-defined standpoint of African-American women. One approach to learning more about a Black women's standpoint is to consult standard scholarly sources for the ideas of specialists on Black women's experiences.[20] But investigating a Black women's standpoint and Black feminist thought requires more ingenuity than that required in examining the standpoints and thought of white males. Rearticulating the standpoint of African-American women through Black feminist thought is much more difficult since one cannot use the same techniques to study the knowledge of the dominated as one uses to study the knowledge of the powerful. This is precisely because subordinate groups have long had to use alternative ways to create an independent consciousness and to rearticulate it through specialists validated by the oppressed themselves.

The contours of an Afrocentric feminist epistemology

Africanist analyses of the Black experience generally agree on the fundamental elements of an Afrocentric standpoint. In spite of varying histories, Black societies reflect elements of a core African value system that existed prior to and independently of racial oppression.[21] Moreover, as a result of colonialism, imperialism, slavery, apartheid and other systems of racial domination, Blacks share a common experience of oppression. These similarities in material conditions have fostered shared Afrocentric values that permeate the family structure, religious institutions, culture and community life of Blacks in varying parts of Africa, the Caribbean, South America and North America.[22] This Afrocentric consciousness permeates the shared history of people of African descent through the framework of a distinctive Afrocentric epistemology.[23]

Feminist scholars advance a similar argument. They assert that women share a history of patriarchal oppression through the political economy of the material conditions of sexuality and reproduction.[24] These shared material conditions are thought to transcend divisions among women created by race, social class, religion, sexual orientation and ethnicity and to form the basis of a women's standpoint with its corresponding feminist consciousness and epistemology.[25]

Since Black women have access to both the Afrocentric and the feminist standpoints, an alternative epistemology used to rearticulate a Black women's standpoint reflects elements of both traditions.[26] The search for the distinguishing features of an alternative epistemology used by African-American women reveals that values and ideas that Africanist scholars identify as being characteristically 'Black' often bear remarkable resemblance to similar ideas claimed by feminist scholars as being characteristically 'female'.[27] This similarity suggests that the material conditions of oppression can vary dramatically and yet generate some uniformity in the epistemologies of subordinate groups. Thus, the significance of an Afrocentric feminist epistemology may lie in its enrichment of our understanding of how subordinate groups create knowledge that enables them to resist oppression.

The parallels between the two conceptual schemes raise a question: is the worldview of women of African descent more intensely infused with the overlapping feminine/Afrocentric standpoints than is the case for either African-American men or white women?[28] While an Afrocentric feminist epistemology reflects elements of epistemologies used by Blacks as a group and women as a group, it also paradoxically demonstrates features that may be unique to Black women. On certain dimensions, Black women may more closely resemble Black men, on others, white women, and on still others, Black women may stand apart from both groups. Black feminist sociologist Deborah K. King describes this phenomenon as a 'both/or' orientation, the act of being simultaneously a member of a group and yet standing apart from it. She suggests that multiple realities among Black women yield a 'multiple consciousness in Black women's politics' and that this state of belonging yet not belonging forms an integral part of Black women's oppositional consciousness.[29] Bonnie Thornton Dill's analysis of how Black women live with contradictions, a situation she labels the dialectics of Black womanhood', parallels King's assertions that this 'both/or' orientation is central to an Afrocentric feminist consciousness.[30] Rather than emphasizing how a Black women's standpoint and its accompanying epistemology are different than those in Afrocentric and feminist analyses, I use Black women's experiences as a point of contact between the two.

Viewing an Afrocentric feminist epistemology in this way challenges analyses claiming that Black women have a more accurate view of oppression than do other groups. Such approaches suggest that oppression can be quantified and compared and that adding layers of oppression produces a potentially clearer standpoint. While it is tempting to claim that Black women are more oppressed than everyone else and therefore have the best standpoint from which to understand the mechanisms, processes and effects of oppression, this simply may not be the case.[31]

African-American women do not uniformly share an Afrocentric feminist epistemology since social class introduces variations among Black women in seeing, valuing and using Afrocentric feminist perspectives. While a Black women's standpoint and its accompanying epistemology stem from Black women's consciousness of race and gender oppression, they are not simply the result of combining Afrocentric and female values – standpoints are rooted in real material conditions structured by social class.[32]

Concrete experience as a criterion of meaning

Carolyn Chase, a thirty-one-year-old inner-city Black woman, notes, 'My aunt used to say, "A heap see, but a few know." '[33] This saying depicts two types of knowing, knowledge and wisdom, and taps the first dimension of an Afrocentric feminist epistemology. Living life as Black women requires wisdom since knowledge about the dynamics of race, gender and class subordination has been essential to Black women's survival. African-American women give such wisdom high credence in assessing knowledge.

Allusions to these two types of knowing pervade the words of a range of African-American women. In explaining the tenacity of racism, Zilpha Elaw, a preacher of the mid-1800s, noted: 'The pride of a white skin is a bauble of great value with many in some parts of the United States, who readily sacrifice their intelligence to their prejudices, and possess more knowledge than wisdom.'[34] In describing differences separating African-American and white women, Nancy White invokes a similar rule: 'When you come right down to it, white women just *think* they are free. Black women *know* they ain't free.'[35] Geneva Smitherman, a college professor specializing in African-American linguistics, suggests that 'from a black perspective, written documents are limited in what they can teach about life and survival in the world. Blacks are quick to ridicule "educated fools," . . . they have "book learning" but no "mother wit," knowledge, but not wisdom.'[36] Mabel Lincoln eloquently summarizes the distinction between knowledge and wisdom: 'To black people like me, a fool is funny – you know, people who love to break bad, people you can't tell anything to, folks that would take a shotgun to a roach.'[37]

Black women need wisdom to know how to deal with the 'educated fools' who would 'take a shotgun to a roach'. As members of a subordinate group, Black women cannot afford to be fools of any type, for their devalued status denies them the protections that white skin, maleness and wealth confer. This distinction between knowledge and wisdom, and the use of experience as the cutting edge dividing them, has been key to Black women's survival. In the context of race, gender and class oppression, the distinction is essential since knowledge without wisdom is adequate for the powerful, but wisdom is essential to the survival of the subordinate.

For ordinary African-American women, those individuals who have lived through the experiences about which they claim to be experts are more believable than those who have merely read or thought about such experiences. Thus, concrete experience as a criterion for credibility is frequently invoked by Black women when making knowledge claims. For instance, Hannah Nelson describes the importance that personal experience has for her: 'Our speech is most directly personal, and every black person assumes that every other black person has a right to a personal opinion. In speaking of grave matters, your personal experience is considered very good evidence. With us, distant statistics are certainly not as important as the actual experience of a sober person.'[38] Similarly, Ruth Shays uses her concrete experiences to challenge the idea that formal education is the only route to knowledge.

> I am the kind of person who doesn't have a lot of education, but both my mother and my father had good common sense. Now, I think that's all you need. I might

not know how to use thirty-four words where three would do, but that does not mean that I don't know what I'm talking about . . . I know what I'm talking about because I'm talking about myself. I'm talking about what I have lived.'[39]

Implicit in Shays's self-assessment is a critique of the type of knowledge that obscures the truth, the 'thirty-four words' that cover up a truth that can be expressed in three.

Even after substantial mastery of white masculinist epistemologies, many Black women scholars invoke their own concrete experiences and those of other Black women in selecting topics for investigation and methodologies used. For example, Elsa Barkley Brown subtitles her essay on Black women's history, 'how my mother taught me to be an historian in spite of my academic training'.[40] Similarly, Joyce Ladner maintains that growing up as a Black woman in the South gave her special insights in conducting her study of Black adolescent women.[41]

Henry Mitchell and Nicholas Lewter claim that experience as a criterion of meaning with practical images as its symbolic vehicles is a fundamental epistemological tenet in African-American thought-systems.[42] Stories, narratives and Bible principles are selected for their applicability to the lived experiences of African-Americans and become symbolic representations of a whole wealth of experience. For example, Bible tales are told for their value to common life, so their interpretation involves no need for scientific historical verification. The narrative method requires that the story be 'told, not torn apart in analysis, and trusted as core belief, not admired as science'.[43] Any biblical story contains more than characters and a plot – it presents key ethical issues salient in African-American life.

June Jordan's essay about her mother's suicide exemplifies the multiple levels of meaning that can occur when concrete experiences are used as a criterion of meaning. Jordan describes her mother, a woman who literally died trying to stand up, and the effect that her mother's death had on her own work:

> I think all of this is really about women and work. Certainly this is all about me as a woman and my life work. I mean I am not sure my mother's suicide was something extraordinary. Perhaps most women must deal with a similar inheritance, the legacy of a woman whose death you cannot possibly pinpoint because she died so many, many times and because, even before she became your mother, the life of that woman was taken. . . . I came too late to help my mother to her feet. By way of everlasting thanks to all of the women who have helped me to stay alive I am working never to be late again.[44]

While Jordan has knowledge about the concrete act of her mother's death, she also strives for wisdom concerning the meaning of that death.

Some feminist scholars offer a similar claim that women, as a group, are more likely than men to use concrete knowledge in assessing knowledge claims. For example, a substantial number of the 135 women in a study of women's cognitive development were 'connected knowers' and were drawn to the sort of knowledge that emerges from first-hand observation. Such women felt that since knowledge comes from experience, the best way of understanding another person's ideas was to try to share the experiences that led the person to form those ideas. At the heart of the procedures used by connected knowers is the capacity for empathy.[45]

In valuing the concrete, African-American women may be invoking not only an Afrocentric tradition, but a women's tradition as well. Some feminist theorists suggest that women are socialized in complex relational nexuses where contextual rules take priority over abstract principles in governing behavior. This socialization process is thought to stimulate characteristic ways of knowing.[46] For example, Canadian sociologist Dorothy Smith maintains that two modes of knowing exist, one located in the body and the space it occupies and the other passing beyond it. She asserts that women, through their childrearing and nurturing activities, mediate these two modes and use the concrete experiences of their daily lives to assess more abstract knowledge claims.[47]

Amanda King, a young Black mother, describes how she used the concrete to assess the abstract and points out how difficult mediating these two modes of knowing can be:

> The leaders of the ROC [a labor union] lost their jobs too, but it just seemed like they were used to losing their jobs. . . . This was like a lifelong thing for them, to get out there and protest. They were like, what do you call them – intellectuals. . . . You got the ones that go to the university that are supposed to make all the speeches, they're the ones that are supposed to lead, you know, put this little revolution together, and then you got the little ones . . . that go to the factory everyday, they be the ones that have to fight. I had a child and I thought I don't have the time to be running around with these people. . . . I mean I understand some of that stuff they were talking about, like the bourgeoisie, the rich and the poor and all that, but I had surviving on my mind for me and my kid.[48]

For King, abstract ideals of class solidarity were mediated by the concrete experience of motherhood and the connectedness it involved.

In traditional African-American communities, Black women find considerable institutional support for valuing concrete experience. Black extended families and Black churches are two key institutions where Black women experts with concrete knowledge of what it takes to be self-defined Black women share their knowledge with their younger, less experienced sisters. This relationship of sisterhood among Black women can be seen as a model for a whole series of relationships that African-American women have with each other, whether it is networks among women in extended families, among women in the Black church, or among women in the African-American community at large.[49]

Since the Black church and the Black family are both woman-centered and Afrocentric institutions, African-American women traditionally have found considerable institutional support for this dimension of an Afrocentric feminist epistemology in ways that are unique to them. While white women may value the concrete, it is questionable whether white families, particularly middle-class nuclear ones, and white community institutions provide comparable types of support. Similarly, while Black men are supported by Afrocentric institutions, they cannot participate in Black women's sisterhood. In terms of Black women's relationships with one another then, African-American women may indeed find it easier than others to recognize connectedness as a primary way of knowing, simply because they are encouraged to do so by Black women's tradition of sisterhood.

The use of dialogue in assessing knowledge claims

For Black women, new knowledge claims are rarely worked out in isolation from other individuals and are usually developed through dialogues with other members of a community. A primary epistemological assumption underlying the use of dialogue in assessing knowledge claims is that connectedness rather than separation is an essential component of the knowledge-validation process.[50]

The use of dialogue has deep roots in an African-based oral tradition and in African-American culture.[51] Ruth Shays describes the importance of dialogue in the knowledge-validation process of *enslaved African-Americans*. 'They would find a lie if it took them a year . . . the foreparents found the truth because they listened and they made people tell their part many times. Most often you can hear a lie. . . . Those old people was everywhere and knew the truth of many disputes. They believed that a liar should suffer the pain of his lies, and they had all kinds of ways of bringing liars to judgement'.[52]

The widespread use of the call and response discourse mode among African-Americans exemplifies the importance placed on dialogue. Composed of spontaneous verbal and nonverbal interaction between speaker and listener in which all of the speaker's statements or 'calls' are punctuated by expressions or 'responses' from the listener, this Black discourse mode pervades African-American culture. The fundamental requirement of this interactive network is active participation of all individuals.[53] For ideas to be tested and validated, everyone in the group must participate. To refuse to join in, especially if one really disagrees with what has been said is seen as 'cheating'.[54]

June Jordan's analysis of Black English points to the significance of this dimension of an alternative epistemology:

> Our language is a system constructed by people constantly needing to insist that we exist. . . . Our language devolves from a culture that abhors all abstraction, or anything tending to obscure or delete the fact of the human being who is here and now/the truth of the person who is speaking or listening. Consequently, *there is no passive voice construction possible in Black English.* For example, you cannot say, 'Black English is being eliminated.' You must say, instead, 'White people eliminating Black English.' The assumption of the presence of life governs all of Black English . . . every sentence assumes the living and active participation of at least two human beings, the speaker and the listener.[55]

Many Black women intellectuals invoke the relationships and connectedness provided by use of dialogue. When asked why she chose the themes she did, novelist Gayle Jones replied: 'I was . . . interested . . . in oral traditions of storytelling – Afro-American and others, in which there is always the consciousness and importance of the hearer.'[56] In describing the difference in the way male and female writers select significant events and relationships, Jones points out that 'with many women writers, relationships within family, community, between men and women, and among women – from slave narratives by black women writers on – are treated as complex and significant relationships, whereas with many men the significant relationships are those that involve confrontations – relationships outside the family and community.'[57] Alice Walker's reaction to Zora Neale Hurston's book, *Mules and Men*, is another example of the use of dialogue in assessing knowlege claims. In *Mules and Men*, Hurston chose not to become a detached observer of the stories and folktales she collected but instead, through extensive dialogues with the people in the communities she studied, placed herself at the center of her analysis. Using a similar process, Walker tests the truth of Hurston's knowledge claims:

> When I read *Mules and Men* I was delighted. Here was this perfect book! The 'perfection' of which I immediately tested on my relatives, who are such typical Black Americans they are useful for every sort of political, cultural, or economic survey. Very regular people from the South, rapidly forgetting their Southern cultural inheritance in the suburbs and ghettos of Boston and New York, they sat around reading the book themselves, listening to me read the book, listening to each other read the book, and a kind of paradise was regained.[58]

Their centrality in Black churches and Black extended families provides Black women with a high degree of support from Black institutions for invoking dialogue as a dimension of an Afrocentric feminist epistemology. However, when African-American women use dialogues in assessing knowledge claims, they might be invoking a particularly female way of knowing as well. Feminist scholars contend that males and females are socialized within their families to seek different types of autonomy, the former based on separation, the latter seeking connectedness, and that this variation in types of autonomy parallels the characteristic differences between male and female ways of knowing.[59] For instance, in contrast to the visual metaphors (such as equating knowledge with illumination, knowing with seeing, and truth with light) that scientists and philosophers typically use, women tend to ground their epistemological premises in metaphors suggesting speaking and listening.[60]

While there are significant differences between the roles Black women play in their families and those played by middle-class white women, Black women clearly are affected by general cultural norms prescribing certain familial roles for women. Thus, in terms of the role of dialogue in an Afrocentric feminist epistemology, Black women may again experience a convergence of the values of the African-American community and woman-centered values.

The ethic of caring

'Ole white preachers used to talk wid dey tongues widdout sayin' nothin', but Jesus told us slaves to talk wid our hearts.'[61] These words of an ex-slave suggest that ideas cannot be divorced from the individuals who create and share them. This theme of 'talking with the heart' taps another dimension of an alternative epistemology used by African-American women, the ethic of caring. Just as the ex-slave used the wisdom in his heart to reject the ideas of the preachers who talked 'wid dey tongues widdout sayin' nothin'', the ethic of caring suggests that personal expressiveness, emotions and empathy are central to the knowledge-validation process.

One of three interrelated components making up the ethic of caring is the emphasis placed on individual uniqueness. Rooted in a tradition of African humanism, each individual is thought to be a unique expression of a common spirit, power or energy expressed by all life.[62] This belief in individual uniqueness is illustrated by the value placed on personal expressiveness in African-American communities.[63] Johnetta Ray, an inner-city resident, describes this Afrocentric emphasis on individual uniqueness: 'No matter how hard we try, I don't think black people will ever develop much of a herd instinct. We are profound individualists with a passion for self-expression.'[64]

A second component of the ethic of caring concerns the appropriateness of emotions in dialogues. Emotion indicates that a speaker believes in the validity of an argument.[65] Consider Ntozake Shange's description of one of the goals of her work: 'Our [Western] society allows people to be absolutely neurotic and totally out of touch with their feelings and everyone else's feelings, and yet be very respectable. This, to me, is a travesty. . . . I'm trying to change the idea of seeing emotions and intellect as distinct faculties.'[66] Shange's words echo those of the ex-slave. Both see the denigration of emotion as problematic, and both suggest that expressiveness should be reclaimed and valued.

A third component of the ethic of caring involves developing the capacity for empathy. Harriet Jones, a sixteen-year-old Black woman, explains why she chose to open up to her interviewer: 'Some things in my life are so hard for me to bear, and it makes me feel better to know that you feel sorry about those things and would change them if you could.'[67]

These three components of the ethic of caring – the value placed on individual expressiveness, the appropriateness of emotions, and the capacity for empathy – pervade African-American culture. One of the best examples of the interactive nature of the importance of dialogue and the ethic of caring in assessing knowledge claims occurs in the use of the call and response discourse mode in traditional Black church services. In such services, both the minister and the congregation routinely use voice rhythm and vocal inflection to convey meaning. The sound of what is being said is just as important as the words themselves in what is, in a sense, a dialogue between reason and emotions. As a result, it is nearly impossible to filter out the strictly linguistic-cognitive abstract meaning from the sociocultural psycho-emotive meaning.[68] While the ideas presented by a speaker must have validity, that is, agree with the general body of knowledge shared by the Black congregation, the group also appraises the way knowledge claims are presented.

There is growing evidence that the ethic of caring may be part of women's experience as well. Certain dimensions of women's ways of knowing bear striking resemblance to Afrocentric expressions of the ethic of caring. Belenky, Clinchy, Goldberger and Tarule point out that two contrasting epistemological orientations characterize knowing – one, an epistemology of separation based on impersonal procedures for establishing truth, and the other, an epistemology of connection in which truth emerges through care. While these ways of knowing are not gender specific, disproportionate numbers of women rely on connected knowing.[69]

The parallels between Afrocentric expressions of the ethic of caring and those advanced by feminist scholars are noteworthy. The emphasis placed on expressiveness and emotion in African-American communities bears marked resemblance to feminist perspectives on the importance of personality in connected knowing. Separate knowers try to subtract the personality of an individual from his or her ideas because they see personality as biasing those ideas. In contrast, connected knowers see personality as adding to an individual's ideas, and they feel that the personality of each group member enriches a group's understanding.[70] Similarly, the significance of individual uniqueness, personal expressiveness and empathy in African-American communities resembles the importance that some feminist analyses place on women's 'inner voice'.[71]

The convergence of Afrocentric and feminist values in the ethic-of-care dimension of an alternative epistemology seems particularly acute. While white women may have access to a women's tradition valuing emotion and expressiveness, few white social institutions except the family validate this way of knowing. In contrast, Black women have long had the support of the Black church, an institution with deep roots in the African past and a philosophy that accepts and encourages expressiveness and an ethic of caring. While Black men share in this Afrocentric tradition, they must resolve the contradictions that distinguish abstract, unemotional Western masculinity from an Afrocentric ethic of caring. The differences among race/gender groups thus hinge on differences in their access to institutional supports valuing one type of knowing over another. Although Black women may be denigrated within white-male-controlled academic institutions, other institutions, such as Black families and churches, which encourage the expression of Black female power, seem to do so by way of their support for an Afrocentric feminist epistemology.

The ethic of personal accountability

An ethic of personal accountability is the final dimension of an alternative epistemology. Not only must individuals develop their knowledge claims through dialogue and present those knowledge claims in a style proving their concern for their ideas, people are expected to be accountable for their knowledge claims. Zilpha Elaw's description of slavery reflects this notion that every idea has an owner and that the owner's identity matters: 'Oh, the abominations of slavery! . . . every case of slavery, however lenient its inflictions and mitigated its atrocities, indicates an oppressor, the oppressed, and oppression.'[72] For Elaw, abstract definitions of slavery mesh with the concrete identities of its perpetrators and its victims. Blacks 'consider it essential for individuals to have personal positions on issues and assume full responsibility for arguing their validity.'[73]

Assessments of an individual's knowledge claims simultaneously evaluate an individual's character, values and ethics. African-Americans reject Eurocentric masculinist beliefs that probing into an individual's personal viewpoint is outside the boundaries of discussion. Rather, all views expressed and actions taken are thought to derive from a central set of core beliefs that cannot be other than personal.[74] From this perspective, knowledge claims made by individuals respected for their moral and ethical values will carry more weight than those offered by less respected figures.[75]

An example drawn from an undergraduate course composed entirely of Black women, which I taught, might help clarify the uniqueness of this portion of the knowledge-validation process. During one class discussion, I assigned the students the task of critiquing an analysis of Black feminism advanced by a prominent Black male scholar. Instead of dissecting the rationality of the author's thesis, my students demanded facts about the author's personal biography. They were especially interested in concrete details of his life such as his relationships with Black women, his marital status and his social class background. By requesting data on dimensions of his personal life routinely excluded in positivist approaches to knowledge validation, they were invoking concrete experience as a criterion of meaning. They used this information to assess whether he really cared about his topic and invoked this ethic of caring in advancing their knowledge claims about his work. Furthermore, they refused to evaluate the rationality of his written ideas without some indication of his personal credibility as an ethical human being. The entire exchange could only have occurred as a dialogue among members of a class that had established a solid enough community to invoke an alternative epistemology in assessing knowledge claims.[76]

The ethic of personal accountability is clearly an Afrocentric value, but is it feminist as well? While limited by its attention to middle-class, white women, Carol Gilligan's work suggests that there is a female model for moral development where women are more inclined to link morality to responsability, relationships and the ability to maintain social ties.[77] If this is the case, then African-American women again experience a convergence of values from Afrocentric and female institutions.

The use of an Afrocentric feminist epistemology in traditional Black church services illustrates the interactive nature of all four dimensions and also serves as a metaphor for the distinguishing features of an Afrocentric feminist way of knowing. The services represent more than dialogues between the rationality used in examining biblical texts/stories and the emotion inherent in the use of reason for this purpose. The rationale for such dialogues addresses the task of examining concrete experiences for the presence of an ethic of caring. Neither emotion nor ethics is subordinated to reason. Instead, emotion, ethics and reason are used as interconnected, essential components in assessing knowledge claims. In an Afrocentric feminist epistemology, values lie at the heart of the knowledge-validation process such that inquiry always has an ethical aim.

Epistemology and Black feminist thought

Living life as an African-American woman is a necessary prerequisite for producing Black feminist thought because within Black women's communities thought is validated and produced with reference to a particular set of historical, material and epistemological conditions.[78] African-American women who adhere to the idea that claims about Black women must be substantiated by Black women's sense of their own experiences and who anchor their knowledge claims in an Afrocentric feminist epistemology have produced a rich tradition of Black feminist thought.

Traditionally, such women were blues singers, poets, autobiographers, storytellers and orators validated by the larger community of Black women as experts on a Black women's standpoint. Only a few unusual African-American feminist scholars have been able to defy Eurocentric masculinist epistemologies and explicitly embrace an Afrocentric feminist epistemology. Consider Alice Walker's description of Zora Neale Hurston: 'In my mind, Zora Neale Hurston, Billie Holiday, and Bessie Smith form a sort of unholy trinity. Zora *belongs* in the tradition of Black women singers, rather than among "the literati." . . . Like Billie and Bessie she followed her own road, believed in her own gods, pursued her own dreams, and refused to separate herself from "common" people.'[79]

Zora Neale Hurston is an exception for, prior to 1950, few Black women earned advanced degrees, and most of those who did complied with Eurocentric masculinist epistemologies. While these women worked on behalf of Black women, they did so within the confines of pervasive race and gender oppression. Black women scholars were in a position to see the exclusion of Black women from scholarly discourse, and the thematic content of their work often reflected their interest in examining a Black women's stand point. However, their tenuous status in academic institutions led them to adhere to Eurocentric masculinist epistemologies so that their work would be accepted as scholarly. As a result, while they produced Black feminist thought, those Black women most likely to gain academic credentials were often least likely to produce Black feminist thought that used an Afrocentric feminist epistemology.

As more Black women earn advanced degrees, the range of Black feminist scholarship is expanding. Increasing numbers of African-American women scholars are explicitly choosing to ground their work in Black women's experiences, and, by doing so, many implicitly adhere to an Afrocentric feminist epistemology. Rather than being restrained by their 'both/and' status of marginality, these women make creative use of their outsider-within status and produce innovative Black feminist thought. The difficulties these women face lie less in demonstrating the technical components of white male epistemologies than in resisting the hegemonic nature of these patterns of thought in order to see, value and use existing alternative Afrocentric feminist ways of knowing.

In establishing the legitimacy of their knowledge claims, Black women scholars who want to develop Black feminist thought may encounter the often conflicting standards of three key groups. First, Black feminist thought must be validated by ordinary African-American women who grow to womanhood 'in a world where the saner you are, the madder you are made to appear'.[80] To be credible in the eyes of this group, scholars must be personal advocates for their material, be accountable for the consequences of their work, have lived or experienced their material in some fashion, and be willing to engage in dialogues about their findings with ordinary, everyday people. Second, if it is to establish its legitimacy, Black feminist thought also must be accepted by the community of Black women scholars. These scholars place varying amounts of importance on rearticulating a Black women's standpoint using an Afrocentric feminist epistemology. Third, Black feminist thought within academia must be prepared to confront Eurocentric masculinist political and epistemological requirements.

The dilemma facing Black women scholars engaged in creating Black feminist thought is that a knowledge claim that meets the criteria of adequacy for one group and thus is judged to be an acceptable knowledge claim may not be translatable into the terms of a different group. Using the example of Black English, June Jordan illustrates the difficulty of moving among epistemologies: 'You cannot "translate" instances of Standard English preoccupied with abstraction or with nothing/nobody evidently alive into Black English. That would warp the language into uses antithetical to the guiding perspective of its community of users. Rather you must first change those Standard English sentences, themselves, into ideas consistent with the person-centered assumptions of Black English.'[81] While both worldviews share a common vocabulary, the ideas themselves defy direct translation.

Once Black feminist scholars face the notion that, on certain dimensions of a Black women's standpoint, it may be fruitless to try to translate ideas from an Afrocentric feminist epistemology into a Eurocentric masculinist epistemology, then the choices become clearer. Rather than trying to uncover universal knowledge claims that can withstand the translation from one epistemology to another, time might be better spent rearticulating a Black women's standpoint in order to give African-American women the tools to resist their own subordination. The goal here is not one of integrating Black female 'folk culture' into the substantiated body of academic knowledge, for that substantiated knowledge is, in many ways, antithetical to the best interests of Black women. Rather, the process is one of rearticulating a pre-existing Black women's standpoint and recentering the language of existing academic discourse to accommodate these knowledge claims. For those Black women scholars engaged in this rearticulation process, the social construction of Black feminist thought requires the skill and sophistication to decide which knowledge claims can be validated using the epistemological assumptions of one but not both frameworks, which claims can be generated in one framework and only partially accommodated by the other, and which claims can be made in both frameworks without violating the basic political and epistemological assumptions of either.

Black feminist scholars offering knowledge claims that cannot be accommodated by both frameworks face the choice between accepting the taken-for-granted assumptions that permeate white-male-controlled academic institutions or leaving academia. Those Black women who choose to remain in academia must accept the possibility that their knowledge claims will be limited to those claims about Black women that are consistent with a white male worldview. And yet those African-American women who leave academia may find their work is inaccessible to scholarly communities.

Black feminist scholars offering knowledge claims that can be partially accommodated by both epistemologies can create a body of thought that stands outside of either. Rather than trying to synthesize competing worldviews that, at this point in time, may defy reconciliation, their task is to point out common themes and concerns. By making creative use of their status as mediators, their thought becomes an entity unto itself that is rooted in two distinct political and epistemological contexts.[82]

Those Black feminists who develop knowledge claims that both epistemologies can accommodate may have found a route to the elusive goal of generating so-called objective generalizations that can stand as universal truths. Those ideas that are validated as true by African-American women, African-American men, white men, white women, and other groups with distinctive standpoints, with each group using the epistemological approaches growing from its unique standpoint, thus become the most objective truths.[83]

Alternative knowledge claims, in and of themselves, are rarely threatening to conventional knowledge. Such claims are routinely ignored, discredited, or simply absorbed and marginalized in existing paradigms. Much more threatening is the challenge that alternative epistemologies offer to the basic process used by the powerful to legitimize their knowledge claims. If the epistemology used to validate knowledge comes into question, then all prior knowledge claims validated under the dominant model become suspect. An alternative epistemology challenges all certified knowledge and opens up the question of whether what has been taken to be true can stand the test of alternative ways of validating truth. The existence of an independent Black women's standpoint using an Afrocentric feminist epistemology calls into question the content of what currently passes as truth and simultaneously challenges the process of arriving at that truth.

Notes

Special thanks go out to the following people for reading various drafts of this manuscript: Evelyn Nakano Glenn, Lynn Weber Cannon, and participants in the 1986 Research Institute, Center for Research on Women, Memphis State University; Elsa Barkley Brown, Deborah K. King, Elizabeth V. Spelman, and Angelene Jamison-Hall; and four anonymous reviewers at *Signs*.

1. For analyses of how interlocking systems of oppression affect Black women, see Frances Beale, 'Double jeopardy: to be black and female', in *The Black Woman*, ed. Toni Cade (Signet, New York, 1970); Angela Y. Davis, *Women, Race and Class* (Random House, New York, 1981); Bonnie Thornton Dill, 'Race, class, and gender prospects for an all inclusive sisterhood', *Feminist Studies*, 9, 1 (1983), pp. 131–50; bell hooks, *Ain't I a Woman? Black Women and Feminism* (South End Press, Boston, 1981); Diane Lewis, 'A response to inequality: black women, racism, and sexism', *Signs: Journal of Women in Culture and Society*, 3, 2 (Winter 1977), pp. 339–61; Pauli Murray, 'The liberation of black women', in *Voices of the New Feminism*, ed. Mary Lou Thompson (Beacon, Boston, 1970), pp. 87–102; and the introduction in Filomina Chioma Steady, *The Black Woman Cross-Culturally* (Schenkman, Cambridge, Mass., 1981), pp. 7–41.

2. See the introduction in Steady, *Black Woman*, for an overview of Black women's strengths. This strength-resiliency perspective has greatly influenced empirical work on African-American women. See, e.g., Joyce Ladner's study of low-income Black adolescent girls, *Tomorrow's Tomorrow* (Doubleday, New York, 1971); and Lena Wright Myers's work on Black women's self-concept, *Black Women: Do They Cope Better?* (Prentice-Hall, Englewood Cliffs, NJ, 1980). For discussions of Black women's resistance, see Elizabeth Fox-Genovese, 'Strategies and forms of resistance: focus on slave women in the United States', in *In Resistance: Studies in African, Caribbean and Afro-American History*, ed. Gary Y. Okihiro (University of Massachusetts Press, Amherst, 1986), pp. 143–65; and Rosalyn Terborg-Penn, 'Black women in resistance: a cross-cultural perspective', in Okihiro, *In Resistance*, pp. 188–209. For a comprehensive discussion of everyday resistance, see James C. Scott, *Weapons of the Weak: Everyday Forms of Peasant Resistance* (Yale University Press, New Haven, Conn., 1985).

3. See Patricia Hill Collins's analysis of the substantive content of Black feminist thought in 'Learning from the outsider within: the sociological significance of black feminist thought', *Social Problems*, 33, 6 (1986), pp. 14–32.

4. Scott describes consciousness as the meaning that people give to their acts through the symbols, norms and ideological forms they create.

5. This thesis is found in scholarship of varying theoretical perspectives. For example, Marxist analyses of working-class consciousness claim that 'false consciousness' makes the working class unable to penetrate the hegemony of ruling-class ideologies. See Scott's critique of this literature.

6. For example, in Western societies, African-Americans have been judged as being less capable of intellectual excellence, more suited to manual labor, and therefore as less human than whites. Similarly, white women have been assigned roles as emotional, irrational creatures

ruled by passions and biological urges. They too have been stigmatized as being less than fully human, as being objects. For a discussion of the importance that objectification and dehumanization play in maintaining systems of domination, see Arthur Brittan and Mary Maynard, *Sexism, Racism and Oppression* (Basil Blackwell, New York, 1984).

7. The tendency for Western scholarship to assess Black culture as pathological and deviant illustrates this process. See Rhett S. Jones, 'Proving blacks inferior: the sociology of knowledge', in *The Death of White Sociology*, ed. Joyce Ladner (Vintage, New York, 1973), pp. 114–35.

8. The presence of an independent standpoint does not mean that it is uniformly shared by all Black women or even that Black women fully recognize its contours. By using the concept of standpoint, I do not mean to minimize the rich diversity existing among African-American women. I use the phrase 'Black women's standpoint' to emphasize the plurality of experiences within the overarching term 'standpoint'. For discussions of the concept of standpoint, see Nancy M. Hartsock, 'The feminist standpoint: developing the ground for a specifically feminist historical materialism', in *Discovering Reality*, ed. Sandra Harding and Merrill Hintikka (D. Reidel, Boston, 1983), pp. 283–310, and *Money, Sex, and Power* (Northeastern University Press, Boston, 1983); and Alison M. Jaggar, *Feminist Politics and Human Nature* (Rowman & Allanheld, Totowa, NJ, 1983), pp. 377–89. My use of the standpoint epistemologies as an organizing concept in this essay does not mean that the concept is problem-free. For a helpful critique of standpoint epistemologies, see Sandra Harding, *The Science Question in Feminism* (Cornell University Press, Ithaca, NY, 1986).

9. One contribution of contemporary Black women's studies is its documentation of how race, class and gender have structured these differences. For representative works surveying African-American women's experiences, see Paula Giddings, *When and Where I Enter: The Impact of Black Women on Race and Sex in America* (William Morrow, New York, 1984); and Jacqueline Jones, *Labor of Love, Labor of Sorrow: Black Women, Work, and the Family from Slavery to the Present* (Basic Books, New York, 1985).

10. For example, Judith Rollins, *Between Women: Domestics and Their Employers* (Temple University Press, Philadelphia, 1985); and Bonnie Thornton Dill, ' "The means to put my children through": child-rearing goals and strategies among black female domestic servants', in *The Black Woman*, ed. LaFrances Rodgers-Rose (Sage Publications, Beverly Hills, Calif., 1980), pp. 107–23, report that Black domestic workers do not see themselves as being the devalued workers that their employers perceive and construct their own interpretations of the meaning of their work. For additional discussions of how Black women's consciousness is shaped by the material conditions they encounter, see Ladner, *Tomorrow's Tomorrow*; Myers, *Black Women* and Cheryl Townsend Gilkes, ' "Together and in harness": women's traditions in the sanctified church', *Signs* 10, 4 (Summer 1985), pp. 678–99. See also Marcia Westkott's discussion of consciousness as a sphere of freedom for women in 'Feminist criticism of the social sciences', *Harvard Educational Review*, 49, 4 (1979), pp. 422–30.

11. John Langston Gwaltney, *Drylongso: A Self-Portrait of Black America* (Vintage, New York, 1980), p. 4.

12. Ibid., p. 33.

13. Ibid., p. 88.

14. Ibid., p. 7.

15. Victoria Byerly, *Hard Times Cotton Mill Girls: Personal Histories of Womanhood and Poverty in the South* (ILR Press, New York, 1986), p. 134.

16. See Peter L. Berger and Thomas Luckmann, *The Social Construction of Reality* (Doubleday, New York, 1966), for a discussion of everyday thought and the role of experts in articulating specialized thought.

17. See Michael Omi and Howard Winant, *Racial Formation in the United States* (Routledge & Kegan Paul, New York, 1986), esp. p. 93.

18. In discussing standpoint epistemologies, Hartsock, in *Money, Sex, and Power*, notes that a standpoint is 'achieved rather than obvious, a mediated rather than immediate understanding' (p. 132).

19. See Scott, *Weapons of the Weak*; and Hartsock, *Money, Sex, and Power*.

20. Some readers may question how one determines whether the ideas of any given African-American woman are 'feminist' and 'Afrocentric'. I offer the following working definitions. I agree with the general definition of feminist consciousness provided by Black feminist sociologist Deborah K. King: 'Any purposes, goals, and activities which seek to enhance the potential of women, to ensure their liberty, afford them equal opportunity, and to permit and encourage their self-determination represent a feminist consciousness, even if they occur within a racial community' (in 'Race, class and gender salience in black women's womanist consciousness, Dartmouth College, Department of Sociology, Hanover, NH, 1987, typescript, p. 22). To be Black or Afrocentric, such thought must not only reflect a similar concern for the self-determination of African-American people, but must in some way draw upon key elements of an Afrocentric tradition as well.

21. For detailed discussions of the Afrocentric worldview, see John S. Mbiti, *African Religions and Philosophy* (Heinemann, London, 1969); Dominique Zahan, *The Religion, Spirituality, and Thought of Traditional Africa* (University of Chicago Press, Chicago, 1979); and Mechal Sobel, *Trabelin' On: The Slave Journey to an Afro-Baptist Faith* (Greenwood Press, Westport, Conn., 1979), pp. 1–76.

22. For representative works applying these concepts to African-American culture, see Niara Sudarkasa, 'Interpreting the African heritage in Afro-American family organization', in *Black Families*, ed. Harriette Pipes McAdoo (Sage, Beverly Hills, Calif., 1981); Henry H. Mitchell and Nicholas Cooper Lewter, *Soul Theology: The Heart of American Black Culture* (Harper & Row, San Francisco, 1986); Robert Farris Thompson, *Flash of the Spirit: African and Afro-American Art and Philosophy* (Vintage, New York, 1983); and Ortiz M. Walton, 'Comparative analysis of the African and the Western aesthetics', in *The Black Aesthetic*, ed. Addison Gayle (Doubleday, Garden City, NY, 1971), pp. 154–64.

23. One of the best discussions of an Afrocentric epistemology is offered by James E. Turner, 'Foreword: Africana studies and epistemology; a discourse in the sociology of knowledge', in *The Next Decade: Theoretical and Research Issues in Africana Studies*, ed. James E. Turner (Cornell University Africana Studies and Research Center, Ithaca, NY, 1984), pp. v–xxv. See also Vernon Dixon, 'World views and research methodology', summarized in Harding, *Science Question*, p. 170.

24. See Hester Eisenstein, *Contemporary Feminist Thought* (G.K. Hall, Boston, 1983). Nancy Hartsock's *Money, Sex, and Power*, pp. 145–209, offers a particularly insightful analysis of women's oppression.

25. For discussions of feminist consciousness, see Dorothy Smith, 'A sociology for women', in *The Prism of Sex: Essays in the Sociology of Knowledge*, ed. Julia A. Sherman and Evelyn T. Beck (University of Wisconsin Press, Madison, 1979); and Michelle Z. Rosaldo, 'Women, culture, and society: a theoretical overview', in *Woman, Culture, and Society*, ed. Michelle Z. Rosaldo and Louise Lamphere (Stanford University Press, Stanford, Calif., 1974), pp. 17–42. Feminist epistemologies are surveyed by Jaggar, *Feminist Politics*.

26. One significant difference between Afrocentric and feminist standpoints is that much of what is termed women's culture is, unlike African-American culture, created in the context of and produced by oppression. Those who argue for a women's culture are electing to value, rather than denigrate, those traits associated with females in white patriarchal societies. While this choice is important, it is not the same as identifying an independent, historic culture associated with a society. I am indebted to Deborah K. King for this point.

27. Critiques of the Eurocentric masculinist knowledge-validation process by both Africanist and feminist scholars illustrate this point. What one group labels 'white' and 'Eurocentric', the other describes as 'male-dominated' and 'masculinist'. Although he does not emphasize its patriarchal and racist features, Morris Berman's *The Reenchantment of the World* (Bantam, New York, 1981) provides a historical discussion of Western thought. Afrocentric analyses of this same process can be found in Molefi Kete Asante, 'International/intercultural relations', in *Contemporary Black Thought*, ed. Molefi Kete Asante and Abdulai S. Vandi (Sage, Beverly Hills, Calif., 1980), pp. 43–58; and Dona Richards, 'European mythology: the ideology of "progress" ', ibid., pp. 59–79. For feminist analyses, see Hartsock, *Money, Sex, and Power*.

Harding also discusses this similarity (see *Science Question*, chap. 7, 'Other "others" and fractured identities: issues for epistemologists', pp. 163–96).

28. Harding, *Science Question*, p. 166.

29. D. King, 'Race, class'.

30. Bonnie Thornton Dill, 'The dialectics of black womanhood', *Signs*, 4, 3 (Spring 1979), pp. 543–55.

31. One implication of standpoint approaches is that the more subordinate the group, the purer the vision of the oppressed group. This is an outcome of the origins of standpoint approaches in Marxist social theory, itself a dualistic analysis of social structure. Because such approaches rely on quantifying and ranking human oppressions – familiar tenets of positivist approaches – they are rejected by Blacks and feminists alike. See Harding, *The Science Question* for a discussion of this point. See also Elizabeth V. Spelman's discussion of the fallacy of additive oppression in 'Theories of race and gender: the erasure of black women', *Quest*, 5, 4 (1982), pp. 36–62.

32. Class differences among Black women may be marked. For example, see Paula Giddings's analysis (*When and Where I Enter*) of the role of social class in shaping Black women's political activism; or Elizabeth Higginbotham's study of the effects of social class in Black women's college attendance in 'Race and class barriers to black women's college attendance', *Journal of Ethnic Studies*, 13, 1 (1985), pp. 89–107. Those African-American women who have experienced the greatest degree of convergence of race, class and gender oppression may be in a better position to recognize and use an alternative epistemology.

33. Gwaltney, *Drylongso*, p. 83.

34. William L. Andrews, *Sisters of the Spirit: Three Black Women's Autobiographies of the Nineteenth Century* (Indiana University Press, Bloomington, 1986), p. 85.

35. Gwaltney, *Drylongso*, p. 147.

36. Geneva Smitherman, *Talkin' and Testifyin': The Language of Black America* (Wayne State University Press, Detroit, 1986), p. 76.

37. Gwaltney, *Drylongso*, p. 68.

38. Ibid., p. 7.

39. Ibid., pp. 27, 33.

40. Elsa Barkley Brown, 'Hearing our mothers' lives'. Paper presented at the Fifteenth Anniversary Faculty Lecture Series, African-American and African Studies, Emory University, Atlanta, 1986.

41. Landner, *Tomorrow's Tomorrow*.

42. Mitchell and Lewter, *Soul Theology*. The use of the narrative approach in African-American theology exemplifies an inductive system of logic alternately called 'folk wisdom' or a survival-based, need-oriented method of assessing knowledge claims.

43. Ibid., p. 8.

44. June Jordan, *On Call: Political Essays* (South End Press, Boston, 1985), p. 26.

45. Mary Belenky, Blythe Clinchy, Nancy Goldberger and Jill Tarule, *Women's Ways of Knowing* (Basic Books, New York, 1986), p. 113.

46. Hartsock, *Money, Sex and Power*, p. 237; and Nancy Chodorow, *The Reproduction of Mothering* (University of California Press, Berkeley and Los Angeles, 1978).

47. Dorothy Smith, *The Everyday World as Problematic* (Northeastern University Press, Boston, 1987).

48. Byerly, *Hard Times*, p. 198.

49. For Black women's centrality in the family, see Steady, *Black Woman Cross-Culturally*; Ladner, *Tomorrow's Tomorrow*; Brown, 'Hearing'; and McAdoo, *Black Families*. See Gilkes, ' "Together and in Harness" ', for Black women in the church; and Ch. 4 of Deborah Gray White, *Ar'n't I a Woman? Female Slaves in the Plantation South* (Norton, New York, 1985). See also Gloria Joseph, 'Black mothers and daughters: their roles and functions in American society', in *Common Differences: Conflicts in Black and White Feminist Perspectives*, ed. Gloria Joseph and Jill Lewis (Anchor, Garden City, NY, 1981), pp. 75–126. Even though Black women play essential roles in Black families and Black churches, these institutions are not free from sexism.

50. As Belenky et al. note, 'Unlike the eye, the ear requires closeness between subject and object. Unlike seeing, speaking and listening suggest dialogue and interaction' (*Women's Ways of Knowing*, p. 18).

51. Thomas Kochman, *Black and White: Styles in Conflict* (University of Chicago Press, Chicago, 1981); and Smitherman, *Talkin' and Testifyin'*.

52. Gwaltney, *Drylongso*, p. 32.

53. Smitherman, *Talkin' and Testifyin'*, p. 108.

54. Kochman, *Black and White*, p. 28.

55. Jordan, *On Call*, p. 129.

56. Claudia Tate, *Black Women Writers at Work* (Continuum, New York, 1983), p. 91.

57. Ibid., p. 92.

58. Alice Walker, *In Search of Our Mothers' Gardens* (Harcourt Brace Jovanovich, New York, 1974), p. 84.

59. Evelyn Fox Keller, *Reflections on Gender and Science* (Yale University Press, New Haven, Conn., 1985), p. 167; Chodorow *Reproduction of Mothering*.

60. Belenky et al., *Women's Ways of Knowing*, p. 16.

61. Thomas Webber, *Deep Like the Rivers* (Norton, New York, 1978), p. 127.

62. In her discussion of the West African Sacred Cosmos, Mechal Sobel (*Trabelin' On*) notes that Nyam, a root word in many West African languages, connotes an enduring spirit, power or energy possessed by all life. In spite of the pervasiveness of this key concept in African humanism, its definition remains elusive. She points out, 'Every individual analyzing the various Sacred Cosmos of West Africa has recognized the reality of this force, but no one has yet adequately translated this concept into Western terms' (p. 13).

63. For discussions of personal expressiveness in African-American culture, see Smitherman, *Talkin' and Testifyin'*; Kochman, *Black and White*, esp. Ch. 9; and Mitchell and Lewter, *Soul Theology*.

64. Gwaltney, *Drylongso*, p. 228.

65. For feminist analyses of the subordination of emotion in Western culture, see Arlie Russell Hochschild, 'The sociology of feeling and emotion: selected possibilities', in Marcia Millman and Rosabeth Kanter (eds), *Another Voice: Feminist Perspectives on Social Life and Social Science* (Anchor, Garden City, NY, 1975), pp. 280–307; and Chodorow, *Reproduction of Mothering*.

66. Tate, *Black Women Writers*, p. 156.

67. Gwaltney, *Drylongso*, p. 11.

68. Smitherman, *Talkin' and Testifyin'*, pp. 135, 137.

69. Belenky et al., *Women's Ways of Knowing*, pp. 100–130.

70. Ibid., p. 119.

71. See ibid., pp. 52–75, for a discussion of inner voice and its role in women's cognitive styles. Regarding empathy, Belenky et al. note: 'Connected knowers begin with an interest in the facts of other people's lives, but they gradually shift the focus to other people's ways of thinking. . . . It is the form rather than the content of knowing that is central. . . . Connected learners learn through empathy' (ibid., p. 115).

72. Andrews, *Sisters of the Spirit*, p. 98.

73. Kochman, *Black and White*, pp. 20, 25.

74. Ibid., p. 23.

75. The sizable proportion of ministers among Black political leaders illustrates the importance of ethics in African-American communities.

76. Belenky et al. discuss a similar situation. They note, 'People could critique each other's work in this class and accept each other's criticisms because members of the group shared a similar experience. . . . Authority in connected knowing rests not on power or status or certification but on commonality of experience' (*Women's Ways of Knowing*, p. 18).

77. Carol Gilligan, *In a Different Voice* (Harvard University Press, Cambridge, Mass., 1982). Carol Stack critiques Gilligan's model by arguing that African-Americans invoke a similar model of moral development to that used by women (see 'The culture of gender: women and men of

color', *Signs*, 11, 2 [Winter 1986]: pp. 321–4). Another difficulty with Gilligan's work concerns the homogeneity of the subjects whom she studied.

78. Black men, white women and members of other race, class and gender groups should be encouraged to interpret, teach and critique the Black feminist thought produced by African-American women.

79. Walker, *In Search of Our Mothers' Gardens*, p. 91.

80. Gwaltney, *Drylongso*, p. 7.

81. Jordan, *On Call*, p. 130.

82. Collins, 'Learning from the outsider within'.

83. This point addresses the question of relativity in the sociology of knowledge and offers a way of regulating competing knowledge claims.

Feminism and Theories of Scientific Knowledge

Sandra Harding

Do feminists have anything distinctive to say about the natural sciences? Should feminists concentrate on criticizing sexist science and the conditions of its production? Or should feminists be laying the foundation for an epistemological revolution illuminating all facets of scientific knowledge? Is there a specifically feminist theory of knowledge growing today which is analogous in its implications to theories which are the heritage of Greek science and of the scientific revolution of the seventeenth century? Would a feminist epistemology informing scientific inquiry be a family member to existing theories of representation and philosophical realism? Or should feminists adopt a radical form of epistemology that denies the possibility of access to a real world and an objective standpoint? Would feminist standards of knowledge genuinely end the dilemma of the cleavage between subject and object or between noninvasive knowing and prediction and control? Does feminism offer insight into the connections between science and humanism? Do feminists have anything new to say about the vexed relations of knowledge and power? Would feminist authority and power to name give the world a new identity, a new story? Can feminists master science? (Haraway, 1981: 470)

A problem

Feminism is a political movement for the emancipation of women. Looked at from the perspective of science's self-understanding, 'feminist knowledge', 'feminist science', 'feminist sociology' – or biology, psychology or economics (or epistemology) – is a contradiction in terms.[1] Scientific knowledge-seeking is supposed to be value-neutral, objective, dispassionate, disinterested. It is supposed to be protected from local political interests, goals and desires by the norms of science. In particular, science's method is supposed to protect the results of research from the social values of the researchers and their cultures. Yet many claims generated through research guided by feminist concerns appear to be more plausible – better supported, more reliable, less false, more likely to be confirmed by evidence – than the

---

From *Women*, 1 (1), 1990, pp. 87–98.

beliefs they replace.[2] Scientific method supposedly permits all things to be represented in their proper, real relations to each other. Scientific method removes the blinders and distorting lenses created by social values. To those who believe science maximally successful at this project, feminism appears to propose – at best – substituting one set of social lenses for another. Yet the substitution appears to be justifiable on empirical grounds. What theory of knowledge could justify this kind of 'method' of inquiry? How can feminist research (such as that mentioned in note 2), grounded in the politics of the women's movement, be increasing the objectivity of research?

Feminist empiricism

An initial response to this problem has been to argue that sexism and androcentrism in scientific research are entirely the consequence of 'bad science'. The distortions in our views of nature and social relations that feminists have revealed are caused by social biases. These prejudices are the result of hostile attitudes and false beliefs arising from superstition, ignorance or miseducation. Androcentric biases enter the research process particularly at the stage when scientific problems are identified and defined, but they also appear in the design of research and in the collection and interpretation of data. (See e.g. Longino and Doell, 1983.) Feminist empiricists argue that sexist and androcentric biases can be eliminated by stricter adherence to the existing methodological norms of scientific inquiry. They try to make honest those who respond to feminist criticism with such persuasive claims about mainstream belief as: 'Everyone knows that permitting only men to interview only men about both men's and women's beliefs and behaviours is just plain bad science.' (Of course, this is the science upon which 99 per cent of the claims of the social sciences rest, and to which no one objected before the women's movement.) 'Everyone knows that both sexes contributed to the evolution of our species.' (Try to find that understanding in Darwin or contemporary textbooks.)

But how can the scientific community come to see that its work *has* been shaped by androcentric prejudices? Feminist empiricists say that here is where we can see the importance of the women's movement. Such a political movement alerts everyone to the social blinders, the distorted and clouded lenses, through which we have been experiencing the world around (and within) us. The women's movement creates conditions that make better science possible. Furthermore, they point out that the women's movement expands opportunities for women researchers and feminist ones (male and female); these people are more likely to notice androcentric biases (see Harding, 1989).[3]

There are great strengths to this theory of how knowledge grows. In the first place, its appeal is obvious: many of the claims emerging from feminist research in biology and the social sciences are capable of accumulating better empirical support than the claims they replace. This research better meets the overt standards of 'good science' than do the purportedly gender-blind studies. Should not the weight of this empirical support be valued more highly than the ideal of value-neutrality that was advanced, we are told, only in order to increase empirical support for hypotheses? It is not that all feminist claims are automatically to be preferred because they are feminist; rather, when the results of such research show good empirical support, the fact that they were produced through politically guided research should not count against them.

Second, feminist empiricism appears to leave intact much of scientists' and philosophers' traditional understanding of the principles of adequate scientific research. It appears to challenge mainly the incomplete way scientific method has been practised, not the norms of science themselves. Many scientists will admit that the social values and political agendas of feminists raise new issues, enlarge the scope of inquiry, and reveal cause for greater care in the conduct of inquiry. But the logic of the research process and the logic of scientific explanation appear to rest fundamentally untouched by these challenges.

In the third place, in defence of feminist empiricism one can appeal to the history of science. After all, wasn't it the bourgeois revolution of the fifteenth to seventeenth centuries – the movement from feudalism to modernity – that made it possible for modern science to emerge? Furthermore, wasn't it the proletarian revolution of the nineteenth century that fostered an understanding of the effects of class struggles on conceptions of nature and social relations? Finally, doesn't the post-1960 decline of North Atlantic colonialism have obvious positive effects on the growth of scientific knowledge? From these historical perspectives, the contemporary international women's movement is just the most recent of these revolutions, each of which moves us yet closer to the goals of the creators of modern science.

There are problems with this justificatory strategy. Its feminism appears to undermine its empiricism in fundamental ways. For one thing, it argues that women, or feminists, as a social group are more likely than others to achieve 'good science'. Thus it implicitly challenges the assumption that the social identity of the observer is irrelevant to the 'goodness' of the results of research. As indicated, it can draw on historical support for this scepticism. For another, appearances to the contrary, feminist empiricism is ambivalent about the potency of science's norms and methods to eliminate androcentric biases. While attempting to fit feminist research within these norms and methods, it also points to the fact that without the challenge of feminism, science's norms and methods regularly failed to detect sexism. Finally, it challenges the belief that science must be protected from all politics. It argues that the politics of movements for emancipatory social change can increase the objectivity of science. These points are not independent, but they draw attention to different problematic facets of empiricism. Are these problems fatal to feminist empiricism – not to mention to empiricism and the liberal theory of human nature on which empiricism is grounded?[4]

Is 'scientific rationality' gender-biased masculine rationality?

More radical than the feminist criticisms of 'bad science' are those that take as their target Western generalizations from masculine to human in the case of ideal reason. Before turning to the standpoint theorists, for whom this critique provides one motivation for the development of a feminist theory of knowledge, I mention several thinkers who intentionally stop short of such a theoretical programme. Philosophers such as Genevieve Lloyd (1984) and Sara Ruddick (1980) and the scientist/historian Evelyn Fox Keller (1984) criticize what has come to be called abstract masculinity. They point out how ideals of Western rationality, including scientific thought, distort and leave partial our understandings of nature and social relations. These ideals devalue contextual modes of thought and emotional components of reason. Empirical support for this criticism is provided by psychologists. Best known is Carol Gilligan's (1982) study of women's moral reasoning. Since scientific reason includes normative judgements (which is the most interesting or potentially fruitful hypothesis or research programme to pursue?), the import of Gilligan's work for philosophy is not restricted to ethics. More recently, the study by Mary Belenky et al. (1986) of developmental patterns in women's thinking about reason and knowledge points to gender bias in philosophic and scientific ideals and suggests its origins in gendered experience. While these critical tendencies do not explicitly address issues about the relationship between feminist politics and feminist research, they do provide additional grounds for questioning the belief that the direction of inquiry by social values can have only bad effects on the growth of knowledge.

Feminist standpoint theory

A second major line of justification of feminist research is provided by the standpoint theorists. Knowledge, they observe, is supposed to be based in some detectable way on experience – highly refined and controlled experience, of course. Thus, the reason the feminist claims can turn out to be scientifically preferable is that they originate in, and are tested against, a more complete and less distorting kind of scientific experience. If we start off our thought, our research (start off our 'experience' in this sense) from women's lives as these are understood through feminist theory, we will be more likely to arrive at more complete and less distorted knowledge claims than if we start off only from the lives of men in the dominant groups (Hartsock, 1983; Smith, 1987; Rose, 1983).

Consider Dorothy Smith's form of the argument. In our society, women have been assigned kinds of work that men do not want to do. Several aspects of this division of activity by gender have consequences for what can be known from the perspective of men's and women's activities. 'Women's work' relieves men of the need to take care of their bodies or of the local places where they exist, freeing men to immerse themselves in the world of abstract concepts. The labour of women thereby articulates and shapes men's concepts of the world into those appropriate for administrative work. Moreover, the more successfully women perform their work, the more invisible does it become to men. Men who are relieved of the need to maintain their own bodies and the local places where these bodies exist can now see as real only what corresponds to their abstracted mental world. Men see 'women's work' not as real human activity – self-chosen and consciously willed – but only as natural activity, an instinctual labour of love. Women are thus excluded from men's conceptions of culture. Furthermore, women's actual experiences of their own activities are incomprehensible and inexpressible within the distorted abstractions of men's conceptual schemes. Women are alienated from their own lives.[5]

However, for women sociologists, a line of fault opens up between their lives and the dominant conceptual schemes. This disjuncture is the break along which much major work in the women's movement has focused. The politics of the women's movement has drawn attention to the lack of fit between women's experiences of our lives and the dominant conceptual schemes. It is to the 'bifurcated consciousness' of women researchers, who see the world as it has been redefined through the politics of the women's movement (and to those who see the world from their perspectives), that we can attribute the greater adequacy of the results of feminist research. Looking at nature and social relations from the perspective of administrative 'men's work' can provide only partial and distorted understandings. (Of course only white, Western, professional/managerial-class men are permitted this work, though it holds a central place in more general conceptions of masculinity.) Research for women must recover the understanding of women, men and social relations available from the perspective of women's activities.

To give an example Smith discusses, the concept housework, which appears in historical, sociological and economic studies and is part of what liberal philosophers include in the realm of the 'private', at least recognizes that what women are assigned to do in the household is work; that is, it is neither instinctual activity nor necessarily always a labour of love. However, it conceptualizes the activity assigned to women in our society on an analogy with the division of men's activities into paid work and leisure. Is housework work? Yes! However, it has no fixed hours or responsibilities, no qualifications, wages, days off for sickness, retirement, or retirement benefits. Is it leisure? No, though even under the worst conditions it has rewarding and rejuvenating aspects. As social scientists and liberal political philosophers use the term, housework includes raising children, entertaining friends, caring for loved ones, and other activities not appropriately understood through the wage-labour versus leisure construct. Smith argues that this activity should be understood through concepts that arise from women's experience of it, not with concepts selected to account for men's experience of their work. Moreover, our understanding of men's activities is also distorted by reliance on conceptual schemes arising only from administrative-class men's experiences. How would our understanding of love, warfare, or how universities operate be expanded and transformed if it were structured by questions and concepts arising from those activities assigned predominantly to women that make possible men's conduct of love, warfare and higher education?

This theory of knowledge is far richer than I can convey in these few lines. Hopefully this excessively brief report will entice readers to pursue these issues further on their own.[6]

Standpoint theories have the virtue of providing a general theory of the potential and actual greater adequacy of research that begins in questions arising from the perspective of women's activities, and that regards this perspective as an important part of the data on which the evidence for all knowledge claims should be based. The standpoint theorists reassert the possibility of science providing less distorted reflections of the world around us, but not a science that myopically beatifies a mythical method and thus is unable to counter the sexist, racist and class biases built into the very social structure and agendas of science (Harding, 1986).

This theory of knowledge resolves more satisfactorily certain problems within feminist empiricism. It sets within larger social theory its explanation of the importance of the origin of scientific problems (of the context of discovery) for the eventual picture of science. It eschews blind allegiance to scientific method, observing that no method, at least in the sciences' sense of this term, is powerful enough to eliminate kinds of social bias that are as widely held as the scientific community itself. Moreover, it draws attention to why feminist politics can be a valuable guide in scientific inquiry, and to the way in which sexist politics is inherently anti-scientific. This theory is certainly not problem-free. But it does encompass within its reach certain aspects of the scientific research process that are dealt with only in an *ad hoc* way by feminist empiricism. Though this epistemology has been formulated to account for social science research, its concerns are clearly applicable also to the natural sciences. If we started off from women's lives – all women's lives – what scientific problems would have the highest priority in physics, chemistry and biology? Ecological rather than military and profit-generating ones? Might not social agendas take higher priority than most of the scientific ones that our taxes support? (see Harding, 1990).

Making choices?

Should one have to choose between these feminist theories of knowledge? I believe not. A theory of knowledge is supposed to be convincing, all things considered, but it is important to notice that these two are likely to appeal to quite different audiences. Feminist empiricism is useful precisely because it stresses the continuities between feminist and traditional justifications of scientific research as the latter would most often be understood by practising scientists and the lay public that stays close to science's self-understandings. In contrast, the feminist standpoint theory stresses the continuities between the radical upheavals in knowledge created by earlier large-scale social movements and by the women's movement. This can be appreciated by social and political theorists, by people interested in the new histories and sociologies of science, and by people involved in the other counter-cultures of science – the ecology, peace, anti-imperialism, and worker-control movements. The two epistemologies also appear to be both locked into dialogue with and talking past each other, paradoxical though that appears. Their relationship reflects the struggles in conventional discourse between liberal and Marxist theories of human nature and politics. Most likely, a preoccupation with choosing one over the other ensures choosing more than we should want of those flawed discourses; we are shaped by what we reject as well as by what we accept.

New histories; postmodernist philosophy

Two more kinds of analysis bearing on feminist epistemology deserve mention: the new histories of science and of philosophy, and the feminist postmodernist critiques of the Enlightenment.

Especially noteworthy among the histories are Merchant's (1980) analysis of the gender dimensions of the shift from organicist to mechanical models of natural order at the birth of modern science, Lloyd's (1984) history of the association of reason with masculinity from Plato to De Beauvoir, Bordo's (1987) study of the origins and dimensions of the 'Cartesian Anxiety' to which modern philosophy has been a response, and Haraway's (1989) study of the history of primatology. These analyses undermine the idea that the problems of traditional epistemology are timeless, universal problems. They are the problems that faced some people in European cultures in the past, and they are your problems or mine only when we choose to live our professional lives in a time warp. The phrase 'science and society' is misleading; science has always been fully *inside* the societies that have supported it. Its internally contradictory progressive *and* regressive tendencies are activated by the social agendas for which it (intentionally or not) provides resources – and the desire to produce 'pure science' is no less a politically identifiable social agenda than is the desire to put science in the service of 'national defence'.

Challenges to both traditional and feminist theories of scientific knowledge are beginning to emerge also from feminists working within and against the postmodernist Enlightenment critiques. They focus on the assumptions feminist thinkers borrow from both Marxist and liberal traditions that feminism can come closer to producing glassy mirror minds capable of reflecting a world that is out there and ready made for the reflecting, and that the science critics' participation in more general feminist commitments to improve the condition of 'women' can avoid both ethnocentrism and replicating humanism's disastrous links of knowledge with disciplinary power. Obviously, these are some of the issues Haraway had in mind in the passage that opened this paper. (See Flax, 1987, 1989; and Nicholson, 1990.)

Conclusion

The focuses created by the eclecticism, the richness, of the feminist epistemological milieux are seen as a flaw by some traditional thinkers. 'When are feminists going to take up the traditional issues that engaged Locke, Berkeley, Kant, and Russell?' In some recent eras, Anglo-American philosophy of science and epistemology have served as havens in a chaotic world that appeared to threaten the purity of these disciplines. Those eras – and thinkers still nostalgically trying to recreate them so that they can relive the Enlightenment (as Richard Rorty has put the point) – would not even identify as legitimate in a theory of knowledge the ways feminists raise issues about the nature of knowers, processes of gaining knowledge, the world to be known, and the purposes of knowledge. These nostalgic sentimentalists forget that modern philosophy itself emerged as part of the social ferment accompanying the transition from feudalism to bourgeois modernity, and, especially, as a meditation on the accomplishments of Galileo, Newton and, later, Einstein, and on the shifts in conceptions of authority about knowledge and the recommended processes of coming to knowledge that their sciences seemed to require. At a minimum, our theories of knowledge have to be able to account for what happens in the sciences. For much of feminist epistemology, as for other strains of contemporary critique of Enlightenment assumptions, Locke, Berkeley, Kant and Russell are part of the problem.

The development of feminist thinking about knowledge is a consequence of women's attempts to explain the world – to become 'agents of knowledge' rather than only passive objects of others' claims to purported knowledge. We have been denied this fundamental human right to know *from the perspective of our lives* by the police, the courts, the health-care system, the economy, the state, and by those who make public policy on 'the family'. Refusal to entertain the possibility of such knowledge distorts women's and men's understandings of ourselves and our lives, as well as our understandings of the rest of the world.

Can we begin to see the outlines of an answer to Haraway's question: 'Would feminist authority and power to name give the world a new identity, a new story?'

Notes

This article has been updated and otherwise slightly revised from its earlier publication in the *American Philosophical Association Newsletter on Feminism and Philosophy*, November 1987, pp. 9–14.

For helpful comments on an earlier draft I am grateful to David Hoekema, Alison Jaggar, Hilary Rose and Sally Ruddick.

1. Sometimes the argument is put in terms of women's knowledge, or of a sociology, science, etc., for women. See, e.g., Smith (1987).

2. Some may still question this claim. Guides to the relevant research reports and theoretical shifts may be found in the review essays for the disciplines that have appeared in *Signs: Journal of Women in Culture and Society* since 1975, and in traditional, as well as feminist, journals in the disciplines. In reading this report, one could keep in mind such claims as that 'woman the gatherer' made important contributions to the dawn of human history; the patterns of thought prevalent in women's moral reasoning are not all examples of inferior reasoning; much of the difference observable in the physical strength and abilities of females and males is the consequence of social practices (and is decreasing with changes in practices, as sports records indicate).

It is not within the domain of this essay to review the now quite large feminist science literature. (Several review essays can be found in Harding and O'Barr, 1987.) Nevertheless, it should be noted that a number of British feminists have made widely cited contributions to it. See, e.g., Sayre (1975), The Brighton Women and Science Group (1980), Sayers (1982), Rose (1983), Cockburn (1985), Birke (1986), and the work of Jalna Hanmer and other authors associated with the *Journal of Reproductive and Genetic Engineering*, including the essays appearing in Spallone and Steinberg (1987).

3. Because those whom I have called feminist empiricists frequently take themselves to be doing nothing epistemologically unusual – they are simply adhering very strictly to the norms of science – they tend not to articulate this theory of knowledge as such. Examples of feminist empiricism can be found in reports of substantive feminist research, especially in their obligatory sections on methods. See, for instance, Jacklin (1981). Fausto-Sterling (1985: 208) intentionally frames her critical evaluation of sex-difference research as addressing a problem of 'poorly done science'; she, like Millman and Kanter (1975: vii), provides an excellent discussion of the necessity of the feminist political movement to the creation of good science.

4. See the last chapter of Jaggar (1983) for discussions of the articulation of epistemologies with theories of human nature and politics.

5. Obviously, patterns of thought created by race, sexuality and class divisions of activity can also be revealed by this kind of analysis. (Standpoint theorists have learned from Hegel and Marx.) This should provide reason to conceptualize better the structure of contemporary patterns of social domination, not to undervalue the force of the feminist analysis here.

6. One more influential analysis of rationality, objectivity, method and women's perspective that is close to but not quite a standpoint theory must be recommended: MacKinnon (1982–3).

References

Belenky, Mary F., Clinchy, Blythe M., Goldberger, Nancy R. and Tarule, Jill M. (1986) *Women's Ways of Knowing: The Development of Self, Voice, and Mind*. New York: Basic Books.

Birke, Linda (1986) *Women, Feminism and Biology: The Feminist Challenge*. New York: Methuen.

Bordo, Susan (1987) *The Flight to Objectivity*. Albany: State University of New York Press.

Brighton Women and Science Group (1980) *Alice Through the Microscope: The Power of Science over Women's Lives*. London: Virago.

Cockburn, Cynthia (1985) *Machinery of Dominance: Women, Men and Technical Know-How*. London: Pluto Press.

Fausto-Sterling, Anne (1985) *Myths of Gender: Biological Theories about Women and Men*. New York: Basic Books.

Flax, Jane (1983) 'Political philosophy and the patriarchal unconscious: a psychoanalytic perspective on epistemology and metaphysics', in S. Harding and M. Hintikka (eds), *Discovering Reality: Feminist Perspectives on Epistemology, Metaphysics, Methodology and Philosophy of Science*. Dordrecht: Reidel.

Flax, Jane (1987) 'Postmodernism and gender relations in feminist theory', *Signs: Journal of Women in Culture and Society*, 12 (4).

Flax, Jane (1989) *Thinking Fragments: Psychoanalysis, Feminism and Postmodernism in the Contemporary West*. Berkeley: University of California Press.

Gilligan, Carol (1982) *In a Different Voice: Psychological Theory and Women's Development*. Cambridge, MA: Harvard University Press.

Haraway, Donna (1981) 'In the beginning was the word: the genesis of biological theory', *Signs: Journal of Women in Culture and Society*, 6 (3): 469–81.

Haraway, Donna (1989) *Primate Visions: Gender, Race, and Nature in the World of Modern Science*. New York: Routledge.

Harding, Sandra (1986) *The Science Question in Feminism*. Ithaca, NY: Cornell University Press.

Harding, Sandra (1987) *Feminism and Methodology: Social Science Issues*, Bloomington: Indiana University Press.

Harding, Sandra (1989) 'How the women's movement benefits science: two views', *Women's Studies International Forum*, 12 (3): 271–83.

Harding, Sandra (1990) 'Why "physics" is a bad model for physics', in R. Elvee (ed.), *The End of Science? Nobel Conference XXV*. New York: Harper & Row.

Harding, Sandra and Hintikka, Merrill (eds) (1983) *Discovering Reality: Feminist Perspectives on Epistemology, Metaphysics, Methodology and Philosophy of Science*. Dordrecht: Reidel.

Harding, Sandra and O'Barr, Jean (eds) (1987) *Sex and Scientific Inquiry*. Chicago: University of Chicago Press.

Hartsock, Nancy (1983) 'The feminist standpoint: developing the ground for a specifically feminist historical materialism', in Harding and Hintikka (1983). See also Chapter 10 of her *Money, Sex and Power*. Boston: Northeastern University Press, 1985.

Jacklin, C.V. (1981) 'Methodological issues in the study of sex-related difference', *Developmental Review*, 1: 266–73.

Jaggar, Alison (1983) *Feminist Politics and Human Nature*. Totowa, NJ: Rowman & Allanheld.

Keller, Evelyn Fox (1984) *Reflections on Gender and Science*. New Haven, Conn.: Yale University Press.

Lloyd, Genevieve (1984) *The Man of Reason: 'Male' and 'Female' in Western Philosophy*. Minneapolis: University of Minnesota Press.

Longino, Helen and Doell, Ruth (1983) 'Body, bias, and behavior: a comparative analysis of reasoning in two areas of biological science', *Signs: Journal of Women in Culture and Society*, 9 (2). (Reprinted in S. Harding and J. O'Barr (eds), *Sex and Scientific Inquiry*. Chicago: University of Chicago Press, 1987.)

MacKinnon, Catharine (1982–3) 'Feminism, Marxism, method and the state', Parts 1 & 2, *Signs: Journal of Women in Culture and Society*, 7 (3); 8 (4). See also her *Feminism Unmodified*. Cambridge, Mass.: Harvard University Press, 1987.

Merchant, Carolyn (1980) *The Death of Nature: Women, Ecology and the Scientific Revolution*. New York: Harper & Row.

Millman, Marcia and Kanter, Rosabeth Moss (1975) 'Introduction' to *Another Voice: Feminist Perspectives on Social Life and Social Science*. New York: Anchor Books. (Reprinted in Harding, 1987.)

Nicholson, Linda J. (ed.) (1990) *Feminism/Postmodernism*. New York: Routledge.

Rose, Hilary (1983) 'Hand, brain and heart: a feminist epistemology for the natural sciences', *Signs: Journal of Women in Culture and Society*, 9 (1). (Reprinted in Harding and O'Barr, 1987.)

Ruddick, Sara (1980) 'Maternal thinking', *Feminist Studies*, 6 (2).

Sayers, Janet (1982) *Biological Politics: Feminist and Anti-Feminist Perspectives*. New York: Tavistock.

Sayre, Anne (1975) *Rosalind Franklin and DNA*. New York: W.W. Norton.

Smith, Dorothy (1987) *The Everyday World as Problematic: A Feminist Sociology*. Boston: Northeastern University Press.

Spallone, Patricia and Steinberg Deborah, (eds) (1987) *Made to Order: The Myth of Reproductive and Genetic Progress*. New York: Pergamon Press.

Tuana, Nancy (ed.) (1989) *Feminism and Science*. Bloomington: Indiana University Press. (Reprint of *Hypatia: A Journal of Feminist Philosophy*, 2 (3), 1987, and 3 (1), 1988.)

SECTION III

REPRESENTATION

The first edition of *The Woman Question* included, in the section on 'Culture and Ideology', articles by Cora Kaplan and Tillie Olsen on issues about the representation of women.[1] Cora Kaplan took issue with Kate Millett's *Sexual Politics*, and in particular with what she described as Millett's failure to 'look more carefully at the complex interrelation of class and gender ideologies in literature by men and women ... [and] theorize imaginative writing as something more specific, strange and fragmented than a "reflection" of either patriarchal ideology or real social relations'.[2] In essence, Kaplan's contention was that literature was more complicated than radical feminism (at least as represented by Kate Millett) suggested.

Since that essay was written (in 1979) the canon of Western literature has been extensively debated and deconstructed, not least by feminists. The 'core' canon of English, European and North American literature has historically always included a number of 'great' women writers (Austen, George Eliot and the Brontës, for example) but the shift in the construction of the canon has now been such as to include women writers from diverse cultures alongside a tradition drawn from white bourgeois society.[3] In recent years this development has not gone unnoticed by opponents of both feminism and multiculturalism; in Britain various right-wing critics of shifts in the curriculum of both schools and higher education have alleged that 'political' considerations now influence cultural and aesthetic judgements. The breathtaking naivety of this view, which assumes a politically neutral past, has been widely questioned and refuted.[4] Nevertheless, what this debate reveals is the lasting contentiousness of aesthetic and cultural standards. Judgements about the 'great' and the 'good' remain as bitterly contested as ever.

Feminism's contribution to this debate has been to extend the parameters of the literary canon. Even though the established 'great' writers have remained as appealing as ever to critics, new, unknown writers have been added to the lists of literature to be read. In the *Bloomsbury Guide to Women's Literature* the entries attest to the diversity and the vitality of women writers and critics.[5] New names are given generous space alongside established writers, and just as new individuals are acknowledged so are forms of literature – such as romantic literature – which had previously received critical dismissal rather than critical attention.

It is here – in the extension of the discussion of forms of culture as much as individuals – that we can see the most significant change in the contemporary study of culture. For at least the first half of the twentieth century, the study of literature (and film, the visual arts and drama) was dominated by the received wisdom of fixed categories of 'good' and 'bad', and 'high' and 'low' culture. The views of Q.D. Leavis were representative of an intellectual tradition which confined much of popular culture to the theoretical wilderness. As far as critics such as Q.D. Leavis were concerned, romantic fiction and popular music were simply not worth attention.[6]

Such a view could not, however, remain dominant in the face of post-war cultural transformation. The new global culture of television, film and popular music brought with it – or to it – critics who were prepared to consider Madonna and soap opera as seriously as *Middlemarch*. In-itially, much of the impetus for this widening of intellectual horizons was derived from a rejection of the political and moral codes of the Western middle class, but this defence of working-class, and minority, culture was rapidly overtaken by structural analysts of culture, for whom any cultural product was as valid an object for interpretation as any other. Thus *Dallas* arrived in the academy, and thus was born the new subject of cultural studies.

With this rethinking of the subject matter of literature came a new agenda for its analysis. For feminists, as much as for the male 'new' critics, the major intellectual inspiration was psychoanalysis, and it is psychoanalysis which has come to dominate contemporary studies of the various forms of the representation of reality. Increasingly, the film or the novel is read as metaphor; the actual text is seen as only a guide to the real meaning of the director or the author. Central to the study of literature is the general psychoanalytic orthodoxy which argues that the acquisition of subjectivity is essentially a psychic and sexual development. Sexuality – and sexual identity – is therefore not merely a part of human activity, but central to it.

The work of Freud has provided feminism with a major theoretical tradition through which to interpret culture. Freud himself is an important source of ideas, but so too is the later work of Lacan.[7] Lacan's work – with its emphasis on language, and the acquisition of identity through language – has proved to be a major force in feminist studies of representation. Because Lacan argues that the symbolic order of representation can release sexual identity from biological definition, his work offers a means of escaping from male/female, man/woman dichotomies, in the study of representation. What becomes central is the revelation of the pattern of relationships in literature (or film) and the articulation of the contradictions and inconsistencies that are expressed through various forms of representation. This form of 'reading' culture allows feminist critics the freedom to explore the dynamics of diverse cultural products. Ideas about 'silences' and 'evasions' in the novel thus become important, as critics identify what is not said as much as the themes which are made explicit.

Inevitably, this form of 'reading' has been contentious and to a certain extent divisive among feminist literary critics. In her influential overview of feminist literary theory, *Sexual/Textual Politics*, Toril Moi argued that

> My reservations about much Anglo-American feminist criticism are thus not primarily that it has remained within the lineage of male-centred humanism but that it has done so without sufficient awareness of the high political costs this entails. The central paradox of Anglo-American feminist criticism is thus that despite its often strong, explicit political engagement, it is in the end not quite political enough; not in the sense that it fails to go far enough along the political spectrum, but in the sense that its radical analysis of sexual politics still remains entangled with depoliticizing theoretical paradigms.[8]

In Moi's view the authors whose work she sees as theoretically deficient include the widely read feminist critics Elaine Showalter, Sandra Gilbert and Susan Gubar.[9] Writing with respect for what these women have accomplished, she nevertheless raises the issue of the extent to which feminist criticism can simply be the conventional history and theory of literature rewritten for women. The radical, and destabilizing, implication of thinking about gender and the words 'woman' and 'man' are lost in an account which reads woman and man as stable and not as endlessly liable to both deconstruction and reconstruction.

The studies of literature – and film – which appeal to a politics of destabilizing the text are those such as Laura Mulvey on film, and Jacqueline Rose on literature.[10] These studies do not just assert the existence of the feminine and of women, they also attempt to explain the shifting relationship between both text and writer and text and reader. Jacqueline Rose, together with Juliet Mitchell, helped to bring the work of Lacan to Anglo-Saxon audiences and her finely textured study of Sylvia Plath, *The Haunting of Sylvia Plath*, demonstrates particularly clearly how his work, and psychoanalysis, can be brought to bear on the study of literature.[11] In a concluding remark to *The Haunting of Sylvia Plath* Jacqueline Rose suggests that 'it is a woman who is most likely to articulate the power – perverse, recalcitrant, persistent – of fantasy as such. Nor would such an insight be in any way incompatible with women's legitimate protest against a patriarchal world.'[12] That idea is central to the whole area of the discussion of women and representation, the issue of *how* women choose to represent experience (their own or that of others) and how that representation is both formed by and often antagonistic to, a patriarchal culture. As Audre Lorde argues in 'the master's tools will never dismantle the master's house' (reproduced on pp. 366–8 of the present book), it is not enough to understand that sexual difference exists, it is also essential to understand sexual difference as a source of creativity.[13]

Notes

1. Cora Kaplan, 'Radical feminism and literature', and Tillie Olsen, 'Silences: when writers don't write', in Mary Evans (ed.), *The Woman Question* (Fontana, London, 1982).

2. Ibid., p. 386.

3. For a discussion of this issue see J. Batsleer et al. (eds), *Rewriting English* (Methuen, London, 1985).

4. Catherine Belsey, 'Re-reading the Great Tradition', in Peter Widdowson (ed.), *Re-reading English* (Methuen, London, 1982), pp. 121–35.

5. Claire Buck (ed.), *The Bloomsbury Guide to Women's Literature* (Bloomsbury, London, 1982).

6. Q.D. Leavis, *Fiction and the Reading Public* (Chatto & Windus, London, 1968).

7. See Jacqueline Rose, 'Feminine sexuality: Jacques Lacan and the *école freudienne*', in Rose, *Sexuality in the Field of Vision* (Verso, London, 1986).

8. Toril Moi, *Sexual/Textual Politics* (Methuen, London, 1985), p. 87.

9. The crucial works in question here are Elaine Showalter's *A Literature of Their Own* (Princeton University Press, Princeton, NJ, 1977) and Sandra Gilbert and Susan Gubar's *The Madwoman in the Attic* (Yale University Press, New Haven, Conn., 1979). All authors have published extensively since the publication of these works.

10. Laura Mulvey, *Visual and Other Pleasures* (Macmillan, London, 1989) and Jacqueline Rose, *The Haunting of Sylvia Plath* (Virago, London, 1992).

11. Jacqueline Rose and Juliet Mitchell (eds), *Feminine Sexuality – Jacques Lacan and the 'école freudienne'* (Verso, London, 1982).

12. Rose, *Haunting of Sylvia Plath*, p. 238.

13. See the interesting essay by Janet Sayers, 'Sex, art and reparation', *Women*, 1, 2 (1990), pp. 135–43.

Sex and Death in the Rational World of Defense Intellectuals

Carol Cohn

'I can't believe *that*,' said Alice.

'Can't you?' the Queen said in a pitying tone. 'Try again: draw a long breath, and shut your eyes.'

Alice laughed. 'There's no use trying,' she said. 'One *can't* believe impossible things.'

'I daresay you haven't had much practice,' said the Queen. 'When I was your age, I always did it for half-an-hour a day. Why, sometimes I've believed as many as six impossible things before breakfast.' (Lewis Carroll, *Through the Looking Glass*)

My close encounter with nuclear strategic analysis started in the summer of 1984. I was one of forty-eight college teachers (one of ten women) attending a summer workshop on nuclear weapons, nuclear strategic doctrine and arms control, taught by distinguished 'defense intellectuals'. Defense intellectuals are men (and indeed, they are virtually all men) who use the concept of deterrence to explain why it is safe to have weapons of a kind and number it is not safe to use.[1] They are civilians who move in and out of government, working sometimes as administrative officials or consultants, sometimes at universities and think tanks. They formulate what they call 'rational' systems for dealing with the problems created by nuclear weapons: how to manage the arms race; how to deter the use of nuclear weapons; how to fight a nuclear war if deterrence fails. It is their calculations that are used to explain the necessity of having nuclear destructive capability at what George Kennan has called 'levels of such grotesque dimensions as to defy rational understanding'.[2] At the same time, it is their reasoning that is used to explain why it is not safe to live without nuclear weapons.[3] In short, they create the theory that informs and legitimizes American nuclear strategic practice.

For two weeks, I listened to men engage in dispassionate discussion of nuclear war. I found myself aghast, but morbidly fascinated – not by nuclear weaponry, or by images of nuclear destruction, but by the extraordinary abstraction and removal from what I knew as reality that characterized the professional discourse. I became obsessed by the question: How can they think this way? At the end of the summer program, when I was offered the

From *Signs*, 12 (4), 1987, pp. 687–712, abridged.

opportunity to stay on at the university's center on defense technology and arms control (hereafter known as 'the Center'), I jumped at the chance to find out how they could think 'this' way.

I spent the next year of my life immersed in the world of defense intellectuals. As a participant observer, I attended lectures, listened to arguments, conversed with defense analysts, and interviewed graduate students at the beginning, middle and end of their training. I learned their specialized language, and I tried to understand what they thought and how they thought. I sifted through their logic for its internal inconsistencies and its unspoken assumptions. But as I learned their language, as I became more and more engaged with their information and their arguments, I found that my own thinking was changing. Soon, I could no longer cling to the comfort of studying an external and objectified 'them'. I had to confront a new question: How can *I* think this way? How can any of us?

Throughout my time in the world of strategic analysis, it was hard not to notice the ubiquitous weight of gender, both in social relations and in the language itself; it is an almost entirely male world (with the exception of the secretaries), and the language contains many rather arresting metaphors. There is, of course, an important and growing body of feminist theory about gender and language.[4] In addition, there is a rich and increasingly vast body of theoretical work exploring the gendered aspects of war and militarism, which examines such issues as men's and women's different relations to militarism and pacifism, and the ways in which gender ideology is used in the service of militarization. Some of the feminist work on gender and war is also part of an emerging, powerful feminist critique of ideas of rationality as they have developed in Western culture.[5] While I am indebted to all of these bodies of work, my own project is most closely linked to the development of feminist critiques of dominant Western concepts of reason. My goal is to discuss the nature of nuclear strategic thinking; in particular, my emphasis is on the role of its specialized language, a language that I call technostrategic.[6] I have come to believe that this language both reflects and shapes the nature of the American nuclear strategic project, that it plays a central role in allowing defense intellectuals to think and act as they do, and that feminists who are concerned about nuclear weaponry and nuclear war must give careful attention to the language we choose to use – whom it allows us to communicate with and what it allows us to think as well as say.

Listening

'Clean bombs' and clean language

Entering the world of defense intellectuals was a bizarre experience – bizarre because it is a world where men spend their days calmly and matter-of-factly discussing nuclear weapons, nuclear strategy and nuclear war. The discussions are carefully and intricately reasoned, occurring seemingly without any sense of horror, urgency or moral outrage – in fact, there seems to be no graphic reality behind the words, as they speak of 'first strike', 'counterforce exchanges' and 'limited nuclear war', or as they debate the comparative values of a 'minimum deterrent posture' versus a 'nuclear war-fighting capability'.

Yet what is striking about the men themselves is not, as the content of their conversations might suggest, their cold-bloodedness. Rather, it is that they are a group of men unusually endowed with charm, humor, intelligence, concern and decency. Reader, I liked them. At least, I liked many of them. The attempt to understand how such men could contribute to an endeavor that I see as so fundamentally destructive became a continuing obsession for me, a lens through which I came to examine all of my experiences in their world.

In this early stage, I was gripped by the extraordinary language used to discuss nuclear war. What hit me first was the elaborate use of abstraction and euphemism, of words so bland that they never forced the speaker or enabled the listener to touch the realities of nuclear holocaust that lay behind the words.

Anyone who has seen pictures of Hiroshima burn victims or tried to imagine the pain of hundreds of glass shards blasted into flesh may find it perverse beyond imagination to hear a class of nuclear devices matter-of-factly referred to as 'clean bombs'. 'Clean bombs' are nuclear devices that are largely fusion rather than fission; they release a somewhat higher proportion of their energy as prompt radiation, but produce less radioactive fallout than fission bombs of the same yield.[7]

'Clean bombs' may provide the perfect metaphor for the language of defense analysts and arms controllers. This language has enormous destructive power, but without emotional fallout, without the emotional fallout that would result if it were clear one was talking about plans for mass murder, mangled bodies and unspeakable human suffering. Defense analysts talk about 'countervalue attacks' rather than about incinerating cities. Human death, in nuclear parlance, is most often referred to as 'collateral damage'; for, as one defense analyst said wryly, 'The Air Force doesn't target people, it targets shoe factories.'[8]

Some phrases carry this cleaning-up to the point of inverting meaning. The MX missile will carry ten warheads, each with the explosure power of 300–475 kilotons of TNT: *one* missile the bearer of destruction approximately 250–400 times that of the Hiroshima bombing.[9] Ronald Reagan has dubbed the MX missile 'the Peacekeeper'. While this renaming was the object of considerable scorn in the community of defense analysts, these very same analysts refer to the MX as a 'damage limitation weapon'.[10]

These phrases, only a few of the hundreds that could be discussed, exemplify the astounding chasm between image and reality that characterizes technostrategic language. They also hint at the terrifying way in which the existence of nuclear devices has distorted our perceptions and redefined the world. 'Clean bombs' tells us that radioactivity is the only 'dirty' part of killing people.

To take this one step further, such phrases can even seem healthful/ curative/corrective. So that we not only have 'clean bombs' but also 'surgically clean strikes' ('counterforce' attacks that can purportedly 'take out' – i.e., accurately destroy – an opponent's weapons or command centers without causing significant injury to anything else). The image of excision of the offending weapon is unspeakably ludicrous when the surgical tool is not a delicately controlled scalpel but a nuclear warhead. And somehow it seems to be forgotten that even scalpels spill blood.[11]

White men in ties discussing missile size

Feminists have often suggested that an important aspect of the arms race is phallic worship, that 'missile envy' is a significant motivating force in the nuclear build-up.[12] I have always found this an uncomfortably reductionist explanation and hoped that my research at the Center would yield a more complex analysis. But still, I was curious about the extent to which I might find a sexual subtext in the defense professionals' discourse. I was not prepared for what I found.

I think I had naively imagined myself as a feminist spy in the house of death – that I would need to sneak around and eavesdrop on what men said in unguarded moments, using all my subtlety and cunning to unearth whatever sexual imagery might be underneath how they thought and spoke. I had naively believed that these men, at least in public, would appear to be aware of feminist critiques. If they had not changed their language, I thought that at least at some point in a long talk about 'penetration aids', someone would suddenly look up, slightly embarrassed to be caught in such blatant confirmation of feminist analyses of What's Going On Here.[13]

Of course, I was wrong. There was no evidence that any feminist critiques had ever reached the ears, much less the minds, of these men. American military dependence on nuclear weapons was explained as 'irresistible, because you get more bang for the buck'. Another lecturer solemnly and scientifically announced 'to disarm is to get rid of all your stuff'. (This may, in turn, explain why they see serious talk of nuclear disarmament as perfectly resistible, not to mention foolish. If disarmament is emasculation, how could any real man even consider it?) A professor's explanation of why the MX missile is to be placed in the silos of the newest Minuteman missiles, instead of replacing the older, less accurate ones, was 'because they're in the nicest hole – you're not going to take the nicest missile you have and put it in a crummy hole'. Other lectures were filled with discussion of vertical erector launchers, thrust-to-weight ratios, soft lay downs, deep penetration, and the comparative advantages of protracted versus spasm attacks – or what one military adviser to the National Security Council has called 'releasing 70 to 80 percent of our megatonnage in one orgasmic whump'.[14] There was serious concern about the need to harden our missiles and the need to 'face it, the Russians are a little harder than we are'. Disbelieving glances would occasionally pass between me and my one ally in the summer program, another woman, but no one else seemed to notice.

If the imagery is transparent, its significance may be less so. The temptation is to draw some conclusions about the defense intellectuals themselves – about what they are *really* talking about, or their motivations; but the temptation is worth resisting. Individual motivations cannot necessarily be read directly from imagery; the imagery itself does not originate in these particular individuals but in a broader cultural context.

Sexual imagery has, of course, been a part of the world of warfare since long before nuclear weapons were even a gleam in a physicist's eye. The history of the atomic bomb project itself is rife with overt images of competitive male sexuality, as is the discourse of the early nuclear phycsists, strategist and SAC commanders.[15] Both the military itself and the arms manufacturers are constantly exploiting the phallic imagery and promise of sexual domination that their weapons so conveniently suggest. A quick glance at the publications that constitute some of the research sources for defense intellectuals makes the depth and pervasiveness of the imagery evident.

Air Force Magazine's advertisements for new weapons, for example, rival *Playboy* as a catalog of men's sexual anxieties and fantasies. Consider the following, from the June 1985 issue: emblazoned in bold letters across the top of a two-page advertisement for the AV-8B Harrier II – 'Speak Softly and Carry a Big Stick'. The copy below boasts 'an exceptional thrust to weight ratio' and 'vectored thrust capability that makes the . . . unique rapid response possible'. Then, just in case we've failed to get the message, the last line reminds us, 'Just the sort of "Big Stick" Teddy Roosevelt had in mind way back in 1901'.[16]

An ad for the BKEP (BLU-106/B) reads:

> The Only Way to Solve Some Problems is to Dig Deep.
> THE BOMB, KINETIC ENERGY
> PENETRATOR
> 'Will provide the tactical air commander with efficient power to deny or significantly delay enemy airfield operations'.
> 'Designed to maximize runway cratering by optimizing penetration dynamics and utilizing the most efficient warhead yet designed'.[17]

(In case the symbolism of 'cratering' seems far-fetched, I must point out that I am not the first to see it. The French use the Mururoa Atoll in the South Pacific for their nuclear tests and assign a woman's name to each of the craters they gouge out of the earth.)

Another, truly extraordinary, source of phallic imagery is to be found in descriptions of nuclear blasts themselves. Here, for example, is one by journalist William Laurence, who was brought to Nagasaki by the Air Force to witness the bombing:

> Then, just when it appeared as though the thing had settled down in to a state of permanence, there came shooting out of the top a giant mushroom that increased the size of the pillar to a total of 45,000 feet. The mushroom top was even more

alive than the pillar, seething and boiling in a white fury of creamy foam, sizzling upward and then descending earthward, a thousand geysers rolled into one. It kept struggling in an elemental fury, like a creature in the act of breaking the bonds that held it down.[18]

Given the degree to which it suffuses their world, that defense intellectuals themselves use a lot of sexual imagery does not seem especially surprising. Nor does it, by itself, constitute grounds for imputing motivation. For me, the interesting issue is not so much the imagery's psychodynamic origins, as how it functions. How does it serve to make it possible for strategic planners and other defense intellectuals to do their macabre work? How does it function in their construction of a work world that feels tenable? Several stories illustrate the complexity.

During the summer program, a group of us visited the New London Navy base where nuclear submarines are homeported and the General Dynamics Electric Boat boatyards where a new Trident submarine was being constructed. At one point during the trip we took a tour of a nuclear-powered submarine. When we reached the part of the sub where the missiles are housed, the officer accompanying us turned with a grin and asked if we wanted to stick our hands through a hole to 'pat the missile'. *Pat the missile?*

The image reappeared the next week, when a lecturer scornfully declared that the only real reason for deploying cruise and Pershing II missiles in Western Europe was 'so that our allies can pat them'. Some months later, another group of us went to be briefed at NORAD (the North American Aerospace Defense Command). On the way back, our plane went to refuel at Offut Air Force Base, the Strategic Air Command headquarters near Omaha, Nebraska. When word leaked out that our landing would be delayed because the new B-1 bomber was in the area, the plane became charged with a tangible excitement that built as we flew in our holding pattern, people craning their necks to try to catch a glimpse of the B-1 in the skies, and climaxed as we touched down on the runway and hurtled past it. Later, when I returned to the Center I encountered a man who, unable to go on the trip, said to me enviously, 'I hear you got to pat a B-1'.

What is all this 'patting'? What are men doing when they 'pat' these high-tech phalluses? Patting is an assertion of intimacy, sexual possession, affectionate domination. The thrill and pleasure of 'patting the missile' is the proximity of all that phallic power, the possibility of vicariously appropriating it as one's own.

But if the predilection for patting phallic objects indicates something of the homoerotic excitement suggested by the language, it also has another side. For patting is not only an act of sexual intimacy. It is also what one does to babies, small children, the pet dog. One pats that which is small, cute, and harmless – not terrifyingly destructive. Pat it, and its lethality disappears.

Much of the sexual imagery I heard was rife with the sort of ambiguity suggested by 'patting the missiles'. The imagery can be construed as a deadly serious display of the connections between masculine sexuality and the arms race. At the same time, it can also be heard as a way of minimizing the seriousness of militarist endeavors, of denying their deadly consequences. A former Pentagon target analyst, in telling me why he thought plans for 'limited nuclear war' were ridiculous, said, 'Look, you gotta understand that it's a pissing contest – you gotta expect them to use everything they've got.' What does this image say? Most obviously, that this is all about competition for manhood, and thus there is tremendous danger. But at the same time, the image diminishes the contest and its outcomes, by representing it as an act of boyish mischief.

Fathers, sons and virgins

'Virginity' also made frequent, arresting, appearances in nuclear discourse. In the summer program, one professor spoke of India's explosion of a nuclear bomb as 'losing her virginity'; the question of how the United States should react was posed as whether or not we should 'throw her away'. It is a complicated use of metaphor. Initiation into the nuclear world involves being deflowered, losing one's innocence, knowing sin, all wrapped up into one. Although the manly United States is no virgin, and proud of it, the double standard raises its head in the question of whether or not a woman is still worth anything to a man once she has lost her virginity.

New Zealand's refusal to allow nuclear-armed or nuclear-powered warships into its ports prompted similar reflections on virginity. A good example is provided by Retired US Air Force General Ross Milton's angry column in *Air Force Magazine*, entitled, 'Nuclear virginity'. His tone is that of a man whose advances have been spurned. He is contemptuous of the woman's protestation that she wants to remain pure, innocent of nuclear weapons; her moral reluctance is a quaint and ridiculous throwback. But beyond contempt, he also feels outraged – after all, this is a woman we have *paid* for, who *still* will not come across. He suggests that we withdraw our goods and services – and then we will see just how long she tries to hold onto her virtue.[19] The patriarchal bargain could not be laid out more clearly.

Another striking metaphor of patriarchal power came early in the summer program, when one of the faculty was giving a lecture on deterrence. To give us a concrete example from outside the world of military strategy, he described having a seventeen-year-old son of whose TV-watching habits he disapproves. He deals with the situation by threatening to break his son's arm if he turns on the TV again. 'That's deterrence!' he said triumphantly.

What is so striking about this analogy is that at first it seems so inappropriate. After all, we have been taught to believe that nuclear deterrence is a relation between two countries of more or less equal strength, in which one is only able to deter the other from doing it great harm by threatening to do the same in return. But in this case the partners are unequal, and the stronger one is using his superior force not to protect himself or others from grave injury but to coerce.

But if the analogy seems to be a flawed expression of deterrence as we have been taught to view it, it is nonetheless extremely revealing about US nuclear deterrence as an operational, rather than rhetorical or declaratory policy. What it suggests is the speciousness of the defensive rhetoric that surrounds deterrence – of the idea that we face an implacable enemy and that we stockpile nuclear weapons only in an attempt to defend ourselves. Instead, what we see is the drive to superior power as a means to exercise one's will and a readiness to threaten the disproportionate use of force in order to achieve one's own ends. There is no question here of recognizing competing but legitimate needs, no desire to negotiate, discuss or compromise, and most important, no necessity for that recognition or desire, since the father carries the bigger stick.[20]

The United States frequently appeared in discussions about international politics as 'father', sometimes coercive, sometimes benevolent, but always knowing best. The single time that any mention was made of countries other than the United States, our NATO allies, or the USSR was in a lecture on nuclear proliferation. The point was made that younger countries simply could not be trusted to know what was good for them, nor were they yet fully responsible, so nuclear weapons in their hands would be much more dangerous than in ours. The metaphor used was that of parents needing to set limits for their children.

Domestic bliss

Sanitized abstraction and sexual and patriarchal imagery, even if disturbing, seemed to fit easily into the masculinist world of nuclear war planning. What did not fit, what surprised and puzzled me most when I first heard it, was the set of metaphors that evoked images that can only be called domestic.

Nuclear missiles are based in 'silos'. On a Trident submarine, which carries twenty-four multiple warhead nuclear missiles, crew members call the part of the submarine where the missiles are lined up in their silos ready for launching 'the Christmas tree farm'. What could be more bucolic – farms, silos, Christmas trees?

In the ever-friendly, even romantic world of nuclear weaponry, enemies 'exchange' warheads; one missile 'takes out' another; weapons systems can 'marry up'; 'coupling' is sometimes used to refer to the wiring between mechanisms of warning and response, or to the psycho-political links between strategic (intercontinental) and theater (European-based) weapons. The patterns in which a MIRVed missile's nuclear warheads land is known as a 'footprint'.[21] These nuclear explosives are not dropped; a 'bus' 'delivers' them. In addition, nuclear bombs are not referred to as bombs or even warheads; they are referred to as 're-entry vehicles', a term far more bland and benign, which is then shortened to 'RVs', a term not only totally abstract and removed from the reality of a bomb but also resonant with the image of the recreational vehicles of the ideal family vacation.

These domestic images must be more than simply one more form of distancing, one more way to remove oneself from the grisly reality behind the words; ordinary abstraction is adequate to that task. Something else, something very peculiar, is going on here. Calling the pattern in which bombs fall a 'footprint' almost seems a willful distorting process, a playful, perverse refusal of accountability – because to be accountable to reality is to be unable to do this work.

These words may also serve to domesticate, to *tame* the wild and uncontrollable forces of nuclear destruction. The metaphors minimize; they are a way to make phenomena that are beyond what the mind can encompass smaller and safer, and thus they are a way of gaining mastery over the unmasterable. The fire-breathing dragon under the bed, the one who threatens to incinerate your family, your town, your planet, becomes a pet you can pat.

Using language evocative of everyday experiences also may simply serve to make the nuclear strategic community more comfortable with what they are doing. 'PAL' (permissive action links) is the carefully constructed, friendly acronym for the electronic system designed to prevent the unauthorized firing of nuclear warheads. 'BAMBI' was the acronym developed for an early version of an antiballistic missile system (for Ballistic Missile Boost Intercept). The president's Annual Nuclear Weapons Stockpile Memorandum, which outlines both short- and long-range plans for production of new nuclear weapons, is benignly referred to as 'the shopping list'. The National Command Authorities choose from a 'menu of options' when deciding among different targeting plans. The 'cookie cutter' is a phrase used to describe a particular model of nuclear attack. Apparently it is also used at the Department of Defense to refer to the neutron bomb.[22]

The imagery that domesticates, that humanizes insentient weapons, may also serve, paradoxically, to make it all right to ignore sentient human bodies, human lives.[23] Perhaps it is possible to spend one's time thinking about scenarios for the use of destructive technology and to have human bodies remain invisible in that technological world precisely because that world itself now *includes* the domestic, the human, the warm and playful – the Christmas trees, the RVs, the affectionate pats. It is a world that is in some sense complete unto itself; it *even* includes death and loss. But it is weapons, not humans, that get 'killed'. 'Fratricide' occurs when one of your warheads 'kills' another of your own warheads. There is much discussion of 'vulnerability' and 'survivability', but it is about the vulnerability and survival of weapons systems, not people.

Male birth and creation

There is one set of domestic images that demands separate attention – images that suggest men's desire to appropriate from women the power of giving life and that conflate creation and destruction. The bomb project is rife with images of male birth.[24] In December 1942, Ernest Lawrence's telegram to the physicists at Chicago read, 'Congratulations to the new parents. Can hardly wait to see the new arrival.'[25] At Los Alamos, the atom bomb was referred to as 'Oppenheimer's baby'. One of the physicists working at Los Alamos, Richard Feynman, writes that when he was temporarily on leave after his wife's death, he received a telegram saying, 'The baby is expected on such and such a day.'[26] At Lawrence Livermore, the hydrogen bomb was referred to as 'Teller's baby', although those who wanted to disparage Edward Teller's contribution claimed he was not the bomb's father but its mother. They claimed that Stanislaw Ulam was the real father; he had the all-important idea and inseminated Teller with it. Teller only 'carried it' after that.[27]

Forty years later, this idea of male birth and its accompanying belittling of maternity – the denial of women's role in the process of creation and the reduction of 'motherhood' to the provision of nurturance (apparently Teller did not need to provide an egg, only a womb) – seems thoroughly incorporated into the nuclear mentality, as I learned on a subsequent visit to US Space Command in Colorado Springs. One of the briefings I attended included discussion of a new satellite system, the not yet 'on line' MILSTAR system.[28] The officer doing the briefing gave an excited recitation of its technical capabilities and then an explanation of the new Unified Space Command's role in the system. Self-effacingly he said, 'We'll do the motherhood role – telemetry, tracking, and control – the maintenance.'

In light of the imagery of male birth, the extraordinary names given to the bombs that reduced Hiroshima and Nagasaki to ash and rubble – 'Little Boy' and 'Fat Man' – at last become intelligible. These ultimate destroyers were the progeny of the atomic scientists – and emphatically not just any progeny but male progeny. In early tests, before they were certain that the bombs would work, the scientists expressed their concern by saying that they hoped the baby was a boy, not a girl – that is, not a dud.[29] General Grove's triumphant cable to Secretary of War Henry Stimson at the Potsdam conference, informing him that the first atomic bomb test was successful read, after decoding: 'Doctor has just returned most enthusiastic and confident that the little boy is as husky as his big brother. The light in his eyes discernible from here to Highhold and I could have heard his screams from here to my farm.'[30] Stimson, in turn, informed Churchill by writing him a note that read, 'Babies satisfactorily born.'[31] In 1952, Teller's exultant telegram to Los Alamos announcing the successful test of the hydrogen bomb, 'Mike', at Eniwetok Atoll in the Marshall Islands, read, 'It's a boy.'[32] The nuclear scientists gave birth to male progeny with the ultimate power of violent domination over female Nature. The defense intellectuals' project is the creation of abstract formulations to control the forces the scientists created – and to participate thereby in their world-creating/destroying power.

The entire history of the bomb project, in fact, seems permeated with imagery that confounds man's overwhelming technological power to destroy nature with the power to create – imagery that inverts men's destruction and asserts in its place the power to create new life and a new world. It converts men's destruction into their rebirth.

William L. Laurence witnessed the Trinity test of the first atomic bomb and

wrote: 'The big boom came about a hundred seconds after the great flash –
the first cry of a new-born world . . . They clapped their hands as they leaped
from the ground – earthbound man symbolising the birth of a new force.'[33]
Watching 'Fat Man' being assembled the day before it was dropped on
Nagasaki, he described seeing the bomb as 'being fashioned into a living
thing.'[34] Decades later, General Bruce K. Holloway, the commander in chief
of the Strategic Air Command from 1968 to 1972, described a nuclear war
as involving 'a big bang, like the start of the universe'.[35]

God and the nuclear priesthood

The possibility that the language reveals an attempt to appropriate ultimate
creative power is evident in another striking aspect of the language of
nuclear weaponry and doctrine – the religious imagery. In a subculture of
hard-nosed realism and hyper-rationality, in a world that claims as a sign of
its superiority its vigilant purging of all nonrational elements, and in which
people carefully excise from their discourse every possible trace of soft
sentimentality, as though purging dangerous nonsterile elements from a lab,
the last thing one might expect to find is religious imagery – imagery of the
forces that science has been defined in *opposition to*. For surely, given that
science's identity was forged by its separation from, by its struggle for
freedom from, the constraints of religion, the only thing as unscientific as the
female, the subjective, the emotional, would be the religious. And yet,
religious imagery permeates the nuclear past and present. The first atomic
bomb test was called Trinity – the unity of the Father, the Son and the Holy
Spirit, the male forces of Creation. The imagery is echoed in the language of
the physicists who worked on the bomb and witnessed the test: 'It was as
though we stood at the first day of creation.' Robert Oppenheimer thought
of Krishna's words to Arjuna in the *Bhagavad Gita*: 'I am become Death, the
Shatterer of World'.[36]

Perhaps most astonishing of all is the fact that the creators of strategic
doctrine actually refer to members of their community as 'the nuclear
priesthood'. It is hard to decide what is most extraordinary about this: the
easy arrogance of their claim to the virtues and supernatural power of the
priesthood; the tacit admission (*never* spoken directly) that rather than being
unflinching, hard-nosed, objective, empirically minded scientific describers
of reality, they are really the creators of dogma; or the extraordinary implicit
statement about who, or rather what, has become God. If this new
priesthood attains its status through an inspired knowledge of nuclear
weapons, it gives a whole new meaning to the phrase 'a mighty fortress is
our God'. [. . .]

Dialogue

It did not take very long to learn the language of nuclear war and much of
the specialized information it contained. My focus quickly changed from

mastering technical information and doctrinal arcana to attempting to understand more about how the dogma was rationalized. Instead of trying, for example, to find out why submarines are so hard to detect or why, prior to the Trident II, submarine-based ballistic missiles were not considered counterforce weapons, I now wanted to know why we really 'need' a strategic triad, given submarines' 'invulnerability'.[37] I also wanted to know why it is considered reasonable to base US military planning on the Soviet Union's military capabilities rather than seriously attempting to gauge what their intentions might be. This standard practice is one I found particularly troubling. Military analysts say that since we cannot know for certain what Soviet intentions are, we must plan our military forces and strategies as if we knew that the Soviets planned to use all of their weapons. While this might appear to have the benefit of prudence, it leads to a major problem. When we ask only what the Soviets *can* do, we quickly come to assume that that is what they *intend* to do. We base our planning on 'worst-case scenarios' and then come to believe that we live in a world where vast resources must be committed to 'prevent' them from happening.

Since underlying rationales are rarely discussed in the everyday business of defense planning, I had to start asking more questions. At first, although I was tempted to use my newly acquired proficiency in technostrategic jargon, I vowed to speak English. I had long believed that one of the most important functions of an expert language is exclusion – the denial of a voice to those outside the professional community.[38] I wanted to see whether a well-informed person could speak English and still carry on a knowledgeable conversation.

What I found was that no matter how well-informed or complex my questions were, if I spoke English rather than expert jargon, the men responded to me as though I were ignorant, simpleminded, or both. It did not appear to occur to anyone that I might actually be choosing not to speak their language.

A strong distaste for being patronized and dismissed made my experiment in English short-lived. I adapted my everyday speech to the vocabulary of strategic analysis. I spoke of 'escalation dominance', 'pre-emptive strikes', and, one of my favorites, 'subholocaust engagement'. Using the right phrases opened my way into long, elaborate discussions that taught me a lot about technostrategic reasoning and how to manipulate it.

I found, however, that the better I got at engaging in this discourse, the more impossible it became for me to express my own ideas, my own values. I could adopt the language and gain a wealth of new concepts and reasoning strategies – but at the same time as the language gave me access to things I had been unable to speak about before, it radically excluded others. I could not use the language to express my concerns because it was physically impossible. This language does not allow certain questions to be asked or certain values to be expressed.

To pick a bald example: the word 'peace' is not a part of this discourse. As close as one can come is 'strategic stability', a term that refers to a balance of numbers and types of weapons systems – not the political, social, economic and psychological conditions implied by the word 'peace'. Not only is there no word signifying peace in this discourse, but the word 'peace' itself cannot be used. To speak it is immediately to brand oneself as a soft-headed activist instead of an expert, a professional to be taken seriously.

If I was unable to speak my concerns in this language, more disturbing still was that I found it hard even to keep them in my own head. I had begun my research expecting abstract and sanitized discussions of nuclear war and had readied myself to replace my words for theirs, to be ever vigilant against slipping into the never-never land of abstraction. But no matter how prepared I was, no matter how firm my commitment to staying aware of the reality behind the words, over and over I found that I could not stay connected, could not keep human lives as my reference point. I found I could go for days speaking about nuclear weapons without once thinking about the people who would be incinerated by them.

It is tempting to attribute this problem to qualities of the language, the words themselves – the abstractness, the euphemisms, the sanitized, friendly, sexy acronyms. Then all we would need to do is change the words, make them more vivid; get the military planners to say 'mass murder' instead of 'collateral damage' and their thinking would change.

The problem, however, is not only that defense intellectuals use abstract terminology that removes them from the realities of which they speak. There *is* no reality of which they speak. Or, rather, the 'reality' of which they speak is itself a world of abstractions. Deterrence theory, and much of strategic doctrine altogether, was invented largely by mathematicians, economists, and a few political scientists. It was invented to hold together abstractly, its validity judged by its internal logic. Questions of the correspondence to observable reality were not the issue. These abstract systems were developed as a way to make it possible to 'think about the unthinkable' – not as a way to describe or codify relations on the ground.[39]

So the greatest problem with the idea of 'limited nuclear war', for example, is not that it is grotesque to refer to the death and suffering caused by *any* use of nuclear weapons as 'limited' or that 'limited nuclear war' is an abstraction that is disconnected from human reality but, rather, that 'limited nuclear war' is itself an abstract conceptual system, designed, embodied, achieved by computer modeling. It is an abstract world in which hypothetical, calm, rational actors have sufficient information to know exactly what size nuclear weapon the opponent has used against which targets, and in which they have adequate command and control to make sure that their response is precisely equilibrated to the attack. In this scenario, no field commander would use the tactical 'mini-nukes' at his disposal in the height of a losing battle; no EMP-generated electronic failures, or direct attacks on command and control centers, or human errors would destroy communications networks. Our rational actors would be free of emotional response to being attacked, free of political pressures from the populace, free from madness or despair or any of the myriad other factors that regularly affect human actions and decision-making. They would act solely on the basis of a perfectly informed mathematical calculus of megatonnage.

So to refer to 'limited nuclear war' is already to enter into a system that is *de facto* abstract and removed from reality. To use more descriptive language would not, by itself, change that. In fact, I am tempted to say that the abstractness of the entire conceptual system makes descriptive language nearly beside the point. In a discussion of 'limited nuclear war', for example, it might make some difference if in place of saying 'In a counterforce attack against hard targets collateral damage could be limited', a strategic analyst had to use words that were less abstract – if he had to say, for instance, 'If we launch the missiles we have aimed at their missile silos, the explosions would cause the immediate mass murder of 10 million women, men and children, as well as the extended illness, suffering and eventual death of many millions more.' It is true that the second sentence does not roll off the tongue or slide across one's consciousness quite as easily. But it is also true, I believe, that the ability to speak about 'limited nuclear war' stems as much, if not more, from the fact that the term 'limited nuclear war' refers to an abstract conceptual system rather than to events that might take place in the real world. As such, there is no need to think about the concrete human realities behind the model; what counts is the internal logic of the system.[40]

This realization that the abstraction was not just in the words but also characterized the entire conceptual system itself helped me make sense of my difficulty in staying connected to human lives. But there was still a piece missing. How is it possible, for example, to make sense of the following paragraph? It is taken from a discussion of a scenario ('regime A') in which the United States and the USSR have revised their offensive weaponry, banned MIRVs, and gone to a regime of single warhead (Midgetman) missiles, with no 'defensive shield' (or what is familiarly known as 'Star Wars' or SDI):

> The strategic stability of regime A is based on the fact that both sides are deprived of any incentive ever to strike first. Since it takes roughly two warheads to destroy one enemy silo, an attacker must expend two of his missiles to destroy one of the enemy's. A first strike disarms the attacker. The aggressor ends up worse off than the aggressed.[41]

'The aggressor ends up worse off than the aggressed'? The homeland of 'the aggressed' has just been devastated by the explosions of, say, a thousand nuclear bombs, each likely to be ten to one hundred times more powerful than the bomb dropped on Hiroshima, and the aggressor, whose homeland is still untouched, 'ends up worse off'? How is it possible to think this? Even abstract language and abstract thinking do not seem to be a sufficient explanation.

I was only able to 'make sense of it' when I finally asked myself the question that feminists have been asking about theories in every discipline: What is the reference point? Who (or what) is the *subject* here?

In other disciplines, we have frequently found that the reference point for theories about 'universal human phenomena' has actually been white men. In technostrategic discourse, the reference point is not white men, it is not human beings at all; it is the weapons themselves. The aggressor thus ends up worse off than the aggressed because he has fewer weapons left; human factors are irrelevant to the calculus of gain and loss.

In 'regime A' and throughout strategic discourse, the concept of 'incentive' is similarly distorted by the fact that weapons are the subjects of strategic paradigms. Incentive to strike first is present or absent according to a mathematical calculus of numbers of 'surviving' weapons. That is, incentive to start a nuclear war is discussed not in terms of what possible military or political ends it might serve but, instead, in terms of numbers of weapons, with the goal being to make sure that you are the guy who still has the most left at the end. Hence, it is frequently stated that MIRVed missiles create strategic instability because they 'give you the incentive to strike first'. Calculating that two warheads must be targeted on each enemy missile, one MIRVed missile with ten warheads would, in theory, be able to destroy five enemy missiles in their silos; you destroy more of theirs than you have expended of your own. You win the numbers game. In addition, if you do not strike first, it would theoretically take relatively few of their MIRVed missiles to destroy a larger number of your own – so you must, as they say in the business, 'use 'em or lose 'em'. Many strategic analysts fear that in a period of escalating political tensions, when it begins to look as though war may be inevitable, this combination makes 'the incentive to strike first' well nigh irresistible.

Incentive to launch a nuclear war arises from a particular configuration of weapons and their hypothetical mathematical interaction. Incentive can only be so narrowly defined because the referents of technostrategic paradigms are weapons – not human lives, not even states and state power.

The fact that the subjects of strategic paradigms are weapons has several important implications. First, and perhaps most critically, there simply is no way to talk about human death or human societies when you are using a language designed to talk about weapons. Human death simply *is* 'collateral damage' – collateral to the real subject, which is the weapons themselves.

Second, if human lives are not the reference point, then it is not only impossible to talk about humans in this language, it also becomes in some sense illegitimate to ask the paradigm to reflect human concerns. Hence, questions that break through the numbing language of strategic analysis and raise issues in human terms can be dismissed easily. No one will claim that the questions are unimportant, but they are inexpert, unprofessional, irrelevant to the business at hand to ask. The discourse among the experts remains hermetically sealed.

The problem, then, is not only that the language is narrow but also that it is seen by its speakers as complete or whole unto itself – as representing a body of truths that exist independently of any other truth or knowledge. The isolation of this technical knowledge from social or psychological or moral thought, or feelings, is all seen as legitimate and necessary. The outcome is that defense intellectuals can talk about the weapons that are supposed to protect particular political entities, particular peoples and their way of life, without actually asking if weapons *can* do it, or if they are the best *way* to do it, or whether they may even damage the entities you are supposedly protecting. It is not that the men I spoke with would say that these are invalid questions. They would, however, simply say that they are separate questions, questions that are outside what they do, outside their realm of expertise. So their deliberations go on quite independently, as though with a life of their own, disconnected from the functions and values they are supposedly to serve.

Finally, the third problem is that this discourse has become virtually the only legitimate form of response to the question of how to achieve security. If the language of weaponry was one competing voice in the discussion, or one that was integrated with others, the fact that the referents of strategic paradigms are only weapons would be of little note. But when we realize that the only language and expertise offered to those interested in pursuing peace refers to nothing but weapons, its limits become staggering, and its entrapping qualities – the way in which, once you adopt it, it becomes so hard to stay connected to human concerns – become more comprehensible.

Notes

1. Thomas Powers, 'How nuclear war could start', *New York Review of Books*, 17 January 1985, p. 33.

2. George Kennan, 'A modest proposal', *New York Review of Books*, 16 July 1981, p. 14.

3. It is unusual for defense intellectuals to write for the public, rather than for their colleagues, but a recent, interesting exception has been made by a group of defense analysts from Harvard. Their two books provide a clear expression of the stance that living with nuclear weapons is not so much a problem to be solved but a condition to be managed rationally. Albert Carnesale and the Harvard Nuclear Study Group, *Living with Nuclear Weapons* (Harvard University Press, Cambridge, Mass., 1984); and Graham T. Allison, Albert Carnesale and Joseph Nye, Jr. (eds), *Hawks, Doves, and Owls: An Agenda for Avoiding Nuclear War* (W.W. Norton, New York, 1985).

4. For useful introductions to feminist work on gender and language, see Barrie Thorne, Cheris Kramarae and Nancy Henley (eds), *Language, Gender and Society* (Newbury, Rowley, Mass., 1983); and Elizabeth Abel (ed.), *Writing and Sexual Difference* (University of Chicago Press, Chicago, 1982).

5. For feminist critiques of dominant Western conceptions of rationality, see Nancy Hartsock, *Money, Sex, and Power* (Longman, New York, 1983); Sandra Harding and Merrill Hintikka (eds), *Discovering Reality: Feminist Perspectives on Epistemology, Metaphysics, Methodology and the Philosophy of Science* (Reidel, Dordrecht, 1983); Evelyn Fox Keller, *Reflections on Gender and Science* (Yale University Press, New Haven, Conn., 1985); Jean Bethke Elshtain, *Public Man, Private Woman: Woman in Social and Political Thought* (Princeton University Press, Princeton, NJ, 1981); Genevieve Lloyd, *The Man of Reason: 'Male' and 'Female' in Western Philosophy* (University of Minnesota Press, Minneapolis, 1984), which contains a particularly useful bibliographic essay; Sara Ruddick, 'Remarks on the sexual politics of reason', in *Women and Moral Theory*, ed. Eva Kittay and Diana Meyers (Rowman & Allanheld, Totowa, NJ, 1988). Some of the growing feminist work on gender and war is explicitly connected to critiques of rationality. See Virginia Woolf, *Three Guineas* (Harcourt, Brace, Jovanovich, New York, 1966); Nancy C.M. Hartsock, 'The feminist standpoint: developing the grounds for a

specifically feminist historical materialism', in Harding and Hintikka, *Discovering Reality*, pp. 283–310, and 'The barracks community in Western political thought: prologomena to a feminist critique of war and politics', in *Women and Men's Wars*, ed. Judith Hicks Stiehm (Pergamon Press, Oxford, 1983); Jean Bethke Elshtain, 'Reflections on war and political discourse: realism, just war and feminism in a nuclear age', *Political Theory*, 13, 1 (February 1985), pp. 39–57; Sara Ruddick, 'Preservative love and military destruction: some reflections on mothering and peace', in *Mothering: Essays in Feminist Theory*, ed. Joyce Trebilcot (Rowman & Allanheld, Totowa, NJ, 1984), pp. 231–62; Genevieve Lloyd, 'Selfhood, war, and, masculinity', in *Feminist Challenges*, ed. E. Gross and C. Pateman (Northeastern University Press, Boston, 1986). There is a vast and valuable literature on gender and war that indirectly informs my work. See, e.g., Cynthia Enloe, *Does Khaki Become You? The Militarization of Women's Lives* (South End Press, Boston, 1984); Stiehm, *Women and Men's Wars*; Jean Bethke Elshtain, 'On Beautiful Souls, Just Warriors, and Feminist Consciousness', in Stiehm, *Women and Men's Wars*, pp. 341–8; Sara Ruddick, 'Pacifying the forces: drafting women in the interests of peace', *Signs: Journal of Women in Culture and Society*, 8, 3 (Spring 1983), pp. 471–89, and 'Drafting women: pieces of a puzzle', in *Conscripts and Volunteers: Military Requirements, Social Values, and the All-Volunteer Force*, ed. Robert K. Fullinwider (Rowman & Allanheld, Totowa, NJ, 1983); Amy Swerdlow, 'Women's strike for peace versus HUAC', *Feminist Studies*, 8, 3 (Fall 1982), pp. 493–520; Mary C. Segers, 'The Catholic bishops' pastoral letter on war and peace: a feminist perspective', *Feminist Studies*, 11, 3 (Fall 1985), pp. 619–47.

6. I have coined the term 'technostrategic' to represent the intertwined, inextricable nature of technological and nuclear strategic thinking. The first reason is that strategic thinking seems to change in direct response to technological changes, rather than political thinking, or some independent paradigms that might be isolated as 'strategic'. (On this point see Lord Solly Zuckerman, *Nuclear Illusions and Reality*, Viking Press, New York, 1982.) Even more important, strategic theory not only depends on and changes in response to technological objects, it is also based on a kind of thinking, a way of looking at problems – formal, mathematical modeling, systems analysis, game theory, linear programming – that are part of technology itself. So I use the term 'technostrategic' to indicate the degree to which nuclear strategic language and thinking are imbued with, indeed constructed out of, modes of thinking that are associated with technology.

7. Fusion weapons' proportionally smaller yield of radioactive fallout led Atomic Energy Commission Chairman Lewis Strauss to announce in 1956 that hydrogen bomb tests were important 'not only from a military point of view but from a humanitarian aspect'. Although the bombs being tested were 1,000 times more powerful than those that devastated Hiroshima and Nagasaki, the proportional reduction of fallout apparently qualified them as not only clean but also humanitarian. Lewis Strauss is quoted in Ralph Lapp, 'The "humanitarian" H-bomb', *Bulletin of Atomic Scientists*, 12, 7 (September 1956), p. 263.

8. I must point out that we cannot know whether to take this particular example literally: America's list of nuclear targets is, of course, classified. The defense analyst quoted, however, is a man who had access to that list for at least two decades. He is also a man whose thinking and speaking is careful and precise, so I think it is reasonable to assume that his statement is not a distortion, that 'shoe factories', even if not themselves literally targeted, accurately, represent a category of target. Shoe factories would be one among many 'military targets' other than weapons systems themselves; they would be military targets because an army needs boots. The likelihood of a nuclear war lasting long enough for foot soldiers to wear out their boots might seem to stretch the limits of credibility, but that is an insufficient reason to assume that they are not nuclear targets. Nuclear targeting and nuclear strategic planning in general frequently suffer from 'conventionalization' – the tendency of planners to think in the old, familiar terms of 'conventional' warfare rather than fully assimilating te ways in which nuclear weaponry has changed warfare. In avoiding talking about the murder, the defense community has long been ahead of the State Department. It was not until 1984 that the State Department announced it will no longer use the word 'killing', much less 'murder', in official reports on the status of human rights in allied countries. The new term is 'unlawful or arbitrary deprivation of life' (*New*

York Times, 15 February 1984, as cited in *Quarterly Review of Doublespeak*, 11, 1 (October 1984), p. 3).

9. Kiloton (or kt) is a measure of explosive power, measured by the number of thousands of tons of TNT required to release an equivalent amount of energy. The atomic bomb dropped on Hiroshima is estimated to have been approximately 12 kt. An MX missile is designed to carry up to ten Mk 21 re-entry vehicles, each with a W-87 warhead. The yield of W-87 warheads is 300 kt, but they are 'upgradable' to 475 kt.

10. Since the MX would theoretically be able to 'take out' Soviet land-based ICBMs in a 'disarming first strike', the Soviets would have few ICBMs left for a retaliatory attack, and thus damage to the United States theoretically would be limited. However, to consider the damage that could be inflicted on the United States by the remaining ICBMs, not to mention Soviet bombers and submarine-based missiles as 'limited' is to act as though words have no meaning.

11. Conservative government assessments of the number of deaths resulting from a 'surgically clean' counterforce attack vary widely. The Office of Technology Assessment projects 2 million to 20 million immediate deaths. (See James Fallows, *National Defense*, Random House, New York, 1981, p. 159.) A 1975 Defense Department study estimated 18.3 million fatalities, while the US Arms Control and Disarmament Agency, using different assumptions, arrived at a figure of 50 million (cited by Desmond Ball, 'Can nuclear war be controlled?' Adelphi Paper no. 169, International Institute for Strategic Studies, London, 1981).

12. The phrase is Helen Caldicott's in *Missile Envoy: The Arms Race and Nuclear War* (Bantam Books, Toronto, 1986).

13. For the uninitiated, 'penetration aids' refers to devices that help bombers or missiles get past the 'enemy's' defensive systems; e.g., stealth technology, chaff or decoys. Within the defense intellectual community, they are also familiarly known as 'penaids'.

14. General William Odom, 'C³I and telecommunications at the policy level'. Incidental Paper, Seminar on C³I: Command, Control, Communications and Intelligence (Harvard University, Center for Information Policy Research, Cambridge, Mass., Spring 1980), p. 5.

15. This point has been amply documented by Brian Easley, *Fathering the Unthinkable: Masculinity, Scientists and the Nuclear Arms Race* (Pluto Press, London, 1983).

16. *Air Force Magazine*, 68, 6 (June 1985), pp. 77–8.

17. Ibid.

18. William L. Laurence, *Down over Zero: The Study of the Atomic Bomb* (Museum Press, London, 1974), pp. 198–9.

19. USAF Retired General T.R. Milton. 'Nuclear virginity', *Air Force Magazine*, 68, 5 (May 1985), p. 44.

20. I am grateful to Margaret Cerullo, a participant in the first summer program, for reporting the use of this analogy to me and sharing her thoughts about this and other events in the program. The interpretation I give here draws strongly on hers.

21. MIRV stands for 'multiple independently targetable re-entry vehicle'. A MIRVed missile not only carries more than one warhead: its warheads can be aimed at different targets.

22. Henry T. Nash, 'The bureaucratization of homicide', *Bulletin of Atomic Scientists* (April 1980), reprinted in E.P. Thompson and Dan Smith (eds), *Protest and Survive* (Monthly Review Press, New York, 1981), p. 159. The neutron bomb is notable for the active political contention that has occurred over its use and naming. It is a small warhead that produces six times the prompt radiation but slightly less blast and heat than typical fission warheads of the same yield. Pentagon planners see neutron bombs as useful in killing Soviet tank crews while theoretically leaving the buildings near the tanks intact. Of course, the civilians in the nearby buildings would be killed by the same 'enhanced radiation' as the tank crews. It is this design for protecting property while killing civilians along with soldiers that has led people in the antinuclear movement to call the neutron bomb 'the ultimate capitalist weapon'. However, in official parlance the neutron bomb is not called a weapon at all; it is an 'enhanced radiation device'. It is worth noting, however, that the designer of the neutron bomb did not conceive of it as an anti-tank personnel weapon to be used against the Russians. Instead, he thought it would be useful in an area where the enemy *did not have* nuclear weapons to use (Samuel T. Cohen, in an

interview on National Public Radio, as reported in Fred Kaplan, 'The neutron bomb: what it is, the way it works', *Bulletin of Atomic Scientists*, October 1981, p. 6).

23. For a discussion of the functions of imagery that reverses sentient and insentient matter, that 'exchange[s] . . . idioms between weapons and bodies', see Elaine Scarry, *The Body in Pain: The Making and Unmaking of the World* (Oxford University Press, New York, 1985), pp. 60–157, esp. p. 67.

24. For further discussion of men's desire to appropriate from women the power of giving life and death, and its implications for men's war-making activities, see Dorothy Dinnerstein, *The Mermaid and the Minotaur* (Harper & Row, New York, 1977). For further analysis of male birth imagery in the atomic bomb project, see Evelyn Fox Keller, 'From secrets of life to secrets of death', paper delivered at the Kansas Seminar, Yale University, New Haven, Conn., November 1986; and Easlea, *Fathering the Unthinkable*, pp. 81–116.

25. Lawrence is quoted by Herbert Childs in *An American Genius: The Life of Ernest Orlando Lawrence* (E. P. Dutton, New York, 1968), p. 340.

26. Feynman writes about the telegram in Richard P. Feynman, 'Los Alamos from below', in *Reminiscences of Los Alamos, 1943–1945*, ed. Lawrence Badash, Joseph O. Hirshfelder and Herbert P. Broida (D. Reidel, Dordrecht, 1980). p. 130.

27. Hans Bethe is quoted as saying that 'Ulam was the father of the hydrogen bomb and Edward was the mother, because he carried the baby for quite a while' (J. Bernstein, *Hans Bethe: Prophet of Energy*, Basic Books, New York, 1980, p. 95).

28. The MILSTAR system is a communications satellite system that is jam resistant, as well as having as 'EMP-hardened capability'. (This means that the electromagnetic pulse set off by a nuclear explosion would theoretically not destroy the satellites' electronic systems.) There are, of course, many things to say about the sanity and morality of the idea of the MILSTAR system and of spending the millions of dollars necessary to EMP-harden it. The most obvious point is that this is a system designed to enable the United States to fight a 'protracted' nuclear war – the EMP-hardening is to allow it to act as a conduit for command and control of successive nuclear shots, long after the initial exchange. The practicality of the idea would also appear to merit some discussion – who and what is going to be communicating to and from after the initial exchange? And why bother to harden it against EMP when all an opponent has to do to prevent the system from functioning is to blow it up, a feat certain to become technologically feasible in a short time? But, needless to say, exploration of these questions was not part of the briefing.

29. The concern about having a boy, not a girl, is written about by Robert Jungk, *Brighter than a Thousand Suns*, trans. James Cleugh (Harcourt, Brace, New York, 1956), p. 197.

30. Richard E. Hewlett and Oscar E. Anderson, *The New World, 1939/46: A History of the United States Atomic Energy Commission*, 2 vols (Pennsylvania State University Press, University Park, 1962), vol. 1, p. 386.

31. Winston Churchill, *The Second World War*, vol. 6: *Triumph and Tragedy* (Cassell, London, 1954), p. 551.

32. Quoted by Easlea, *Fathering the Unthinkable*, p. 130.

33. Laurence, *Dawn over Zero*, p. 10.

34. Ibid., p. 188.

35. From a 1985 interview in which Holloway was explaining the logic of a 'decapitating' strike against the Soviet leadership and command and control systems – and thus how nuclear war would be different from World War II, which was a 'war of attrition', in which transportation, supply depots and other targets were hit, rather than being a 'big bang' (Daniel Ford, 'The button', *New Yorker Magazine*, 61, 7 [8 April, 1985], p. 49).

36. Jungk, *Brighter than a Thousand Suns*, p. 201.

37. The 'strategic triad' refers to the three different modes of basing nuclear warheads: on land, on intercontinental ballistic missiles; at sea, on missiles in submarines; and 'in the air', on the Strategic Air Command's bombers. Given that nuclear weapons based on submarines are 'invulnerable' (i.e., not subject to attack), since there is not now nor likely to be in the future any reliable way to find and target submarines, many commentators (mostly from outside the community of defense intellectuals) have suggested that the Navy's leg of the triad is all we need to ensure a capacity to retaliate against a nuclear attack. This suggestion that submarine-based

missiles are an adequate deterrent becomes especially appealing when it is remembered that the other basing modes – CBMs and bombers – act as targets that would draw thousands of nuclear attacks to the American mainland in time of war.

38. For an interesting recent discussion of the role of language in the creation of professional power, see JoAnne Brown, 'Professional language: words that succeed', *Radical History Review*, 34 (1986), pp. 33–51.

39. For fascinating, detailed accounts of the development of strategic doctrine, see Fred Kaplan, *The Wizards of Armageddon* (Simon & Schuster, New York, 1983); and Gregg F. Herken, *The Counsels of War* (Alfred A. Knopf, New York, 1985).

40. Steven Kull's interviews with nuclear strategists can be read to show that on some level, some of the time, some of these men are aware that there is a serious disjunction between their models and the real world. Their justification for continuing to use these models is that 'other people' (unnamed, and on asking, unnameable) believe in them and that they therefore have an important reality ('Nuclear nonsense', *Foreign Policy*, 58 (Spring 1985), pp. 28–52).

41. Charles Krauthammer, 'Will Star Wars kill arms control?', *New Republic*, 3,653 (21 January 1985), pp. 12–16.

She's Gotta Have It: The Representation of Black Female Sexuality on Film

Felly Nkweto Simmonds

The black man . . . particularly since the Black Movement has been in a position to define the black woman. He is the one who tells her whether or not she is a woman and what it is to be a woman. And therefore, whether he wishes it or not, he determines her destiny as well as his own. (Wallace, 1979: 14)

I think this film should be the antidote to how the black male is perceived in 'The Color Purple' . . . the film's black men . . . are just one-dimensional animals . . . because if you read Alice Walker, that's the way she feels about black men. She really has problems with them . . . To me, it's justifying everything they say about black people and black men in general that we are animals. (Lee, 1986: 48)

She's Gotta Have It (*SGHI*) has been hailed as the new face of black American cinema by critics both in America and Europe. Its writer and director, Spike Lee, young, gifted and black, has been dubbed the black Woody Allen and, in 1986, *SGHI* won the Prix de Jeunesse at Cannes. *Film and Filming* concluded its review of the film with the words:

Only time will tell if he is going to make it as a mainstream American film-maker. But if he does, and can do it without compromising, then he won't only become the first important Black film-maker America has produced, but the first of any colour, to tell it as it really is in Black America. (*Film and Filming*, 1987: 42–3)

Spare Rib, while acknowledging some of the film's more obvious limitations, called it a 'well observed and humorous film . . . about a sexually liberated woman . . . [which] offers a refreshing alternative to the stereotyped and peripheral roles and concerns which have become the domain of Black people' (Alexander, 1987).

The film

The focus of the film is the sexual life of a young black American woman, Nola Darling. She is economically independent and works as a graphic artist.

From *Feminist Review*, 29, May 1988, pp. 10–22, abridged.

She has her own apartment in Brooklyn. Nola Darling wishes to remain a sexually free woman. She has three male lovers: Jamie Overstreet, Mars Blackmon (played by Spike Lee) and Greer Childs. There is also a woman, Opal Gilstrap, who would like to have Nola Darling as her lover.

In various ways – its use of black and white photography, direct address to camera and so on – the film departs in form from the conventional feature. This, combined with the fact that it has an all-black cast, gives *SGHI* the air of being a different, and more acceptable film about black experience in America.

Throughout, *SGHI* is a humorous film. An early sequence, for example, shows a series of stereotyped male figures making direct, comical sexual advances to women. The same play on sexual behaviour as a source of humour is returned to throughout the film, especially by Mars Blackmon. The characters use humour to maximum advantage, since each is given the opportunity directly to address the camera, and thus the audience. We are invited to laugh with them.

Nola Darling's three male lovers spend most of the film trying to convince her, and us, why each is best for Nola, and why she should give up her other lovers. In defence of their own positions, they spend much time telling us what they think is wrong with her because she refuses to choose between them. Nola is presented to us as odd because she chooses to have more than one lover. Even her father agrees she is odd.

Most of the time, the lovers' attempts to persuade Nola to give up their rivals are light and playful. Towards the end, however, one of Nola's lovers rapes her, to teach her a lesson.

The majority of the scenes are shot in Nola's apartment, where her lovers come to her. The central feature in her apartment is her bed. It is from here that she addresses the camera at the beginning of the film. In the opening sequence, Nola states what for her is the purpose of the film. She wants to clear her name. Her position, however, has already been undermined by the title of the film, *She's Gotta Have It*, which frames our subsequent perceptions of Nola. The 'it' that she has to have is sex. Lots of it. Spike Lee as the writer and director defines Nola's sexuality, exercising what Andrea Dworkin defines as the male power of naming:

> Men have the power of naming, a great and sublime power. This power of naming enables men to define experience, to articulate boundaries and values, to designate to each thing its realm and qualities, to determine perception itself. (Dworkin, 1981: 17)

By naming the film in the way that he has, the writer invites the viewer – even if she is a black woman herself – to view Nola Darling from the outside. The title is value laden, for the word 'it' carries male-defined sexual meaning:

> Commonly referred to as 'it', sex is defined in action only by what the male does with his penis. Fucking – the penis thrusting – is the magical, hidden meaning of

'it', the reason for sex, the expansive experience through which the male realises his sexual power. (Dworkin, 1981: 23)

Spike Lee's use of 'it' in his title demonstrates his assent to the notion that all a woman really needs is a man who can fuck her. *SGHI*, then, is not a woman-centred film, and it is a mistake to classify it, as *City Limit*'s Saskia Baron has done, as a 'feminist sex-comedy' (Baron, 1987: 15).

Spike Lee is quite specific in his reasons for making the film. In the summer of 1985 he had failed to make a different film, *The Messenger*, and, in his own words, 'out of that devastation and disaster . . . out of desperation . . . we came up with the idea to do *SGHI*. I was determined to do another film for as little money as possible' (Lee, 1986: 47). He therefore needed to make a film that would guarantee some return. Sex it seemed, was not a bad place to start. He also wanted to make a film that would appeal to black men, and counter what he saw as the exploitation of black men by black women writers such as Alice Walker and Ntozake Shange:

> Within recent years, the quickest way for a black playwright, novelist or poet to get published had been to say that black men are shit. If you say that, then you are definitely going to get media, your book published, your play done . . . that's why they put Alice Walker out there. That's why she won the Pulitzer Prize. That's why Hollywood leaped the pond to seize this book and had it made. (Lee, 1986: 47)

Thirdly, Spike Lee wanted to make a film about black sexuality:

> I think a lot of people, particularly black Americans, have been waiting for a film like this for a long time. They never saw black people kissing on the screen or making love. (Lee, 1987)

Spike Lee, as a black film director, wanted to challenge the notion that white film directors, such as Spielberg, could define the black experience on film. He used down-to-earth Brooklyn humour to make his audience accept the sexual experiences of a black woman and her three male at lovers at face value.

The use of an all-black cast is significant. It releases the film from the race issues that surface in any film with a black and white cast. The lack of racial tension in *SGHI*, and the humour of the film, give it a fresh, relaxed air, and help us to swallow what would otherwise be bitter and painful messages about black sexual politics.

Spike Lee alone created the film. He wrote, directed and edited it. It is exactly as he labels it in the humorous credits: a 'Spike Lee Joint'. It is therefore safe to assume that the views and messages of the film are predominantly his. Yet he admits himself that, as a black man, he can never be a spokesperson for black women: 'To me this film is about various men's views on this type of woman . . . [it is] not meant to represent every single black woman in the United States' (Lee, 1987). As he (alias Mars Blackmon) would have said, it is mighty black of him to acknowledge that he can neither speak for, nor represent, black female experience. And yet, the very expression 'this type of woman' starts to define categories of women. The film explicitly defines one particular woman and classifies her experience as unnatural. The words 'freak', 'nympho' and 'bogus' are all used in the film to define and categorize. Whether or not it was so intended, the film has been received as a film about a sexually promiscuous black woman, and this is what brings the crowds to the cinemas. Spike Lee could not have been unaware of the attraction a black woman on the screen, presented as an erotic being, would have for an American audience. This is why he makes Nola the central figure. It is around Nola, not around male sexuality, and certainly not around black women's views on sexually promiscuous young men, that the film revolves.

To understand the attraction of *SGHI*, we have to move beyond the image of Nola Darling on screen, and examine the combination of black + woman + sex in the context of the politics of gender and race, both in the historical and current political context. These, then, are the questions on which the following section focuses.

The black woman and sexuality

Black sexuality has historically been defined by white racism to justify its perception of the inferiority of black people. That perception has always been explicit. Blacks, considered lower on the evolutionary ladder, have always been considered more sexually active than whites. In the United States that notion of black sexuality has its roots in the history of slavery. Black sexuality was used to the economic advantage of white slavers, particularly after the banning of direct importation of enslaved Africans, when the reproduction of an enslaved workforce had to be ensured. The image of the black woman as breeder played a crucial role in the reproduction of the workforce. As T.F. Gossett suggests:

> The market required that a brutal emphasis be placed upon the stud capabilities of the black man and upon the black woman's fertility . . . she was labeled sexually promiscuous because it was important that her womb supply the labor force. (Gossett, 1965: 48)

Black women were, therefore, subjected to ruthless exploitation of their sexuality. The rape of black women by white slavers was one of the more acute manifestations of this exploitation. The perception of a black woman's sexuality was damaged for all time, and out of this exploitation grew the image of a black woman as 'not only emotionally callous but physically invulnerable' (Wallace, 1979: 138).

Through history, the image of the black female as breeder has remained dominant. Even black resistance movements have failed to address, let alone unseat, this view. In the 1960s the black power movement never challenged dominant images of black female sexuality. Black power was explicitly expressed as the pursuit of black manhood. The manhood that black male activists like Malcolm X proclaimed was black patriarchy, and the black woman had only one place in it – on her back. Even the young George Jackson wrote from his prison cell: 'Black Mama, you're going to have to stop making cowards . . . Black Mama, your overriding concern with the survival of our sons is mistaken if it is a survival at the cost of their manhood' (Jackson, 1971: 220). He talked of a manhood that excluded women, for he too had heard Malcolm X, Stokely Carmichael and Eldridge Cleaver all proclaim black manhood as the essence of black power. The black woman was asked not to do anything that would stand in his way and, more importantly, not to threaten his manhood. As Michelle Wallace points out:

> The message of the Black Movement was that I was being watched, on probation as a Black woman, that any signs of aggressiveness, intelligence or independence would mean I'd be denied even the one role still left open to me – my man's woman. . . . Black men were threatening me with being deserted, with being alone. (Wallace, 1979: 138)

This message produced its own antagonisms, within black sexual politics, between black men and black women. This position remains largely unchanged in the 1980s. It is, however, a position that has started to change as black women, influenced by feminist politics, are trying to define their own reality as black women. A reality that can be uncomfortable for black men and which requires a re-examination of black sexual politics, a task which the black power movement of the 1960s singularly failed to address. Women were defined then as men's possessions and 'as a possession, the black woman was of little use to the revolution except as a performer of drudgery' (Wallace et al., 1982: 7).

Today, black women such as Alice Walker are trying to redefine black sexual politics, and it is in this context that the film *SGHI* has been made, in an attempt once again to restrict a black woman's ability to assert her independence. Nola Darling, beautiful, independent and black, is the very embodiment of a black woman's threat to black manhood. Spike Lee speaks of his film as being 'an antidote' to Alice Walker, and it is on this basis that he justifies making *SGHI*.

Notes

Felly Nkweto Simmonds is from Zambia and has lived and worked as a teacher in Zambia, Tanzania and Sierra Leone, and as a development education worker in Britain. She has recently completed an MA in Interdisciplinary Women's Studies at Warwick University, and she is currently living in Tanzania and researching a book on women and education in Zambia.

This article arises out of initial discussions in Birmingham in March 1987: discussions about whether issues of black female sexuality have a place in black politics. As part of the International Women's Day celebrations, Vokani Film Circuit showed a series of films on and about women. *She's Gotta Have It* was one of the films shown. Since then it has gone into general circulation and beyond all-women viewings, but has been discussed privately by many women, especially black women.

I could not have written this article without the support of my friends, Helle Johansen and especially Inge Blackman, who in the end bore the brunt of some of the anger aroused in some men by our daring to discuss black female sexuality in public.

References

Alexander, Karen (1987) review of *She's Gotta Have It, Spare Rib*, 176 (March): 32.

Attille, Martina and Blackwood, Maureen (1986) 'Black women and representation', in C. Brunsdon (ed.), *Films for Women*. London: BFI.

Baron, Saskia (1987) 'Kiss me in black and white', *City Limits*, 282 (26 February–5 March): 15, 17.

Brunsdon, C. (ed.) (1986) *Films for Women*. London: BFI.

Dworkin, Andrea (1981) *Pornography: Men Possessing Women*. London: Women's Press.

Gossett, T.F. (1965) *Race: The History of an Idea in America*. New York: Schocken Books.

Haskell, Molly (1975) *From Reverence to Rape: The Treatment of Women in the Movies*. London: New English Library.

Jackson, George (1971) *Soledad Brother: The Prison Letters of George Jackson*. Harmondsworth: Penguin.

Kramarae, C. and Treichler, P.A. (1985) *A Feminist Dictionary*. London: Pandora Press.

Lee, S. (1986) *Film Comment* (October). Film Society of Lincoln.

Lee, S. (1987) *Ebony* BBC 1: transcript ref. 1/NBM JH 646T.

Wallace, Michelle (1979) *Black Macho and the Myth of the Superwoman*. London: John Calder.

Wallace, M., Tull, G., Scott, P.B. and Smith, B. (1982) *But Some of Us Are Brave*. New York: Feminist Press.

Reading Buchi Emecheta: Contests for Women's Experience in Women's Studies

Donna Haraway

I am regularly responsible for teaching 'Methological Issues in the Study of Women', a required course in a women's studies major. In the present potent political moment, the intense intersections and co-constructions of feminist theory, the critique of colonial discourse, and anti-racist theory have fundamentally restructured individually and collectively the always contested meanings of what counts as 'women's experience' . . . Here I want to inspect a small part of the apparatus for the discursive production of women's experience in the women's studies classrooms which I inhabit and for which I am accountable to and with others in the circuits of women's movement.

A typical class might begin with the serious logical joke that, especially for the complex category and even more complex people called 'women', A and not-A are likely simultaneously true. This correct exaggeration insists that even the simplest matters in feminist analysis require contradictory moments and a wariness of their resolution, dialectically or otherwise. 'Situated knowledges' is a shorthand term for this insistence. Situated knowledges build in accountability.[1] Being situated in an ungraspable middle space characterizes actors whose worlds might be described by branching bushes like the map or bush of consciousness I have drawn in Figure 1.[2] Situated knowledges are particularly powerful tools to produce maps of consciousness for people who have been inscribed within the marked categories of race and sex that have been so exuberantly produced in the histories of masculinist, racist and colonialist dominations. Situated knowledges are always *marked* knowledges; they are re-markings, reorientings, of the great maps that globalized the heterogeneous body of the world in the history of masculinist capitalism and colonialism.

From *Women*, 1 (3), 1990, pp. 240–55.

AaBbCcDdEeFfGgHhIiJjKkLlMmNnOoPpQqRrSsTtUuVvWwXxYyZz

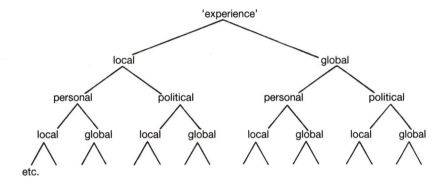

Figure 1   *'Bush' or 'map' of women's consciousness/experience*

The 'bush of women's consciousness' or the 'bush of women's experience' is a simple diagrammatic model for indicating how feminist theory and the critical study of colonial discourse intersect with each other in terms of two crucial binary pairs; i.e. *local / global* and *personal / political*. While the tones of personal/political sound most strongly in feminist discourse, and local/global in the critical theory of colonial discourse, both binaries are tools essential to the construction of each. Also, of course, each term of the binary constructs its opposite. I have put the pair 'local/global' at the top of the diagram. To begin, drawing from a particular descriptive practice (which can never simply be innocently available; descriptions are *produced*) place an account of 'women's experience' or 'women's consciousness' at the top. The simple 'dichotomizing machine' immediately bifurcates the experience into two aspects, 'local/global' or 'personal/ political'. Wherever one begins, each term in turn bifurcates: the 'local' into 'personal/political' and the 'global' into 'personal/political'. Similarly, continuing indefinitely, every instance of the analytical pair 'personal/ political' splits on each side into 'local/global'.

The bush plainly does not guarantee unmediated access to some unfixable referent of 'women's experience'. However, the bush does guarantee an open, branching discourse with a high likelihood of reflexivity about its own interpretative and productive technology. Its very arbitrariness and its inescapable encrustings within the traditions of Western rhetoric and semantics are virtues for feminist projects that simultaneously construct the potent object, 'women's experience', and insist on the webs of account-ability and politics inherent in the specific form that this artefact takes on.

I suggest that this simple little diagram-machine is a beginning geometry for sketching some of the multiple ways that anti-colonial and feminist discourses speak to each other and require each other for their own analytical progress. One can work one's way through the analytical/ descriptive bush, making decisions to *exclude* certain regions of the map; for example, by concentrating only on the global dimension of a political aspect of a particular local experience. But the rest of the bush is implicitly present, providing a resonant echo chamber for any particular tracing through the bush of 'women's experience'.

So, risking falling into the 'tourism of the soul' that Wendy Rose warned against, I will outline three different readings of a popular author, most of whose readers probably have no interest in women's studies, but whose fiction appears in women's studies' courses and is also an object of contention in womanist/feminist literary criticism and politics. Before engaging these three readings, consider a short construction of the text of the text of the author's life, a text that will become part of my stakes in reading her fiction. The author is Buchi Emecheta, born in Nigeria in 1944 of Ibuza background. Emecheta married in 1962 and went to London with her husband, who had a student fellowship. In England, the couple had five children in difficult circumstances, and the marriage ended painfully. Emecheta found herself a single mother in London, Black, immigrant, on welfare, in public housing, and going to school for a degree in library science and then for a PhD in sociology.[3]

Emecheta also became a writer. Her becoming a writer was constituted from those webs of 'experience' implicit in the biographical text in the last paragraph. She was a mother, an immigrant, an independent woman, an African, an Ibo, an activist, a 'been to', a writer. It is said that her husband destroyed her first manuscript because he could not bear the idea that his wife was thinking and acting for herself (Schipper, 1984: 44). She published a series of novels that are simultaneously pedagogical, popular, historical, political, autobiographical, romantic – and contentious.

Let us study the dust jackets and reference library text on Emecheta's life a little further. Besides learning about the academic degrees, a job as a sociologist, and her habit of rising to write in the early hours of the day, we learn that in addition to children's novels she has written eight other novels, including *The Joys of Motherhood* (1979), available in the prestigious African Writers Series, whose founding editor was Chinua Achebe, author of *Things Fall Apart* and other internationally renowned fiction. In the UK, Emecheta's work is published by Allen & Unwin and by Allison & Busby, in the US by Braziller, and in Nigeria by Ogwugwu Afor. Until recently, it was easier to purchase Emecheta's fiction in the UK or the US than in Nigeria. Emecheta's writing is read as mass market paperbacks on subways in Britain more than it is read in classrooms. Her work is now published simultaneously in Africa and the West, and it is part of debates among African Anglophone readers. In part because of its treatment of African women's issues by an expatriate identified with feminism, Emecheta's writing is controversial, perhaps especially in Nigeria and among political academics everywhere it is read.

The Dutch critic, Mineke Schipper (1985: 46), claimed that 'Emecheta's novels are extremely popular in Nigeria and elsewhere, but they have sometimes been coolly received or even ignored by African critics'. Emecheta's relations to feminism and the relations of her readers to feminism are very much at the heart of this matter. Adopting a perspective that bell hooks in the United States named intrinsic to feminist movement, in an interview in 1979 Emecheta in an account of her writing explicitly refused to restrict her attention only to women:

> The main themes of my novels are African society and family: the historical, social, and political life in Africa as seen by a woman through events. I always try to show that the African male is oppressed and he too oppresses the African woman . . . I have not committed myself to the cause of African women only, I write about Africa as a whole. (Bruner, 1983: 49)

The Joys of Motherhood, set roughly in the 1920s and 1930s in Nigeria, treated the conflicts and multi-layered contradictions in the life of a young married woman who was unable to conceive a child. The woman subsequently conceived all too many children, but only after she lost access to her own trading networks and so lost her own income. The mother moved from village to city; and her children emigrated to Canada, the United States and Australia. Although she had many sons, she died childless in an extraordinarily painful story of the confrontation of urban and village realities for women in early twentieth-century Nigeria.

But, as for Achebe, for Emecheta also there is no moment of innocence in Africa's history before the fall into the conflict between 'tradition' and 'modernity'. Much of Emecheta's fiction is set in Ibuza early in the twentieth century, where the great patterns of cultural syncretism in Africa were the matrix of the characters' lives. In *The Bride Price* (1976) and *The Slave Girl* (1977), Emecheta explored fundamental issues around marriage, control of one's life from different women's points of view, and the contradictory positions, especially for her Ibuza women characters, in every location on the African cultural map, whether marked foreign or indigenous. Life in Europe was no less the locus of struggle for Emecheta's characters. *Second-Class Citizen* (1975) explored the breakup of the protagonist's marriage in London. *In the Ditch* (1972, 2nd edn 1979) followed the main character as a single mother into residence in British public housing and her solidarity with white and coloured, working-class, British, women's and feminist organizations challenging the terms of the welfare state. *The Double Yoke* (1983) returned to Nigeria in the late twentieth century to take up again Emecheta's interrogation of the terms of women's struggles in the local and global webs of the African diaspora, viewed from a fictional reconstruction of the paths of travel from and to a minority region in Nigeria.[4]

In a course that I taught in 1987 called 'Methodological Issues in the Study of Women', the students read politically engaged essays by two literary theorists who placed Emecheta in their paradigms of women's fiction and women's unity in the African diaspora. One was by Barbara Christian, a professor of Afro-American Studies at the University of California at Berkeley and a pioneer of Black feminist literary criticism, and the other was by Chikwenye Okonjo Ogunyemi, a professor teaching Afro-American and African literature in the English Department at the University of Ibadan in Nigeria. With women from Ibadan and Ife, Ogunyemi participated in 1988 in a group developing women's studies in Nigeria (Tola Olu Pearce, personal communication). She has published on Emecheta's fiction elsewhere (in a German journal); but in the text we read in class, it was Ogunyemi's explicit marginalization of Emecheta that organized our reading of her essay in its particular publishing context and in other political aspects. Barbara Christian published *Black Feminist Criticism* (1985) in the Athena series of Pergamon Press, a major feminist series in British and US women's studies publishing. The third reading was my own, developed from the perspectives of a Euro-American women's studies teacher in a largely white state university in the United States, and first delivered in a conference co-constructing the critical study of colonial discourse and feminist theory. I wanted my women's studies undergraduate students to read, misread, reread, and so reflect on the field of possible readings of a particular contested author, including the discursive constructions of her life on the literal surfaces of the published novels themselves. These readings were directed to fictions in which many people had considerable stakes – the publishers, Emecheta, Ogunyemi, Christian, myself, each of the students, and those anonymous readers of thousands of paperbacks in several nations. I wanted us to watch how those stakes locate readers in a map of women's self-consciously liberatory discourses, including constructions, such as 'womanism', that place 'feminism' under erasure and propose a different normative genealogy for women's movement. The goal was to make these critically reflexive readings open up the complexities of location and affinities in partially allied, partially oppositional drawings of maps of women's consciousness in the local/ global, personal/political webs of situated knowledges.

First, let us examine how Ogunyemi (1985: 66–7) read – or declined to read – Emecheta in an essay published for a largely non-African audience in *Signs: Journal of Women in Culture and Society*, a major scholarly organ of feminist theory in the United States. Out of seventeen international correspondents for *Signs* in 1987, one was from Africa – Achola Pala of Kenya. Many *Signs* essays are assigned in women's studies courses, where most, but by no means all, of the students would be Euro-Americans. Ogunyemi's essay was an argument to distance herself from the label 'feminist' and to associate herself with the marker 'womanist'. She argued that she had independently developed that term and then found Alice Walker's working of it. Ogunyemi produced an archaeology or mapping of African and Afro-American Anglophone women's literature since the end of colonization, roughly from the 1960s. The map led to a place of political hope, called 'womanism'. Ogunyemi used the word to designate a woman committed to the survival of the wholeness of the 'entire people', men and women, Africa and the people of its diaspora. She located her discourse on Emecheta in the diaspora's joining of Afro-Caribbean, Afro-American and African Anglophone literatures. Ogunyemi argued that a womanist represents a particular moment of maturity that affirms the unity of the whole people through a multi-layered exploration of the experiences of women as 'mothers of the people'. The mother binding up the wounds of a scattered people was an important image, potent for womanist movement away from both Black male chauvinism and feminist negativism, iconoclasm and immaturity.

But Ogunyemi's principal image was somewhat oblique to that of the mother; it was a *married woman*. Ogunyemi read the fiction since the 1960s in order to construct the relationships of women in the diaspora as 'amicable co-wives with an invisible husband' (1985: 74). Since her archaeology of Anglophone African and African-American literature located the traces of womanism in Black foremothers-as-writers, Ogunyemi rejected Emecheta. Her fiction did not affirm marriage as the image of full maturity that could represent the unity of Black people internationally. Quite the opposite, Emecheta's explorations frequently involved an account of the failure of marriage. In particular, far from recuperating polygamy as an image for liberatory women's movement, Emecheta regarded the practice as a 'decaying institution' that would disappear 'as women became more and more educated and free to decide for themselves' (Bruner, 1983: 49). Emecheta's fiction has a sharp edge on marriage throughout, even where it is most affirmed, as in *The Double Yoke*. Seeing the novelist's characters as merely rebellious, Ogunyemi treated Emecheta's fictional and personal relation to marriage harshly, even scornfully, stating that she started to write 'after a marital fiasco', that her writing feminizes Black men, and that she finally kills off her heroines in childbirth, enslavement in marriage, insanity, or abandonment by their children. Ogunyemi went so far as to claim, 'Emecheta's destruction of her heroines is a feminist trait that can be partly attributed to narcissism on the part of the writer' (1985: 67).

Emecheta in political action allied herself with Irish and British feminists and developed an international discourse quite different from Ogunyemi's account of womanism. In addition to criticizing Emecheta's discourse on and history in relation to marriage, Ogunyemi highlighted Emecheta's exile status. Having lived abroad for twenty years, Emecheta returned to Nigeria to teach in 1980–81 as a senior research fellow at the University of Calabar. In her article, Ogunyemi problematized Emecheta's 'authenticity' as a returned emigrant writer. In Ogunyemi's archaeology of African Anglophone literature, socialism, feminism and lesbianism all stood explicitly for an immature moment, perhaps recuperable later, but for the moment not incorporable within the voices of the 'co-wives', who figured a normative kind of Black women's unity. Womanism meant that the demands of 'culture' take precedence over those of 'sexual politics'. Because of that relationship, for the womanist writer who still does not forget the inequities of patriarchy, 'the matrilineal and polygynous societies in Africa are dynamic sources for the womanist novel' (1985: 76). Ogunyemi proposed a logic of inclusion and exclusion in an emerging literary canon as part of a politics about nationalism, gender and internationalism, argued through the central images of polygynous African marriage.

Barbara Christian had very different stakes in reading Emecheta. In *Black Feminist Criticism* (1985) Christian read *The Joys of Motherhood* (1979) in close relation with Alice Walker's *Meridian* (1976), in order specifically to reclaim a matrilineal tradition around the images of a particular feminism that Christian's text foregrounds. Christian located this discourse on matrilineal connection and mothering in these two important novels of the 1970s in order to discuss the simultaneous exaltation and disruption/ destruction of mothering for Black women in African traditions, in Afro-American slavery, and in post-slavery and post-civil rights movement contexts in the United States.[5] She uncovered the contradictions and complexities of mothering, reflecting on the many ways in which it is both enjoyed, celebrated, enforced, and turned into a double bind for women in all of those historical locations. So while Christian sounded a faint note of a lost utopian moment of mothering before the 'invaders' came, the invaders were not only the white slave traders. Rather the invaders seemed to be coeval with mothering; the world is always already fallen apart.

But the mother was no more Christian's fundamental image for the unity of women in the African diaspora through time and space than the mother was for Ogunyemi. Christian read *Meridian* and *The Joys of Motherhood* in delicate echo with each other in order to foreground a particular kind of feminism that also carried with it an agenda of affirming lesbianism within Black feminism and within the model of the inheritance from Africa of the tie between mother and daughter, caring for each other in the impossible conditions of a world that constantly disrupts the caring. Barbara Christian was committed to forbidding the marginalization of lesbianism in feminist discourse by women of colour, and she subtly enlisted Emecheta as one of her texts, for precisely the same reasons that Ogunyemi excluded Emecheta from her genealogy of womanism in the African diaspora. But like Ogunyemi, Christian proposed a narrative of maturation in the history of the writing of her literary foremothers. . . .

Christian's narrative schematized the history of Afro-American women writers' consciousness in terms of a chronology with suggestive similarities to and differences from Ogunyemi's. Christian argued that, before about 1950, American Black women wrote for audiences that largely excluded them-selves. Christian characterized the fiction as other-directed, rather than inward-searching, in response to the dominating white society's racist definitions of Black women. (Zora Neale Hurston was the exception to the pattern.) Christian traced a process of initial self-definition in the 1950s and the emergence of attention to the ordinary dark-skinned Black women. Roughly, the 1960s was a decade of finding unity in shared Blackness, the

1970s a period of exposure of sexism in the Black community, and the 1980s a time of emergence of a diverse culture of Black women engaged in finding selfhood and forming connections among women that promised to transcend race and class in a worldwide community patterned on the ties of mother and daughter. In the 1980s, the terrain for the growing understanding of the personhood of Black women, figured in the fictions of the diaspora, was worldwide.

I will conclude by suggesting a third non-innocent reading of Emecheta's fiction – my own, as a Euro-American, middle-class, university-based feminist, who produced this reading as part of a pedagogical practice in US women's studies in the 1980s, in a class in which white students greatly outnumbered students of colour and women greatly outnumbered men. Enmeshed in the debates about postmodernism, the multiplicity of women's self-crafted and imposed social subjectivities, and questions about the possibility of feminist politics in late twentieth-century global and local worlds, my own stakes were in the potent ambiguities of Emecheta's fiction and of the fictions of her life. My reading valorized her heterogeneous statuses as exile, Nigerian, Ibo, Irish-British feminist, Black woman, writer canonized in the African Writers Series, popular writer published in cheap paperback books and children's literature, librarian, welfare mother, sociologist, single woman, reinventor of African tradition, deconstructor of African tradition, member of the Advisory Council to the British Home Secretary on race and equality, subject of contention among committed multiracial womanist and feminist theorists, and international figure. As for Ogunyemi and Christian, there was a utopian moment nestled in my reading, one that hoped for a space for political accountability and for cherishing ambiguities, multiplicities and affinities without freezing identities. These risk being the pleasures of the eternal tourist of experience in devastated postmodern terrains. But I wanted to stay with affinities that refused to resolve into identities or searches for a true self. My reading naturalized precisely the moment of ambiguity, the exile status and the dilemma of a 'been-to' for whom the time of origins and returns is inaccessible. Contradiction held in tension with the crafting of accountability was my image of the hoped for unity of women across the holocaust of imperialism, racism and masculinist supremacy. This was a feminist image that figured not mothers and daughters, co-wives, sisters or lesbian lovers, but adopted families and imperfect intentional communities, based not so much on 'choice' as on hope and memory of the always already fallen apart structure of the world. I valued in Emecheta the similarities to the post-holocaust reinvented 'families' in the fiction of Afro-American SF writer, Octavia Butler, as tropes to guide 'us' through the ravages of gender, class, imperialism, racism and nuclear exterminist global culture.

My reading of Emecheta drew from *The Double Yoke* (1983), in which the incoherent demands on and possibilities for women in the collision of 'tradition' and 'modernity' are interrogated. At the same time, what counts as 'traditional' or 'modern' emerges as highly problematic. The fictions important to the intersection of postmodernism, feminism and post-colonial local/global webs begin with the book as a material object and the biographical fragments inscribed on it that construct the author's life for international Anglophone audiences. In the prose of the dust-jacket, the author metamorphosed from the earlier book-jackets' accounts of the woman with five children, on welfare and simultaneously going to school, who rose at 4 a.m. in order to write her first six novels, into a senior research fellow at Nigeria's University of Calabar and a member of the Arts Council of Great Britain. There are many Emechetas on the different dust-jackets, but all of these texts insist on joining the images of a mother, writer and émigré Nigerian in London.

A short synopsis must serve to highlight the multiple criss-crossing worlds of ethnicity, region, gender, religion, 'tradition' and 'modernity', social class, and professional status in which Emecheta's characters reinvent their senses of self and their commitments and connections to each other. In *The Double Yoke*, a 'been-to', Miss Bulewao, taught creative writing to a group of mainly young men at the University of Calabar. Framed by Miss Bulewao's assignment to the students and her response to the moral dilemmas posed in one man's story, the core of the novel was the essay submitted by Ete Kamba, who had fallen in love with a young woman, Nko, who lived a mile from his village. Nko, a young Efik woman, came from a different ethnic group from Ete Kamba, an Ikikio. Hoping to marry, both were at the university on scholarship and both had complicated obligations to parents as well as ambitions of their own. But gender made their situations far from symmetrical. . . . Emecheta sketched the University of Calabar as a microcosm of the contending forces within post-independence Nigeria, including the New Christian movement, Islamic identities, demands of ethnic groups, economic constraints from both family and national locations in the global economy, contradictions between village and university, and controversy over 'foreign' ideologies such as feminism.

All of these structured the consequences of the love between Ete Kamba and Nko. The pair had intercourse one night outside the village, and afterwards he was consumed with worry over whether Nko was or was not still a virgin, since they had had intercourse with their clothes on and standing up. It was crucial to him that she was still a virgin if he was to marry her. Nko refused to answer his obsessive questions about her virginity. This novel rejects images of matrilineality linking mother and daughter and of the community of women as co-wives as emblems of collective unity. Instead a deconstruction of 'virginity' structures this novel's arguments about origins, authenticity and women's positions in constructing the potent unit called 'the people' in the heterogeneous worlds of post-independence Nigeria. The young man went for advice to an elder of Nko's village, who was also a faculty member and a leader of the American-inspired, revivalist, New Christian movement at the university. The professor, religious leader, and model family man had been sexually harassing Nko, who was also his student; and following Ete Kamba's visit, the elder man forced her into a sexual relation in which she became pregnant.

Nko told Ete Kamba that whether he called her 'virgin', 'prostitute' or 'wife', those were all his names. She came to the university to get a degree by the fruits of her own study. If she were forced to get her degree through negotiating the tightening webs of sexualization drawn around her, she would still not flatten into the blank sheet on which would be written the text of post-colonial 'woman'. She would not allow the local/global and personal/political contradictions figured in Ete Kamba's need for her to be an impossible symbol of non-contradiction and purity to define who she – and they – might be. Perhaps Emecheta's fiction should be read to argue that women like Nko struggle to prevent post-colonial discourse being written by others on the terrain of their bodies, as so much of colonial discourse was. Perhaps Emecheta is arguing that African women will no longer be figures for any of the great images of Woman, whether voiced by the colonizer or by the indigenous nationalist – virgin, whore, mother, sister or co-wife. Something else is happening for which names have hardly been uttered in any region of the great Anglophone diaspora. Perhaps part of this process will mean that, locally and globally, women's part in the building of persons, families and communities cannot be fixed in any of the names of Woman and her functions.

Ete Kamba related his dilemma and Nko's story in his assigned essay for Miss Bulewao, who called him in to talk. In a wonderful depiction of a faculty–student meeting where the personal, political and academic are profoundly interwined, Miss Bulewao advised Ete Kamba to marry the woman he loved. The young man was absent when the papers were passed back; he had gone to join Nko, who had returned to her village to bury her father. Their marriage was left open.

Ogunyemi's, Christian's, and my readings of Emecheta are all grounded in the texts of the published fiction; and all are part of a contemporary struggle to articulate sensitively specific and powerfully collective women's liberatory discourses. Inclusions and exclusions are not determined in advance by fixed categories of race, gender, sexuality or nationality. 'We' are accountable for the inclusions and exclusions, identifications and separations, produced in the highly political practices called reading fiction. *To whom* we are accountable is part of what is produced in the readings, imposed readings, and imagined readings of a text that is originally and finally never simply there. Just as the world is *originally* fallen apart, the text is always already enmeshed in contending practices and hopes. From our very specific, non-innocent positions in the local/global and personal/ political terrain of contemporary mappings of women's consciousness, each of these readings is a pedagogic practice, working through the naming of the power-charged differences, specificities and affinities that structure the potent, world-changing artefacts called 'women's experience'. In difference is the irretrievable loss of the illusion of the one.

Notes

A slightly shortened version of an essay published in Donna Haraway, *Simians, Cyborgs, and Women: The Reinvention of Nature* (London, Free Association Books, 1990 and New York: Routledge, 1991).

This paper has been revised from a talk at the Feminism and the Critical Study of Colonial Discourse Conference at UCSC in the spring of 1987. Proceedings were published in *Inscriptions*, 3/4 (1988). Thanks especially to organizers of the conference (Deborah Gordon, Lisa Bloom, Vivek Dareshawar) and co-member of the panel (Teresa de Lauretis).

1. At the heart of US feminist theory in the 1980s has been an effort to articulate the specificity of location from which politics and knowledge must be built.

2. Trinh T. Minh-ha (1986–7: 3–38; 1988: 71–7; 1989) discusses this ungraspable middle space and develops her theory of the 'inappropriate/d other' as a figure for post-colonial women.

3. On Emecheta see Schipper (1985: 44–6), Bruner (1983: 49–50). See also Brown (1981), Taiwo (1984), Davies and Graves (1986), Jameson (1986).

4. Caren Kaplan (1986–7, 1987) movingly and incisively theorized the 'deterritorializations' in feminist discourse and the importance of displacement in the fictions constructing post-colonial subjectivity. Writing of Alicia Dujovne Ortiz's novel *Buenos Aires*, Kaplan formulated a reading practice that might also be engaged for Emecheta's novels: '*Buenos Aires* reinvents identity as a form of self-conscious cultural criticism. Displacement is a force in the modern world which can be reckoned with, not to heal splits but to explore them, to acknowledge the politics and limits of cultural processes' (Kaplan, 1986–7: 98).

5. *The Nation* for 24–31 July 1989, edited and written by Black women, examines 'The scapegoating of the Black family'. See especially Jewell Handy Gresham, 'The politics of family in America' (pp. 116–22). See also Collins (1989b) for an analysis of the attacks on Black mothers and families in the last twenty years in the US and the use of gender to demonstrate racial inferiority. Carby (1987) analyses Black women's discourse on mothering and racial uplift in the late nineteenth and early twentieth centuries in terms of a specific non-racist and non-patriarchal reconstruction of womanhood. The contested and heterogeneous discourse of US 'Black feminist criticism' could be traced from Smith (1977).

References

Brown, Lloyd (ed.) (1981) *Women Writers of Black Africa*. Westport, CT: Greenwood Press.

Bruner, Charlotte H. (ed.) (1983) *Unwinding Threads: Writing by Women in Africa*. London and Ibadan: Heinemann.

Carby, Hazel (1987) *Reconstructing Womanhood: The Emergence of the Afro-American Woman Novelist*. New York: Oxford University Press.

Christian, Barbara (1985) *Black Feminist Criticism: Perspectives on Black Women Writers*. New York: Pergamon.

Collins, Patricia Hill (1989a) 'The social construction of Black feminist thought', *Signs*, 14 (4): 745–73.

Collins, Patricia Hill (1989b). 'A comparison of two works on Black family life', *Signs*, 14 (4): 875–84.

Davies, Carole Boyce and Graves, Anne Adams (eds) (1986) *Ngambika: Studies of Women in African Literature*. Trenton: Africa World.

Emecheta, Buchi (1979) *The Joys of Motherhood*. New York: Braziller.

Emecheta, Buchi (1983) *Double Yoke*. New York: Braziller; London and Ibuza: Ogwugwu Afor.

Haraway, Donna J. (1989) 'Review of A. Ong, *Spirits of Resistance and Capitalist Discipline*', *Signs*, 14 (4): 945–7.

hooks, bell (1981) *Ain't I a Woman*. Boston: South End.

hooks bell (1984) *Feminist Theory: From Margin to Center*. Boston: South End.

Jameson, Frederic (1986) 'Third World literature in the era of multinational capitalism', *Social Text*, 151: 65–88.

Kaplan, Caren (1986–7) 'The politics of displacement in *Buenos Aires*', *Discourse*, 8: 84–100.

King, Katie (1986) 'The situation of lesbianism as feminism's magical sign: contests for meaning and the US women's movement, 1968–72', *Communication*, 9 (1): 65–92.

King, Katie (1988) 'Audre Lorde's lacquered layerings: the lesbian bar as a site of literary production', *Cultural Studies*, 2 (3): 321–42.

King, Katie (forthcoming) 'Producing sex, theory, and culture: gay/straight remappings in contemporary feminism', in Marianne Hirsch and Evelyn Keller (eds), *Conflicts in Feminism*.

De Lauretis, Teresa (1984) *Alice Doesn't: Feminism, Semiotics, Cinema*. Bloomington: Indiana University Press.

Lorde, Audre (1982) *Zami, a New Spelling of My Name*. Trumansberg, NY: Crossing.

Minh-ha, Trinh T. (1986–7) 'Introduction', and 'Difference: "a special third world women issue" ', *Discourse*, 8 (Winter): 3–38.

Minh-ha, Trinh T. (1988) 'Not you/like you: post-colonial women and the interlocking questions of identity and difference', *Inscription*, 3/4: 71–7.

Minh-ha, Trinh T. (1989) *Woman, Native, Other: Writing Postcoloniality and Feminism*. Bloomington: Indiana University Press.

Mohanty, Chandra Talpade (1984) 'Under western eyes: feminist scholarship and colonial discourse', *Boundary*, 2, 3 (12/13): 333–58.

Mohanty, Chandra Talpade (1988) 'Feminist encounters: locating the politics of experience', *Copyright*, 1: 30–44.

Ogunyemi, Chikwenye Okonjo (1985) 'Womanism: the dynamics of the contemporary Black female novel in English', *Signs*, 11 (1): 63–80.

Reagon, Bernice Johnson (1983) 'Coalition politics: turning the century', in B. Smith (ed.), *Home Girls: A Black Feminist Anthology*. New York: Kitchen Table, Women of Color Press. pp. 356–68.

Rich, Adrienne (1986) 'Notes toward a politics of location', in *Blood, Bread, and Poetry: Selected Prose, 1979–85*. New York: Norton. pp. 210–31.

Schipper, Mineke (1985) 'Women and literature in Africa', in Mineke Schipper (ed.), *Unheard Words: Women and Literature in Africa, the Arab World, Asia, the Caribbean and Latin America*, trans. Barbara Potter Fasting. London: Allison & Busby. pp. 22–58.

Smith, Barbara (1977) 'Toward a Black feminist criticism', in Elaine Showalter (ed.) (1985), *The New Feminist Criticism: Essays on Women, Literature and Theory*. New York: Pantheon. pp. 168–85.

Smith, Barbara (ed.) (1983) *Home Girls: A Black Feminist Anthology*. New York: Kitchen Table, Women of Color Press.

Taiwo, Oladele (1984) *Female Novelists of Modern Africa*. New York: St Martin's.

Feminism and Culture – the Movie: A Critical Overview of Writing on Women and Cinema

Maria Lauret

Stage one: images of women, realism and semiotics

The first book-length studies of women in film appeared in the early to mid-1970s and were an integral part of the women's movement's push for cultural and political change. These studies concentrated on images of women, a type of criticism which views films as cultural forms imbued with sexist ideology. This sexism was traced in the stereotyping of women (the madonna/whore dichotomy of classic Hollywood is a well-known example), and critics implicitly or explicitly called for an authentic women's cinema which would portray *real women* as they *really* are. The titles of Marjorie Rosen's *Popcorn Venus* (1973) and Molly Haskell's *From Reverence to Rape* (1974) indicate this concern with images; both books aim at giving a survey of representations of women in Hollywood film. Haskell was almost immediately criticized, however, for operating on an untheorized assumption of a direct relation between *representations of women*, in the world of cinematic fantasy (the 'dream-machine') and *real women* in the world of social and economic relations. As part of a journalistic and sociological school of film-viewing, Haskell's work tended to ask 'why *this* film *now*?'; this approach assumes by and large that unambiguous answers can be given, that ideology (sexism) can be 'read off' the film text, as, for example, in Haskell's well-known argument that the violence against women and the absence of big female leading parts in the films of the 1970s was a matter of a backlash against an emerging women's movement. (Haskell, 1974; Kuhn, 1982)

On the production side the early phase of feminist film was characterized by an interest in realism, whether in man-made liberal feminist Hollywood efforts such as *An Unmarried Woman* (Mazursky, 1977), *A Woman Under the Influence* (Cassavetes, 1974) and *Alice Doesn't Live Here Anymore*

From *Women*, 2 (1), 1991, pp. 52–69.

(Scorsese, 1975), or in the making of documentary. The latter, facilitated by the arrival of the cheaper 16 mm and 8 mm formats, represented an exciting departure for feminist film-makers. Often working in small cooperatives and adopting the techniques of the earlier *cinéma vérité* (fly on the wall), feminists engaged in the filming of women by women. Unlike traditional documentary, the authority of voice-over was replaced with the autobiographical discourse of women talking on camera about themselves as simply and directly as possible. Personal testimonies were presented in films such as *Joyce at 34* and *Janie's Janie*, but there were also collective 'her' stories. *Union Maids, The Life and Times of Rosie the Riveter* and, in this country, *Women of the Rhondda* are products of early feminist oral history, often interspersed with historical documentary footage. Critique followed hot on the heels of this pioneering work. Films such as Citron's *Daughter Rite* adopted a format borrowed from the personal testimony (the diary, the autobiographical voice) but exposed the illusory nature of 'unmediated' film-making by revealing in the credits that the two women who had been reminiscing in the film were in fact actresses *playing* sisters (Feuer, 1986; Lesage, 1986).[1]

Problematization of 'images of women' criticism and its counterpart in realist documentary film-making became a major theme in feminist film criticism of the mid- to late 1970s, on the grounds that realism created an illusory notion of transparency which could only reaffirm, not undermine dominant commonsense notions of the subject as (bourgeois) individual and of reality as fixed, accessible and 'there'. A typical statement of this position was Claire Johnston's argument that in realist feminist film 'what the camera in fact grasps is the "natural" world of dominant ideology' (Johnston, 1976: 214).

Here the role of film-viewer came into play as well, for critics of realist practices argued that the reproduction of 'reality' in documentary film encouraged passive viewing behaviour, reducing spectators to mere consumers of the dominant ideology. B. Ruby Rich's critical comments on *Not a Love Story*, a documentary film about the pornography industry and one of the big hits of feminist realist film-making, were especially powerful in this respect. In an analysis of camera angles Rich demonstrated that despite its ostensible anti-porn content *Not a Love Story* in fact reproduced the voyeuristic position which lends pornography its appeal (Rich, 1986).

In Britain the work of Claire Johnston and Pam Cook on Hollywood films by 1930s and 1940s women directors established an alternative brand of feminist writing on film, introducing criticism which drew on both Marxist theory of ideology (especially Althusser) and on French structuralism and semiotics (Barthes, Lévi-Strauss). Broadening the field of feminist film criticism to include theory, Johnston and Cook sought to understand film as a process of *signification* with its own 'relatively autonomous' ways and means of constructing meanings. These meanings, they insisted, were *not* derived directly from social formations; the 'relative autonomy' of cultural practices (a concept appropriated from the neo-Marxist theory of Louis

Althusser) prohibited any such simple translation from film image to social reality. Using a Barthesian notion of myth, i.e. seeing myth as the signifying process by which ideology is naturalized, and film therefore as a myth-making medium, Johnston and Cook's work was concerned with classic Hollywood cinema. Taking their terms of analysis from the burgeoning new field of semiotics and arguing against an earlier conception of Hollywood as a lost cause for feminism, Johnston and Cook reread the films of women directors such as Ida Lupino and Dorothy Arzner. Focusing on the 'ideological cracks', such as internal contradictions of the film text, they made a case for a women's discourse where it was previously thought none could possibly exist.

However influential, this feminist appropriation of some Hollywood women's films has remained an area of controversy. Any transgression or hidden resistance in films by women directors is, it is argued, in the end always contained by the characteristic movement of narrative closure in Hollywood films made during the studio period, in which women tend to lose out or are victimized.[2]

Stage two: the gaze

As Annette Kuhn has argued, Hollywood as a 'dream-machine' under the studio system worked as a configuration of forces acting together, of which cinematic characteristics, as well as the institutional framework of economic structures and power relations in the industry were an important part. The debate as to whether this institutional framework exercised a determining (ideological) influence on film output has been an ongoing one, but the importance of Claire Johnston's contribution to it in the mid-1970s is that she argued for a *reading* of Hollywood entertainment films which made a space for 'collective fantasies of women's desire' (Johnston, 1976: 217). At more or less the same time, Laura Mulvey took the discussion of women's desire and fantasy out of the realm of the ideological/symbolic. Her article 'Visual pleasure and narrative cinema' (1975) radically changed the terms of the debate on feminism and film and focused them on the (male) gaze. Using psychoanalytical theory, Mulvey argued that narrative fiction film constructs a male gaze, regardless of the gender of the individual spectator. It does this not only in its narrative preoccupations (active male protagonist, with woman as victim or sexual object) but also – and crucially – in its conventions, in the way the camera moves and produces the image on the screen.

> In a world ordered by sexual imbalance, pleasure in looking has been split between active/male and passive/female. The determining male gaze projects its fantasy onto the female figure, which is styled accordingly. In their traditional exhibitionist role women are simultaneously looked at and displayed, with their appearance coded for strong visual and erotic impact so that they can be said to connote *to-be-looked-at-ness*. (Mulvey, 1989: 366)

Using psychoanalysis 'as a political weapon' to understand the *unconscious* determinants of the dominant imaging of women, Mulvey's concern with pleasure in looking took its cue from Freud's theory of scopophilia in early childhood. I outline this theory very briefly here. As the small child tries to find out about other people's bodily functions and especially their genitalia, its pleasure in looking is active and eroticized. Knowledge of sexual difference is thus established in looking. Later in life this early thrill (a combination of pleasure and shock) is reproduced in voyeuristic activities as well as in its converse: narcissism and exhibitionism – presenting oneself to the gaze of the self and others.

Mulvey combined this Freudian explanation of pleasure in looking with the theory of the mirror stage in the work of Jacques Lacan, in which the child's first recognition of itself in the mirror is called a misrecognition, because what the child sees in the mirror is an idealized whole and rounded image at odds with the child's diffuse bodily experience of itself at that stage in its development – it cannot yet control its movements, let alone its environment. This misrecognition later becomes the 'ego ideal' which affords identification with idealized others, and it is this possibility of identification which constitutes another aspect of pleasure in film-viewing, as well as the voyeuristic mode posited by Freud.

Mulvey analysed the mechanism of the filmic gaze as composed of *identification* with the idealized male protagonist on the one hand, and on the other of voyeuristic distanced viewing, a private pleasure which the setting of cinema (the darkened room) encourages. She distinguished three aspects to the gaze: that of the eye of the camera registering the pro-filmic event, that of the spectator viewing the film, and that of the characters on screen looking at each other. Classic narrative film, said Mulvey, constructs a male viewer by privileging the look of the male protagonist at the woman character(s): as the camera follows this fictional male gaze so also is the spectator's look directed at woman as object. Thus the spectator's gaze is 'sewn into', sutures, that of the male.[3]

As if this indictment of classic cinema were not enough, Mulvey also drew attention to the role of castration anxiety in the unconscious dynamic of pleasure and unpleasure of film-viewing. If strong women characters do appear in Hollywood film, this is no consolation for feminists. For the woman as sexual object, displayed as spectacle on the screen in Hollywood cinema, is not just a source of pleasure but also imbued with threat since her lack of a penis implies castration. For the male two responses are possible: dismantling this threat by making the woman submit to his will, or fetishizing her. The image of the 'phallic woman' (such as Dietrich or Mae West) is the product of this latter strategy, whereas the frequent victimization and punishment of women in Hollywood movies is an effect of the former.

Narrative cinema, Mulvey concluded, is a dead loss for feminists. She saw the only viable feminist film practice to be one that breaks up the familiar structures of visual pleasure, thus exposing and problematizing the habitual violence which is the male gaze.

The debate on the male gaze has continued ever since and has had an impact on feminist film-making as well as on theory and criticism. 'Theory films' such as Sally Potter's *Thriller* (1979), Laura Mulvey's own *Amy!* (1980) and *Riddles of the Sphinx* (1976), both made in collaboration with Peter Wollen, and theory-informed documentaries like Michelle Citron's *Daughter Rite* (1978) and Susan Clayton and Jonathan Curling's *Song of the Shirt* (1979) all tried to forge a new film language outside of the established structures of mainstream cinema. These films were often independently funded and distributed through a network of art-house cinemas and educational establishments; but whilst trying to create an alternative circuit they were also subject to the dangers of marginalization and exclusivism. This was not just an effect of small-scale distribution, but perhaps particularly due to their explicit problematization of realism and of the conventional pleasures of cinema-viewing within the film text. Some of them, such as Mulvey's films, and Tyndall, McCall, Pajaczkowska and Weinstock's *Sigmund Freud's Dora* (1979), presupposed a knowledge of psychoanalytical theory which necessarily limited their appeal. On the other hand though, it must be noted that this was an important phase of feminist film-making because it established a foothold in Britain for avant-garde work, extending an already existing interest in (and audience for) the films of continental women directors such as Agnes Varda and Marguerite Duras.

'Theory films' demanded a different, more active and critical mode of viewing from that invited by realist documentary and classic fiction film. This new dialectical relationship between spectator and screen image led some critics and film-makers to make large claims for the avant-garde film as inherently more progressive and political, because of its self-reflexiveness and because of its refusal to give in to the tendency of mainstream film to construct an 'imaginary identity'.[4]

Although some feminists rejected psychoanalytical theory on the grounds that it is inherently woman-unfriendly, many feminist film theorists after Mulvey saw Lacan's work on the psychic formation of gendered identity in relation to specularity (gazing in the mirror), the unconscious and language as central to their concerns. Lacanian psychoanalysis, they argued, offered the best understanding of the objectification of woman in film, of the way film constructs a gendered viewer, and of the complex of perversions – voyeurism, exhibitionism, fetishism – which because of their prominence in mainstream cinema are pertinent to the feminist engagement with film. Since the mid-1980s, therefore, Lacanian psychoanalysis, often in combination with some brand of semiotics, has been pretty well dominant in Anglo-American feminist film theory. Kaplan's *Women and Film: Both Sides of the Camera* (1983), Teresa de Lauretis's *Alice Doesn't: Feminism, Semiotics, Cinema* (1984), and Constance Penley's more recent *Feminism and Film Theory* (1988), and *The Future of an Illusion: Film, Feminism and Psychoanalysis* (1989) all privilege the question of the gaze and the (im)possibility of feminist meanings in the white Western traditions of mainstream and avant-garde cinema.

This does not mean that a consensus has been reached about either the inescapability of the male gaze or its centrality in feminist film analysis. Critique and modification have come from both within and without psychoanalytical film theory, and have centred on different aspects of the gaze. Mary Ann Doane's argument concerning the 'women's films' of the 1940s, for example, was that these products of mainstream fiction cinema *were* directed at a female audience and thus did construct a female gaze. Unfortunately, Doane's conclusion was no less pessimistic than Mulvey's as to the radical potential of this gaze, since she argued that the film narrative in these cases effectively forced the female spectator into a masochistic identification with the female protagonist (Doane, 1984). The issue of the female viewer's possibilities for identification was taken up in a different way in the work of Janet Bergstrom and in Laura Mulvey's own 'Afterthoughts on "Visual pleasure and narrative cinema" '. Making a case for the complexity of woman's position as spectator, both critics stated that spectators are not necessarily locked into identification with their own gender but are able to take up multiple identifications, whether simultaneously or in succession (Bergstrom, 1988: 181–2; Mulvey, 1988: 74).

Finally, from within psychoanalytical criticism but from outside the Anglo-American paradigm, Gertrud Koch has drawn attention to a different theorization of the gaze, one that does not link it to voyeuristic (peeping through the keyhole) pleasure but rather to the earlier, pre-symbolic stage in which the small child gazes openly at the world and at its mother: 'We may in fact owe the invention of the camera not to the keyhole but to the baby-carriage' (Koch, 1985a: 149).

Koch and others have stressed that because this conception of the gaze goes back to the Freudian idea of an originary bisexuality it therefore affords a better explanation of women's *actual* viewing behaviour, e.g. their multiple identifications with either gender (Koch, 1985b: 111).

It is almost inevitable that a critical overview of feminist writing on film reproduces the dominant features of existing debate, even as it tries to displace them. It is, therefore, all the more important to round off this discussion of the privileging of the gaze by looking at the work of critics who positioned themselves outside the psychoanalytical framework. Terry Lovell's *Pictures of Reality* was a seminal text in this respect, since it presented a scrupulous critique of the semiotic and psychoanalytical preoccupations of film theory even before they came into full swing in feminism. From Lovell's Marxist perspective the feminist debates outlined above are misdirected for a variety of reasons. As regards the feminist critique of realism, Lovell pointed to the failure to relate realism as a mode of signification to realism as an epistemology. Likewise she argued that the feminist versions of Althusserian concepts of ideology overemphasized textuality at the expense of social and economic analysis. All too often in this work, Lovell maintained, ideological effects were 'read off' from the film text itself, thus conflating the *constructed* or implied reader with actual viewers – and leaving the latter out of account altogether. Finally and perhaps most importantly, Lovell criticized the narrowness of Lacanian psychoanalytic concerns because of their focus on the construction of individual subjectivity rather than on ways in which a collective subject can be constituted, and because the Lacanian subject was seen as ultimately powerless. Pleasure should have an important place in Marxist aesthetics, Lovell concluded, but theoretical work on pleasure should be connected with the political and with analysis of popular culture as a prime site of ideological contestation:

> The pleasure of the text stems at least in part from collective utopias, social wish fulfillment and social aspirations, and these are not simply the sublimated expression of more basic sexual desires. (Lovell, 1983: 61)

Christine Gledhill's 'Developments in feminist film criticism' touched on many of the same points. Starting from the position that the dominant framework of feminist film criticism was 'too restrictive in the kinds of questions it asks of cinema', Gledhill gave a convincing defence of feminist realist practices and concluded with a plea for a kind of cultural analysis which could 'hold the extra-discursive and the discursive together as a complex and contradictory interrelation' (Gledhill, 1984: 44). This demand for a wider and less myopic frame of analysis has only recently and partially begun to be met, primarily in a shift towards an interest in *actual* spectatorship, but also in related issues such as the experience of viewing and the role of cultural differences in film reception and production.

Stage three: spectatorship and differential contexts

The multi-interpretability of film (polysemy) and the realization that spectators can and do adopt diverse identificatory positions in watching film has led to a new and more complex conception of film-viewing. It is true that in film the 'image', however symbolically intended or perceived, is always 'literalized' by the medium itself. In this respect the cinematic sign differs radically from the language of literature, where images are less likely to be taken at only the literal level (Doane, 1984: 6). But this does not mean either that film-viewers are not also *active* readers of film who can produce their own meanings, or that identification with mainstream fiction film characters means unconditional surrender to bourgeois ideology (Penley, 1988: 11). Teresa de Lauretis has described this shift towards a greater interest in reception as in part a delayed effect of feminism's construction of a new social subject – women – who may be and are legitimately addressed in cinematic practices (De Lauretis, 1984: 163). The impact of this shift on film-making has been that except for overtly feminist films, cinematic practices in the independent sector no longer necessarily can be said to construct a male gaze. Whatever one may think of *Sex, Lies and Videotape* – and it doesn't have to be much – it does at least address the question of the gaze and of masculine sexuality. In ways more amenable to women's visual pleasure, off-beat films which then made it into the mainstream distribution circuit such as *Lianna* (Nelson/Renzi), *Desert Hearts, I've Heard the Mermaids Singing* (Rozema) and Percy Adlon's work with Marianne Sagebrecht in *Baghdad Café* and *Sugar Baby* have achieved a degree of success in changing the dynamics of female objectification and sexual fantasy in an entertainment setting. Where lesbian love and sexuality are addressed, however 'delicately and discreetly', a public space is nevertheless created for discussion and analysis.

Women's pleasure in viewing then is high on the agenda in recent feminist work on film. This is welcome not only because women's desires are being taken more seriously in cultural production or because a less purist feminist film practice and criticism is simply more fun, but perhaps particularly because it is in relation to the audience, and in the context of film reception, that issues of race, class and sexual orientation can at last find their rightful place in feminist theory and criticism. Charlotte Brunsdon's excellent collection *Films for Women* (1986) and E. Deirdre Pribram's equally useful *Female Spectators* (1988) both emphasize the heterogeneity of female spectatorship, whilst at the same time seeing film-viewing as very much a social *practice* rather than something which individuals undergo, passively, in the dark. Thus it is not the case that the spectator's experience of a film is wholly determined by atomized viewing in the cinema – discussion afterwards with friends or groups, reviews and other contextual factors play their parts in the construction of meanings too.

Racial and cultural difference are addressed in this context both as determinants in the production of meanings and as a means of putting the concerns of white Western feminist film criticism into perspective. These concerns must be recognized as *specific*, which doesn't mean that semiotics or Lacanian film theory has no relevance outside the established framework of Anglo-American and European cinema, but rather that their legitimacy should not automatically be assumed or their dominance remain uncontested in the light of developments within feminism at large.[5] For example, Brunsdon notes that 'Hollywood, as the world-dominant cinema, exports ideals of White femininity worldwide', yet feminist critics have rarely looked at this aspect of the Hollywood dream-machine in their copious critiques of it (Brunsdon, 1986: 55).

In relation to the production of more differentiated cultural meanings, Jacqueline Bobo's article in *Female Spectators* (1988) on Black women's viewing of Spielberg's *The Color Purple* offers a good example of where feminist film criticism might go next. Bobo draws attention to the role of cultural groups functioning as interpretative communities in the construction of oppositional readings of films which are regarded as reactionary by a theoreticist criticism refusing to see signification as a two-way *social* process. She makes a useful distinction between three types of film-viewing: dominant readings, negotiated readings which are critical of what is on offer but nevertheless accept the underlying ideology, and oppositional readings which can range from outright rejection to the creation of subversive meanings. Finally, Bobo notes that the recent popularity of Black women's writing is one of those extra-discursive factors which must be taken into account when looking at cultural practices such as *The Color Purple.*[6]

Feminist film debate: truly global issues

This brief discussion of the differential positioning of Black women as spectators was clearly reflected in a Channel 4 debate which was part of a season on women and film. Here the different ways of seeing 'women in film', especially in the controversies over realism, over documentary film-making, over the gaze and over representations of sexuality, converged, for once, in the serious questions four women asked about the feminist film debate.

Christine Gledhill's forceful defence of realist film-making is of immediate relevance to the Channel 4 debate between four women film-makers: Deepa Dhanraj (India), Marilou Diaz-Abaya (Philippines), Jocelyne Saab (Lebanon) and Ana Carolina (Brazil). 'Politically the issue is very important,' Gledhill argued: 'an assertion of realism is the first recourse of any oppressed group wishing to combat the ideology promulgated by the media in the interests of hegemonic power' (Gledhill, 1984: 19).

The discussion opened with the (as it turned out) vexed question of politics in women's film-making. Dhanraj began by stating unequivocally that she saw film-making as a tool for sociopolitical challenge (she would not go so far as to say change) and that documentary was best suited to this purpose. This immediately raised the question of whether documentary realism is therefore inherently more political than fiction or avant-garde cinema – a useless question, as it turned out. National histories and political contexts have to be taken into account; Marilou Diaz-Abaya explained for example that the Marcos regime had encouraged and subsidized an indigenous entertainments fiction-film industry in the Philippines, but had put severe restrictions upon the making of documentary. For Carolina in Brazil the non-controversial fiction film was likewise the only option left if she wanted to go on working at all: she had been jailed several times for the making of political films.

Entwined with the question of politics and of film-making as self-expression – a matter of class privilege (Diaz-Abaya) or cultural struggle (Dhanraj) – was the issue of women's sexual objectification. Working in India in a film industry which thrives on the sexual exploitation of women, Dhanraj spoke of the impossibility of positing a desiring female subject. Jocelyne Saab, on the other hand, took issue with the question itself, which she saw as confined to the typically limited preoccupations of white, Western, middle-class feminists. There is, said Saab, 'nothing wrong with the representation of women as objects of desire'; she found them attractive and strong. But again this statement was problematized as soon as specific conditions of production and national/cultural traditions were brought into play. In Brazil, according to Carolina, 'either you do sex films or you die professionally', because of the politically repressive climate in which little other than sex films pleases the eye of the censor. With regard to their own work, three of the four women said they had been criticized by white feminists for 'too much sex' or for 'collusion in the exploitation of women for the male gaze', a criticism which they all felt was inappropriate and indicative not just of Western ignorance *vis-à-vis* questions of representation and cultural difference, but also of institutional and political constraints. None of these constraints, incidentally, had much to do with the novelty of women directors within their national traditions; all four could point to predecessors, especially in the earlier part of this century when the film industry was being established.[7]

Feminism and cinema is indeed a global issue. It encompasses a great diversity of questions around film as a signifying practice, as a locus of pleasure and entertainment, and as an instrument of dominant ideology, or, conversely, as a tool for political resistance and subversion. As a cultural practice it is embedded in national traditions and subject to institutional constraints, but it is also a multi-interpretable art form, which may be opaque in its meanings, or a window on the world (for feminist windows *are* different). The film as film, as 'text', as visual artefact, takes up only a small place amidst this kaleidoscope of angles – and I haven't even touched on the economic aspects of production and reception, such as box office pressures, state subsidies, distribution and exhibition.[8] These do not always yield the most interesting insights into feminism and film, but they are indispensable for a full understanding of the factors at play, material and cultural. Add to this the broader questions of feminism itself – its heterogeneity and contradictions, its activist and theoretical incarnations, its diverse and chequered histories, its multiple definitions and its uncertain future – and the stage is set. 'Women and film' would make a great movie if it had an international, multicultural cast and would address all these questions at once. I would not want to direct it, but I do think it would be a shame if Lacan, Althusser, Freud and Foucault yet again were allowed to bag the best parts. Not because they could not be useful – but they wouldn't give us, as desiring female spectators, *that* much to look at.

Notes

This article is a much extended version of a talk given at the Southampton Film Club's day conference 'Women and Film' in April 1990. I would like to thank Jeanne Butterfield, Bill Marshall and Erica Carter for their help.

1. Just how slippery the use of the autobiographical discourse can be is demonstrated in two recent films: *When Harry Met Sally* and *Sex, Lies and Videotape*. The former incorporates the device of 'people talking simply and directly' merely by way of counterpoint to the main

fictional narrative, whilst the latter uses it – rather more problematically – in the form of women's sexual confessions on camera.

2. See for a more detailed account of these arguments E. Ann Kaplan (1983), Chapter 10, 'The Realist debate in the feminist film', pp. 125–41, and Constance Penley (1988), 'Introduction: The Lady Doesn't Vanish: Feminism and Film Theory', pp. 1–24.

3. Suture is often achieved with the technique of using a shot (woman looks 'out of the screen' at the audience) and then a reverse shot (man is seen looking at her), so that the woman's look is contained and mastered by that of the male. Suture has almost come to be seen as synonymous with shot–reverse shot.

4. Both Terry Lovell and Susan Hayward mention this phenomenon in critical comments on the work of Colin MacCabe and Jacqueline Rose respectively (Lovell, 1983: 84; Hayward, 1990: 285).

5. See for a similar argument in connection with Black film-makers and feminist film criticism Martine Attille and Maureen Blackwood in Brunsdon (1986), and Alile Sharon Larkin in Pribram (1988).

6. The context of Black women's writing is relevant to Spike Lee's work as well. *She's Gotta Have It* gains another dimension when viewed as an update of Zora Neale Hurston's *Their Eyes Were Watching God*.

7. Useful documentation of these histories can be found in the booklet, edited by Penny Ashbrook, which accompanied the Channel 4 *Women Call the Shots* series.

8. For an insight in these matters, Charlotte Brunsdon's *Films for Women* contains a section on distribution and exhibition.

Bibliography

Ashbrook, Penny (ed.) (1990) *Women Call the Shots*. London: Channel 4 Television.

Attille, Martine and Blackwood, Maureen (1986) 'Black women and representation', in Charlotte Brunsdon (ed.), *Films for Women*. London: British Film Institute. pp. 202–8.

Bergstrom, Janet (1988) 'Rereading the work of Claire Johnston', in Constance Penley (ed.), *Feminism and Film Theory*. London: Routledge. pp. 80–8.

Bobo, Jacqueline (1988) '*The Color Purple*: black women as cultural readers', in E. Deirdre Pribram (ed.), *Female Spectators*. London: Verso. pp. 90–109.

Brunsdon, Charlotte (ed.) (1986) *Films for Women*. London: British Film Institute.

Doane, Mary Ann (1984) 'The "woman's film": possession and address', in Doane et al. (eds), *Re-Vision*. pp. 67–82.

Doane, Mary Ann (1988) 'Woman's stake: filming the female body', in Constance Penley (ed.), *Feminism and Film Theory*. London: Routledge. pp. 216–28.

Doane, Mary Ann, Mellencamp, Patricia and Williams, Linda (eds) (1984) *Re-Vision: Essays in Feminist Film Criticism*. Los Angeles: American Film Institute.

Ecker, Gisela (1985) *Feminist Aesthetics*. London: Women's Press.

Feuer, Jane (1986) '*Daughter Rite*: living with our pain and love', in Charlotte Brunsdon (ed.), *Films for Women*. London: British Film Institute. pp. 24–30.

Gledhill, Christine (1984) 'Developments in feminist film criticism', in Mary Ann Doane et al. (eds), *Re-Vision*. Los Angeles: American Film Institute. pp. 18–48.

Haskell, Molly (1974) *From Reverence to Rape: The Treatment of Women in the Movies*. New York: Holt Rinehart & Winston.

Hayward, Susan (1990) 'Beyond the gaze and into *Femme-Filmécriture*: Agnes Varda's *Sans Toit Ni Loi* (1985)', in Susan Hayward and Ginette Vincendeau (eds), *French Film*. London: Routledge. pp. 285–96.

Hayward, Susan and Vincendeau, Ginette (eds) (1990) *French Film: Texts and Contexts*. London: Routledge.

Johnston, Claire (1976) 'Women's cinema as counter-cinema', in Bill Nicholls (ed.), *Movies and Methods*. London: University of California Press. pp. 208–18.

Kaplan, E. Ann (1983) *Women and Film: Both Sides of the Camera*. London: Methuen.

Koch, Gertrud (1985a) 'Ex-changing the gaze: revisioning feminist film theory', *New German Critique*, 34 (Winter): 139–53.

Koch, Gertrud (1985b) 'Why women go to men's films', in Gisela Ecker (ed.), *Feminist Aesthetics*. London: Women's Press. pp. 108–19.

Kuhn, Annette (1982) *Women's Pictures: Feminism and Cinema*. London: Routledge & Kegan Paul.

Kuhn, Annette (1986) 'Hollywood and the new women's cinema', in Charlotte Brunsdon (ed.), *Films for Women*. London: British Film Institute. pp. 125–30.

Larkin, Alile Sharon (1988) 'Black women film-makers defining ourselves: feminism in our own voice', in E. Deirdre Pribram (ed.), *Female Spectators*. London: Verso. pp. 157–73.

Lauretis, Teresa de (1984) *Alice Doesn't: Feminism, Semiotics, Cinema*. London: Macmillan.

Lauretis, Teresa de (1985) 'Aesthetic and feminist film theory: rethinking women's cinema', *New German Critique*, 34 (Winter): 154–75.

Lesage, Julia (1986) 'Political aesthetics of the feminist documentary film', in Charlotte Brunsdon (ed.), *Films for Women*. London: British Film Institute. pp. 14–26.

Lovell, Terry (1983) *Pictures of Reality: Aesthetics, Politics and Pleasure*. London: British Film Institute.

Mulvey, Laura (1975) 'Visual pleasure and narrative cinema', *Screen*, 16 (3): 16–18.

Mulvey, Laura (1988) 'Afterthoughts on "Visual pleasure and narrative cinema", inspired by *Duel in the Sun*', in Constance Penley (ed.), *Feminism and Film Theory*. London: Routledge. pp. 69–79.

Mulvey, Laura (1989) *Visual and Other Pleasures*. Basingstoke: Macmillan.

Nicholls, Bill (ed.) (1976) *Movies and Methods*. London: University of California Press.

Penley, Constance (ed.) (1988) *Feminism and Film Theory*. London: Routledge.

Penley, Constance (1989) *The Future of an Illusion: Film, Feminism and Psychoanalysis*. London: Routledge.

Pribram, E. Deirdre (ed.) (1988) *Female Spectators: Looking at Film and Television*. London: Verso.

Rich, B. Ruby (1986) 'Anti-porn: soft issue, hard world', in Charlotte Brunsdon (ed.), *Films for Women*. London: British Film Institute. pp. 31–43.

Rosen, Marjorie (1973) *Popcorn Venus: Women, Movies and the American Dream*. New York: Coward McCann & Geoghehan.

Williams, Linda (1984) 'When the woman looks', in Mary Ann Doane et al. (eds), *Re-Vision*. Los Angeles: American Film Institute. pp. 83–99.

SECTION IV

REALITY

The previous sections of this reader all attest to the intellectual creativity and vitality of contemporary feminism. Whilst aspects of Western academic and intellectual life have recently appeared moribund, feminism and feminist thinking have demonstrated a constant, lively engagement with debate and discussion. But, as suggested in the introduction to this collection, whatever the intellectual heights achieved, the material situation of women as a whole remains markedly unequal to that of men. In the West, the differences in social and material expectations between women are related first and foremost to class differences: women who are born into middle-class families, for example, are far more likely to go on to higher education than those born into the working class. Equally, income differences still persist between white-collar and blue-collar occupations, and recent evidence throughout the West demonstrates the close relationship between material prosperity and health and life expectancy.[1]

However, even though social class remains of fundamental importance in understanding the different expectations and aspirations of women, the class structure – particularly of Britain and the United States – has to be seen in the light of two factors which complicate the assumption that social class is the only determinant of an individual's life chances. The first factor is the growing complexity of determining the definition of a person's social class. Divorce, remarriage and separation have shattered the once comfortable view that social class could be determined by the occupation of the head of the household. In the 1990s the first obvious problem about this definition is the issue of which household, in an age of step-parents and extended families, is being described. The second failing of the head-of-the-household view of class, especially for feminists, is that this definition is based on assumptions about male heads of households, male occupations and a single male wage-earner for a family.[2] The majority of British families now include at least two 'economically active' members (who are, of course, likely to be the mother and father), and the standard of living of many families is dependent upon the existence of two incomes. As feminist historians have pointed out, this has always been the case for many working-class households and the idea that married women, either with or without children, did not work outside the home was only ever partly true.[3]

Nevertheless, the 'Janet and John' construction of the Western family, in which two (white) children lived in a stable situation in which Mummy stayed at home while Daddy went out to work was a potent ideal. Moreover, it was an ideal which had a basis in reality, since in the period immediately after the Second World War the cult of domesticity, general prosperity and high levels of wages and employment in the West combined to ensure that at least a substantial proportion of families could, and did, conform to this norm.[4] But growing rates of male unemployment, a falling birth rate and shifts in women's perception of their social role contributed to changes in the organization of the family. New ideologies of marriage and sexuality brought a shift in expectations about domestic life. The growth of a 'sex industry' and the idea of sex as recreation undermined the traditional expectation that marriage was primarily about the construction of a household.[5] The household, it became apparent, could be made and remade. Indeed, in an era of increasing consumer affluence and an ethic of instant hedonism, it was inevitable that expectations about the family and marriage should change.

So in the United States half of all first marriages end in divorce; for the United Kingdom the figure is approximately one-third. Other European societies have significantly lower figures for divorce, but from this it would be fanciful to conclude that separation and the reordering of households does not occur. What is also known, as established fact, about divorce, is that it makes women poor. A mass of evidence (largely from the United States) demonstrates that after divorce, men very rapidly regain the economic status they had when married, whilst for women divorce brings an overall decrease in prosperity.[6] On both sides of the Atlantic divorce petitions are, on the whole, brought by women, so feminists have argued that, for women, increased poverty is infinitely preferable to intolerable marriages.

Whatever the reasons for the increase in Western divorce rates, one fact of social life remains absolutely clear amongst the competing interpretations of the evidence. It is that whatever the changing relationship between adult women and men in the household, the bond between mothers and children remains absolute and unbroken. Again, evidence from both sides of the Atlantic reiterates the ease with which ties between fathers and children are broken, but the durability of ties between mothers and children.[7] What appears to be happening throughout the West is that the relationship of men to the family is changing, whilst the family, as a continuous and constant group, is increasingly constituted by women and children. A considerable number of feminists might well argue that this was always the case, but without making complex historical comparisons what we can say is that the 'Janet and John' family so beloved of advertisers – and indeed of many on the political right – is becoming increasingly rare.

However rare our 'Janet and John' family is, it nevertheless remains a deeply emotive fantasy about how family life should be organized. Even though it may have disappeared in reality, it is still a powerful normative fantasy, from which many find it impossible to escape. Amongst the diverse consequences of the strength of this ideal are the continuing marginalization of the single-parent family (including families in which the parent or parents are homosexual) and the persistence of the view that mothers are financially supported by the fathers of the children. The Beveridge ideal of the stable nuclear family with a male wage-earner and a dependent wife and children is still the ideal in the minds of many policy-makers, despite overwhelming evidence which suggests that many people (especially women) both do not, and do not want to, live in this particular family form.[8] The implicit authoritarianism and dependence of the single-male-earner family are no longer found supportive by many women.

The problem with women's rejection of the traditional family is that it has occurred, in both Britain and the United States, in societies in which there is almost no state provision which might enable women with dependent children to become financially self-supporting. The 'welfare mothers' of right-wing demonology are created out of a rejection of traditional forms of financial support which occurs in this context of non-existent alternative support. The problem of childcare in Britain and the United States is that it consists of a patchwork of imperfect arrangements, with women attempting to juggle the demands of children and the labour market. Given that the majority of women have a lower level of occupational skills than men, it is hardly suprising that the Western poor include a disproportionate number of women – and of children growing up in female-headed households.

So staying married to, or in a stable relationship with, an employed man offers the majority of women a greater chance of financial stability. The numbers of women who combine motherhood with professional or managerial careers remains tiny, yet a potent myth has developed in the West of the ease with which women can now 'have it all'. Having that 'all' is, however, dependent on access to higher education (which is becoming increasingly expensive in the West as levels of state support diminish) and subsequently on an income substantial enough to support the substitute care which is necessary for small children. Given that such care is both difficult to find (and expensive to pay for) it is hardly surprising that drop-out rates for women in the professions are high, and that women are virtually unrepresented in senior management.

The recent shifts in the organization of the Western family suggest that increasingly large numbers of people (especially women) are voting with their feet against a form of family life which they find unacceptable. In 1884 Engels attacked the bourgeois nuclear family as a form of the prostitution of women, and argued for the increasing intervention of the state in the support of children.[9] He argued passionately against what he described as the 'stifling boredom' of the bourgeois family, with its enforced dependence of women on men. The key to the emancipation of women from this patriarchal form of the family lay, he argued, in the entry of women into paid work and the assumption by the state of responsibility for the material support of children. What has happened throughout the West – and in the once Soviet-dominated states of Eastern Europe – is that increasing numbers of women are in paid work, but there has been little movement by the state towards the role of provider of childcare. In Eastern Europe such provision was always more generous than in the West, but the collapse of state socialism has brought a decrease in this provision. Whatever the society, or its ruling ideology, all the evidence suggests that little has shifted since 1884 in the allocation of responsibility for caring in the family – women were, and are, quite literally the primary caretakers of mankind.

Western policy towards the family, and women, has long been a combination of reality and fantasy – and largely fantasies by men about how they would like the family and domestic life to be organized. Although the consequences of this less than dispassionate account of family life have often been against the interests of Western women, the West has been relatively prosperous and women within it have had some room for negotiation and manoeuvre. It is in the application of Western assumptions about the family to the world outside the industrial West that we can see the most damaging and pernicious impact of fantasies about the ideal family. The West has exported, through government agencies and development agencies, models of the nuclear family and male heads of household, to societies where women are the primary earners, the family is a group of kin, and the kinship structure is matriarchal.[10]

What this transposition of ideals of social life so aptly demonstrates is the degree to which the socially powerful can impose on others their perception of social normality. In the case of social relations between women and men this remains a persistent feature of all societies. It is not that women do not, and have not, consistently challenged male definitions of law, normality and social order, but these definitions often originally represent a narrow, patriarchal view of what is socially desirable. In accounts of the family, of women's fertility, of reproductive rights, the welfare of children and many other areas of social life, there is an inherent contest between the interests of women and men which gives rise to fiercely fought battles for control of the definition of the situation.[11] In recent years the debates around fertility and the family demonstrate clearly the different perceptions and interests of women and men.

The plurality and diversity of forms of personal relations throughout the world is now widely recognized in the academy. Unfortunately, the academy exists in a world in which homogeneity is an increasingly prized feature of social life. Homogeneity is, simply, more convenient for the bureaucracies that are now essential for the organization of the complex societies in which we live. One of the paradoxes of the contemporary world is that just as the world's diversity is recognized (and experienced by large numbers of people) so accommodating that diversity within political and economic structure becomes more difficult. For women, whose political voice and influence has historically been less powerful than that of men, a crucial and urgent problem is to ensure the recognition of the diversity of the condition of women.

Notes

1. On the relationship between women and the British Health Service, see Lesley Doyal, 'Carers and the careless', *Feminist Review*, 27 (1987), pp. 49–55.

2. See Christine Delphy and Diana Leonard, 'Class analysis, gender analysis and the family', in Rosemary Crompton and Michael Mann (eds), *Gender and Stratification* (Polity, Oxford, 1986), pp. 57–73.

3. There is an interesting debate within feminism on the motives for excluding women in Britain from the labour force – see, in particular, Jane Humphries, 'Protective legislation, the capitalist state and working class men', *Feminist Review*, 7 (1980), pp. 1–33.

4. Elizabeth Wilson, *Only Halfway to Paradise* (Tavistock, London, 1980).

5. Barbara Ehrenreich, *The Hearts of Men* (Pluto, London 1983).

6. Lenore Weitzman, *The Divorce Revolution* (Free Press, Menuchen, NJ, 1985).

7. An extensive and extremely useful discussion of motherhood (with a very full bibliography) is given in Ann Snitow, 'Feminism and motherhood: an American reading', *Feminist Review*, 40 (Spring 1992), pp. 32–51.

8. The now classic literature on this issue includes Hilary Land, 'The myth of the male breadwinner', *New Society*, 9 October 1975. Other essays on this issue are included in Clare Ungerson (ed.), *Women and Social Policy* (Macmillan, London, 1985).

9. F. Engels, *The Origin of the Family, Private Property and the State* (Penguin, Harmondsworth, 1985).

10. An extensive literature on this subject now exists. See Georgia Ashworth (ed.), *A Diplomacy of the Oppressed* (Zed Books, London, 1993); Maria Mies, *Patriarchy and Accumulation on a World Scale* (Zed Books, London, 1992); and Bina Agarwal (ed.), *Structures of Patriarchy* (Zed Books, London, 1991).

11. See the essays in Michelle Stanworth (ed.), *Reproductive Technologies* (Polity, Cambridge, 1987).

Women's Unwaged Work – the Heart of the Informal Sector

Selma James

At the 1985 World Conference of the UN Decade for Women in Nairobi, Housewives in Dialogue presented evidence[1] which helped government delegates to agree to the amended paragraph 120 of *Forward-Looking Strategies*, the final document of the Decade. Paragraph 120 commits governments to counting the GNP (Gross National Product) women's 'unremunerated' – unpaid or unwaged – work in 'agriculture, food production, reproduction and household activities'. The decision came after almost two decades of grassroots campaigning and determined lobbying pioneered by the International Wages for Housework Campaign elaborating the wide implications of unwaged work which, though uncounted, is *counted on* by every individual and institution.

The present

There are signs that we are moving slowly but surely towards implementation of paragraph 120: pilot projects, such as that on 'Measuring unpaid household work' in Australia; a national policy in Trinidad and Tobago; a bill in the British parliament; a resolution in the European Parliament; and Recommendation V by the 1990 UN Commission on the Status of Women that counting women's unwaged work be prioritized in national policies by 1995, and that methods of counting be developed by the UN.

Despite this progress towards acknowledging unwaged work, which is estimated to produce as much as 50 per cent of GNP,[2] Third World women are urged to 'get into the development process', and metropolitan women are urged to get 'out to work'. In fact, with the economic crisis, which for women never seems to cease, fewer and fewer women anywhere can afford to refuse to do at least two jobs. The so-called 'double day' is an international phenomenon which ironically goes hand in hand with the 'feminization of poverty': a rise in workload, a fall in living standards. But while women in metropolitan countries who do two jobs – housework and

From *Women*, 2 (3), 1991, pp. 267–71.

work outside the home – get one wage, women in Third World countries, even with two jobs – housework and, for example, subsistence farming – can still be without wages and even perhaps without food. To add insult to injury, the woman anywhere who doesn't secure a wage may enter statistics as 'economically inactive'.

In 1982 the ILO (International Labour Organization) 'for purposes of international comparisons, [classified] all members of the armed forces . . . as employed'. On the other hand they introduced 'a separate category . . . to account for persons not economically active but contributing to output and welfare. This category includes homemakers, community and volunteer workers and persons engaged in certain subsistence activities.'[3] The person whose business is death is named a worker, but the person whose business is life is not. This definition of work and productiveness says much about the priorities which have resulted in, or at least permitted, the increase of world poverty in the 1980s[4] and the death, injury or dislocation of 80 million people in 105 wars since 1945, and before the Gulf War.[5]

Despite such 'disregard'[6] and 'discounting', every sector of every economy is dependent on women's unwaged housework for its basic ingredient: its workforce. *Unwaged housework is the heart of every economic sector, formal, informal, waged or unwaged*, not merely presenting commerce and industry with a new generation of workers, but each day reproducing the human mind and muscle which have been exhausted and consumed by the day's work. Overwhelmingly, the burden of this reproductive work has been carried by the female half of humanity, consuming our time – which happens to be our life. And yet this work is hidden from history, politics and economic statistics.

In order to meet reproductive obligations to family and community, women face daily a mass of unavoidable immediate tasks. The woman who has to cook the food may have to grow it first. In this situation, agricultural work is also reproductive work. Some metropolitan definitions of housework are too narrow to encompass this reality. Definitions rarely include time squandered in waiting rooms and standing in queues which bleed not only hours but months and years from the life of women; in some areas of the world older women, whose time has less exchange value, are condemned to do this vital but tedious work. All of it must be counted.

The past

It may be useful to recall that the informal sector and even the question of development, as international questions, arose in the second half of the twentieth century. In 1947 India, the jewel in the British Crown, became independent. A decade later the Gold Coast became Ghana, the first Black African country to break from colonial rule. It was at first assumed that once political independence had been achieved, the aspirations of the population had been met. But then what was called 'the revolution in rising expectations' made clear that political independence aimed at more than a flag, a national anthem and local personnel inheriting positions of power and prestige. The formerly colonized people wanted to enter what appeared to be a wonderland of consumer goods which the transistor radio was anxious to advertise to them. Pressure from this explosion of hopes was used to propel the economies of newly independent countries further into the money economy. When exchange value became the measure of wealth, power moved from the farmer in the countryside – often a woman – to the city, and women found themselves deprived of their economic power base. Esther Boserup's pioneering work in the 1960s indicated how women fought the erosion of their traditional power.[7] 'There are many reports from Africa about husbands whose wives refuse to help them in the production of cash crops, or to perform household chores, unless they are paid for their work.'

The statistics which exclude women workers reflect the dominant view that the unwaged work a woman does, on which her social power and very existence depend, stands in the way of 'progress'. 'Progress' has won, depriving the rural woman of a living from the land (but not freeing her from agricultural work). Women have therefore tried in every possible way to enter the waged sector. In the Third World and in the metropolitan world, women's thirst for the economic and social independence of waged work has been misread. Women may be delighted to have gained waged employment, especially on Friday afternoon, but they're less thrilled on Monday morning after a weekend of housework. Despite great efforts, including becoming 'economic refugees' – immigrants hundreds or even thousands of miles from home – for millions of women (and men) the informal sector is the only place they can find jobs, even in metropolitan countries. One occupation which many must turn to yet again is housework.

Devaluation of domestic workers is replicated internationally. As a consequence, women must take on additional informal work, such as prostitution, with its burden of criminalization, that is, further devaluation. In 1987 the ILO decided not to list prostitution as a job in the International Standard of Classification of Occupations. Yet it keeps many families alive, and is an important source of foreign currency in some Eastern economies, the largest in Thailand.[8]

While women move up into the informal sector, capital enterprises develop by moving down to rest on it. The Japanese industrial miracle is a classic example. Subcontractors employ casual labour, mainly women, whose low wages and poor working conditions subsidize the industrial giants they make components for. Thus unseen women in precarious employment are the miracle-workers who bestow permanent employment on men. As the *Independent* (11 March 1991) said, 'Japan is the world's richest poor country. . . . Because of the country's bias towards production instead of consumption, some of the benefits that consumers take for granted in other developing countries are just missing here. Only 42 per cent of households in Japan were connected to the sewers. And 13 per cent of households have no bath.' This 'dual industrial structure',[9] the formal resting directly on the informal, is spreading with Japanese investment, carrying an aspect of underdevelopment to metropolitan countries.

And how can we distinguish work in the informal sector from the work of women employed by multinationals operating in free trade zones? Women, often treated as casual workers and working without labour protection codes, form up to 95 per cent of this workforce.[10]

The future

To sum up. The housewife producing the labour force is considered marginal. The informal sector is considered marginal. Subsistence farming is considered marginal. We now know that this work is not marginal to the economy. But the people who do it have less social power to insist that their needs be met and are therefore called 'marginal'. What can statistics do to help?

Statistics shape and reflect a hierarchy of social values by the categories into which people, their activities and their products are placed, and by what is being measured – and not measured. Statistics about women can only reflect their needs by accounting for their entire working day and what they gain from it.

When we say that women's unwaged work should be counted, we mean that the actual number of hours women work should be quantified, and that the output of this work should be valued and included in the GNP. And since a woman's working day is often supplemented by children's work, especially in Third World countries, this work too must be quantified and valued. The gulf widens between expenditure of time and energy on the one hand, and output and return on the other, the further we get from metropolitan centres, but is always wider for women than for men of the same social sector or class.

The level of northern military technology is dazzling; yet in the south there are scant resources for piped water, solar cookers and non-polluting technology which would both relieve the burden of labour and protect the environment. Counting women's unwaged work would value a woman's time by valuing the cost to her in hours of her life which she spends in ensuring everyone's survival. This cost is borne by women not only where starvation is imminent but where life is less threatened but still a grim struggle. This encompasses most of the world's population, Third World and metropolitan, including the Third World in the metropolis and the metropolis in the Third World.

Such a cost accounting would make clear that communities need not justify their claim to survival by proving their productiveness. The disparity between labour and productivity reflects not on them but on social and economic priorities which counting and renaming women's work would help transform.

Notes

Selma James on behalf of Housewives in Dialogue, a non-governmental organization in consultative status with the UN Economic and Social Council, presented this paper in Rome in March 1991 to a consultative meeting of the United Nations research institute on women, INSTRAW (United Nations International Research and Training Institute for the Advancement of Women).

1. Selma James, *The Global Kitchen*, Housewives in Dialogue, 1985.

2. *Valuing Domestic Activities*. Second ECE/INSTRAW joint meeting on Statistics of Women, UN (Economic Commission for Europe, Geneva, November 1989), p. 2.

3. *Labour Force, Employment, Unemployment and Underemployment*, Report II ICLS/13/ 11 (Thirteenth International Conference of Labour Statisticians, ILO, 1982), p. 42.

4. *World Bank, 1990 World Development Report*, cited in *The Independent*, 19 July 1990, p. 21.

5. 'Five million civilians have died in recent conflicts', *The Guardian*, 29 January 1991, p. 9.

6. 'We have been oppressed a great deal, we have been exploited a great deal, we have been disregarded a great deal.' *The Arusha Declaration*, Tanzania, 5 February 1967.

7. Esther Boserup, *Woman's Role in Economic Development* (Earthscan Publications, London, 1970), p. 64.

8. Thanh-Dam Thong, *Sex, Money and Morality: Prostitution and Tourism in South East Asia* (Zed Books, London, 1990), p. 163.

9. Mary Saso, *Women in the Japanese Workplace* (Hilary Shipman, London, 1990), p. 81.

10. *Women Working Worldwide: the International Division of Labour in the Electronics, Clothing and Textile Industry* (War on Want, 1988).

Sex and Race in the Labour Market

Irene Bruegel

On average white men earn substantially more than black men, whereas there is little difference in the case of women. (Brown, 1984: 167)

We know from our everyday experience that black women have some of the worst jobs. Yet this is not quite what published statistics suggest. Official data certainly show marked differences between men's and women's jobs and between the jobs that black and white men hold, but racial differences *between* women appear slight in national survey results.

This article attempts to unravel the reasons for the apparent conflict between the evidence of our eyes and those of surveys such as Colin Brown's. One critical difference is the fact that black women are more often full-time workers; they are also concentrated in the London area and in jobs where redundancies have been particularly high. To uncover the true scale of race inequalities these points have to be considered as well as the qualifications of black women and the inadequacies of standard socioeconomic/occupational classification systems. This article also draws out the key effects of the recession on black and white women's working lives using the evidence of the Greater London Council's (GLC) London Living Standards Survey (LLSS) between 1981 and 1986. This survey shows that black women are not only at the bottom of the pile, but that their position has got worse relative both to black men and white women over the last few years.[1]

Black women in labour market surveys

The first comprehensive national survey to distinguish adequately by both race and sex in Britain was Colin Brown's survey for the Policy Studies Institute (PSI) (Brown, 1984). Previous PSI surveys of race in Britain focused on differences between black and white men. The national Department of Employment/Office of Population Censuses and Surveys (OPCS) survey of

---

From *Feminist Review*, 32 (1989), pp. 50–68.

women at work (Martin and Roberts, 1984) included black women in its sample but in insufficient numbers to make reliable comparisons. The EEC Labour Force Survey (LFS) and the OPCS General Household Survey do collect ethnic group information, but the sample numbers of different ethnic groups are usually too small to provide reliable estimates by ethnic group and sex. In analysing the position of black women in Britain's labour force, the Department of Employment was therefore forced to amalgamate information from three consecutive Labour Force Surveys 1984/5/6 (Department of Employment, 1988); even so there are doubts as to how accurate a picture is presented.

Outside London and the major conurbations, the 'problem' is that there are too few black women for a 0.5 per cent sample survey to pick up sufficient numbers for reliable analysis. As a result, most studies of the position of black women are surveys of small areas or studies of particular workplaces and/or types of work (see for example Hoel, 1982; Stone, 1983; Westwood and Bhachu, 1988; Dex, 1983) and even these studies are relatively rare. Such studies cannot be generalized to portray the national position and are not usually able to demonstrate changes in the position of particular groups over time. It is for such reasons that the PSI deliberately 'over-sampled' the black population, using smaller sampling fractions for them than for the white population. Once the Census of Population includes ethnic group information this particular problem should be overcome, but the earliest such information from the 1991 Census is likely to be available is 1993–4; nor will it overcome the deficiency of information on race and income. Moreover, the form in which 'ethnic' information is collected by the Census and the LFS will still make it impossible to analyse the position of 'white' ethnic minorities. The effects of colour as against ethnic group discrimination cannot therefore be discerned from official statistics. (See Yuval-Davis, 1988, for a discussion of this issue.)

The PSI survey reported in Brown (1984) made strenuous efforts to achieve a good response from black women, employing interviewers matched with respondents by ethnic group and sex and seeking help from community leaders to get the survey accepted. As a result, their sample is more representative than earlier ones, with response rates for Asian men and women which are as high as for white adults. However the survey still estimated that only 18 per cent of Muslim women were in the labour market (and only 10 per cent were employed). Although this figure accords with that of the Labour Force Survey for Pakistani and Bangladeshi women, there are good grounds for suspecting that in both cases the surveys missed many women's involvement in homeworking, in family employment in shops and elsewhere, and in paid childcare. Certainly OPCS are known to be concerned with the representativeness of their sample of ethnic minorities in the LFS and the General Household Survey (GHS). The Labour Force Survey has been shown to under-record the number of black- and female-headed households in the population (Morris, 1987) and is most likely to miss the poorer black households. Taking these points together, it is likely

that the PSI survey also under-records homeworking and family employment and that therefore pay and job levels of black women are likely to have
been overestimated in the survey.[2] Since Muslim women were almost half
the PSI sample of Asian women, Brown's picture of the job levels and pay of
Asian women could be seriously distorted.

Pay differentials

Colin Brown's apparently perverse findings on pay are partly due to such
biases in response rates and under-reporting of low-paid work. His figures
(Table 1) give the impression that black women earn more in a week than
white women. They also suggest that wage differences are greater between
white men and women than between black men and women.

Table 1   *Gross earnings of full-time women employees Great Britain 1983*

	White	Black
Median weekly earnings	£77.50	£78.50
(as a proportion of male)	60%	71%

Source: Brown (1984)

It is interesting that Brown's results on pay differentials by sex and race
appear to mirror those identified in the USA. US Census data, quoted by
Wallace (1980), appear to confirm Oaxaca's historical interpretation that
between 1955 and 1971 'black women gained access to traditionally white
female jobs faster than black males entered white male jobs' (Oaxaca, 1977).
Wallace's figures[3] suggest that between 1939 and 1976 black women closed
their earnings gap with white women far more than black men did in relation
to white men. By 1976 race appeared to add nothing to the disadvantages
faced by black *women* over and above their sex. However, Malveaux
(1987), argues that the 'convergence' theory makes selective use of statistics,
using raw data to avoid comparing like with like.

A similar argument is being advanced in this article. Before we can accept
Brown's 'convergent' thesis as a true picture of the situation in Britain, his
figures require further scrutiny. Aside from the possibility of sample bias,
discussed above, Brown's results, reproduced in Table 1, provide only a
partial, and to some extent inaccurate, account of racial divisions between
women in the labour market.

There are three critical differences between white and black women in
Britain which qualify Colin Brown's findings. Firstly black women work
longer hours, in both full-time and part-time work; secondly black women
are concentrated in London; thirdly they have a younger and hence better
qualified age profile. Once these points are allowed for, the relative earnings
position of black women in the British labour market begins to look very
different.

The effect of allowing for the longer hours worked by black full-time workers is shown in Table 2. On an hourly comparison, black women full-time workers in Brown's sample earned 3p *less* per hour on average, as against 26 per cent *more* in weekly rates.

Table 2   *Relative value of full-time women's earnings by race*

	Black women : White women
Weekly pay	
(Brown, 1984)	126 : 100
Weekly pay (aged 25–54)	
(Brown, 1984)	88 : 100
Weekly pay (London graduates)	
(LLSS, 1986)	71 : 100
Hourly pay	
(Brown, 1984)	97 : 100
Hourly pay (London)	
(LLSS, 1986)	77 : 100

Sources: Brown (1984) and London Living Standards Survey (LLSS)

Considering the real value or buying power of their earnings, the discrepancy may be even greater. Part of the reason why Colin Brown finds little difference between women in wage rates is that black women are concentrated in London where women's pay is higher than average. As many as 51 per cent of economically active black women live in London (Department of Employment, 1988). But higher prices in London reduce the overall spending power of black women compared to that of white women workers. Evidence of pay differences in London by sex and race for those in employment show that once regional differences and working-hour differences are allowed for, white women earn 23 per cent more per hour than black.[4] Moreover, black women in London earn only 63 per cent of the average black man's weekly earnings, less than the equivalent proportion for whites (72 per cent); emphasizing that disadvantages of race do not cancel out disadvantages of sex for black women.

For a variety of reasons black women with jobs are much more likely to be in the 25–54 age group,[5] at the hump of the age/earnings profile. If comparisons are restricted to women in that age group, the race gap in weekly rates becomes clearer. Similarly, if differences in qualifications levels are abstracted, the gap also widens. Table 2 shows that black women graduates in London earn on average only 71 per cent as much a week as white women graduates.

Black women are also more likely to work shifts. On Brown's evidence 16 per cent of black women do, compared to 11 per cent of white. West Indian women indeed work night shifts much more frequently than white men. Our evidence from London also shows that black women are less likely to have fringe benefits[6] and more likely to work in poorer physical conditions. So in terms of the 'total employment package', black women can be seen to be considerably worse off than white women.

Differences in occupational status

At first sight the occupational profile of black women as compared to white looks promising (Table 3 from the Department of Employment, 1988). But a similar 'deconstruction' can be carried out, for these figures are subject to all the distortions considered above, and to two further major problems.

Table 3 *Women's employment by occupation and ethnic origin*

	White %	Black %
All non-manual	65	59
Managerial and professional	25	27
Clerical, etc.	30	25
Other non-manual	10	7
Manual		
Craft, etc.	4	9
Other manual	31	31

Source: Labour Force Survey (LFS) 1984/5/6

Firstly, these figures, unlike the pay data considered above, are for full- and part-time workers together. For reasons we shall discuss below, black women with jobs are generally more likely to work full time. However, amongst white women poor employment is heavily concentrated in part-time jobs. Ninety per cent of white women in manual and personal service work in London are part time. Amongst black women, however, poor jobs are very often full-time jobs – 38 per cent of full-time black women workers in London are in manual and personal service work (see Table 4).

Secondly, socioeconomic categories used in these types of analysis can obscure large differences in the actual employment position of women. This problem is a legacy of the sexist bias in socioeconomic and occupational categories which differentiate finely between levels of male work but which bunch together widely different types of work for women because they were never designed to measure class differentiation between women (see Hunt, 1981; Thomas, 1986).

Over half the female labour force in this country (56.7 per cent) are classified into just eight of the 100+ occupational units which form the basis of socioeconomic group classification. Some of these units – for example 46.3 other clerks and cashiers; 49 receptionists, typists, secretaries; 16 nurse administrators and nurses – cover a very wide range of jobs and have rather ambiguous class or SEG status. If, as is likely, black women are particularly concentrated in the poorer types of jobs *within* these occupational units, much of the class status difference between them and white women will have been obscured by the classification process. Data from the London Survey 1986 reinforce this supposition. The average pay for black women within non-manual jobs in London was only £137 a week, £31 less than 'non-manual' white women.

Nurses are one example of the obscuring of status differentials. Black nurses tend to be State Enrolled, rather than State Registered Nurses or RGNs (Hicks, 1982), though even this is difficult to establish from the official statistics which differentiate only by place of birth, not race. As SENs their pay and prospects are considerably worse, but they are classed in the same occupation and socioeconomic group as predominantly white RGNs/SRNs.

Similarly, observation of clerical and secretarial work shows a distinct differentiation between the routine, boring keyboarding jobs often held by black women, and the true secretaries and personal assistants, the majority of whom are white (GLC, 1985). Yet the classification system lumps them all together, again obscuring real differences.

If the socioeconomic group and social-class categories better reflected the differences *within* women's work, then official statistics would show up greater race differences between women than they do. In this instance, sexism in social categorizations serves also to obscure racial divisions in real life. Some of the effects of bias in response can be seen from comparing the results Brown obtained to those of the 1985 LFS. For example, Brown's survey identifies 44 per cent of Asian women as semi-skilled and 6 per cent as skilled, whereas the small LFS 1985 sample found 34 per cent semi-skilled and 12 per cent skilled.

The comparison between London and Great Britain as a whole suggests that the relatively high proportion of black women in non-manual jobs is very much an outcome of their concentration in the London labour market. Outside London only about 40 per cent of black women appear to be non-manual workers (and only 6 per cent professionals). For white women outside London the proportions are around 57 per cent non-manual and 20 per cent professional.[7]

The effect of standardizing for differences in the amount of part-time work once regional differences are excluded are shown in Table 4.

Table 4 *Socioeconomic group of women by race and hours, London 1986 (%)*

| | All women | | Full-time workers | | Part-time workers | |
	Black	White	Black	White	Black	White
Prof., employers and managers	4	18	5	24	[0]	4
Intermediate non-manual	30	25	28	29	[40]	6
Junior non-manual	26	35	25	33	[40]	32
Skilled manual	6	4	8	4	[0]	3
Personal service	13	11	13	5	[10]	23
Semi-skilled manual	15	4	15	4	[10]	4
Unskilled	5	4	2	0	[15]	11
White-collar	42	68	58	86	[80]	44
Manual	33	19	30	9	[35]	41
Total sample	80	590	60	392	20	198

Source: LLSS

Table 4 shows that race differences are much starker if part-time women workers are separated off. Amongst full-time workers, a black woman is three times more likely than a white woman to be a manual worker, though for the female workforce as a whole, the ratio of black to white manual workers is just over 3 : 2.

While black women part-time workers are disadvantaged relative to black women full-timers, data from the LLSS (Table 4) suggest that differences are small, though sample sizes make this difficult to establish conclusively. More important is the observation that white women who work full time are to some extent able to avoid the lowest-paid areas of work, and that this is much less true of black women full-timers. Avoiding part-time work does not bring black women the same gains. Statistically speaking, black women as a group do benefit from their tendency to work full time − that is, their socioeconomic group profile is partly a reflection of this tendency − but the degree of discrimination they face may be underestimated if comparisons are not made separately for full-time and part-time work. Further evidence on this point comes from a more detailed look at fringe benefits in relation to race and part-time status.[8]

In what follows we consider how the picture of racial differences between women in Britain is affected by the pattern of part-time and full-time working and differences in age and qualifications. We then go on to consider the importance of unemployment as a critical factor differentiating the experiences of women of different racial backgrounds in the London labour market and what the effects of economic crisis have been on women of different races in London.

The size of the London sample precludes any detailed differentiation *between* black women by ethnic group and, as with all other surveys which do not distinguish white women by ethnic group, our sample of *white* women includes women from ethnic minority groups suffering from racial disadvantage, such as the Cypriots and Chinese (See Yuval-Davis, 1988; Westwood and Bhachu, 1988). To some degree, then, our information underestimates the effects of racial disadvantage amongst women in the London labour market, but it is impossible to gauge the degree, given the lack of information on non-black ethnic minorities in employment.

Race and part-time work

The emphasis white feminists have placed on part-time work as a determinant of the sexual division of labour and of differential rewards between men and women's paid work can be seen as ethnocentric (Amos and Parmar, 1984; Barrett and McIntosh, 1985). For white women, rewards, prospects and the quality of work vary greatly between those who work full time and those who work part time (Table 4; Martin and Roberts, 1984; Bruegel, 1983; GLC, 1986). Occupation by occupation, part-timers earn less per hour than full-timers, but part-time working is not a major factor in keeping black women's pay and prospects so far below those of white men.

White women who work full time tend to be free of immediate childcare responsibilities and those with childcare responsibilities tend to work part time, but that standard picture of the way women have negotiated their 'double burden' does not apply to black women and suggests that we need to rethink the 'domestic responsibilities' model of women's position in the labour market. Interestingly, the strength of the link between childcare responsibilities and part-time work seems to have declined nationally over the last ten years; our figures for London also suggest that it is much less pronounced in London than elsewhere.

In the light of this, it may be time to revise the generalized view of part-time work reflecting constrained choices. The low pay associated with it might better be seen as a price part-timers have to pay for the relative freedom of having some (unpaid) time for housework and childcare. In comparison, black women – especially West Indian women – appear to be constrained to working full time.

It is increasingly clear that in Britain today black women are more likely to be 'economically active' and much less likely to work part time than white women (Stone, 1983). This is true irrespective of age, childcare responsibilities and area, though there are important differences between ethnic minority groups, according to both the LFS (Table 5) and Brown (1984).[9] Black women are also more likely to be unemployed than white women, a point which will be considered in more detail below.

Table 5 *Proportion of economically active women working full or part time*

Ethnic group	% Full-time employees	% Part-time	% Self-employed
White	52	40	6
West Indian	71	24	2
Indian	66	21	8
Pakistani/Bangladeshi	[55]	[27]	[18]
All black	65	25	7

Source: LFS 1984/5/6

One reason for the greater participation of black women in the labour market might be considered to be the higher rate of single parenthood amongst West Indian women (Colin Brown's figures for the country as a whole suggest that nearly a third of West Indian households with children are headed by single parents, compared to 10 per cent of white and 5 per cent of Asian households with children). However, this is not a satisfactory explanation, for two reasons: Colin Brown's figures show that West Indian lone parents are *less* likely to have a job and are *more* dependent on supplementary benefit/unemployment benefit than white single parents.[10] Secondly, he finds that Asian women are unlikely to work part time and yet single parenthood is rare amongst them.

Our London sample is too small to distinguish between West Indian and Asian women but it does show part-time working to be much commoner amongst white mothers than amongst black mothers, even when single parents are excluded (Table 6). On this basis, it is clear that high levels of single parenthood cannot explain the greater propensity of black women to work full time.

Table 6   *Women in employment: proportion working part time by race and childcare responsibilities, London 1986*

Age and childcare	White %	Black %
With pre-school children	61	29
With school children	57	38
No children		
Age under 30	3	0
Age 30–50	20	4
Age over 50	54	49

Source: LLSS

Nevertheless, the evidence is that the high rate of full-time employment amongst black women is to be explained by the economic situation of black households. Colin Brown tends to a 'culturist' explanation, rather than a material one, following other writers on the position of black women in Britain (Stone, 1983; Haynes, 1983).

While it is clear that cultural background does affect whether women seek employment, and to some extent the type of employment they seek, this explanation is always in danger of falling into outdated stereotypes, sometimes with tinges of almost racist essentialism. As Wallace points out in relation to the USA, much of the research on black women undertaken by white economists and sociologists suffers from 'unwarranted inferences; for example the tendency to speculate about the psychosociological characteristics of individuals, the inheritance of economic status, or the structure of black families' (Wallace, 1980: 2). It is interesting to note, with this in mind, that Cain (1966) sought to explain the high rates of labour-force participation of black women in the USA between 1940 and 1960 by the *greater* prevalence of part-time work amongst them.

In the British context, in particular, there is a need to take account of the wide diversity of origins of the black population. While cultural norms clearly influence the desire and ability of women to seek paid work, once that decision has been made, the choice between part-time and full-time work hardly varies between black women. Part-time working is as uncommon amongst employed women from the Hindu, Sikh and Muslim communities as amongst West Indian women (Table 5), even though Hindu, Muslim and Sikh women have at least as many childcare responsibilities. If a cultural explanation for differences in the part-time/full-time divide were sufficient, it would have to be one which noted the 'deviance' of white women in working part time, rather than that of black women seeking full-time work. The pattern of full-time working amongst women from ethnic minority communities with widely varying rates of participation in the labour market, is perhaps another example of the need for a much more *dynamic* approach to the understanding of cultural constraints, a position argued by Westwood and Bhachu (1988) and Warrier (1988).

The racism faced by black people in employment means, possibly paradoxically, that black households rely much more heavily on the income that women can bring in, irrespective of cultural traditions (Cook and Watt, 1987). Again the US experience (which has generated a much richer data source on race and economic welfare) is instructive (Malveaux, 1987). In 1976, 34 per cent of black US household income was earned by women, compared to 26 per cent of white household income, even ignoring single-adult households (Wallace, 1980).

In Britain in each type of household (apart from lone parents) income per head is lower for black households than white, even after women's incomes are included.[11]

The London Survey also shows that there is a great gulf in the assets available to black households;[12] quite simply they are poorer and more in need of women's earnings. Where supplementary benefit is available, as in the case of single mothers, it makes less sense for black women to seek employment, especially if childcare is costly. Where supplementary benefit is not available, as with most married or cohabiting couples, black women are more likely to seek full-time work, despite their poorer prospects. An analysis which focuses on the effects of racism on men's earnings is probably the best way of reconciling these differences.

The propensity for white women to work part time suggests that, in a sense, they can afford to, or at least it is often not worth their while to seek full-time work. Of course where a woman has access to reasonably well-paid work, these constraints are much less binding and what we find is that women with qualifications are much more likely to work full time, even when they have children, than women without recognized skills. In London both part-time women workers and full-time housewives were much less well qualified than women in full-time work.[13]

White women without qualifications seem to get 'stuck' in part-time jobs. In particular, it is possible to identify a group of older women whose children have grown up who nevertheless continue to work part time. This draws us to the conclusion that earnings potential and earning needs are much more important in explaining the pattern of women's employment than many writers allow. The pattern does vary with domestic responsibilities and ethnic background, but by less than the accepted stereotypes.

Racial exclusion in the market for 'women's work'

Sexual discrimination is an important issue for black women as well as white. Other things being equal, sex differences in pay may be *greater* in the black communities, despite the fact that black men's pay is lower than white men's. We have already established, contrary to some observers, that racial discrimination between women is also important for black women. This is particularly evident if we look more closely at women with some qualifications.

Black women in the British labour market today are not especially badly qualified, despite the stereotype. The LFS found no difference in the proportion of black and white women with higher qualifications (12 per cent) (Department of Employment, 1988). Nationally, both the LFS and Colin Brown (1984) show West Indian women to be better qualified than white women. In London, black women hold fewer higher qualifications than white women, but they are more likely to have gained some qualifications at school.[14] In each age group black women are less qualified, but their younger age profile compensates; older women – black and white – lack formal qualifications on a massive scale.

What is clear, however, is that, for the most part, black women earn less relative to their qualifications than white women (see Table 7).

Table 7 *Weekly pay by qualifications, sex and race: London 1986 (£)*

Highest qualification	Men		Women	
	White	Black	White	Black
Degree	293	298	224	159
Other post-school	224	191	152	144
School qualifications	200	173	150	114
No qualifications	195	165	133	109

Source: LLSS

The reasons why pay rates should be so much lower for black women than white, once qualifications are taken into account, are not immediately obvious. We examine below how far it might stem from the greater exclusion of black women with qualifications from higher-level work and from higher-paying industries, finance and banking in particular. The figures suggest that it is not the result of any concentration in small non-unionized workplaces, since the evidence available to us is that black women are not more likely to work in small establishments. As discussed earlier, there may be some undercounting of black women working in small workplaces, but they would also be excluded from the qualifications figures, so the argument is not affected.

Although black women are less likely to be in a workplace where the union is recognized, when they are, they are more likely to join than white women (66 per cent to 62 per cent; the same is true of black men in comparison to white men: 84 per cent to 76 per cent). Two-thirds of black women workers in London are union members, compared to 64 per cent of white men, 76 per cent of black men and 70 per cent of white women. So much for the stereotype of the typical trade unionist: over 40 per cent of London trade union members are not white men.

Table 8 shows the proportion of the London Living Standards Survey sample who had school and/or post-school qualifications who were in unskilled, semi-skilled and personal service jobs at the time of interview. The greater degree of 'overqualification' identified amongst black people is likely to arise from racial exclusion and discrimination.

Table 8 *Comparison of 'overqualification' by sex and race (%)*

| | Men | | Women | |
	White	Black	White	Black
People in unskilled/semi-skilled & personal service jobs as a % of those:				
with post-school qualifications	0.6	20.0	10.7	20.0
with school qualifications	11.8	40.0	8.9	13.5
with any qualification	9.5	31.6	9.6	15.2

As many as one in five of black men and women with qualifications beyond A level (including apprenticeships as well as degrees) is working in a job which in the main does not demand such qualifications, compared to less than 1 per cent of white men and 10 per cent of white women (including part-time workers). In this respect racial discrimination is at least as important, if not more important than sex discrimination in determining the opportunities open to black women.

Black women are much more likely to work in manufacturing, especially in food processing and clothing, and in transport, and much less likely to work in banking, insurance and finance than white women.[15] A higher proportion of black women do work in the public sector (35 per cent to 30 per cent for white women) when the nationalized industries and recently privatized concerns like British Telecom are included, but the proportion in public sector *services* like education, health, local government – taken as a whole – is similar to that for white women (28 per cent to 26 per cent).

Brown found, on the other hand, that a higher proportion of black women work in the public services. Whether this is because these are less discriminatory or because job for job they offer poorer pay is not clear.

Our evidence is, then, that a substantial part of the racial discrimination experienced by black women in the labour market is concealed when researchers fail to allow for the relative youth of the black female workforce and when part-time work is not distinguished from full-time. In London, at any rate, the concentration of black women in the manufacturing sector, and their relative exclusion from banking and finance, contributes to an under-utilization of their skills and qualifications and hence to their lower pay.

Unemployment and its impact on black women

Since manufacturing is the sector most in decline and finance and banking is the fastest-growing sector, it is not surprising to find that black women have experienced far more unemployment than white (Table 9). This is probably why we also found that over the years 1981–6, black women experienced the greatest decline in living standards.

Table 9 *Women's unemployment by age and race: unemployed* as a proportion of economically active*

	London		GB	
	All ages	Under 30**	All ages	16–24
White	3	7	10	15
Black	13	33	19	31
West Indian	–	–	18	29
Indian	–	–	18	28
Pakistani/Bangladeshi	–	–	38	–

* self-defined. ** excluding those with children.
Source: LLSS 1986 and LFS 1984/5/6

Racial differences in unemployment rates between women seem to be especially pronounced in London, possibly because of the industrial and occupational divisions of women by race. Differences again are particularly marked for the younger age group, despite the fact, noted above, that qualification differences between younger black and white women are not large. The LFS shows that unemployment rates for black women with qualifications are over twice the rate for qualified white women for every age group.

There can be no real mystery as to why this is so, but it is interesting to observe the differences in long-term effects of unemployment. The long-term effects of unemployment on men's incomes and prospects have increasingly been recognized, but for women, and specifically white women, such effects are overshadowed by the 'deskilling' effects of childcare breaks. Our earlier discussions of activity rates suggested that breaks for childcare are less important for black women, but our evidence is that black women find their longer-term prospects and relative incomes reduced following experiences of unemployment.

The London Living Standards Survey collected information from three-quarters of the survey members on their jobs and pay in 1981, five years before the survey.[16] Recall information of this type is never as reliable as recent data, nevertheless the results shown in Table 10 are indicative.

Table 10 *Increase in earnings 1981–6 (%)*

All individuals	49		
All men	53	All women	45
White men	57	White women	53
Black men	22	Black women	5

Source: LLSS

The whole sample, excluding only those not employed in 1981, were asked about their subjective judgements of the change in the value of their (own) take-home pay. Again black women came out considerably worse than any other group, despite the high increase in unemployment levels in the period for both white and black men.

The evidence from the London Living Standards Survey is of increasing polarization in income and living standards between households and individuals in London since 1980–1. This is in line with, and indeed greater than, the experience over the country as a whole (Townsend et al., 1987). The London Survey also shows that polarization of income *between* women has been greater than that between men. Some women, on the London evidence, have done relatively well in recent years and some have done particularly badly. Race would appear to be one important distinguishing factor. For black women direct discrimination appears to be conflated by their concentration in manual work and their consequent greater risk of unemployment.

In general, unemployment was the greatest source of income loss amongst the sample who were in work in 1981. The incomes of those unemployed at the time of the survey declined on average by 52 per cent, compared to an increase in income amongst those in work of 75 per cent over the same period. As many as a tenth of all black women who had jobs in 1981 found that they were much worse off in 1986, compared to 8 per cent of white women and 7 per cent of all men. This may well be explained by their much higher vulnerability to unemployment.

Even amongst those who had jobs in 1986 (many of whom had had some experience of unemployment) only 6 per cent of black women found that their incomes went 'much further', compared to 19 per cent of white men and 11 per cent of white women. At the other end of the scale, 39 per cent of black women in work judged themselves to be worse off, compared to 32 per cent of white men and 37 per cent of white women.

For both men and women the differences in the experiences of manual and non-manual workers were marked. Amongst those in non-manual work in 1981, average income (for both men and women) increased by 40 per cent; against this manual workers – a much higher proportion of whom had experienced unemployment – increased their average incomes by no more than 21 per cent. So the concentration of black women in manual work has contributed in at least two ways to a deterioration in earning power relative to many white women, both directly as non-manual incomes grew faster (by 65 per cent, as compared to 51 per cent on National Economic Survey figures) and as redundancies and unemployment hit manual workers harder.

Conclusions

Many black women have rightly criticized the ethocentrism of much of the feminist literature on women's position in Britain (Amos and Parmar, 1984). This criticism holds particularly for the emphasis that has been placed on the importance of the part-time/full-time divide in characterizing the position of women in the labour market and the associated importance attached to domestic responsibilities as the prime determinant of that position. As I hope

I have shown, where black women are concerned other factors, primarily racism as it affects unemployment and the earning levels of both black men and women, are at least as important in determining women's place in the labour market. The existing literature, structured as it is by standard categorizations of occupations and by standard approaches to gathering information, especially through household surveys, presents a false picture of the position of black women in relation to white. Both groups are affected by sexual discrimination in labour markets, but black women are also subject to racial discrimination, much of which remains hidden by conventional approaches to the gathering and analysis of labour market information.

It does not follow that better research methods will help to improve the position of black women, and many black people are, understandably, wary of the inclusion of racial information in the Population Census. It is an open question as to whether the extensive monitoring of the position of black people in individual workplaces has done much over the last few years to radically improve their position. However, without an adequate baseline to measure differences, it is difficult to see where and how improvements can be identified. For this reason alone it is important to demystify existing analyses and to show how, and in what ways, they serve to obscure the real experience of black women.

Notes

1. Definitions of 'black' in the LLSS rely on self-assessment. The overall sample of black women in the London Living Standards Survey was 173. Of these 77 described themselves as Asian, 45 as Afro-Caribbean, 35 as 'Black British' and 16 were from other black groups.

2. Allen and Wolkowitz (1987) summarize the 'numbers debate' in relation to homeworkers, showing the limitations of official statistics, but they guard against the all too prevalent assumption that this only affects ethnic minority women. It is also important not to underestimate the economic power that working in the small family business may give some ethnic minority women *vis-à-vis* their relatives. See Westwood and Bhachu (1988) for a discussion of the problems of assessing levels of exploitation of women engaged in ethnic minority businesses.

3. Wallace quotes the following figures:

Relative earnings by race: USA 1939 and 1976, men and women (%)

	1939	1976
Black men : white men	45	74
Black women : white women	30	97

Source: Wallace (1980: 59)

4. The figures from the London Living Standards Survey are as follows:

Full-time women workers: earnings by race, London 1986

	Weekly earnings	Hourly earnings	% of male	
			Weekly pay	Hourly pay
White	£160.1	£4.3	72	78
Black	£124.5	£3.3	63	72

Source: LLSS

The London Living Standards Survey identified only 20 women homeworkers in all; it may be that, as with Brown's survey and the LFS, there has been some under-recording of homeworking, and therefore of poorly paid work amongst our black respondents. The survey may also underestimate black women nurses and teachers in London; it did not trace any professional workers amongst the black female sample.

5. Information from the LFS in Department of Employment, 1988, shows that 46 per cent of white women in employment were aged 25–44, compared to 53 per cent of black women in employment.

6. The proportion of full-time women workers with 'fringe' benefits, was as follows:

Full-time women workers, London 1986

% with	Black	White
Training	36	44
Paid holiday	80	84
2 weeks' notice	70	76
Sick pay	64	73
Union coverage	45	50

Source: LLSS

7. Differences in socioeconomic group are affected by the concentration of black women in London, as the following comparison shows:

Socioeconomic group by ethnic origin, national : London comparisons, all employed women

	GB (LFS 1985)		London (LLSS 1986)	
	White	Black*	White	Black
Prof., employers and managers	9	5	18	4
Other non-manual	54	46	40	56
Skilled manual	8	9	4	6
Semi-skilled manual	21	32	15	28
Unskilled	8	5	4	5
Total sample	9,318	205	590	80

* West Indian/Guyanese/Indian/Pakistani and Bangladeshi only.

8. The figures from the London Living Standards Survey are as follows:

Fringe benefits for women workers by race and hours, London 1986

% with	White women		Black women	
	Full-time	Part-time	Full-time	Part-time
Training	52	28	34	[39]
Holiday	92	68	82	[75]
1 week's notice	84	59	73	[63]
Meal subsidy	46	31	45	[25]
Company pension	63	12	55	[16]
Car	7	2	8	[0]
Sick pay	85	49	68	[50]
TU coverage	53	46	47	[35]
Total sample	388	60	196	20

Source: LLSS

9. Brown gives the following figures:

Women's part-time work as a proportion of employment by ethnic group, 1983

			Asian		
	White	West Indian	Hindu	Sikh	Muslim
% part time	45	29	18	14	[14]

Source: Brown (1984)

10. Brown gives the following figures:

Lone parents by employment status and benefit by race, GB 1983

	White	West Indian	Asian
% with earner in household	53	49	39
% unemployment benefit	7	11	10
% supplementary benefit	45	50	45
Total sample	85	203	71

Source: Brown (1984)

11. Brown gives the following figures:

Earnings per household member by family type and race, GB 1983

	Family type			
			Other	
Race	Extended	Lone parent	with children	w/o children
White	£46	£20	£37	£59
West Indian	£37	£24	£32	£51
Asian	£27	£21	£27	£50

Source: Brown (1984)

12. The average value of assets (other than houses) owned by black women in the survey was £1,330, compared to £3,519 for white women.

13. Analysis of the London Survey gives the following picture:

Educational experience by economic activity, London 1986

Current economic activity	Left school at 17+ %	No qualifications %
Full-time work	54	22
Part-time work	33	49
Housewife	26	60
Unemployed	31	50

All women N=1,457

Source: LLSS

14. The London Survey figures for highest qualifications are as follows:

Highest qualifications (at school and college) of women by race and economic activity

% with	All women		Full-time workers	
	White	Black	White	Black
Degree	8	5	15	6
Other post-school	13	10	14	14
A Levels	8	7	15	7
O Levels	17	22	26	32
CSE	6	9	9	14
None	49	45	21	29
Total sample	1,224	163	387	60

Source: LLSS

15. The figures from the London Living Standards Survey broadly reflect those found elsewhere:

Industrial distribution of women workers by race

Industry	White %	Black %
Energy, water, metal manuf. & chemical	1	1
Engineering etc.	3	4
Other manufacture*	5	14
Construction	2	0
Distribution	13	10
Transport & communications	2	10
Finance and banking	21	10
Other services	44	41
Private	70	65
Public	30	35

* Includes clothing, food, plastics, toys as sizeable employers of women.
Source: LLSS

16. Those not questioned were those who had stayed in the same job throughout the period.

References

Allen, Sheila and Wolkowitz, Carol (1987) *Homeworking: Myths and Realities*. London: Macmillan.
Amos, Valerie and Parmar, Pratibha (1984) 'Challenging imperial feminism', *Feminist Review*, 17.
Anwar, M. (1979) *The Myth of Return*. London: Heinemann.
Barrett, Michèle and McIntosh, Mary (1985) 'Ethnocentrism and socialist feminist theory', *Feminist Review*, 20.
Brown, Colin (1984) *White and Black in Britain*. London: Policy Studies Institute.
Bruegel, Irene (1983) 'Women's employment, legislation and the labour market', in Lewis (1983).

Cain, Glen (1966) *Married Women in the Labor Force: An Economic Analysis*. Chicago: University of Chicago Press.

Cook, Juliet and Watt, Shantu (1987) 'Racism, women and poverty', in Glendinning and Millar (1987).

Davis, Mike, Marable, Manning, Pfiel, Fred and Sprinkler, Michael (eds) (1987) *The Year Left 2: Essays on Race, Ethnicity, Class and Gender*. London: Verso.

Department of Employment (1988) 'Ethnic origins and the labour market', *Employment Gazette*, March: 164.

Dex, Shirley (1983) 'The second generation: West Indian female school-leavers', in Phizacklea (1983).

Glendinning, Caroline and Millar, Jane (1987) *Women and Poverty in Britain*. Brighton: Wheatsheaf.

Greater London Council (1985) 'Office work and information technology', in *London Industrial Strategy*. London: GLC.

Greater London Council (1986) *London Labour Plan*. London: GLC.

Haynes, A. (1983) *The State of Black Britain*. London: Root Books.

Hoel, Barbro (1982) 'Contemporary clothing sweatshops', in West (1982).

Hicks, Cheryll (1982) 'Racism in nursing', *Nursing Times*, May.

Hunt, Audrey (1981) 'Women and government statistics', *EOC Research Bulletin*, 3.

Juster, F. Thomas (1987) *The Distribution of Economic Well-Being*. Cambridge, Mass.: Ballinger.

Kamdin, Ron (1987) *The Making of the Black Working Class in Britain*. Aldershot: Wildwood House.

Lewis, Jane (ed.) (1983) *Women's Welfare, Women's Rights*. London: Croom Helm.

Malveaux, Julianne (1987) 'The political economy of black women', in Davis et al. (1987).

Martin, Jean and Roberts, Ceridwen (1984) *Women and Employment: A Lifetime Perspective*. London: HMSO.

Morris, Peter (1987) 'The Labour Force Survey: a study in differential response', Central Statistical Office, *Statistical News*, 79, November.

Oaxaca, Ronald (1977) 'The persistence of male–female earnings differentials', in Juster (1987).

Phizacklea, A. (ed.) (1983) *One Way Ticket*. London: Routledge & Kegan Paul.

Stone, Karen (1983) 'Motherhood and waged work: West Indian, Asian and white mothers compared', in Phizacklea (1983).

Thomas, Roger (1986) 'The classification of women's occupation', *EOC Research Bulletin* 10, Autumn.

Townsend, Peter, Corrigan, Paul and Kowarzik, Ute (1987) *Poverty and Labour in London*. London: Low Pay Unit.

Wallace, Phyllis (1980) *Black Women in the Labor Force*. Cambridge Mass.: MIT Press.

Warrier, Shrikala (1988) 'Marriage, maternity and female economic activity: Gujarati mothers in Britain', in Westwood and Bhachu (1988).

West, Jackie (ed.) (1982) *Work, Women and the Labour Market*. London: Routledge & Kegan Paul.

Westwood, Sallie and Bhachu, Parminder (eds) (1988) *Enterprising Women: Ethnicity, Economy and Gender Relations*. London: Routledge & Kegan Paul.

Wilson, Amrit (1978) *Finding a Voice*. London: Virago.

Yuval-Davis, Nira (1988) 'Racism, anti-racism and "blackness" in contemporary Britain', paper to Conference of Socialist Economists, July.

Out But Not Down: Lesbians' Experience of Housing

Jayne Egerton

Lesbians and 'home'

> City-center, mid-traffic
> I wake to your public kiss. Your name
> is Judith, your kiss a sign
> to the shocked pedestrians, gathered
> beneath the light that means
> stop
> in our culture
> where red is a warning.
> (Broumas, 1977: 62)

> When it comes to work it always
> seemed to me that you gave the
> appearance of being a very lonely
> person having no social life at all,
> because you can't talk about it.
> (Hall Carpenter Archives, 1989: 58)

Lesbians do not have an undifferentiated experience of the world of work and family, but we share a sense of not belonging, of being 'apart' in many public, social and familial situations. Many lesbians are not 'out' to their families, workmates, the doctor, or even friends. Few of us are 'out' in every situation. We all make choices every day. Lack of recognition and support for our lives as lesbians means that our search for 'home' has a psychic as well as a practical dimension.

The psychological effects of chronic housing problems cannot be under-estimated. Feminists have described the way in which being homeless or living in poor-quality housing contributes to women's feelings of failure and worthlessness (Austerberry and Watson, 1980). We often internalize anger and blame ourselves for the problems we experience, whether they be battery and abuse, or homelessness (Eichenbaum and Orbach, 1982). Denise Marshall of Stonewall Housing Association told me that homeless

From *Feminist Review*, 36, 1990, pp. 75–88.

women who contact them often do not define themselves as homeless, or they attempt to hide the fact. It is as if they believe it reflects badly on them rather than on our society.

The inability to obtain decent and secure housing when combined with rarely being in living situations where one is able to be open as a lesbian can have disastrous effects on lesbians' self-esteem and mental health. I once advised a Glaswegian lesbian in her seventies who had been driven from one squalid and impermanent home after another as a result of harassment from neighbours. Her family would have nothing to do with her and her only friend had been her lover who had recently died. She had never experienced the pleasures of a genuine 'home' in her entire life and had taken tranquillizers for 'depression' for twenty years. Many of the lesbians who are resident in the worst and most institutionalized women's hostels would tell similar tales about their housing histories; tales full of the grief of rootlessness and 'nonbelonging'.

Home represents a great deal to me – touching a woman without a trace of defiance or self-consciousness, feeling 'real' and having my life witnessed. For women who do not have my lesbian networks or public existence as a lesbian, home is the place they can forget the habit of self-concealment and constant vigilance which spring from having a 'secret' self. Home, for all lesbians, is the real or imaginary place where we feel safe, loved and validated.

There has been little research conducted into lesbian housing need and experience, and existing feminist research has often ignored lesbians entirely (Austerberry and Watson, 1983). This article cannot hope to redress this omission in any definitive way. It combines statistics, anecdotes and impressions to convey what I see as some of the major housing problems facing lesbians, and considers whether this issue is part of a larger feminist agenda. In addition, it looks at the housing experiments of the 1970s in the light of changes over the past ten years in housing policy and the economic context. It asks whether or not 'home' is becoming an increasingly elusive reality for many lesbians.

Feminism and housing

Women's housing struggles

Women's access to decent accommodation is frequently determined by their relationship with a male wage-earner. Single, divorced and widowed women invariably have greater financial and housing problems than married or cohabiting women (Austerberry and Watson, 1983). Women's average hourly earnings continue to be only 74 per cent of male earnings, and 68 per cent of the low-paid are women (Small, 1985–6). The 1981 census revealed that, in London, where house prices have escalated, 54 per cent of households headed by men and only 32 per cent of households headed by women were homeowners (CHAR, 1988). The vast majority of women are economically in no position to break into the private rented sector, let alone owner occupation. Independent women have little choice but to rely on a shrinking public sector to meet their housing needs and those without children are rarely eligible for council accommodation.

Women have historically often been at the 'sharp end' of bad housing. The fact that most women are restricted to the private sphere for significant periods of their life – as mothers, housewives and carers – has given them an intimate awareness of the miseries of overcrowding, damp and disrepair, poor lighting and vandalism on council estates, bad design and lack of play space for children. From the 1915 rent strike on the Clyde to the housing struggles of Docklands in the late 1980s women have often initiated and played a leading role in community housing politics. In the 1970s, many Black and white working-class women found their political voice in tenants' organizations and housing campaigns. As the authors of a book documenting the lives of Black women in Britain point out:

> At the hands of unscrupulous landlords or racist local councils, we faced – and still do face – the worst housing conditions in Britain. By 1978 the proportion of Black people living in homes without baths, running hot water or an inside toilet was more than twice the national average, and three times as many Black families as white were living in sub-standard privately furnished accommodation. Because of the discriminatory policies of local authorities growing numbers of Black women were being housed in high rise blocks of problem estates – particularly if they were single parents. (Bryan et al., 1985: 160)

Few of these campaigns were self-consciously 'feminist' but many of the demands which were articulated did address female inequality and oppression. Some women developed a feminist consciousness as a result of involvement in housing politics. An organizer from a flat-dweller's action group at Netherley, Liverpool told *Spare Rib*:

> I have faced male chauvinism I failed to see existed before . . . we came to understand politics, usually thought of as a man's world, and expected more of ourselves – knew more about what we could and couldn't do for ourselves. People now call us women's libbers. I never realized but, we must have become just that. (*Spare Rib*, 1977)

A feminist issue?

The politics of housing was a recurrent part of the agenda of the women's liberation conferences of the 1970s. There was never a housing demand formulated as such, but perhaps this is because so many of the issues which were debated and organized around could not be considered in isolation from women's lack of access to secure, decent and affordable accommodation. There may also have been some ambivalence about defining housing as a feminist issue if this meant a capitulation to the idea of women as exclusively located in the home (Austerberry and Watson, 1983). One of the most notable, and long-lasting achievements of 1970s feminism was the creation of Women's Aid. Our recognition of many women's economic inability to leave violent relationships with men led to the creation of the refuge movement. Lesbians formed the backbone of Women's Aid (in my experience many women came out in this context) but were often invisible to the extent that we were there as feminists rather than as lesbians. There was a diverse range of feminist housing initiatives from the late 1970s. Women organized as housing workers, builders, architects and designers. There was a strong lesbian presence within most of these initiatives, but no explicitly lesbian agenda. Looking back I would say this is because lesbian feminists of the time were primarily 'active' as women rather than as lesbians. Many of the needs we identified were of equal relevance and importance to women as a whole, and single women in particular.

Lesbian-feminist housing experiments

There was a significant trend amongst lesbian feminists in the 1970s towards squatting and communal living. It coincided in time with the anti-statism prevalent in the anarchist and libertarian left. Many feminists came from this political background and had a passionate commitment to lifestyle politics. Direct action and resistance were championed in movement writings as ways of seizing control of one's own life. 'In and against the state' notions were not in the ascendant. The state was, in some quarters, seen as uniformly oppressive and unsusceptible to demands. (This is long before the days of the lesbian 'femocrat'.)

When I first came out in the early 1980s, most of the lesbians I met lived in communal, women-only households. These houses were occasionally owner occupied, but more commonly were squats, housing co-ops and housing associations. Few women lived with their lovers. The desire to live communally was not, of course, uniquely lesbian any more than it was specific to that period of women's liberation history. Anarchists, socialists and gay liberationists had also celebrated a lifestyle predicated on a critique of exclusive relationships and the nuclear family. Kollontai had declared:

> The stronger the collective, the more firmly established becomes the way of life. The closer the emotional ties between the members of the community, the less the need to seek refuge from loneliness in marriage. (cited in Holt, 1977: 231)

Few of the communal households of the 1970s, whether gay, women only or mixed socialist, still survive. As one feminist writer has lamented, 'The debris of innumerable communal households litters our social arena' (Clarke, 1983: 174). One woman I spoke to commented: 'It was a particular moment and it had a political content that was quite specific.' The time has passed. Squats are often repossessed within three months these days and, although there are more co-ops and housing associations than there used to be, there is also a greater housing crisis. A major concern of many of these women was safety and security. She concludes those people allocated a low status by society are allocated the worst housing. And for women, and lesbians, such housing exacerbates risks and vulnerability to attack (Anlin, 1989: 31). Amongst the direct reasons which were cited as contributing to their housing problems were several examples of appalling harassment and violence:

> One lesbian couple had had excreta put through the letterbox of their council flat, had had break ins, and were subsequently forced to sleep with a knife by their bedside . . . another lesbian was verbally harassed (the threat of actual physical violence was also real) by National Front supporters in adjacent neighbouring flats . . . another, living in a hostel for young single homeless people, was harassed by other residents who targeted both her and a gay male resident as Aids carriers, refusing to use crockery and cutlery that they had touched. (Anlin, 1989: 5)

Stonewall Housing Association, which caters for young homeless lesbians and gay men, confirm that the lesbians who approach them for housing are more likely to have experienced violence than gay applicants. Between May 1988 and February 1989 49 out of 261 applicants had experienced violence, and three-quarters of these were women. At the CHAR housing for lesbians and gay men conference in 1988:

> Security was one of the major unmet needs voiced by the women's caucus, a number of lesbians there expressing fears about isolation and vulnerability in terms of harassment and eviction. (CHAR, 1988: 7)

This fear of isolation has led historically to lesbians (and gay men) gravitating towards cities which offer the possibility of social networks and support. In the Homeless Action survey:

> All the twenty-eight respondents either do or wanted to live in areas where they have other lesbian friends, or in areas they know to have a high proportion of lesbians. This makes many lesbians reluctant to leave London (Anlin, 1989: 29)

Sarah Green, a PhD student currently researching into lesbian feminism in London, has found that, in her sample, housing is the single, most chronic practical problem facing lesbians in London. Many of her interviewees live in short-life accommodation, and most of those who live in secure accommodation are council tenants. Those who do live relatively securely tended to express enormous relief to her and an acknowledgement that they were fortunate. The problem of housing was a recurrent theme in these interviews. The anxiety these women expressed about living in sub-standard and insecure housing perhaps testifies to the extent to which 'home' has a special significance for us as an antidote to the hostility and invisibility which we may experience 'outside'.

Lesbians and gay men

Joint lesbian and gay housing initiatives in the voluntary and statutory sector are a mid-to-late-1980s phenomenon. The yoking together of lesbian and gay concerns gained its original impetus from the 'rainbow-coalition'-style politics of the Greater London Council, and, subsequently, a handful of other Labour-controlled local authorities.

Lesbian and gay working parties and support groups now exist in a number of local councils and voluntary housing projects and campaigns. It is undeniably true that lesbians and gay men do have some housing problems in common. We suffer as a result of the refusal by most housing providers and managers to recognize 'family units' as self-defined (CHAR, 1988: 3). Same-sex couples still often face discrimination when attempting to obtain double mortgages from building societies (gay men in particular are having problems in this area because so many insurance companies want information about HIV testing and status). Large numbers of young people are thrown out of the parental home once their parents know about their sexuality (Trenchard and Warren, 1985). Lesbian and gay partners do not have the same rights as heterosexuals to succeed to a tenancy if the tenant dies. The law, at present, gives little protection to anyone who experiences harassment, but harassment on racial or sexual grounds can be challenged in law, unlike harassment on the grounds of sexuality (CHAR, 1988). Many lesbians and gay men experience harassment in both the private and public sector. As we get older we may fear ending our lives in residential homes which do not recognize our sexual and emotional histories and lives. (This is more likely for lesbians since the majority of pensioners are women.) We all need a home, at times, as a defence against homophobia and lack of recognition by the dominant heterosexual culture.

I would argue, nevertheless, that gender is a more crucial determinant of housing choice and experience than sexuality. A survey in the United States found that white gay men were the single most affluent minority in the States (Jay and Young, 1979). Research in this country suggests a similar picture. Their lack of financial commitments in terms of responsibility for 'dependants' means that they have far greater spending power than heterosexual men. We may share an experience of certain forms of anti-gay discrimination in housing, but our initial capacity to obtain decent and secure accommodation is determined by our position in the labour market.

In addition to the material advantages which accrue to gay men on a basis of their gender, the social and symbolic meaning of being men unconnected to women can be positive. Women, conversely, are expected to derive their sense of self from connections with men. Feminist psychotherapists have noted that:

> Our culture does not have a positive image of a woman on her own. It is never seen as a choice. It always appears as something that befalls her and engenders sympathy. . . . [Women alone] are out of the ordinary and somewhat frightening. (Eichenbaum and Orbach, 1982: 2)

The tendency to too readily conflate lesbian and gay oppression is, I believe, symptomatic of the current weakness of organized feminism, and of the lack of support lesbians have often received from heterosexual feminists. Section 28 and the creeping moralism of the 1980s have also given mixed gay organizing a new lease of life but, I believe, our experience as 'women' has frequently been lost within these politics.

Lesbians' experience of housing

Many of the housing difficulties which lesbians encounter overlap with those of single women in general. Race, class and a host of other material factors can also play a critical part in determining lesbians' experience of housing.

Recent research amongst workers, residents and management committee members at Homeless Action, a women's housing organization with a 30 per cent lesbian target, found that twenty-seven of the total sample (of twenty-eight women) believed that single women generally have difficulty getting housing (Anlin, 1989: 35). The majority of the respondents, however, also felt that lesbians have greater difficulty in obtaining housing than other single women.

> Twenty out of the total sample did believe that being a lesbian, or becoming one, had contributed either directly or indirectly to their being homeless or in unsatisfactory housing conditions on one or more occasions, either now or in the past. (Anlin, 1989: 5)

There was a strong awareness amongst the interviewees of factors other than sexuality which had a significant influence in their lives. Half of the women said other influences such as having children, race, cultural background, class, physical and mental health, prison records, family, or political affiliations were as important to them. When questioned about the relationship between sexuality and discrimination in housing one woman commented, 'Single Black women might find it harder than a white lesbian, who at least has the option to "hide" her sexuality to avoid discrimination' (Anlin, 1989: 36).

This research does suggest that sexuality can lead women into forms of housing which they would not otherwise choose:

> For many of the lesbians in the sample, although ghettos were seen to constitute bad housing, this was preferable because it meant they could be with other lesbians. Many often put up with unsatisfactory housing even if it is in conflict with what they would really like, because they can create a lesbian community there. (Anlin, 1989: 31)

In addition, there is no longer the same feminist context which bred the desire for communal living with other women:

> It was a women's community. We were very accountable to each other in terms of how we behaved in relationships, with money, etc. It was a whole social and sexual context that is hard to imagine now. Now my home is my refuge. Yes, it provided support but it was a political location and now it's a refuge from everything – classic Thatcherism.

These communes were overloaded with impossible expectations, none more so in my experience than lesbian-feminist households. It had been noted by 1970s researchers that mixed-sex communes often simply reproduced the existing sexual division of labour, albeit on a larger scale (Abrams and McCulloch, 1976). Our households, too, in their own way, were unable to resolve the inequalities that existed amongst us. They tended to be exclusively white and could not banish differences of class and culture. There were honest attempts, however, to deal with these issues:

> Women who did come from backgrounds of economic privilege often acted in good faith. Money was often shared. It wasn't just playing around. It was politically serious.

There was a strong sense of being part of a general political struggle:

> We felt the struggle for lesbian housing was part of the same struggle as for single women's housing and for all women to have the right to choose how they would live and have autonomy. It wasn't just wanting housing for us. We helped a lot of women to squat. We were on the crest of Women's Liberation. Housing didn't seem like a separate area.

The first lesbian squat I went to seemed to me to be teeming with messy and hectic life. It was a far cry from the 'pressure cooker' atmosphere and tidy sterility of my parents' bourgeois home. I had been to mixed-sex communal homes before, but the absence of men made a pleasing difference. Living without men was the *raison d'être* of this way of life. Women's houses seemed to offer community, an escape from 'coupledom', the chance to be free from the gaze or control of men (at least within four walls), the opportunity to acquire 'male' skills, the sense of living as if the revolution had already happened. I never squatted, however, since part of me was alarmed by the lack of comfort in some of these houses. Amongst some of the middle-class lesbians I knew there was a self-punishing, anti-consumerist ethos which, I think, came from a position of class privilege. One writer condemned the way in which middle-class women enthusiastically embraced squalor. She described it as the 'Ms Steptoe, Ph.D' syndrome and declared that she did not find 'poverty, dirt or ugliness groovy' (Tension, 1978: 87).

For some women, though, the hardships of squatting were inspiring:

> The squat we lived in was falling down but, like Patience and Sarah, we tackled our problems with a pioneering spirit. We saw it as an opportunity to demystify the male world of plumbing, electricity and carpentry. We read and experimented until we could stride into a builders' suppliers and ask for one-way cistern inlet valves, 1.5 mm triple-core insulated or three-inch steel angle brackets, just as though we were born knowing all about it like men! (Dixon, 1988: 79)

Although a few, according to one woman, 'treated squatting and maybe even being lesbians as a stage in their personal "growth", as a dilettante thing, as slumming it a bit', it was also true that most of these women had few alternatives:

> Although we had roofs over our heads we were very discontented. We were living in bedsitters or small flats, and we wanted to live collectively. We wanted control over our own living space. None of us would have been able to buy, and at that

time it would have been against all we believed in. We were disallowed from living in groups and that was what we wanted.

The desire to create new, non-possessive relationships was paramount:

For a while there was a rather frenetic phase, rotating beds and clothes and lovers which was rather unfortunate for me as everyone else was tall and thin! There was lots of sex, sometimes it was difficult to winkle people out of their respective beds to go on demonstrations! 'Desire' wasn't invented in the 1980s.

Some women inevitably became 'burnt out' by the stress and discomfort of this life:

You were not legal, you were never on safe ground. The houses were mostly in very poor condition. There was a hepatitis outbreak because of our lack of plumbing . . . I remember having cups of tea which fleas would jump into.

The constant moving around as households broke up and squats were lost could also lose its attractions:

Since 1971 I've lived at about twenty different addresses with about thirty-seven different people. I got a lot out of the variety but I now want to be more secure. I've felt increasingly insecure as the years have gone by. The prolonged struggles of meetings and negotiations and wondering if it's the police or the LEB at the door, I couldn't go on living like that, it's just too nerve-wracking.

Inevitably, you get to the stage where you just want to be able to take where you live for granted and get on with other things, and not make housing your main political work in life. It was a full-time occupation.

The division between self-help and making demands on the state was, for some women, blurred. They felt they did both:

We didn't have housing rights to lose, but we were very visible and we did insist they take notice of us. In the end the councils declared an amnesty on squatting and we were all made legitimate.

There is a sense in which these experiments were the product of a specific historical moment as well as being possible only at a certain time of women's lives:

Many of us were on the dole, or doing bits and pieces of work. We could have affairs during the day, sit up at night. It was very different from the position women I know today are in, in terms of work and income.

Looking back, the women I talked to clearly felt that lesbian access to housing has not improved to any significant degree. We expressed ambivalence about the changes in the ways in which lesbian feminists live in the 1980s in comparison to that earlier more experimental era. We noted the trend towards more women living with their lovers and having children as well as the increase in owner occupation amongst those who can afford it: 'Are we duplicating some of the things about family which we wanted to get away from? How do we get the security we need?'

The recognition that most lesbians are poor should not make us oblivious to the fact that we are not immune to the general economic polarization which has occurred under Thatcherism. 'Home' is a less distant reality for some of us. As Sarah Green observed during the course of her research: 'There are rich dykes around. One lesbian removals firm told me how pissed off they were with moving the same women first from co-ops to their own flats and then, later, out of London to buy bigger property in the north.'

The lesbian-feminist housing experiments of the past decade may seem remote and anachronistic for women living in such different times, but the women I spoke with agreed that there had been a positive legacy:

> At an ideological level, even if there hasn't been a corresponding material change, single women and lesbians do now get mentioned as being in housing need. Women without men just weren't a category at all at that time, you just didn't 'fit in'.

The effects of national housing policy

The Housing Act 1988

The Housing Act 1988 is a crucial part of the government's overall privatization programme. It is a continuation of the policies of the Housing Act 1980 which instituted the 'Right to Buy' policy which led to a severe depletion of local authorities' best housing stock:

> London has lost £777 million in capital in the last eight years; 1,000,000 homes have been sold under the Right To Buy scheme; council housing stock is under new pressure through the Housing Act – from Housing Action Trusts and transfers to new landlords – and many local authorities have no money for new building. (CHAR, 1988: 9)

The notion that local authorities have any special role to play in providing homes for working-class people has finally been jettisoned with this legislation. Local authorities under the new provisions are to become 'enablers' rather than 'providers': 'The belief behind this policy is that the system of public housing provision and management is bankrupt, and that private money and management is the key to the future' (Burrows, 1989: 7). The 'hidden agenda' is, arguably, to prepare the way for a public housing sector which caters for the same disenfranchised and voiceless 'underclass' who some government ministers see as the future consumers of the NHS.

The avowed intention of the Act is to revitalize the private rented sector through deregulation, that is, through less security for tenants and more powers for landlords. This sector declined from 90 per cent of the housing stock in 1914 to about 10 per cent in 1986. There has been a corresponding increase in owner occupation, which has risen steeply from 10 per cent to 65 per cent. The private sector may receive a small boost as a result of the Act, but these new tenancies will be at 'market' rather than 'fair' rents which are registered with the council. Single women and lesbians will, for the most part, find this sector increasingly out of their financial reach. Lesbians who depend on co-ops and housing associations for their housing may also suffer as a result of the contraction of council short-life property and housing associations' increased reliance on private funds which will lead to higher rents.

Although it would be mistaken to assume that the government has an entirely systematic and coherent strategy behind its new legislation, it seems clear that the promotion of owner occupation is a way of ensuring that a majority of people in this country have a material and ideological investment in the promise of Thatcherism. It has the potential of creating a class of voters who attend the anarchic fluctuations of the interest rate at the expense of any interest in social justice and inequality. There is no doubt that support for owner occupation is also support for the traditional nuclear family at the expense of those who live for much of their life within a different social unit.

Other legislative disasters

In addition to the Housing Act there is a range of other changes in social policy which further restrict lesbians' options. Changes in the tax law, preventing unmarried house-owners from each qualifying for tax relief, hit low earners who want to live together. The poll tax also affects alternative households' capacity to survive. Changes in the way in which benefits are paid to hostels could, in the long term, result in their closure. Many lesbians rely on hostels at some point in our lives, particularly when we are in crisis situations. There are serious implications for the future of Women's Aid and for women leaving violent men. Social security measures over the last two years have had the effect of making it extremely difficult for young people to leave the parental home and survive independently. This has led to a sharp and dramatic increase in the number of young women who are 'sleeping out' in our towns and cities. Young lesbians who are thrown out by their parents inevitably form a significant percentage of these homeless women. All of these developments have significance for different groups of lesbians. Whilst some lesbians will increasingly be unable to choose the kind of household they wish to live in, others will be unable to leave their existing home and can only face the prospect of temporary shelters and the street.

How are lesbians affected?

I believe that the most disturbing aspect of the last ten years has been the extent to which the material conditions which make a lesbian life and identity possible are progressively being undermined. I do not hold with the view that there a fixed number of lesbians in the world. The ability any of us have to choose a lesbian life is invariably determined by the social and economic status of women as a whole. In countries where the conditions for women's autonomy from men do not exist lesbianism is a statistically negligible phenomenon and heterosexuality is compulsory. As Thatcherism bites deeper, many more women may feel forced into, or unable to leave, undesired relationships with men.

The struggle for secure, decent and affordable housing links lesbians with other groups whose needs are also marginalized by current housing policy and therefore to a larger feminist and socialist agenda. But we should also hang on to our own agenda.

We all carry within us a memory of our first home, for better or worse. Feminists now and in the past have interrogated the myth of familial bliss, peeling back the Christmas card images to reveal the violence, inequality and isolation which too many women experience within the privacy of four walls. Yet the lure and promise of the conventional family is as potent as ever, beckoning us with its offer of eternal safety, shelter and community. In our attempts to redefine and escape restricted definitions of 'home' we go well beyond the narrow 'rights'-based discourse of housing campaigns; we begin to articulate radical desires and possibilities, to speak of a better life. The struggle has never been about bricks and mortar alone.

Notes

Jayne Egerton worked with young homeless people for three years in Piccadilly Advice Centre. She has been a member of the Hall Carpenter Lesbian Oral History Group and chair of Stonewall Housing Association.

Thanks to Lynn Alderson and Frankie Green for their racy and fascinating accounts of lesbian squatting. Thanks also to Sarah Green, Denise Marshall, Gilly Green and Sandra Anlin. The title for this article is taken from Anlin's research.

References

Abrams, Philip and McCulloch, Andrew (1976) *Communes, Sociology and Society*. Cambridge: Cambridge University Press.
Anlin, Sandra (1989) *Out But Not Down*. London: Homeless Action.
Austerberry, Helen and Watson, Sophie (1980) 'Homewoman', *Spare Rib*, 91.
Austerberry, Helen and Watson, Sophie (1983) *Women on the Margins: A Study of Single Women's Housing Problems*. London: Housing Research Group, City University.
Broumas, Olga (1977) *Beginning with O*. New Haven and London: Yale University Press.
Bryan, Beverley, Dadzie, Stella and Scafe, Suzanne (1985) *The Heart of the Race*. London: Virago.
Burrows, Les (1989) *The Housing Act 1988*. London: Shelter.
Cant, Bob and Hemmings, Susan (1988) *Radical Records: Thirty Years of Lesbian and Gay History*. London: Routledge.
CHAR (1988) *Lesbian and Gay Housing Conference Report*. London: CHAR.
Clarke, Wendy (1983) 'Home thoughts from not so far away: a personal look at family', in Segal (1983).
Dixon, Janet (1988) 'Separatism' in Cant and Hemmings (1988).
Eichenbaum, Luise and Orbach, Susie (1982) *Outside In Inside Out*. Harmondsworth: Penguin.
Feminist Anthology Collective (eds) (1981) *No Turning Back*. London: Women's Press.
Hall, Carpenter Archives, Lesbian Oral History Group (eds) (1989) *Inventing Ourselves: Lesbian Life Stories*. London: Routledge.
Holt, Alix (ed.) (1977) *Alexandra Kollontai: Selected Writings*. London: Allison & Busby.
Jay, Karla and Young, Allen (1979) *The Gay Report*. New York: Simon & Schuster.
O'Reilly, Maria (1977) 'Netherly United: women take on the Housing Corporation', *Spare Rib*, 56.

Segal, Lynne (ed.) (1983) *What Is To Be Done About the Family?*, Harmondsworth : Penguin.

Small, Robin (1985–6) 'The price of low pay', *Low Pay Review*, 24.

Tension, Evelyn (1978) 'You don't need a degree to read the writing on the wall', in Feminist Anthology Collective (1981).

Trenchard, Lorraine and Warren, Hugh (1985) *Something To Tell You*. London: Gay Teenage Group.

Narrow Definitions of Culture: The Case of Early Motherhood

Ann Phoenix

The 1960s restrictions on black adult workers' entry to Britain meant that a large proportion of new black migrants were the children and spouses of workers who were already resident. New migrants were permitted entry to Britain for the purposes of 'family reunification' (Phizacklea, 1983), if it could be proved that the proposed entrant was economically dependent on the resident worker and could be supported by them.

These increasingly stringent immigration controls have meant that a growing proportion of black adults in Britain have either been born here or have lived most of their lives here. They are not therefore faced with the task of settling in Britain and coping with the migration process. Rather, they are black people who have been through the British education system and are familiar with a range of British cultures and institutions. For the majority of them there is no question of 'returning' to the countries in which their parents grew up. These black adults are not 'between two cultures' (Watson, 1977) as has commonly been believed. Instead they are situated in their social networks as well as in the wider society, and in that sense are clearly British.

This article argues that concentration on cultural differences between black people and white people has frequently obscured the fact that cultural beliefs, identities and practices necessarily embody the structural forces that affect people's lives, and that culture itself is dynamic rather than static. In particular, analyses of class, race,[1] and gender are crucial to the understanding of British society and of individual behaviours, since the intersection of these structural forces serves to locate individuals in their social positions and also to produce social constructions of beliefs and identities. Much of the discussion would be equally relevant to black people of South Asian origin. However, here I concentrate on black people of Afro-Caribbean origin because literature on early motherhood (discussed here) has focused on black women who are 'West Indian' rather than South Asian.

From S. Westwood and P. Bhachu (eds), *Enterprising Women*, Routledge, London, 1988, pp. 153–75.

The first part of the article is concerned with reasons why simplistic views of cultural influence are inadequate for the understanding of young black women's lives. The second part uses empirical material as a way of exploring how analyses which rely on such simplistic views of culture (referred to here as narrow definitions of culture) obscure the similarities between black women and white women who become pregnant before they are twenty years of age. In order to do so it focuses on the areas of paid employment and mother–daughter relationships. Particular attention is given to class, race and gender as forces that simultaneously structure young women's lives. Although it is generally thought that race only influences black women, what it means to be 'white' can only be understood in contradistinction from what it means to be 'black'. White women's lives are as racially structured as black women's lives (Frankenberg, unpublished), although the effects are of course vastly different. The article concludes that young black women and young white women become pregnant for the same sorts of reasons, and that this is because they share the same socioeconomic contexts. A more dynamic definition of culture would therefore necessarily include analyses of material factors.

Cultural influence and young black women

Young black women have rarely been the subjects of academic study. The category 'youth' has tended to be applied almost exclusively to young men, both black and white. Similarly the term 'black' has tended to be used as if it were either gender neutral or male. When 'women' have been written about it is almost exclusively white women who have been discussed, yet the term has been used as if it were colour neutral. The net effect of this is to render black women, and young black women in particular, invisible (hooks, 1982).

There are some exceptions to this omission of black women. Over the last decade black women have increasingly documented and theorized their experiences themselves (see for example Parmar, 1982; Carby, 1982; *Feminist Review*, 1984; hooks, 1984; Bryan et al., 1985), and the experiences of young black women (Amos and Parmar, 1981). By way of contrast, white academics who have focused on young black women have tended to treat them as if they were pathological. Thus, while black women have frequently been omitted from work which has sought to gain an understanding of 'normal' women, black women have frequently been the focus of research which studies devalued groups.

Studies of 'teenage mothers' provide examples of this negative focus on young black women. These studies often either compare black mothers (of African descent in the USA, and of Afro-Caribbean origin in Britain) with white mothers, or concentrate only on black mothers. This focus on black women as 'teenage mothers' occurs within a context in which early motherhood is stigmatized and devalued. 'Young motherhood' has been associated with a variety of negative outcomes both for the women themselves and for their children. These poor outcomes include postnatal depression, poor educational qualifications and 'welfare dependence' for the women, and risks of perinatal mortality, child abuse and developmental delay for their children (Scott et al., 1981; Butler et al., 1981).

The attention given to young black women as members of a devalued group, 'teenage mothers', has to be considered in the context of the routine exclusion of black women from psychological studies which explore the processes of normal child development, and hence concentrate on mother–child interactive processes. That exclusion helps constitute black women as abnormal mothers and means that they are visible only as members of stigmatized groups.

One of the few contexts in which young black women (of Afro-Caribbean origin) are explicitly discussed in this society and in the USA is thus as 'young mothers'. (Young black women of Asian origin become visible in a similar way at the point at which it is thought likely that they will experience 'arranged marriages'. See Brah and Minhas, 1985 for discussion of this.) The following section will consider how young black women are socially constructed in the literature on 'teenage mothers'.

Young black women and studies of 'teenage motherhood'

In literature on 'teenage mothers' black 'teenage mothers' are presumed to be different from white 'teenage mothers'. Phipps-Yonas in a 1980 review of American literature pointed out that psychological explanations, to do, for example, with problems in individual mother–daughter relationships, tend to be advanced for the incidence of early motherhood in white, middle-class women. For black, lower-class women however, sociocultural explanations, suggesting that early motherhood occurs for 'cultural reasons', tend to be invoked. Phipps-Yonas suggested that this common approach was unjustified because there was no evidence that black teenagers and white teenagers became pregnant for different reasons or that their families were more accepting of early motherhood than white mothers.

By comparison with the USA, Britain has produced little research on early motherhood. However, the North American model of black 'teenage mothers' and white 'teeange mothers' becoming pregnant for different reasons has been reproduced in British research. Examples of these different types of explanation for early motherhood in black women and in white women are provided by two British studies (Skinner, 1986; Ineichen, 1984–5). Both these papers start by considering whether 'West Indian' cultural patterns account for there being proportionally more black mothers of Afro-Caribbean origin who are under twenty years of age than of white mothers of British origin. To do this both researchers discuss family patterns that have been observed in the Caribbean (in fact almost exclusively in Jamaica).

While Skinner states in her introduction that she found no evidence to support the hypothesis that young black women have children for cultural reasons, she nonetheless makes consistent reference to 'West Indian' family patterns as a means of explaining the behaviour of the black women in her study. Much of the material for the typologies she uses is drawn from Clarke's (1957) study done in Jamaica and Fitzherbert's (1967) work on 'West Indian family patterns'. The implicit assumptions underlying this use of work which is thirty and twenty years old respectively are twofold. They are first, that the behaviour of British people of Afro-Caribbean origin can only be understood by making reference to behaviour in Jamaica (one of many Caribbean countries). This suggests that the British context in which black people live is irrelevant to an understanding of their behaviour. The second assumption is that 'the West Indian family' is timeless and remains unchanged over decades.

Skinner herself recognizes that problems are presented by the use of an explanatory framework that is derived from work which is geographically and historically removed from the black British sample whose behaviour she is trying to explain. She says, for example:

> It would be misleading to describe early pregnancies in the UK black teenagers as being attempts to prove fertility on the grounds that similar behaviour observed in the West Indies has, in the past, been interpreted in this way. (1986: 97)

The recognition of the problematic nature of such explanations does not prevent Skinner from drawing parallels between 'Jamaica and West Indian society in the UK' (p. 99). She does so because in academic writing this is the usual way of understanding black British people's behaviour. In the absence of equally long-established alternative discourses to draw upon, she reverts to these comparisons.

This readiness to draw parallels between the behaviour of black people in the Caribbean and that of black people in Britain is further illustrated by the study done by Ineichen (1984–5). In his study Ineichen claims that:

> the contrasts between these two groups of teenagers (white and black) can best be illustrated by prefacing a consideration of their situation by quoting from recent writers . . . on attitudes to and patterns of youthful fertility in the Caribbean. (1984: 52)

Ineichen then lists eight Caribbean traits which he considers particularly relevant to 'West Indian patterns' of fertility. His black British samples are discussed under the headings provided by these eight traits. The Caribbean traits he identifies (from the literature) thus provide the framework for the analysis of the behaviour of his black British sample.

The first trait on which Ineichen compares his black British sample with Caribbean women is 'frequency of teenage motherhood'. He concludes that:

> This ['teenage motherhood'] appears to be commoner among Afro-Caribbean girls. They formed one-fifth of our sample, but a much smaller proportion of the teenage population of the Bristol Health District, although precise figures are not available. (Ineichen, 1984–5)

It is in fact difficult to establish whether, and if so by how much, black British rates of early motherhood exceed white ones. In the USA the rate is known to be higher among black women than among white women, but because white women are more numerous than black women in the USA, the majority of births to women in their teenage years are to white women. Unlike the USA, Britain does not produce national statistics broken down according to the mother's colour. Very few studies of early motherhood have been done in Britain, and Ineichen and Skinner have so far conducted the only research which has shown a higher rate of early pregnancy in black women than white women. Since national figures are not available, the conclusion that early motherhood is more common among black women than among white women must be a tentative one. However, Ineichen draws this conclusion from a study of only eighteen women of Afro-Caribbean origin (with Afro-Caribbean partners). Why does he feel confident on the basis of such slight evidence?

One reason is probably to do with Ineichen's belief that Caribbean patterns of fertility behaviour are likely to be reproduced in black British women of Afro-Caribbean origin. Any evidence in the correct direction, however slight, is considered to provide confirmation of this hypothesis without it being felt necessary to discuss factors such as class, which influence the incidence of early motherhood (in both black women and white women) and provide the context in which is occurs. The absence of discussion of this sort makes it necessary to question Ineichen's analytical framework and his interpretations of his data.

Problems with explanations of black British behaviour based on comparisons with the Caribbean

This emphasis on the Caribbean as providing the key to understanding young black British women's behaviour is inappropriate for the following reasons.

It excludes black people from the category 'British'

A major implication of this concentration on the Caribbean is that black people of Afro-Caribbean origin are not really British. Their behaviour does not have its roots in Britain and can only be understood by reference back to the Caribbean as their place of origin.

It oversimplifies Caribbean cultures

The use of narrow cultural explanations implies that 'West Indian' culture is unitary and static. Class differences and urban/rural divisions in the Caribbean are not given serious consideration. Thus differences in behaviour between the peasantry (on whom much of the work which informs a narrow cultural perspective has been done) and the middle classes are not discussed. Neither are differences between islands addressed, even though they differ greatly in many ways, for example the degree of urbanization and industrialization and the relative proportions of African and Asian people who are nationals. Skinner relies on work that is thirty years old. The assumption here seems to be that lifestyles in the Caribbean are not likely to change with time. Thus the description of Caribbean culture presented is extremely simplistic. Particular elements of behaviour (such as 'pro-fertility values') are singled out as if they were definitive of Caribbean society.

It starts from the assumption that all black people are different from all white people

Culture becomes a primary focus only when black women's behaviour is being explained. This helps maintain the social construction of white people as the norm and black people as deviations from that norm, because it emphasizes that only black people's behaviour needs justification. However it also falsely implies that culture does not influence white people's lives as crucially as black people's. White people also have a diversity of cultural backgrounds. The focus on young black women as culturally influenced only by the Caribbean, and young white women as being acultural, serves to exaggerate differences and underplay similarities.

It confuses colour with culture while ignoring issues of power

Work which is structured around the narrow definition of culture frequently confuses colour and culture. White people are treated as if they were culturally homogeneous and British whatever their ancestry or religion (although there is sometimes an ambivalence about the Irish!). Black people are treated as similar to other black people whose ancestry lies roughly in the same region, but not as British. It is colour not culture which is being represented in such instances (although vague notions of ancestry are included). This is done without any reference to the differential social and power positions which black people and white people occupy.

This issue illustrates one way in which power relations permeate social relations. In this case people from the dominant social group (white British) infer the importance of cultural influences for a subordinate social group (black people), without *ever* asking them how *they* perceive culture to influence them. At the same time they fail to acknowledge cultural influences on their own group's behaviour. This illustrates Freire's (1971) point that it is difficult for people in a position of political dominance to recognize how culture influences their own group's actions. Hence in studies of 'teenage mothers', culture is implicity accepted as an important influence on young black women, but not on young white women. Class is sometimes recognized as an important influence on white people, but in these cases, white working-class people have frequently been studied (in the sociology of community) as if they were deviant in comparison with white middle-class people.

It oversimplifies the notion of culture

Cultures are necessarily dynamic (Saifullah Khan, 1982). The culture (as shared systems of meaning) that young black adults now subscribe to has some roots in, but is not precisely that of their parents. Given that the young black women described in the above studies were either born in or have lived most of their lives in Britain, their cultural roots are likely to lie at least as much in British society as in the Caribbean (which most have never visited).

Furthermore, culture is not a discrete entity. It cannot be divorced from its socioeconomic, political and historical contexts (Westwood, 1984). Since all societies have a plurality of socioeconomic groupings it is inaccurate to describe a country as having one culture. The non-unitary nature of culture is particularly relevant for the Caribbean which is composed of dozens of countries, extends 1,500 miles, contains a variety of languages, has a varied mix of ethnic groupings, different musical traditions and cuisine. To speak of 'West Indian culture' is thus rather inaccurate. This inaccuracy is compounded by the fact that many writers generalize from observations made only in Jamaica to people from the whole of the Caribbean.

In so far as the category 'West Indian' has any cultural reality in Britain it demonstrates not only that people in the Caribbean share common histories, but also the dynamic nature of culture (in that people who have previously had very few dealings with one another can relatively quickly form a cultural synthesis). Migration to Britain has meant that structural forces of class stratification and racism force black people to dwell on their commonalities. Experiences of 'outsider' status with respect to white British people serve to unify black people of Afro-Caribbean origin.

The broader meaning of culture

Work which perpetuates the narrow definition of culture has tended to be carried out in isolation from the theoretical advances in cultural studies made, for example, by those who have worked in the Centre for Contemporary Cultural Studies. Work of this kind has taken a dynamic, structural view of culture by theorizing it as lived experience, inextricably linked with race, sex and class, and only having meaning in the context of the society in which it occurs (in this case Britain). Hence everyday features of society and of behaviour like the media, styles of dress and music, as well as what these mean to and for, the groups under study are closely examined. In this way the notion of culture is broadened to include the idea of 'cultures of resistance', rather than being narrow versions of cultural influence. (See for example Hall and Jefferson, 1976; McRobbie, 1984; Centre for Contemporary Cultural Studies, 1978, 1982.)

It seems likely that white children and young adults from the working classes share more cultural features with their black peers than either do with white children and young adults from the middle classes. Inner-city London schools in which white working-class children interact with black peers allow the sharing of cultural knowledge and practices. Evidence for this is provided by the pattern of language use in such schools, which tends to incorporate elements of both black Afro-Caribbean and white Cockney styles of talk (Hewitt, 1986). The cultures that working-class young people share are therefore new, combining features from many groups. This does not mean that they do not also have cultural patterns and identifications that are not shared across black–white groupings, but it does mean that explanations of similar behaviour in young people (early motherhood, for example) should not automatically presume different aetiologies.

The case of early motherhood

The second part of this article uses data from a longitudinal study, done at the Thomas Coram Research Unit, of women who were between 16 and 19 years of age when they gave birth (between 1983 and 1984).[2] Interviews done when the women were heavily pregnant will be used to illustrate how the presumption that early motherhood in black women is the result of narrowly defined cultural influences obscures the similarities between black women's and white women's reasons for becoming pregnant. It will also explore whether, as would be suggested by narrowly defined cultural explanations, relationships with mothers are different for young black women and young white women. (Because of lack of space the similarities in black women's and white women's relationships with their male partners are not addressed here.) About a quarter of the women in this study were black.

This study was originally designed to compare 'West Indian' women with white women. It quickly became evident during piloting and the early stages of data collection however, that black women and white women responded similarly to questions other than those which expressly dealt with racial discrimination. Partly for this reason it was decided to analyse the data from everyone in the study together rather than dividing the sample into a black 'West Indian' group and a white group. There were two additional reasons for analysing the sample in this way.

First, comparisons between black people and white people tend to construct white people as the norm, and black people as deviant by comparison (see discussion above); and second, it is difficult to satisfactorily operationalize the categories 'West Indian' and 'white' as analytical constructs. This is partly because 'West Indian' and 'white' are not equivalent terms in that one describes certain countries of origin and is used as a shorthand for cultural heritage, while the other describes colour. It is also partly because many people do not in reality fit neatly into these categories. Most of the women in our sample (black and white) for example, were British born (as are most of their age peers), but their parents came from a variety of places, had been in Britain for varied amounts of time, and had different religions. Several respondents had parents who came from different places and/or were different colours. If racial discrimination were the subject of study, these problems would be avoided in that this would not necessitate consideration of countries of origin or cultural differences. But narrow cultural analyses cannot represent that diversity, and in addition require that some respondents be placed in groups which do not adequately represent them.

Thus while some percentages which apply to the sample as a whole are presented here, statistical analyses which divide the sample into groups according to colour are not available. Instead qualitative analyses are used to illustrate what black women and white women actually said. The aim of the analysis section is to give some indication of whether similar factors influence black women's and white women's behaviour.

Why become a mother before twenty?

Current dominant reproductive ideologies would suggest that women who are under twenty years of age should not become pregnant. This is partly because mothers are meant to be indisputably adult, and it is not clear whether or not teenage women are adult (Murcott, 1980). It is also partly because marriage is expected to precede motherhood (Busfield, 1974), and women who are under twenty years of age are more likely to be single than married when they give birth (63 per cent of mothers under twenty years of age who gave birth in 1985 were single: Office of Population Censuses and Surveys, 1986). A third reason is that parents are meant to be economically independent of the state, with mothers and children being dependent on the economic provision fathers make for them. Increasing unemployment has however meant that young people from the working classes are more likely to be reliant on state provision of money and housing than they were in the past. Young women's position as dependants is not new, since they have long been expected to be dependent on their male partners. However, as their dependence has been increasingly transferred from male partners to the state, mothers who are under twenty years of age have received more public attention as deviants from social norms.

Given this negative social construction it is important to attempt to understand the reasons why about 3 per cent of women in this age group have become mothers each year of this decade. If simple 'perpetuation of cultural norms' hypotheses are to be confirmed, then black women and white women should become pregnant for different reasons, with black women having more 'pro-natalist tendencies' and being more desirous of having children early in their life course (Ineichen, 1984–5). However, black women and white women give remarkably similar accounts of reasons for and responses to early pregnancy. The socioeconomic contexts within which they live crucially influence these reasons and responses. These contexts are largely similar for black women and white women who become mothers early in their lives in that the majority come from the working classes.

Pregnant women's orientations to motherhood at the point of conception are usually treated as if they were bipolar. Either they were 'trying' to become pregnant, that is they intended to conceive, or they became pregnant accidentally. But orientations to motherhood are rather more complex than this. Nearly half of the women in the Thomas Coram study either did not mind whether or not they became pregnant, or had not thought about pregnancy as something that might affect them. This challenges two widely held assumptions about the conception of children: first that there is a clear dichotomy between wanting and not wanting a child, and second, that women always make clear and conscious decisions about whether or not to conceive. Asked whether it had been important to them not to become pregnant, this group commonly replied, 'I wasn't bothered.' Those who had no conscious thoughts about conception had just started their sexual careers. They illustrate the clear separation that some women (and no doubt some men) make between sexual intercourse and pregnancy, and motherhood.

Women's feelings about motherhood were influenced by how they thought pregnancy and motherhood would affect their lives. Employment and education prospects, relationships with parents as well as with male partners, whether or not they had previously been pregnant, their orientations to contraception, when other people in their social networks tended to give birth as well as their perception of the ideal time to give birth all affected how they felt about motherhood. While women in the study reported here could not be dichotomized into a group which 'planned' its pregnancies and a group for whom pregnancy was 'accidental', they did nonetheless have general views about the best time to have children.

The following section will consider this sample's views about the ideal time to conceive.

Ideal time to conceive

Within the narrow version of cultural influence (that it is separable from structural factors so that 'West Indians' can be picked out as automatically different from 'whites') it is expected that black women of Afro-Caribbean origin believe it to be acceptable and ideal to have children early in life, while white women do not share these beliefs. However, most of the women in this study, whether black or white, reported that they thought it better to have children earlier rather than later in life. This is aptly illustrated by considering some quotations from white women:

> If you have a baby when you're older you're tied down . . . I'll still be able to do what I want to. (Jan, seventeen years old)

> 'I think they look down on women who don't have a child by 30 but there's no set time for anybody to have a baby by. (*What do you think is the ideal age to have a baby?*) I think about now is all right . . . I don't want to get too old and have children. (Mary, nineteen years old)

> Yeah I think I'm young and people say I'm young but I don't think it makes any difference how old you are . . . whether you're thirty or sixteen you can still give it as much love . . . She's twenty-six [R's sister] but she's getting on to have a baby when you think of it. The younger you are the more likely that it's going to be healthier. (Alice, seventeen years old)

From what these women say, it is clear that they consider it preferable to have children earlier rather than later in life. Their reasons for this come from prevalent 'commonsense' frameworks regarding entry into motherhood. Appeals are made to 'not being tied down', and to beliefs about when is the ideal age to have a child. The argument about not being tied down is one also used by older mothers as a reason for not having had children earlier, while the argument about retaining enough youth to enjoy life after the children are grown up (as well as still being young enough to understand their children) is the converse of what older mothers would argue. They also consider themselves to be physically better able to bear and cope with children than younger women are.

This did not mean that all the women in the study considered that theirs was the ideal age at which to reproduce. However, only one fifth considered that the ideal age was over twenty-one years. The general feeling was that women should start to have children early in their life course. It could be argued that since the interviews were conducted in late pregnancy, these women's responses about ideal ages are simply *post hoc* justifications of a situation which is inevitable. Nevertheless, they illuminate the differences between 'insider' and 'outsider' perceptions of early motherhood.

It is also important to note that early motherhood was common rather than unusual in the women's social networks. Nearly half of the sample's mothers had themselves had their first child before they were twenty, as this white respondent illustrates: 'Well me mum had me when she was seventeen. I find I am a bit young to have a baby, but there are some girls here [mother and baby home] who are fifteen years of age' (Sandra, nineteen years old).

In this study attachment to early motherhood was not culturally specific to young black women. White women were similar to black women in wanting to have children early in life, and knowing many other women (including their own mothers) who had done similarly. In addition the mothers in this study, both black and white, generally considered that motherhood conferred high status on women and so felt that having a child would improve their social status.

The experience of (un)employment

Women's feelings about the timing of motherhood was influenced by how they anticipated that it would affect other aspects of their lives. Dominant reproductive ideologies suggest a conflictual model of employment and motherhood in which motherhood should be deferred until the employment career is well established. The rationale for this is that mothers ought not to be employed while their children are young. Therefore unless they are well established in their careers, they will be unable to return to the same occupational position.

This deferment of motherhood makes sense only if women have managed to obtain and keep employment which has built-in career progression, and for many women this is not the case. The jobs which women commonly do, in factories, shops, catering and the health service, give few opportunities for career progression. Less than one-quarter of women in this study had at least one O level or equivalent. Their lack of formal qualifications meant that they were not well placed to obtain employment with career prospects. Indeed only 39 per cent of our sample were employed when they became pregnant. A further 6 per cent were on MSC (Manpower Services Commission) schemes, and 16 per cent were in full-time education. This means that 39 per cent were unemployed at the start of pregnancy.

For women who are unemployed, childbearing does not threaten the current employment career, and may well appear a welcome alternative to unemployment. More than a third of the sample had done more than one job since they started working (one woman had had eight jobs since leaving school). This was either due to redundancy (which some women in the study had experienced more than once in their short employment careers) or because they hoped to get more money or better working conditions in another job. Many women (black and white) had experienced difficulty finding work. This means that for the majority of the sample it was not possible to be continually employed for the necessary two years in order to qualify for statutory maternity leave. This explains why only eight women qualified for maternity leave in late pregnancy. The following examples vividly illustrate how hard it has been for this cohort of women to get established in employment:

> When I was looking for work after I left my job, in the job centre it was all 'eighteen' or 'sixteen with experience', and I couldn't understand that. I know my boyfriend is finding it really hard to get a job. (Linda, a white seventeen-year-old)

> I don't know. If you go to the job centre they want people with 'O' levels and CSEs and things like that and you have to be a certain age. (Ruth, a white seventeen-year-old)

> First of all they say that you need education to get a job and then when – I think you just got to be lucky really. . . . When you go they say you haven't got enough – or they want someone with at least two years' experience. (Fay, a black nineteen-year-old)

When we went up to look [at the banks] they had given out forms to be filled in, and you just sent off for interviews. I got interviews, but I just didn't get no job. I tried one of those youth schemes, but you had to take a test first and get a certain per cent to pass through it. And I failed it by 3 per cent. It was learning computer work. And I went to a few other factories. Towards the end I was giving up a bit, but my mum wouldn't let me sign on. She said if I did, I wouldn't go out and find work. [This woman tried for over twenty jobs before getting one in a supermarket where she stayed for three years.] (Judy, a white nineteen-year-old)

White women and black women alike had difficulty getting jobs because of the general unavailability coupled with their lack of qualifications, and their youth (which partly signalled lack of experience). However, while prospects were poor for the majority of this group, racial discrimination made the situation worse for black women. This was mostly mentioned by black women, but some white women also commented on it.

It was only when I got to the interviews and I didn't used to get the job I used to think I was unfairly treated because when I'd leave and they'd turn me down I used to hear that a white person got it and that she didn't have as much going for her like what I did. (Joyce, a black nineteen-year-old)

I think they would rather take on a white person than a black person. I don't know why that is. They just would. (Tracey, a white eighteen-year-old)

They [friends' siblings] say like how it's harder . . . you could have the same qualifications as a white person and you could go in an office and get all their little exams and everything like that and you get a higher score than a white person but because you're black, you just don't get the job. (Hayley, a black sixteen-year-old)

These accounts illustrate the intersection of race and class in that while all the sample found it difficult to get jobs because of their class position, black women were less likely than white women to get jobs.

The respondents not only shared certain features of their class position, they were also all women. Some responses to questions about employment illustrated the intersection of class, race and gender in that black women were also likely to experience difficulties getting jobs in traditionally male occupations: 'Like my twin, she's a qualified motor mechanic and she can't get a job, so I don't know' (Debbie, a black nineteen-year-old).

At [motor-car manufacturers] I passed the interview maths test along with two boys who had done woodwork but not metalwork like I had done. I didn't get it, but I found out when I met the same boys at another interview that they had an offer. I thought [motor-car manufacturers] was nasty because I had metalwork. I think it's because I'm a girl, because I had seven letters of rejection saying that I couldn't be employed because I was a girl . . . . My dad was annoyed because he thought they had to accept a certain proportion of girls. My mum couldn't believe it. That was a bit *race* discriminatory [my emphasis]. (Claudette, a black nineteen-year-old who later qualified as a mechanical fitter when her daughter was one year old)

In the above examples the women involved were likely to perceive the failure to get jobs to be the result of racial rather than sexual discrimination. Racial discrimination operates both directly and indirectly. In the employment field jobs gained through social network contacts probably provide the clearest example of this indirect discrimination. Many women in this study had obtained jobs through social network contacts.

> The friend that worked at the factory, she told me about that job. And when she left, she worked at Jamesons – they wanted someone there – she told me about that one. She knew I wanted to leave so I had that one straight on. (Clare, a white seventeen-year-old)

> My mum found me a [temporary] job where she worked. (Hayley, a black sixteen-year-old)

> My nan got me the job. (Ruth, a white seventeen-year-old)

> Because my mum worked there you see. So she knew there was a job vacant, so I went for it. (Tracey, a white eighteen-year-old)

The usefulness of social network contacts probably meant that the 33 per cent of women who had unemployed mothers, and the 23 per cent who had unemployed fathers were at a disadvantage when it came to getting employment. Since black people tend to suffer more from unemployment (Brown, 1984) than white people do, it probably also meant that the black women were at a disadvantage in comparison with the white women when it came to finding employment.

In summary, the women in this study were clearly not in occupations which had career progression. Their difficulty in finding (and keeping) jobs meant that few were eligible for maternity leave in late pregnancy. Deferring motherhood would have made little difference to this since the types of employment they were eligible for tended not to be ones which provided career prospects. For these women the intersection of the motherhood career and the employment career does not fit a conflictual model in that childbearing would make little difference to their employment prospects. In the late pregnancy interview it remained to be seen how many women in this group would actually participate in the labour market post-birth. Black women's and white women's experiences of the employment market were largely similar. Difference could more readily be attributed to racial discrimination than to narrowly defined cultural differences.

Mothers and daughters

A narrowly defined cultural approach to the question of why 'West Indian' women become pregnant early in their life course would suggest that whatever their mothers' initial responses to their pregnancy, they can confidently expect their mothers eventually to accept, and even 'mother', their children. The having of children does not mean that they bear full responsibility. White women would be faced with a rather different, and less accepting, reaction. Studies of 'West Indian youth' (usually male) have also suggested that they suffer from pronounced intergenerational conflict as the result of a 'clash of cultures' (West Indian and white British). If these things are true, then black mothers and white mothers should have qualitatively different relationship with their daughters, and react differently to their daughters' pregnancies.

In the Thomas Coram study most women, regardless of colour, were dependent on their parents, particularly mothers, for social support. This was partly because many still lived with their parents. Forty-seven per cent of the sample were living with their mothers when they became pregnant. A further 31 per cent saw their mothers at least weekly. Most of the sample were therefore in frequent contact with their parents, and in addition were more likely to be rated as having a confiding, supportive relationship with their mothers than with their male partners or their fathers.

> Any problems or that I could tell her if I feel like I wanted to tell her . . . Most of the time I did tell her . . . We're like sisters really . . . I wouldn't change her for anything in the world. She's a very good mother. (Geraldine, a black nineteen-year-old living at home)

> Me and my mum were always best friends . . . I never used to go to my dad with my troubles, I always used to go to my mum. (Jan, a white seventeen-year-old living with her husband)

> Oh fantastic! We were very close, and we talked about everything. Everything. (Sandra, a white eighteen-year-old living with parents)

> We were like sisters to tell you the truth, even though I had my little brothers and sisters. Because I could talk to my mum. (Pamela, a black sixteen-year-old living at home)

Good relationships with mothers were not a universal feature. In late pregnancy 21 per cent of the sample were mainly negative about their relationships with their mothers (compared with 37 per cent who were mainly negative about their relationships with their fathers). While black women and white women in the sample said similar things about their relationships with their mothers, some black women perceived these relationships to be similar to white women's relationships with their mothers, while others saw them as different.

Racism as a structural force means that black people are socially constructed as 'outsiders' with respect to white British society. As a result black people recognize that their situation and experiences are similar to those of other black people but different from those of white people. White people similarly experience themselves as different from black people, and perceive black people (who tend to be focused on in discussions of 'race') as 'being all the same', even though they do not perceive all white people to be the same. These notions of similarity and difference are also emphasized by the media, and by academic work which uses the sorts of narrow cultural definitions described earlier.

Implicit within such descriptions of black groups and white groups are issues of power and solidarity. White society demonstrates its power to construct black people as deviant from its behavioural norms while maintaining solidarity between white people in their difference from black people. In a similar way, black people by concentrating on their similarities with other black people show the solidarity which allows them to exert influence on society by use of collective power. However, as discussed earlier, any comparison of groups serves to highlight differences and obscure similarities between them. Difference does not need to be established or proved, but can be taken for granted.

Such taken-for-granted beliefs in the unitary nature of black people and their difference from white people can lead to the simultaneous holding of contradictory beliefs about how black people compare with white people. When asked directly whether she thought that black mothers treated their daughters differently from white mothers, one respondent replied that she felt they did: 'After speaking to some of my friends I realized it was a thing – all black women were the same in the age group . . . because they all have the same beliefs, and the way they've been brought up.' However, she then went on to describe the overlap rather than the differences between black mothers and white mothers:

> Some of them [white mothers] couldn't care two hoots, but some of them – I mean they don't say the same thing, but I mean they hold the same principles as some black people. And some black mothers don't really care two hoots what their daughters do neither. (Angela, a black nineteen-year-old)

This respondent illustrates the contradictions which permeate the mother–daughter relationship. She indicates that while she found her mother's restrictions on her social life irksome, she also experienced them as caring. She also perceived black mothers and white mothers to hold similar principles, whether those were caring or otherwise.

White respondents were also asked to compare their relationships with their mothers with those of their age peers. They tended to report individual, but not group differences. This probably reflects the fact that the prevalence of narrow definitions of culture means that black women are familiar with accounts which are concerned with the 'pathological culture' of black families and so are likely to make comparisons between black families and white families. In contrast white women are unlikely to be familiar with such cultural explanations of their household organizations, and are less likely to compare white families with black families (although in other contexts they may compare black families with white ones).

The causes of friction between mothers and daughters in this study were, perhaps not surprisingly, to do with boyfriends, going out, and helping around the house. Arguments about these issues and inability to discuss them with parents were common (and not confined to black women, although black 'youth' have frequently been described as having severe intergenerational conflict). The following white respondent sums the reasons up very neatly.

> [We would argue] about silly little things. Washing up and going out . . . things about the house. My friends. What I should be doing at night. Where I should be going. Who I should be going with. What time I should be in an all this. (Linda, a white seventeen-year-old)

Although these cannot adequately be discussed here, black parents and white parents were reported to be similar in their attitudes to what their daughters should and should not do before conception. They also did not differ in their hopes for, and expectations of their daughters prior to pregnancy, or their reactions to the pregnancy.

Prior to pregnancy many women (both black and white) knew that their parents wanted them to get jobs they liked, and also to enjoy themselves. When they first learned that their daughters were pregnant, the majority of mothers (both black and white) were initially likely to be unhappy, but by late pregnancy they had generally become enthusiastic. Mothers' and fathers' reactions were initially similar, so that in early pregnancy only 27 per cent of mothers were enthusiastic about it, compared with 30 per cent of fathers. By late pregnancy, however, their responses to their daughters' pregnancies diverged, with mothers being more likely to be perceived as happy about it. As birth approached 62 per cent of mothers were wholly positive, compared with only 46 per cent of fathers. Most parents did, however, have some positive feelings towards the end of the pregnancy with only 8 per cent of mothers and 8 per cent of fathers being wholly negative.

An examination of relationships between mothers and daughers, and maternal responses to a daughter's pregnancy suggests that mother–daughter relationships share many similarities across black families and white families. This reinforces the point, made earlier, that narrow cultural accounts which explain black women's behaviour by relating it to (often outdated) Caribbean patterns of behaviour are inadequate. Meaningful accounts of young women's behaviour need to take account of the structural influences of sex, race and class as well as their intersection.

Conclusion

Studies that focus on black British people of Afro-Caribbean origin have frequently used a narrow definition of cultural influence to explain their behaviour. Such explanations are unsatisfactory because they oversimplify cultural influence, and in doing so serve to reinforce the social construction of black people as deviant from the norms of white British behaviour.

Research on women who become pregnant early in their life course had tended to use such narrow definitions of culture to explain why young black women of Afro-Caribbean origin become pregnant, but not why young white women become pregnant. This approach masks the similarities in experiences and perceptions between black mothers and white mothers. Consideration of the accounts given by women who become mothers early in their life course suggests that their shared experiences of being women from the working classes influence their behaviour more than do patterns of behaviour in the countries from which their parents come. Apart from racial discrimination (which only black women in this study reported experiencing), pregnant black women and white women under twenty years of age cannot easily be differentiated in their attitudes to and experiences of pregnancy, employment, or relationships with parents.

This does not mean that culture is irrelevant to the study of young people's behaviour or that it is never legitimate either to focus solely on black people or to compare black people and white people. However, complex (rather than simple) representations of culture need to be used. Such complex definitions encompass structural influences of class, gender and race, which influence white people's as well as black people's lives. This sort of approach allows the representation of differences in style among young black women and young white women. It takes account of the common experiences that young white women share as the result of being of the same sex and of similar class positions. It recognizes that racism divides white people from black people and stops them from being aware of their similarities. The narrow representations of cultural influence discussed in this article cannot portray these complexities, and are therefore inadequate for the explanation of human behaviour.

Notes

Without the women who took part in the Thomas Coram study this article would not have been possible. To them my grateful thanks. The research was funded by a grant from the Department of Health and Social Security. The project has an advisory group of black women psychologists and sociologists who also have an interest in early motherhood. They have been very helpful throughout this project. My thinking on the issues covered here was greatly sharpened by discussions with them. Their input has been invaluable. As a member of a project team I have benefited from the help and support that Julia Brannen, Peter Moss and Ted Melhuish have provided in general, and more specifically with this article. Thanks also to Barbara Tizard and Charlie Owen who each commented on drafts. The final responsibility for the article must of course be mine.

1. 'Race' is used here to refer to the social construction of black people and white people as belonging to different races. This article concentrates on black women of Afro-Caribbean origin, and white women, most of whom have been born and brought up in Britain. The term as used here connotes the differential treatment that black people and white people in British society receive. As such it refers to racial discrimination on the basis of colour rather than to cultural differences on the basis of ethnicity.

2. The sample was recruited from the antenatal clinics of two large, inner-city London hospitals. Apart from the age criterion women had to be having the first child they intended to rear themselves. Any woman who met these criteria and agreed to participate was included in the study. Seventy-nine women were given in-depth interviews, and the other 101 women were given shorter interviews. The quotations used here all come from the longer interviews, but some of the percentages given refer to the whole sample. All names used are pseudonyms.

References

Amos, V. and Parmar, P. (1981) 'Resistance and responses: the experience of black girls in Britain', in A. McRobbie and T. McCabe (eds), *Feminism for Girls: An Adventure Story*. London: Routledge & Kegan Paul.

Brah, A. and Minhas, R. (1985) 'Structural racism or cultural difference: schooling for Asian girls', in G. Weiner (ed.) *Just a Bunch of Girls*. Milton Keynes: Open University Press.

Brown, C. (1984) *Black and White in Britain: The Third PSI Survey*. London: Heinemann.

Bryan, B, Dadzie, S. and Seafe, S. (1985) *The Heart of the Race*. London: Virago.

Busfield, J. (1974) 'Ideologies and reproduction', in *The Integration of a Child into a Social World*. Cambridge: Cambridge University Press.

Butler, N., Ineichen, B., Taylor, B. and Wadsworth, J. (1981) *Teenage Mothering*. Report to DHSS, University of Bristol.

Carby, H. (1982) 'White woman listen! Black feminism and the boundaries of sisterhood', in Centre for Contemporary Cultural Studies (eds), *The Empire Strikes Back, Race and Racism in 70s Britain*. London: Hutchinson.

Centre for Contemporary Cultural Studies (eds) (1978) *Woman take Issue*. London: Hutchison.

Centre for Contemporary Cultural Studies (eds) (1982) *The Empire Strikes Back, Race and Racism in 70s Britain*. London: Hutchinson.

Clarke, E. (1957) *My Mother Who Fathered Me*. London: Allen & Unwin.

Feminist Review (1984) 'Many voices, one chant, black feminist perspectives', *Feminist Review*, 17.

Fitzherbert, K. (1967) *West Indian children in London* (Occasional Papers on Social Administration 19).

Frankenberg, R. (unpublished) 'Growing up white: feminism, racism and the social geography of childhood', History of Consciousness, University of California, Santa Cruz.

Freire, P. (1971) *Pedagogy of the Oppressed*. New York: Herder & Herder.

Hall, S. and Jefferson, T. (eds) (1976) *Resistance through Rituals: Youth Subcultures in Post-War Britain*. London: Hutchinson.

Hewitt, R. (1986) *White Talk Black Talk. Inter-Racial Friendship and Communication amongst Adolescents*. Cambridge: Cambridge University Press.

hooks, B. (1982) *Ain't I a Woman? Black Women and Feminism*. London: Pluto Press.

hooks, B. (1984) *Feminist Theory from Margin to Center*. Boston: South End Press.

Ineichen, B. (1984–5) 'Teenage motherhood in Bristol: the contrasting experience of Afro-Caribbean and white girls', *New Community*, 12 (1): 52–8.

McRobbie, A. (1984) 'Dance and social fantasy', in A. McRobbie and M. Nava (eds), *Gender and Generation*. London: Macmillan.

Murcott, A. (1980) 'The social construction of teenage pregnancy', *Sociology of Health and Illness*, 2 (1): 1–23.

Office of Population Censuses and Surveys Monitor (1986) FMI 86/2.

Parmar, P. (1982) 'Gender, race and class: Asian women in resistance', in Centre for Contemporary Cultural Studies (eds), *The Empire Strikes Back: Race and Racism in 70s Britain*. London: Hutchinson.

Phipps-Yonas, S. (1980) 'Teenage pregnancy and motherhood, a review of the literature, *American Journal of Orthopsychiatry*, 50 (3): 403–31.

Phizacklea, A. (1983) 'Introduction', in A. Phizacklea (ed.), *One Way Ticket. Migration and Female Labour*. London: Routledge & Kegan Paul.

Phoenix, A. (1987) 'Theories of gender and black families', in G. Weiner and M. Arnot (eds), *Gender under Scrutiny*. London: Hutchinson.

Saifullah Khan, V. (1982) 'The role of the culture of dominance in structuring the experience of ethnic minorities', in G. Husband (ed.), *Race in Britain*. London: Hutchinson.

Scott, K.G., Field, T. and Robertson, E. (1981) *Teenage Parents and their Offspring*. New York: Grune & Stratton.

Skinner, C. (1986) *Elusive Mister Right. The Social and Personal Context of a Young Woman's Use of Contraception*. London: Carolina Publications.

Watson, J. (ed.) (1977) *Between Two Cultures: Migrants and Minorities in Britain*. Oxford: Basil Blackwell.

Westwood, S. (1984) *All Day Every Day: Factory and Family in the Making of Women's Lives*. London: Pluto.

Wilmott, P. and Young, M. (1960) *Family and Class in a London Suburb*. London: Routledge & Kegan Paul.

SECTION V

WOMEN AND THE STATE

In 1989 the Berlin Wall was taken down and with it disappeared a number of assumptions about the stability of the political map of Western Europe. Anyone with the most minimal historical knowledge has long known that states can be made, and remade, but in the years after 1945 it was widely taken for granted that the boundaries of Europe were fixed, and that the iron curtain between West and East was a final frontier. Even though new states appeared throughout Africa and Asia as a result of decolonization, it was seldom seriously thought that, for example, Germany could be reunited or that civilian access to the Soviet satellite states would be entirely open.

However, once the hidden, and secret, states of Europe had been entered, what was discovered was a pattern of absolute state domination and frequently brutal regimes. It was a widely accepted view in the West that standards of living for the general population were lower in the East, but exactly how much lower, and how much more impoverished the citizens of these countries, was only fully revealed after 1989. Tourist and official visitors to the Soviet Union, the Baltic and Central Europe had brought back tales of scarce consumer goods, but the degree of shortage of basic commodities was recognized only when more people were able to travel and experience these societies outside official 'protection'. It then began to be clear that not only did people in the East lack access to luxury goods, they lacked reliable access to ordinary goods which are taken for granted in the industrial West. In Slavenka Drakulić's *How We Survived Communism and Even Laughed* the author notes that for her, and other Yugoslav women, basic emancipation and liberalization would have been provided by the regular supply of sanitary towels. Ms Drakulić writes of meeting a Western feminist, who earnestly requested her views on feminism and postmodernism. To this Ms Drakulić responded:

> Sitting in that luncheonette on Seventy-fifth Street with B, I resented the questions she asked me, the way she asked them, as if she didn't understand that menstrual pads and Tampax are both a metaphor for the system and the reality of women living in Eastern Europe. Or as if she herself were not a woman – slim, tall, smart-looking and, surprisingly, dressed with style. Feeling the slick plastic cup in my hand, it came to my mind that her questions are like that – cold, artificial, slippery, not touching my reality.[1]

This example, of the failure of an apparently 'advanced' society to supply even the most basic of women's needs, is one demonstration of the growing body of opinion among feminists that the state – whether of the East or West, North or South – generally puts the specific needs of women at the bottom of its agenda. The state, when reasonably liberal, is able to provide basic legal protection and welfare and educational support for its citizens, but it does not consider these needs as gendered. Thus the debate within feminism has shifted from the discussion about the ways in which the state discriminates against women to a more general debate about the way in which the state itself is constructed through, and by, gendered assumptions.[2] Even ideas taken as 'gender neutral', such as citizen and natural rights, have been found to be constructed out of male perceptions of the world. For example, in recent years the term 'citizen' has received much critical attention in the West. Partly because of the impetus given to the construction, and reconstruction, of democracy in Eastern Europe, political scientists have attempted to theorize the nature of the contract between the individual and the state. These discussions have inevitably involved the negotiation of political differences; the political right has usually been of the view that whilst the individual may have responsibilities towards the state, the state has few obligations (especially welfare obligations) towards its citizens. The left has generally contested this view, and argued for a state/citizen contract in which the state as a community of interests has a duty to provide for its members.

The point about these discussions and debates in this context is that on the whole they have assumed that all members of society have the same needs, and an absolute identity of interests. Few would contest that women, just as men, benefit from habeas corpus and access to a free press, but in other ways the interests of women and men may differ. How they differ in their needs is not, however, merely a matter of distinct empirical needs (women, for example, require recognition of their role as mothers and carers) but in the overall construction of apparently gender-neutral terms such as 'rights'.[3] A construction of the citizen as a formally free individual with the 'right' to move house and change jobs is inadequate for men, but even more inappropriate for women who may be involved in absolute, binding ties with children and dependent others. The ties-that-bind are a complex issue for women and the state. On the one hand, women might wish for recognition and support of their particular role as mothers. On the other hand, there lies the danger that with protection comes inequality – the assumption that because many women are mothers they are in some sense distinct from other citizens, and have to be considered in a different way. As became apparent in debates about women's access to paid work, in both the nineteenth and the twentieth centuries, it was almost impossible for women both to be protected and to be equal.[4] Within feminism different schools of thought exist about the political strategies to be pursued in women's negotiations with the state. Demonstrating women's specific concerns has for so long carried with it the implicit assumption that difference equals inferiority that many women have become wary of stressing the different social realities of women and men.

However, the meaning of the state, and its policies, is now widely regarded as gender related. The case of Eastern Europe demonstrated just how extensive state misogyny could be. As well as the virtually non-existent provision of consumer goods, state policies, especially on fertility and childbirth, were brutal in the extreme. The documentation of the nature of contraceptive provision in the Soviet Union and Romania (with its emphasis on savage abortion practices in the former and non-existent birth-control facilities in the latter) bore adequate testament to the possibilities of a state unwilling to recognize the needs of women.

The gains fought for by women in the West in health care related to the biology of women were largely absent from the old Soviet empire. Even though childcare was often widely available in the Soviet satellite states, this was tied to the state's policy of compulsory participation by women in paid work. The case put by Engels – that entry into production was the foundation for the liberation of women – had been implemented in Eastern Europe, but without the transformation in patriarchal practice and ideology which Engels had somewhat optimistically assumed would follow.[5] Women, in all these societies, still bore the major share of domestic responsibility and had little or no role in central government.[6]

As the curtain of secrecy was lifted on Eastern Europe, it became clear to feminists in the West that no such movement as feminism existed in the East. There were official organizations of women, but no groups or networks which would have constituted feminism in the Western sense. Indeed, one of the lessons of the world after 1989 was that feminism, as a social movement and a social phenomenon, was more or less exclusively Western. The virtual non-existence of feminism in the South had long been assumed by feminists in the West; with certain exceptions (such as the feminist movement in India and its strong presence in the rejection of the Raj and the pacifist/feminist movement in Japan) the feminist map of the world had to record absence in many countries. What this raised were the issues of exactly how feminism is defined and in what conditions it develops. The answer to the latter would seem to be that essential to the development of a coherent and cumulative tradition of feminism is a society's account of the place of the individual. Bourgeois liberalism seems to be the ideal starting place. This does not mean that other societies do not include powerful or influential women, but that the power and influence of those women is essentially not constructed in individual terms but is related to a specific female identity. Thus Western feminism can date its beginnings from the Protestant Reformation, and the articulation – albeit contested – of the equality of all citizens, whether female or male.[7]

For societies, and states, outside the influence of bourgeois liberalism, the relations of women and men to the state are more problematic. Of first importance is the history of European colonialization, whereby a number of the world's societies and cultures were made subject to European government. In these societies it was (and is) inevitable that struggles for national independence and autonomy should take precedence over competition between the interests of women and men. But just how dangerous it can be for women to subordinate their interests to those of national identity can be demonstrated by events in the 1980s in Iran. In that country, many women were involved in the struggle to overthrow the feudal despotism and autocracy of the Shah, but the government which replaced the Shah had a strict, and non-negotiable, view of the position of women. So whilst women may have welcomed the new independence they rapidly found that independence for the country was accompanied by a decrease in the personal independence of women.

The lessons of Iran alerted Western feminists to the dangers both of fundamentalism and of over-hasty judgements about political change.[8] It has become clear that in order to secure, not to mention maintain, the interests of women, feminism – however loosely constructed – must exist in a society. Even if feminism has different meanings in different societies, certain fundamentals in the organization of civil society seem to be essential: the recognition of sexual difference, a social and political culture which respects, at least formally, democratic representation, and a political tradition which respects the rights, as well as the duties, of individuals. Alongside these civil preconditions of feminism has to be placed a minimal level of general material provision. To speak of feminism in societies where women have no access to clean water or primary health care for their children seems self-indulgent. Yet without feminism the provision of these necessities is too often relegated to a position of little importance, while the 'macho' projects of development and aid agencies are given precedence. It is of lasting credit to feminists that this is now recognized, as is the crucial role of women in development. Thinking about gender is no longer a luxury for a state, but a vital process for any political system which wishes to intervene effectively in the social world.

Notes

1. Slavenka Drakulic, *How We Survived Communism and Even Laughed* (Hutchinson, London, 1992), p. 126.

2. For a classic statement of the first argument, see Mary McIntosh, 'The state and the oppression of women', in A. Kuhn and A. Wolpe (eds), *Feminism and Materialism* (Routledge & Kegan Paul, London, 1978).

3. See Carole Pateman, *The Sexual Contract* (Blackwell, Oxford, 1989).

4. See P. Piva and C. Ingrao, 'Equality and difference', *Feminist Review*, 16 (1984), pp. 51–5.

5. F. Engels, *The Origin of the Family, Private Property and the State* (Penguin, Harmondsworth, 1985).

6. See the various articles in *Feminist Review*, 39 (Autumn 1991). Many include suggestions for further reading.

7. On the links between the Protestant Reformation and feminism see Keith Thomas, 'Women in the Civil War sects', *Past and Present*, 13 (1958).

8. For discussions of feminism and fundamentalism see Clara Connolly, 'Washing our linen: one year of women against fundamentalism', *Feminist Review*, 37 (1991), pp. 68–77.

The Sexual Contract:
The End of the Story?

Carole Pateman

An old anarchist slogan states that 'no man is good enough to be another man's master'. The sentiment is admirable, but the slogan is silent on one crucial issue. In modern civil society all men are deemed good enough to be women's masters; civil freedom depends on patriarchal right. The failure to see patriarchal right as central to the political problem of freedom, mastery and subordination is so deep-seated that even the anarchists, so acutely aware of subjection among men, have had few quarrels with their fellow socialists about sexual domination. From the beginning of the modern era, when Mary Astell asked why, if all men were born free, all women were born slaves, feminists have persistently challenged masculine right; but, despite all the social changes and legal and political reforms over the past 300 years, the question of women's subordination is still not seen as a matter of major importance, either in the academic study of politics or in political practice. Controversy about freedom revolves round the law of the state and the law of capitalist production: silence is maintained on the law of male sex-right.

The original contract is merely a story, a political fiction, but the invention of the story was also a momentous intervention into the political world; the spell exerted by stories of political origins has to be broken if the fiction is to be rendered ineffective. The continuing fascination with origins is well illustrated by the conjectural histories of the origins of patriarchy produced by the contemporary feminist movement. Many feminists believe that to tell a story of matriarchy 'in the beginning' provides a precedent to show that the 'world historical defeat of the female sex' will not have been final and absolute for all time, but preoccupation with mother-right and father-right merely perpetuates patriarchal structures of thought. No doubt the fact that *the* human beginning – or even if there was one – is a mystery, helps explain the allure of stories of political genesis, but there is also another reason for their popularity. The stories express the specifically masculine creative power, the capacity to generate, to give birth to, new forms of political life.

Extract from *The Sexual Contract*, Polity Press, Cambridge, 1988, pp. 219–34.

To begin to understand modern patriarchy the whole story of the original contract must be reconstructed, but to change modern patriarchy, to begin to create a free society in which women are autonomous citizens, the story must be cast aside. Indeed, fully to understand modern patriarchy requires a very different undertaking from the task I have attempted here. The political fiction of an original contract is part of the history of modern patriarchy, but modern patriarchy did not begin with a dramatic act of contract; there is no origin, in that sense, from which to begin an historical investigation. One might plausibly argue that modern patriarchy began in the seventeenth century when the contractual institutions familiar today first began to develop, but the 'beginning' was not clear cut. Historians often say that a particular event, whether a battle, an Act of Parliament, a popular uprising or a natural disaster, was a turning-point, a beginning, but a great deal has always gone before, other events can be cited and such origins are always open to continual reinterpretation.

Talk of founding has been in vogue in recent years among political theorists, especially in the United States, but how should the real historical 'foundings' of two of the countries with which I am concerned be interpreted? When the First Fleet arrived in Australia in 1788, the men unloaded the ships and built shelters, then, five days later, the female convicts were allowed ashore and into the men's hands. By 1809, the colony was being described as 'little better than an extensive brothel'. As more women convicts were transported, 'the inhabitants of the colony each [selected] one at his pleasure, not only as servants but as avowed objects of intercourse'.[1] Exactly which conjectural history of origins could appropriately be told about these events? The bicentennial of the founding is being celebrated in 1988, but the indigenous people of Australia, like their counterparts in the United States in 1976, see nothing to celebrate. Examples of acts that resemble contractual beginnings can be found in the first white settlements in America, but the 'founding' of white America and Australia took protracted campaigns of conquest and forcible seizure of vast areas of land from indigenous inhabitants.

In order to bring out as sharply as possible something of what is at stake in alternative readings of the original contract, I have exaggerated and described the sexual contract as half the story. The story of political genesis needs to be told again from yet another perspective. The men who (are said to) make the original contract are *white* men, and their fraternal pact has three aspects: the social contract, the sexual contract and the slave contract that legitimizes the rule of white over black. I have touched on the slave contract only where germane to retrieval of the story of the sexual contract.

The political fiction of the original contract tells not only of a beginning, an act of political generation, but also of an end, the defeat of (the classic form of) patriarchy. Moreover, the story is not merely about ends and beginnings, but is used by political theorists and, in more popular versions, by politicians, to represent social and political institutions to contemporary citizens and to represent citizens to themselves. Through the mirror of the original contract, citizens can see themselves as members of a society constituted by free relations. The political fiction reflects our political selves back to us – but who are 'we'? Only men – who can create political life – can take part in the original pact, yet the political fiction speaks to women, too, through the language of the 'individual'. A curious message is sent to women, who represent everything that the individual is not, but the message must continually be conveyed because the meaning of the individual and the social contract depend on women and the sexual contract. Women must acknowledge the political fiction and speak the language even as the terms of the original pact exclude them from the fraternal conversation.

The standard readings of the classic texts (readings that underwrite contract argument that makes no explicit reference to the classics) fail to show in what kind of enterprise the classic theorists were engaged. Instead of interrogating the texts to see how it came about that a certain conception of free political relations became established, the standard interpretations take their departure from the assumption that sexual difference, relations between the sexes and the private sphere are paradigmatically non-political. The classics are thus read in the light of the construction of modern civil society in the texts themselves! The manner in which the classic theorists set about their tasks and the multitude of problems, contradictions and paradoxes about women and contract that they bequeathed never come to the surface. No hint is ever given that, although men and women associate with each other in many different ways, the classic theorists have left a legacy within which the complex, varied dealings and relations between the sexes are ruled outside of critical inquiry. Chapters and passages in the texts dealing with marriage and relations between men and women typically are passed over altogether or presented as peripheral to political theory, of interest only because great men thought such questions worth discussing.

The familiar readings of the texts neither acknowledge, nor can answer, the question of how the classic contract theorists began from premises that rendered illegitimate any claim to political right that appealed to nature, and then went on to construct the difference between men and women as the difference between natural freedom and natural subjection. The argument that the subjection of women to men has a foundation in nature, and Hobbes's rejection of any such masculine right, are both tacitly accepted without examination. To retrieve the story of the sexual contract is not, therefore, merely to add something to the standard accounts, to add a chapter to the story of the social contract. The sexual contract is part of the original contract, and to tell the whole story is to transform the reading of the texts, which can no longer be interpreted from within the patriarchal confines established by the classic contract theorists themselves. And if the texts are reinterpreted, so, too, must the contractual relations of civil society be re-examined.

Feminists have not always appreciated the full extent of the paradox and contradiction involved in women's incorporation into civil society. If women had been merely excluded from civil life, like slaves, or wives when coverture held sway, the character of the problem would have been self-evident. But women have been incorporated into a civil order in which their freedom is apparently guaranteed, a guarantee renewed with each telling of the story of the social contract in the language of the individual. Freedom is enjoyed by all 'individuals', a category that, potentially, pertains to everyone, men and women, white and black alike. In the fullness of time, any historical, accidental exceptions to the principle of freedom will be removed. Women's capacity eventually to take their rightful place is demonstrated by the fact that they are parties to the marriage contract. Women, too, are participants in the act – contract – that constitutes freedom. Feminists seized on the apparently unambiguous guarantee of emancipation offered by contract; thus, in 1791, Olympe de Gouges included a 'Form for a Social Contract Between Man and Woman', which set out the conditions of their marital union, in her *Declaration of the Rights of Woman and the Female Citizen*. The guarantee seems all the firmer now that the feminist movement has succeeded in removing most of the formal juridical barriers to women's civil equality.

The appeal of contract as the enemy of patriarchy, striking the death-blow against sexual domination, is strengthened by contractarianism and the idea of the individual as owner, an individual who is so like all others as to be interchangeable. Critics have remarked that this individual is disembodied and so, they argue, has no identity; a self with an identity is, necessarily, an embodied self. The criticism is valid, but the critics miss the same point as feminists attracted by contract. The individual as owner is separated from a body that is of one sex or the other. A human body, except through misfortunes of birth, is not male and female at the same time, no matter how the body is dressed or positioned in the social structure, although now it can be stripped of both male and female characteristics; if dissatisfied with their 'gender orientation', men can become 'transsexuals' and turn themselves into simulacra of women. The 'individual' is constructed from a male body so that his identity is always masculine. The individual is also a unitary figure; a being of the other sex can only be a modification of the individual, not a distinctive being, or his unity and masculine identity is endangered. In effect, as Rawls's version of the state of nature shows, there is only one individual, duplicated endlessly. How the duplication takes place is a mystery.

Critics of the individual as owner do not consider his genesis (the story of the primal scene and the creation of the private sphere are absent from the tales of fathers, sons and original pacts); their attention is directed to the finished product of the classic contract theorists, the individual in his civil world. Rousseau asked how the new men required for a free social order were to be created in advance of a new society, and, ever since, men have puzzled over this central political question. But the new men always look remarkably like the old men – their civil freedom does not disturb patriarchal right. A free society is still held to stand apart from sexual relations and have no connection with sexual identity, to manhood and womanhood. Movements for free work, for example, for industrial democracy, workers' control or self-management, have taken for granted the masculinity of the 'worker' and the existence of a (house) wife rendering him domestic service. The long history of socialist attempts to restore or recreate the community, solidarity or fraternity that is lost when the individual is stripped bare of social relations have uncovered his masculinity plainly enough – yet the sex of the individual is still not noticed because 'fraternity' is interpreted as (universal) community. And even socialist criticism is now muted; the individual as owner has made a spectacular entry into socialist argument with the development of rational choice or analytical Marxism.

An exploration of contracts about property in the person to which women must be a party – the marriage contract, the prostitution contract and the surrogacy contract – show that the body of a *woman* is precisely what is at issue in the contract. Furthermore, when women are a party to the men's contract, the employment contract, their bodies are never forgotten. Women can attain the formal standing of civil individuals but as embodied feminine beings we can never be 'individuals' in the same sense as men. To take embodied identity seriously demands the abandonment of the masculine, unitary individual to open up space for two figures: one masculine, one feminine.

The body, sex and sexual difference are inseparable from civil subordination, but the body and sex must be separated from the individual if civil subordination is to be created and called freedom. The general assumption is that sex and subordination stand at opposite poles. Sex is consensual; after all, is not rape – enforced sexual submission – a criminal offence (at least outside of marriage)? Some feminists have argued that rape is not sex but violence, but this approach serves to reinforce the separation of sex from subordination; where there is no consent there is only violence, not sex. Sex may be conjured away, but the question remains why such difficulty is encountered in distinguishing women's consent from enforced submission, and why men demand to buy women's sexual submission in the capitalist market. An answer is unlikely to be forthcoming all the time that sex is divided up into discrete, watertight areas of discussion – and never discussed as sex. Rape, discussed here, is about violence; prostitution, discussed there, is about free access to employment; pornography is about freedom expression; and sado-masochism is about consent and equality. The stories of the sexual contract and the primal scene allow questions to be asked about the meaning of sex in late twentieth-century patriarchy and allow the fragmented structure of sexual subordination to be put back together. An answer to the question whether sex means men's mastery is writ large from all sides in the books, magazines, films, videos, peep-shows and other commodities of the sex industry. One of the more remarkable features of contemporary political relations is that the answer is so seldom connected to the question.

Sex is central to the original contract. The brothers make the agreement to secure their natural liberty, part of which consists in the patriarchal right of men, the right of one sex. Only one sex has the capacity to enjoy civil freedom. Civil freedom includes right of sexual access to women and, more broadly, the enjoyment of mastery as a sex – not a gender. The term 'gender' is now ubiquitous but frequently lies idle, used merely as an often not very apt synonym for 'women'. 'Gender' was introduced as a crucial weapon in the struggle against patriarchy. The patriarchal claim is that women are naturally subject to men, subject, that is, because of their biology, their sex. To refer to gender instead of sex indicates that women's position is not dictated by nature, by biology or sex, but is a matter of social and political contrivance. True; what men and women are, and how relations between them are structured, depends on a good deal more than their natural physiology and biology. It is also true, however, that the meaning of men's and women's natures, even the depiction of male and female skeletons and physiology, has depended on the political significance accorded to manhood and womanhood. To use the language of gender reinforces the language of the civil, the public and the individual, language that depends on the repression of the sexual contract.

The meaning of the 'individual' remains intact only so long as the dichotomies (internal to civil society) between natural/civil, private/public, women/individual – and sex/gender – remain intact. Women's inclusion into civil society as members of a gender, as individuals, is also their inclusion as members of a sex, as women. The new surrogacy contract illustrates the mutual dependence of sex and the individual/gender in the most dramatic fashion. Two sexually indifferent individuals (owners, representatives of the genders) must be party to the contract or the contract will be illegitimate, nothing more than a case of baby-selling. On the other hand, the surrogacy contract is only possible at all because one party is a woman; only a woman has the requisite capacity (property) to provide the service demanded, a capacity integral to (natural to) her sex.

For feminists to argue for the elimination of nature, biology, sex in favour of the 'individual' is to play the modern patriarchal game and to join in a much wider onslaught on nature within and beyond the boundaries of civil societies. Nature is represented not only by women, but also, for example, by land, indigenous peoples, the descendants of the slaves whom the Reverend Seabury imagined to have contracted with their masters, and animals (and the latter may become property in a new fashion; the Patent and Trademark Office in the United States will now take applications for patents for genetically altered animals, which are being given the same status as any other human invention). To suppose that the patriarchal appeal to nature and natural, sexual difference implies that patriarchal theories and institutions follow directly from what is given by nature (from physiology, from biology, from sex) is to remain locked within patriarchal confines. The classic contract theorists are instructive here; they did not simply take their pictures of the state of nature and the natural inhabitants of the original condition from nature. Nothing about political relations can be read directly from the two natural bodies of humankind that must inhabit the body politic. The state of nature is drawn by each theorist in a manner that enables him to reach 'the desired solution' – the political solution he has already formulated. Sexual difference in the classic contract theories is, and can only be, a political construct.

To ask whether sexual difference is politically significant is to ask the wrong question; the question is always how the difference is to be expressed. One reason why the wrong question is so often posed is that a good deal of contemporary feminist argument assumes that a choice has to be made between femininity as subordination and the ostensibly sex-neuter 'individual'. In modern patriarchy, as a (re)reading of the texts of classic contract theory makes clear, these are *not alternatives*; to choose one is to choose the other too. The classic theorists, unlike some patriarchal extremists in the nineteenth century, did not have any doubts about women's humanity. They did not, for example, suggest that women were at a lower stage of evolution than men. They argued that sexual difference was the difference between subordination and freedom, but, at the same time, the classic theorists had to grant that women possessed the capacities of naturally free beings, the capacities of individuals.

If the claim that civil society was an order of universal freedom was to be plausible, women had to be incorporated through contract, the act that, at one and the same time, signifies freedom and constitutes patriarchal right. The perception of women (subordination, sex) and the individual (freedom, gender) as alternatives rather than the two inseparable spheres of civil society, underlies a significant historical shift in feminist argument. The juridical equality and legal reform so central to contract doctrine (and which, contrary to the impression cultivated on all sides, has not yet been completely achieved) is invariably seen today as a matter of women acting like men. The suffrage, and more recent reforms such as the participation of women on juries, equal-pay and anti-discrimination legislation, reform of marriage and rape law, decriminalization of prostitution, are all seen as allowing women to become citizens like men and owners of property in their persons like men. Historically, this form of argument is unusual; until recently, most feminists demanded civil equality in the expectation that they would give their equal standing a distinctive expression as women.

Contemporary feminists often treat such a presumption as no more than an illustration of their predecessors' inability to see beyond their own immersion in the private sphere and as a sign that feminists in the past merely accepted the patriarchal appeal to natural sexual difference. To be sure, for feminists to demand a re-evaluation of the (private) tasks undertaken by women when, in modern patriarchy, what counts as 'citizenship' and 'work' takes place in the civil masculine world, is to ask for something that cannot be granted. Nevertheless, when feminists in the past demanded juridical equality and recognition *as women*, and proclaimed that what they did as women in the private sphere was part of their citizenship, they grappled with the political problem of expressing sexual difference; they did not attempt to deny political significance to womanhood. They may have had a different view of the relation between private and public from feminists today, but the perception of the division between private and public (civil) as a *political* problem is a recent development, possible, perhaps, only after a considerable measure of civil equality had been won.

After a century or more of legal reform women are near juridical equality with men and all but a few reminders of coverture have been swept away, but men still enjoy extensive power as a sex and have gained some new advantages, for example as fathers. The series of 'gender neutral' reforms over the past decade or so highlight the problem. The reforms enable women to enjoy equality of opportunity, to enter all areas of paid employment, to engage in freedom of contract, contracting out any of the property in their persons, and to wage 'the battle of Venus' alongside men. But, at the same time, 'sexual harassment' has been discovered in the workplace and the patriarchal division of labour has not been greatly upset, except where men use anti-discrimination legislation to enter the few high-status jobs once reserved for women; women's economic circumstances still place them at a disadvantage in the termination of the marriage contract; sexuality and sexual freedom have been subsumed under 'the sex act' and encompassed within capitalism in the sex industry, which provides men with new forms of access to women's bodies.

Men are, once again, also being seen as the 'principal agents' in human generation. Ironically, one of the central tenets of classic patriarchalism is being summoned up in the onward march of the individual and freedom of contract. No one could doubt until a few years ago that if the human species was to reproduce women had to become pregnant and give birth. Technological developments have now cast doubt on this seemingly natural necessity of human existence. If there is indeed the prospect that reproduction could take place outside the human body (or inside men's bodies), women's natural capacity would no longer be needed – and nor would women. The latter possibility may be no more than a figment of sensational imaginations, but I raise it because nature, biology and sex place limits on contract. Contract theory both rejects and requires those very limits. In a social order constituted by nothing but contract, all the way down, freedom is limitless. There can be no limitation on the jurisdiction of the individual over the property in his person, no restriction on freedom of contract. All the old limits of nature, status, ascription or paternalism must be abandoned. That is to say, in the movement from the old world of status to the new world of contract, the freedom of the individual consists in *emancipation* from the old bonds and constraints, whether those of absolutism, the *patria potestas*, the state – or sexual difference.

From the perspective of the opposition between the old world of status and the new civil world, or the opposition between the state of nature and civil society – the perspective of contract theory (save for Rousseau's arguments) – the problem of freedom is solved, or will be solved when the movement to contract is complete. The individual is emancipated from old restrictions or the endemic insecurity of the natural condition. Freedom is exhibited and expressed through contract, an 'original' act that can always be performed anew, and which is limited only by the legitimate constraint of the jurisdiction of the individual. Freedom is an act . . . an act that establishes new bonds even as the old limitations are overthrown. Freedom is limitless but the act that signifies the end of the old constraints also creates the new civil limits of mastery and obedience. In the new world, the act of emancipation creates civil subordination and patriarchal right.

The premise of natural individual freedom and equality is necessary to create the civil world, and as an abstract universal principle, individual freedom can be appealed to by everyone. Abolitionists and defenders of the slave contract alike could talk of natural freedom; the premise could generate Hobbes's Leviathan, Rousseau's participatory order and the early feminist attack on marital despotism. The idea of individual freedom can be used so promiscuously because of the inherent ambiguity of the meaning of 'civil' society. The ambiguity obscures the fact that critics of contract theory adopt a different perspective from the theorists they criticize and understand freedom differently. The critics argue from a vantage-point within civil society. They do not look back to the old world but at the bifurcation of civil society into private and public spheres, albeit that they typically concentrate on the class division between the spheres. The critics are concerned with freedom as *autonomy*, with a structure of free social relations among political equals, but their criticism, like Rousseau's attack on his fellow contract theorists, is fatally compromised. Their argument remains caught within the dichotomies that are under attack, bouncing back and forth within the boundaries established by the story of the original contract. Socialist critics of contract, followed by many feminists, focus on the inadequacy of juridical equality in a context of social inequality. There is no doubt about the inadequacy, or the cogency of their criticisms, but the combination of public equality and private inequality, as the story of the sexual contract shows, is not a contradiction of modern patriarchy. Juridical equality and social inequality – public/private, civil/natural, men/women – form a coherent social structure. If the complicity of feminists and socialists with contract is to end, attention must turn to subordination and the contradiction of slavery.

Contract theory is haunted by the contradiction of slavery in a variety of guises, and the critics of contract have failed to exorcize the spectre. The contradiction of slavery lies at the heart of the construction of civil society in the classic contract theorists' simultaneous denial and affirmation of women's freedom, and continually reappears because freedom as autonomy is still coupled to sexual mastery. The embrace of the sexual contract by the critics of contract is readily apparent in the legacy that Rousseau and Hegel gave to socialism. Rousseau rejected wage slavery and advocated a non-statist, participatory political order, but his apparently thoroughgoing alternative to the 'individual' and the social contract (couched in contractual language) depended on the natural foundation of women's subjection. Similarly, Hegel's famous dialectic of the master and slave overcomes slavery only to replace slave-masters by (free) sexual masters, who gain recognition of their freedom from the brotherhood and recognition of their patriarchal right from wives. Contractarianism claims to have overcome the contradiction of slavery. The unlimited freedom of the individual as owner to contract out property in his person (his labour power or services) entails that he can rightfully contract himself into civil slavery, an exemplification of freedom. The contradiction disappears – a civil slave is juridically free – then immediately reappears. Property in the person is a political fiction. A civil slave provides a service merely; but what use is a disembodied service to a master? The delights of mastery, including civil mastery, can be obtained only from jurisdiction over a living man or woman.

The marriage and prostitution contracts, contracts to which women are necessarily a party, have always been tainted by the odour of slavery, and provide an embarrassing reminder of 'brutal origins'. The reminder is shrugged off as politically irrelevant, and the analogy with slavery is not taken really seriously. Feminist criticism of the two contracts usually proceeds along the lines of socialist criticism of the employment contract – but without the assistance of the idea of wage slavery. Feminists are thus in the curious position of presupposing that the worker stands in the same position as a wife or prostitute, but failing to ask how the subordination of the worker comes about. The ground is thus conceded to contract doctrine on a vital point; the political fiction of labour power, property in the person, is tacitly accepted, and the paradoxes of women and contract and the contradiction of slavery then continue to be played out.

Civil subordination depends upon the capacity of human beings to act *as if* they could contract out labour power or services rather than, as they must, contract out themselves and their labour to be used by another. If contract is not to be a vain endeavour, the means must be available to ensure that the service contracted for is faithfully performed. The party who demands the service (the employer, the husband, the client) must have the right to command that a body is put to use, or access to the body is made available, in the requisite manner. Contracts about property in the person must always create obedience and constitute a man as a civil master. Exactly what form subordination takes, to what use the body is put or what kind of access is granted, depends on whether a man or a woman is constituted as a subordinate. The buyer is never indifferent to the sex of the owner of property in the person. He contracts for jurisdiction over a masculine or feminine body and forms of subjection differ according to the sex of the body.

A brilliant piece of political inventiveness has given the name of freedom to civil subordination and repressed the interdependence of civil freedom and patriarchal right. If the spectre of slavery is ever, finally, to be laid to rest, political theory and practice has to move outside the structure of oppositions established through the story of the original contract. The move would not diminish the importance of juridical freedom as advocates of contract doctrine often assert. On the contrary, the achievement of juridical freedom and equality is a necessary step towards women's autonomy and necessary to safeguard our bodily integrity. The achievement will, with one important caveat, help in the task of creating the social conditions for the development of an autonomous femininity; the caveat is that women's equal standing must be accepted as an expression of the freedom of women *as women*, and not treated as an indication that women can be just like men. Much feminist energy over the past three centuries has gone into the attempt to show that women have the same capacities as men and so are entitled to the same freedom. In one sense, of course, the efforts were all too necessary; women had to fight against, and must continue to fight against, coverture and the multitude of legal and social supports for masculine right, and continue to fight for access to the social resources required to gain their livelihood and to exercise their citizenship. In another sense, the need to wage this battle helps repress the fact that there is no need to try to show that women are (have the capacities of) free beings. Modern contractual patriarchy both denies and *presupposes women's freedom* and could not operate without this presupposition. The retrieval of the story of the sexual contract allows access to this profoundly important insight.

Political argument must leave behind stories of origins and original contracts and move from the terrain of contract and the individual as owner. To look to an 'original' act of contract is systematically to blur the distinction between freedom and subjection. A free social order cannot be a contractual order. There are other forms of free agreement through which women and men can constitute political relations, although in a period when socialists are busy stealing the clothes of contract little political creativity is directed towards developing the necessary new forms. If political relations are to lose all resemblance to slavery, free women and men must willingly agree to uphold the social conditions of their autonomy. That is to say, they must agree to uphold limits. Freedom requires order and order requires limits. In modern civil society individual freedom is unconstrained – and order is maintained through mastery and obedience. If men's mastery is to be replaced by the mutual autonomy of women and men, individual freedom must be limited by the structure of social relations in which freedom inheres.

A great deal has been heard about freedom from the governments of the Right in Britain and the United States in the 1980s. The rhetoric of private enterprise and freedom from the constricting paternalistic embrace of the state dominates official political debate and the same refrain is now being heard from the Labor government in Australia. At the same time the old dream of the anarchists and Marx that the state will 'wither away' is no longer fashionable. Yet the sexual contract and the social contract, the 'individual' and the state, stand and fall together. Perhaps the dream has faded for good reason; despite the prevailing rhetoric of rolling back the state and diminishing state power, the military and surveillance capacity of the state has increased very rapidly in recent years. The figure of the individual is now all too often dressed in combat uniform and brandishing weapons. The conjuncture of the rhetoric of individual freedom and a vast increase in state power is not unexpected at a time when the influence of contract doctrine is extending into the last, most intimate nooks and crannies of social life. Taken to a conclusion, contract undermines the conditions of its own existence. Hobbes showed long ago that contract – all the way down – requires absolutism and the sword to keep war at bay. If the fiction of the original contract is not to come to an end from which there can be no beginning, or if force instead of will is not to be the principle of the postmodern era, a new story about freedom is urgently needed.

To retrieve the story of the sexual contract does not, in itself, provide a political programme or offer any short cuts in the hard task of deciding what, in any given circumstances, are the best courses of action and policies for feminists to follow, or when and how feminists should form alliances with other political movements. Once the story has been told, however, a new perspective is available from which to assess political possibilities and to judge whether this path or that will aid or hinder (or both) the creation of a free society and the creation of sexual difference as diverse expressions of freedom. When the repressed story of political genesis is brought to the surface the political landscape can never look the same again. Nature, sex, masculinity and femininity, the private, marriage and prostitution become political problems; so, therefore, does the familiar, patriarchal understanding of work and citizenship. New anti-patriarchal roads must be mapped out to lead to democracy, socialism and freedom.

In any case, the political landscape has changed substantially over the past two decades. The story of the original contract must now be told in a less hospitable political context. Patriarchal structures and divisions are no longer as solid as they were between, say, the 1867 Reform Act and the turmoil of 1968. The old manufacturing industries and other arenas in which the worker, his unions and his class solidarity and fraternity flourished are disappearing and the idea of the 'employment society' now looks utopian; 'the family' – the breadwinner, dependent wife and children – now forms a small minority of households in the United States, Australia and Britain; the separation/integration of private and public has been raised as a political problem; and long-standing political allegiances are crumbling and new social movements raise some similar questions to feminism, but from different vantage-points. Men have a vested interest in maintaining the silence about the law of male sex-right, but the opportunity exists for political argument and action to move outside the dichotomies of patriarchal civil society, and for the creation of free relations in which manhood is reflected back from autonomous femininity.

Baudelaire once wrote that 'there is a world of difference between a "completed" subject and a "finished" subject and that in general what is "completed" is not "finished".'[2] I have completed what I have to say about the sexual contract, but the story is far from finished. The political fiction is still showing vital signs and political theory is insufficient to undermine the life-supports.

Notes

1. In a letter from a settler to Colonel Macquarie in London; cited in A. Summers, *Damned Whores and God's Police: The Colonization of Women in Australia* (Penguin Books, Harmondsworth, 1975), p. 269.

2. Cited in R. Hayman, *Nietzsche: A Critical Life* (Penguin Books, Harmondsworth, 1982), p. 360.

Toward Feminist Jurisprudence

Catharine MacKinnon

Happy above all Countries is our Country where that equality is found, without destroying the necessary subordination. (Thomas Lee Shippen, 1788)

If I fight, some day some woman will win. (Michelle Vinson, 1987)

A jurisprudence is a theory of the relation between life and law. In life, 'woman' and 'man' are widely experienced as features of being, not constructs of perception, cultural interventions or forced identities. Gender, in other words, is lived as ontology, not as epistemology. Law actively participates in this transformation of perspective into being. In liberal regimes, law is a particularly potent source and badge of legitimacy, and site and cloak of force. The force underpins the legitimacy as the legitimacy conceals the force. When life becomes law in such a system, the transformation is both formal and substantive. It re-enters life marked by power.

In male supremacist societies, the male standpoint dominates civil society in the form of the objective standard — that standpoint which, because it dominates in the world, does not appear to function as a standpoint at all. Under its aegis, men dominate women and children, three-quarters of the world. Family and kinship rules and sexual mores guarantee reproductive ownership and sexual access and control to men as a group. Hierarchies among men are ordered on the basis of race and class, stratifying women as well. The state incorporates these facts of social power in and as law. Two things happen: law becomes legitimate, and social dominance becomes invisible. Liberal legalism is thus a medium for making male dominance both invisible and legitimate by adopting the male point of view in law at the same time as it enforces that view on society.

Through legal mediation, male dominance is made to seem a feature of life, not a one-sided construct imposed by force for the advantage of a dominant group. To the degree it succeeds ontologically, male dominance does not look epistemological: control over being produces control over consciousness, fusing material conditions with consciousness in a way that is

---

Extract from *Toward a Feminist Theory of the State*, Harvard University Press, Cambridge, MA, 1989, pp. 237–49.

inextricable short of social change. Dominance reified becomes difference. Coercion legitimized becomes consent. Reality objectified becomes ideas; ideas objectified become reality. Politics neutralized and naturalized becomes morality. Discrimination in society becomes nondiscrimination in law. Law is a real moment in the social construction of these mirror-imaged inversions as truth. Law, in societies ruled and penetrated by the liberal form, turns angle of vision and construct of social meaning into dominant institution. In the liberal state, the rule of law – neutral, abstract, elevated, pervasive – both institutionalizes the power of men over women and institutionalizes power in its male form.

From a feminist perspective, male supremacist jurisprudence erects qualities valued from the male point of view as standards for the proper and actual relation between life and law. Examples include standards for scope of judicial review, norms of judicial restraint, reliance on precedent, separation of powers, and the division between public and private law. Substantive doctrines like standing, justiciability and state action adopt the same stance. Those with power in civil society, not women, design its norms and institutions, which become the status quo. Those with power, not usually women, write constitutions, which become law's highest standards. Those with power in political systems that women did not design and from which women have been excluded write legislation, which sets ruling values. Then, jurisprudentially, judicial review is said to go beyond its proper scope – to delegitimize courts and the rule of law itself – when legal questions are not confined to assessing the formal correspondence between legislation and the constitution, or legislation and social reality, but scrutinize the underlying substance. Lines of precedent fully developed before women were permitted to vote, continued while women were not allowed to learn to read and write, sustained under a reign of sexual terror and abasement and silence and misrepresentation continuing to the present day are considered valid bases for defeating 'unprecedented' interpretations or initiatives from women's point of view. Doctrines of standing suggest that because women's deepest injuries are shared in some way by most or all women, no individual woman is differentially injured enough to be able to sue for women's deepest injuries.

Structurally, only when the state has acted can constitutional equality guarantees be invoked.[1] But no law gives men the right to rape women. This has not been necessary, since no rape law has ever seriously undermined the terms of men's entitlement to sexual access to women. No government is, yet, in the pornography business. This has not been necessary, since no man who wants pornography encounters serious trouble getting it, regardless of obscenity laws. No law gives fathers the right to abuse their daughters sexually. This has not been necessary, since no state has ever systematically intervened in their social possession of and access to them. No law gives husbands the right to batter their wives. This has not been necessary, since there is nothing to stop them. No law silences women. This has not been necessary, for women are previously silenced in society – by sexual abuse, by not being heard, by not being believed, by poverty, by illiteracy, by a language that provides only unspeakable vocabulary for their most formative traumas, by a publishing industry that virtually guarantees that if they ever find a voice it leaves no trace in the world. No law takes away women's privacy. Most women do not have any to take, and no law gives them what they do not already have. No law guarantees that women will forever remain the social unequals of men. This is not necessary, because the law guaranteeing sex equality requires, in an unequal society, that before one can be equal legally, one must be equal socially. So long as power enforced by law reflects and corresponds – in form and in substance – to power enforced by men over women in society, law is objective, appears principled, becomes just the way things are. So long as men dominate women effectively enough in society without the support of positive law, nothing constitutional can be done about it.

Law from the male point of view combines coercion with authority, policing society where its edges are exposed: at points of social resistance, conflict and breakdown. Since there is no place outside this system from a feminist standpoint, if its solipsistic lock could be broken, such moments could provide points of confrontation, perhaps even openings for change. The point of view of a total system emerges as particular only when confronted, in a way it cannot ignore, by a demand from another point of view. This is why epistemology must be controlled for ontological dominance to succeed, and why consciousness raising is subversive. It is also why, when law sides with the powerless, as it occasionally has,[2] it is said to engage in something other than law – politics or policy or personal opinion – and to delegitimize itself.[3] When seemingly ontological conditions are challenged from the collective standpoint of a dissident reality, they become visible as epistemological. Dominance suddenly appears no longer inevitable. When it loses its ground it loosens its grip.

Thus, when the [US] Supreme Court held that racial segregation did not violate equality rights, it said that those who felt that to be segregated on the basis of race implied inferiority merely chose to place that construction upon it. The harm of forced separation was a matter of point of view.[4] When the Supreme Court later held that racial segregation violated equality rights, it said that segregation generated a feeling of inferiority in the hearts and minds of Black children which was unlikely ever to be undone. Both courts observed the same reality: the feelings of inferiority generated by apartheid. *Plessy* saw it from the standpoint of white supremacy; *Brown* saw it from the standpoint of the Black challenge to white supremacy, envisioning a social equality that did not yet exist. Inequality is difficult to see when everything tells the unequal that the status quo is equality – for them. To the Supreme Court, the way Black people saw their own condition went from being sneered at as a point of view within their own control, a self-inflicted epistemological harm, to being a constitutional measure of the harm a real social condition imposed upon them. Consciousness raising shifts the episteme in a similar way, exposing the political behind the personal, the dominance behind the submission, participating in altering the balance of power subtly but totally. The question is, what can extend this method to the level of the state for women?

To begin with, why law? Marx saw the modern state as 'the official expression of antagonism in civil society'.[5] Because political power in such a state could emancipate the individual only within the framework of the existing social order, law could emancipate women to be equal only within 'the slavery of civil society'.[6] By analogy, women would not be freed from forced sex, but freed to engage in it and initiate it. They would not be freed from reproductive tyranny and exploitation, but freed to exercise it. They would not be liberated from the dialectic of economic and sexual dominance and submission, but freed to dominate. Depending upon the substantive analysis of civil dominance, either women would dominate men, or some women (with all or some men) would dominate other women. In other words, the liberal vision of sex equality would be achieved. Feminism unmodified, methodologically post-Marxist feminism, aspires to better.

From the feminist point of view, the question of women's collective reality and how to change it merges with the question of women's point of view and how to know it. What do women live, hence know, that can confront male dominance? What female ontology can confront male epistemology; that is, what female epistemology can confront male ontology? What point of view can question the code of civil society? The answer is simple, concrete, specific and real: women's social inequality with men on the basis of sex, hence the point of view of women's subordination to men. Women are not permitted fully to know what sex equality would look like, because they have never lived it. It is idealist, hence elitist, to hold that they do. But they do not need to. They know inequality because they have lived it, so they know what removing barriers to equality would be. Many of these barriers are legal; many of them are social; most of them exist at an interface between law and society.

Inequality on the basis of sex, women share. It is women's collective condition. The first task of a movement for social change is to face one's situation and name it. The failure to face and criticize the reality of women's condition, a failure of idealism and denial, is a failure of feminism in its liberal forms. The failure to move beyond criticism, a failure of determinism and radical paralysis, is a failure of feminism in its left forms. Feminism on its own terms has begun to give voice to and describe the collective condition of women as such, so largely comprised as it is of all women's particularities. It has begun to uncover the laws of motion of a system that keeps women in a condition of imposed inferiority. It has located the dynamic of the social definition of gender in the sexuality of dominance and subordination, the sexuality of inequality: sex as inequality and inequality as sex. As sexual inequality is gendered as man and women, gender inequality is sexualized as dominance and subordination. The social power of men over women extends through laws that purport to protect women as part of the community, like the rape law; laws that ignore women's survival stake in the issue, like the obscenity law, or obscure it, like the abortion law; and laws that announce their intent to remedy that inequality but do not, like the sex equality law. This law derives its authority from reproducing women's social inequality to men in legal inequality, in a seamless web of life and law.

Feminist method adopts the point of view of women's inequality to men. Grasping women's reality from the inside, developing its specificities, facing the intractability and pervasiveness of male power, relentlessly criticizing women's condition as it identifies with all women, it has created strategies for change, beginning with consciousness raising. On the level of the state, legal guarantees of equality in liberal regimes provide an opening. Sex inequality is the true name for women's social condition. It is also, in words anyway, illegal sometimes. In some liberal states, the belief that women already essentially have sex equality extends to the level of law. From a perspective that understands that women do *not* have sex equality, this law means that, once equality is meaningfully defined, the law cannot be applied without changing society. To make sex equality meaningful in law requires identifying the real issues, and establishing that sex inequality, once established, matters.

Sex equality in law has not been meaningfully defined for women, but has been defined and limited from the male point of view to correspond with the existing social reality of sex inequality. An alternative approach to this mainstream view threads through existing law. It is the reason sex equality law exists at all. In this approach, inequality is a matter not of sameness and difference, but of dominance and subordination. Inequality is about power, its definition, and its maldistribution. Inequality at root is grasped as a question of hierarchy, which – as power succeeds in constructing social perception and social reality – derivatively becomes categorical distinctions, differences. Where mainstream equality law is abstract, this approach is concrete; where mainstream equality law is falsely universal, this approach remains specific.[7] The goal is not to make legal categories that trace and trap the status quo, but to confront by law the inequalities in women's condition in order to change them.

This alternate approach centers on the most sex-differential abuses of women as a gender, abuses that sex equality law in its sameness/difference obsession cannot confront. It is based on the reality that feminism, beginning with consciousness raising, has most distinctively uncovered, a reality about which little systematic was known before 1970: the reality of sexual abuse. It combines women's sex-based destitution and enforced dependency and permanent relegation to disrespected and starvation-level work – the lived meaning of class for women – with the massive amount of sexual abuse of girls apparently endemic to the patriarchal family, the pervasive rape and attempted rape about which nothing is done, the systematic battery of women in homes, and prostitution – the fundamental condition of women – of which the pornography industry is an arm. Keeping the reality of gender in view makes it impossible to see gender as a difference, unless this subordinated condition of women is that difference. This reality has called for a new conception of the problem of sex inequality, hence a new legal conception of it, both doctrinally and jurisprudentially.

Experiences of sexual abuse have been virtually excluded from the mainstream doctrine of sex equality because they happen almost exclusively to women and because they are experienced as sex. Sexual abuse has not been seen to raise sex *equality* issues because these events happen specifically and almost exclusively to women as women. Sexuality is socially organized to require sex inequality for excitement and satisfaction. The least extreme expression of gender inequality, and the prerequisite for all of it, is dehumanization and objectification. The most extreme is violence. Because sexual objectification and sexual violence are almost uniquely done to women, they have been systematically treated as the sex difference, when they represent the socially situated subjection of women to men. The whole point of women's social relegation to inferiority as a gender is that this is not generally done to men. The systematic relegation of an entire people to a condition of inferiority is attributed to them, made a feature of theirs, and read out of equality demands and equality law, when it is termed a 'difference'. This condition is ignored entirely, with all the women who are determined by it, when only features women share with the privileged group are allowed to substantiate equality claims.

It follows that seeing sex equality questions as matters of reasonable or unreasonable classification of relevant social characteristics expresses male dominance in law. If the shift in perspective from gender as difference to gender as dominance is followed, gender changes from a distinction that is ontological and presumptively valid to a detriment that is epistemological and presumptively suspect. The given becomes the contingent. In this light, liberalism, purporting to discover gender, has discovered male and female in the mirror of nature; the left has discovered masculine and feminine in the mirror of society. The approach from the standpoint of the subordination of women to men, by contrast, criticizes and claims the specific situation of women's enforced inferiority and devaluation, pointing a way out of the infinity of reflections in law-and-society's hall of mirrors where sex equality law remains otherwise trapped.

Equality understood substantively rather than abstractly, defined on women's own terms and in terms of women's concrete experience, is what women in society most need and most do not have. Equality is also what society holds that women have already, and therefore guarantees women by positive law. The law of equality, statutory and constitutional, therefore provides a peculiar jurisprudential opportunity, a crack in the wall between law and society. Law does not usually guarantee rights to things that do not exist. This may be why equality issues have occasioned so many jurisprudential disputes about what law is and what it can and should do. Every demand from women's point of view looks substantive, just as every demand from women's point of view requires change. Can women, demanding actual equality through law, be part of changing the state's relation to women and women's relation to men?

The first step is to claim women's concrete reality. Women's inequality occurs in a context of unequal pay, allocation to disrespected work, demeaned physical characteristics, targeting for rape, domestic battery, sexual abuse as children, and systematic sexual harassment. Women are daily dehumanized, used in denigrating entertainment, denied reproductive control, and forced by the conditions of their lives into prostitution. These abuses occur in a legal context historically characterized by disenfranchisement, preclusion from property ownership, exclusion from public life, and lack of recognition of sex-specific injuries.[8] Sex inequality is thus a social and political institution.

The next step is to recognize that male forms of power over women are affirmatively embodied as individual rights in law. When men lose power, they feel they lose rights. Often they are not wrong. Examples include the defense of mistaken belief in consent in the rape law, which legally determines whether or not a rape occurred from the rapist's perspective; freedom of speech, which gives pimps rights to torture, exploit, use and sell women to men through pictures and words, and gives consumers rights to buy them; the law of privacy, which defines the home and sex as presumptively consensual and protects the use of pornography in the home; the law of child custody, which purports gender neutrality while applying a standard of adequacy of parenting based on male-controlled resources and male-defined norms, sometimes taking children away from women but more generally controlling women through the threat and fear of loss of their children. Real sex equality under law would qualify or eliminate these powers of men, hence men's current 'rights' to use, access, possess and traffic in women and children.

In this context, many issues appear as sex equality issues for the first time – sexual assault, for example. Rape is a sex-specific violation. Not only are the victims of rape overwhelmingly women, perpetrators overwhelmingly men, but also the rape of women by men is integral to the way inequality between the sexes occurs in life. Intimate violation with impunity is an ultimate index of social power. Rape both evidences and practices women's low status relative to men. Rape equates female with violable and female sexuality with forcible intrusion in a way that defines and stigmatizes the female sex as a gender. Threat of sexual assault is threat of punishment for being female. The state has laws against sexual assault but it does not enforce them. Like lynching at one time, rape is socially permitted, though formally illegal. Victims of sex crimes, mostly women and girls, are thus disadvantaged relative to perpetrators of sex crimes, largely men.

A systemic inequality between the sexes therefore exists in the social practice of sexual violence, subjection to which defines women's status, and victims of which are largely women, and in the operation of the state, which *de jure* outlaws sexual violence but *de facto* permits men to engage in it on a wide scale. Making sexual assault laws gender neutral does nothing to address this, nothing to alter the social equation of female with rapable, and may obscure the sex specificity of the problem. Rape should be defined as sex by compulsion, of which physical force is one form. Lack of consent is redundant and should not be a separate element of the crime.[9] Expanding this analysis would support as sex equality initiatives laws keeping women's sexual histories out of rape trials,[10] and publication bans on victims' names and identities.[11] The defense of mistaken belief in consent – which measures whether a rape occurred from the standpoint of the (male) perpetrator – would violate women's sex equality rights by law because it takes the male point of view on sexual violence against women.[12] Similarly, the systematic failure of the state to enforce the rape law effectively or at all excludes women from equal access to justice, permitting women to be savaged on a mass scale, depriving them of equal protection and equal benefit of the laws.

Reproductive control, formerly an issue of privacy, liberty or personal security, would also become a sex equality issue. The frame for analysing reproductive issues would expand from focus on the individual at the moment of the abortion decision to women as a group at all reproductive moments. The social context of gender inequality denies women control over the reproductive uses of their bodies and places that control in the hands of men. In a context of inadequate and unsafe contraceptive technology, women are socially disadvantaged in controlling sexual access to their bodies through social learning, lack of information, social pressure, custom, poverty and enforced economic dependence, sexual force, and ineffective enforcement of laws against sexual assault. As a result, they often do not control the conditions under which they become pregnant. If intercourse cannot be presumed to be controlled by women, neither can pregnancy. Women have also been allocated primary responsibility for intimate care of children yet do not control the conditions under which they rear them, hence the impact of these conditions on their own lives.

In this context, access to abortion is necessary for women to survive unequal social circumstances. It provides a form of relief, however punishing, in a life otherwise led in conditions that preclude choice in ways most women have not been permitted to control. This approach also recognizes that whatever is done to the fetus is done to a woman. Whoever controls the destiny of a fetus controls the destiny of a woman. Whatever the conditions of conception, if reproductive control of a fetus is exercised by anyone but the woman, reproductive control is taken only from women, as women. Preventing a woman from exercising the only choice an unequal society leaves her is an enforcement of sex inequality. Giving women control over sexual access to their bodies and adequate support of pregnancies and care of children extends sex equality. In other words, forced maternity is a practice of sex inequality.[13] Because motherhood without choice is a sex equality issue, legal abortion should be a sex equality right. Reproductive technology, sterilization abuse and surrogate motherhood, as well as abortion funding, would be transformed if seen in this light.

Pornography, the technologically sophisticated traffic in women that expropriates, exploits, uses and abuses women, also becomes a sex equality issue. The mass production of pornography universalizes the violation of the women in it, spreading it to all women, who are then exploited, used, abused and reduced as a result of men's consumption of it. In societies pervaded by pornography, all women are defined by it: this is what a woman wants, this is what a woman is. Pornography sets the public standard for the treatment of women in private and the limits of tolerance for what can be permitted in public, such as in rape trials. It sexualizes the definition of male as dominant and female as subordinate. It equates violence against women with sex and provides an experience of that fusion. It engenders rape, sexual abuse of children, battery, forced prostitution and sexual murder.

In liberal legalism, pornography is said to be a form of freedom of speech. It seems that women's inequality is something pornographers want to say, and saying it is protected even if it requires doing it. Being the medium for men's speech supersedes any rights women have. Women become men's speech in this system. Women's speech is silenced by pornography and the abuse that is integral to it. From women's point of view, obscenity law's misrepresentation of the problem as moral and ideational is replaced with the understanding that the problem of pornography is political and practical. Obscenity law is based on the point of view of male dominance. Once this is exposed, the urgent issue of freedom of speech for women is not primarily the avoidance of state intervention as such, but getting equal access to speech for those to whom it has been denied. First the abuse must be stopped.[14] The endless moral debates between good and evil, conservative and liberal, artists and philistines, the forces of darkness and repression and suppression and the forces of light and liberation and tolerance, would be superseded by the political debate, the abolitionist debate: are women human beings or not? Apparently, the answer provided by legal mandates of sex equality requires repeating.

The changes that a sex equality perspective provides as an interpretive lens include the law of sex equality itself. The intent requirement would be eliminated. The state action requirement would weaken. No distinction would be made between nondiscrimination and affirmative action. Burdens of proof would presuppose inequality rather than equality as a factual backdrop and would be more substantively sensitive to the particularities of sex inequality. Comparable worth would be required. Statistical proofs of disparity would be conclusive. The main question would be: does a practice participate in the subordination of women to men, or is it no part of it? Whether statutes are sex specific or gender neutral would not be as important as whether they work to end or reinforce male supremacy, whether they are concretely grounded in women's experience of subordination or not. Discrimination law would not be confined to employment, education and accommodation. Civil remedies in women's hands would be emphasized. Gay and lesbian rights would be recognized as sex equality rights. Since sexuality largely defines gender, discrimination based on sexuality is discrimination based on gender. Other forms of social discrimination and exploitation by men against women, such as prostitution and surrogate motherhood, would become actionable.

The relation between life and law would also change. Law, in liberal jurisprudence, objectifies social life. The legal process reflects itself in its own image, makes be there what it puts there, while presenting itself as passive and neutral in the process. To undo this, it will be necessary to grasp the dignity of women without blinking at the indignity of women's condition, to envision the possibility of equality without minimizing the grip of inequality, to reject the fear that has become so much of women's sexuality and the corresponding denial that has become so much of women's politics, and to demand civil parity without pretending that the demand is neutral or that civil equality already exists. In this attempt, the idealism of liberalism and the materialism of the left have come to much the same for women. Liberal jurisprudence that the law should reflect nature or society and left jurisprudence that all law does or can do is reflect existing social relations are two guises of objectivist epistemology. If objectivity is the epistemological stance of which women's sexual objectification is the social process, its imposition the paradigm of power in the male form, then the state appears most relentless in imposing the male point of view when it comes closest to achieving its highest formal criterion of distanced aperspectivity. When it is most ruthlessly neutral, it is most male; when it is most sex blind, it is most blind to the sex of the standard being applied. When it most closely conforms to precedent, to 'facts', to legislative intent, it most closely enforces socially male norms and most thoroughly precludes questioning their content as having a point of view at all.

Abstract rights authoritize the male experience of the world. Substantive rights for women would not. Their authority would be the currently unthinkable: nondominant authority, the authority of excluded truth, the voice of silence. It would stand against both the liberal and left views of law. The liberal view that law is society's text, its rational mind, expresses the male view in the normative mode; the traditional left view that the state, and with it the law, is superstructural or epiphenomenal, expresses it in the empirical mode. A feminist jurisprudence, stigmatized as particularized and protectionist in male eyes of both traditions, is accountable to women's concrete conditions and to changing them. Both the liberal and the left view rationalize male power by presuming that it does not exist, that equality between the sexes (room for marginal corrections conceded) is society's basic norm and fundamental description. Only feminist jurisprudence sees that male power does exist and sex equality does not, because only feminism grasps the extent to which antifeminism is misogyny and both are as normative as they are empirical. Masculinity then appears as a specific position, not just the way things are, its judgments and partialities revealed in process and procedure, adjudication and legislation.

Equality will require change, not reflection – a new jurisprudence, a new relation between life and law. Law that does not dominate life is as difficult to envision as a society in which men do not dominate women, and for the same reasons. To the extent feminist law embodies women's point of view, it will be said that its law is not neutral. But existing law is not neutral. It will be said that it undermines the legitimacy of the legal system. But the legitimacy of existing law is based on force at women's expense. Women have never consented to its rule – suggesting that the system's legitimacy needs repair that women are in a position to provide. It will be said that feminist law is special pleading for a particular group and one cannot start that or where will it end. But existing law is already special pleading for a particular group, where it has ended. The question is not where it will stop, but whether it will start for any group but the dominant one. It will be said that feminist law cannot win and will not work. But this is premature. Its possibilities cannot be assessed in the abstract but must engage the world. A feminist theory of the state has barely been imagined; systematically, it has never been tried.

Notes

1. In the United States, the 'state action' requirement restricts review under the Fourteenth Amendment. See Lawrence Tribe, *American Constitutional Law* (Foundation Press, Mineola, NY, 1978), pp. 1688–720, for summary. In Canada, under the Canadian Charter of Rights and Freedoms, Section 32 restricts charter review to acts of government.

2. *Brown* v. *Board of Education*, 347 US 483 (1954); *Swann* v. *Charlotte-Mecklenburg Board of Education*, 402 US 2 (1971); *Griggs* v. *Duke Power*, 401 US 424 (1971).

3. Herbert Wechsler, 'Toward neutral principles of constitutional law', *Harvard Law Review*, 73, I (1959).

4. *Plessy* v. *Ferguson*, 163 US 537, 551 (1896); Wechsler, 'Toward neutral principles', p. 33.

5. Karl Marx, *The Poverty of Philosophy* (International Publishers, New York, 1963), p. 174.

6. Karl Marx and Friedrich Engels, *The Holy Family*, trans. R. Dixon (Progress Publishers, Moscow, 1956), p. 157. See generally M. Cain and A. Hunt, *Marx and Engels on Law* (Academic Press, London, 1979).

7. Examples are *Loving* v. *Virginia*, 388 US I (1967); *Brown* v. *Board of Education* 347 US 483 (1954); some examples of the law against sexual harassment (e.g., *Barnes* v. *Costle*, 561 F. 2d 983 [DC Cir. 1977]; *Vinson* v. *Taylor*, 753 F. 2d 141 [DC Cir. 1985], aff'd. 477 US 57 (1986); *Priest* v. *Rotary*, 98 F.R.D. 755 [D. Cal. 1983]), some athletics cases (e.g., *Clark* v. *Arizona Interscholastic Assn.*, 695 F. 2d 1126 [9th Cir. 1986]), some affirmative action cases (e.g., *Johnson* v. *Transportation Agency, Santa Clara County*, 480 US 616 [1987]), and *California Federal Savings and Loan Association* v. *Guerra*, 492 US 272 (1987).

8. This context was argued as the appropriate approach to equality in an intervention by the Women's Legal Education and Action Fund (LEAF) in *Law Society of British Columbia* v. *Andrews* (22 May 1987) before the Supreme Court of Canada. This approach to equality in general, giving priority to concrete disadvantage and rejecting the 'similarly situated' test, was adopted by the Supreme Court of Canada in that case (1989) – DLR (3d) –.

9. See III, Rev. Stat. 1985, ch. 38, par. 12–14; *People* v. *Haywood*, 515 NE 2d 45 (III. App. 1987) (prosecution not required to prove nonconsent, since sexual penetration by force implicitly shows nonconsent); but cf. *People* v. *Coleman*, 520 NE 2d 55 (III, App. 1987) (state must prove victim's lack of consent beyond reasonable doubt).

10. This is argued by LEAF in its intervention application with several groups in *Seaboyer* v. *The Queen* (12 July 1988) and *Gayme* v. *The Queen* (18 November 1988), both on appeal before the Supreme Court of Canada. The rulings below are *The Queen* v. *Seaboyer and Gayme* (1986) 50 C.R. (3d) 395 (Ont. C.A.).

11. LEAF and a coalition of rape crisis centers, groups opposing sexual assault of women and children, and feminist media made this argument in an intervention in *The Queen* v.

Canadian Newspapers Co., Ltd. The Canadian statute was upheld by a unanimous court. (1988) – D.L.R. (3d) –.

12. This is argued by LEAF intervening in *The Queen* v. *Gayme*.

13. This argument was advanced by LEAF in an intervention in *Borowski* v. *Attorney General of Canada* (7 October 1987).

14. The Anti-Pornography Civil Rights Ordinance aims to do this. See Andrea Dworkin and Catharine A. MacKinnon, *Pornography and Civil Rights: A New Day for Women's Equality* (Organizing Against Pornography, Minneapolis, 1988).

Pornography

Andrea Dworkin

She was thirteen. She was at a Girl Scout camp in northern Wisconsin. She went for a long walk in the woods alone during the day. She had long blond hair. She saw three hunters reading magazines, talking, joking. One looked up and said: 'There's a live one.' She thought they meant a deer. She ducked and started to run away. They meant her. They chased her, caught her, dragged her back to where they were camped. The magazines were pornography of women she physically resembled: blond, childlike. They called her names from the pornography: Little Godiva, Golden Girl, also bitch and slut. They threatened to kill her. They made her undress. It was November and cold. One held a rifle to her head; another beat her breasts with his rifle. All three raped her – penile penetration into the vagina. The third one couldn't get hard at first so he demanded a blow job. She didn't know what that was. The third man forced his penis into her mouth; one of the others cocked the trigger on his rifle. She was told she had better do it right. She tried. When they were done with her they kicked her: they kicked her naked body and they kicked leaves and pine needles on her. '[T]hey told me that if I wanted more, that I could come back the next day.'

She was sexually abused when she was three by a boy who was fourteen – it was a 'game' he had learned from pornography. '[I]t seems really bizarre to me to use the word "boy" because the only memory I have of this person is as a three year old. And as a three year old he seemed like a really big man.' When she was a young adult she was drugged by men who made and sold pornography. She remembers flashing lights, being forced onto a stage, being undressed by two men and sexually touched by a third. Men were waving money at her: 'one of them shoved it in my stomach and essentially punched me. I kept wondering how it was possible that they couldn't see that I didn't want to be there, that I wasn't there willingly.'

She had a boyfriend. She was twenty-one. One night he went to a stag party and watched pornography films. He called her up to ask if he could have sex with her. She felt obligated to make him happy. 'I also felt that the refusal would be indicative of sexual quote unquote hang-ups on my part and that I was not quote unquote liberal enough. When he arrived, he informed me that the other men at the party were envious that he had a girlfriend to fuck. They wanted to fuck too after watching the pornography. He informed me of this as he was taking his coat off.' He had her perform oral sex on him: 'I did not do this of my own volition. He put his genitals in my face and he said "Take it all."' He fucked her. The whole encounter took about five minutes. Then he dressed and went back to the party. 'I felt ashamed and numb and I also felt very used.'[1] [. . .]

I've quoted from statements, all made in public forums, by women I know well. [. . .] I can vouch for them; I know the stories are true. The women who made these particular statements are only a few of the thousands of women I have met, talked with, questioned: women who have been hurt by pornography. The women are real to me. I know what they look like

From the new introduction to *Pornography: Men Possessing Women*, Dutton, New York, 1989, pp. xiii–xl, abridged.

standing tall; I've seen the fear; I've watched them remember; I've talked with them about other things, all sorts of things: intellectual issues, the weather, politics, school, children, cooking. I have some idea of their aspirations as individuals, the ones they lost during the course of sexual abuse, the ones they cherish now. I know them. Each one, for me, has a face, a voice, a whole life behind her face and her voice. Each is more eloquent and more hurt than I know how to convey. Since 1974, when my book *Woman Hating* was first published, women have been seeking me out to tell me that they have been hurt by pornography; they have told me how they have been hurt in detail, how much, how long, by how many. They thought I might believe them, initially, I think, because I took pornography seriously in *Woman Hating*. I said it was cruel, violent, basic to the way our culture sees and treats women – and I said the hate in it was real. Well, they knew that the hate in it was real because they had been sexually assaulted by that hate. One does not make the first tentative efforts to communicate about this abuse to those who will almost certainly ridicule one. Some women took a chance on me; and it was a chance, because I often did not want to listen. I had my limits and my reasons, like everyone else. For many years, I heard the same stories I have tried to encapsulate here: the same stories, sometimes more complicated, sometimes more savage, from thousands of women, most of whom hadn't dared to tell anyone. No part of the country was exempt; no age group; no racial or ethnic group; no 'life-style' however 'normal' or 'alternative'. The statements I have paraphrased here are not special: not more sadistic, not chosen by me because they are particularly sickening or offensive. In fact, they are not particularly sickening or offensive. They simply are what happens to women who are brutalized by the use of pornography on them. [. . .]

In the fall of 1983, something changed. The speech of women hurt by pornography became public and real. It, they, began to exist in the sphere of public reality. Constitutional lawyer Catharine A. MacKinnon and I were hired by the City of Minneapolis to draft an amendment to the city's civil rights law: an amendment that would recognize pornography as a violation of the civil rights of women, as a form of sex discrimination, an abuse of human rights. We were also asked to organize hearings that would provide a legislative record showing the need for such a law. Essentially, the legislators needed to know that these violations were systematic and pervasive in the population they represented, not rare, peculiar anomalies.

The years of listening to the private stories had been years of despair for me. It was hopeless. I could not help. There was no help. I listened; I went on my way; nothing changed. Now, all the years of listening were knowledge, real knowledge that could be mined: a resource, not a burden and a curse. I knew how women were hurt by pornography. My knowledge was concrete, not abstract: I knew the ways it was used; I knew how it was made; I knew the scenes of exploitation and abuse in real life – the lives of prostitutes, daughters, girlfriends, wives; I knew the words the women said when they dared to whisper what had happened to them; I could hear their voices in my mind, in my heart. I didn't know that there were such women all around me, everywhere, in Minneapolis that fall. I was heartbroken as women I knew came forward to testify: though I listened with an outer detachment to the stories of rape, incest, prostitution, battery, and torture, each in the service of pornography, inside I wanted to die.

The women who came forward to testify at the hearings held by the Minneapolis City Council on December 12 and 13, 1983, gave their names and specified the area of the city in which they lived. They spoke on the record before a governmental body in the city where they lived; there they were, for family, neighbors, friends, employers, teachers, and strangers to see, to remember. They described in detail sexual abuse through pornography as it had happened to them. They were questioned on their testimony by Catharine MacKinnon and myself and also by members of the city council and sometimes the city attorney. There were photographers and television cameras. There were a couple of hundred people in the room. There was no safety, no privacy, no retreat, no protection; only a net of validation provided by the testimony of experts – clinical psychologists, prosecutors, experimental psychologists, social scientists, experts in sexual abuse from rape crisis centers and battered women's shelters, and those who worked with sex offenders. The testimony of these experts was not abstract or theoretical; it brought the lives of more women, more children, into the room: more rape, more violation through pornography. They too were talking about real people who had been hurt, sometimes killed; they had seen, known, treated, interviewed, numbers of them. A new social truth emerged, one that had been buried in fear, shame, and the silence of the socially powerless: no woman hurt by pornography was alone – she never had been; no woman hurt by pornography would ever be alone again because each was – truly – a 'living remnant of the general struggle'.[2] What the survivors said was speech; the pornography had been, throughout their lives, a means of actively suppressing their speech. They had been turned into pornography in life and made mute; terrorized by it and made mute. Now, the mute spoke; the socially invisible were seen; the women were real; they mattered. This speech – their speech – was new in the world of public discourse, and it was made possible by the development of a law that some called censorship. The women came forward because they thought that the new civil rights law recognized what had happened to them, gave them recourse and redress, enhanced their civil dignity and human worth. The law itself gave them *existence*: I am real; they believed me; I count; social policy at last will take my life into account, validate my worth – me, the woman who was forced to fuck a dog; me, the woman he urinated on; me, the woman he tied up for his friends to use; me, the woman he masturbated in; me, the woman he branded or maimed; me, the woman he prostituted; me, the woman they gang-raped.

The law was passed twice in Minneapolis in 1983 and 1984 by two different city councils; it was vetoed each time by the same mayor, a man active in Amnesty International, opposing torture outside of Minneapolis. The law was passed in 1984 in Indianapolis with a redrafted definition that targeted violent pomography – the kind 'everyone' opposes. The city was sued for passing it; the courts found it unconstitutional. The appeals judge said that pomography did all the harm we claimed – it promoted insult and injury, rape and assault, even caused women to have lower wages – and that these effects proved its power as speech; therefore, it had to be protected. In 1985, the law was put on the ballot by popular petition in Cambridge, Massachusetts. The city council refused to allow it on the ballot; we had to sue for ballot access; the civil liberties people opposed our having that access; we won the court case and the city was ordered to put the law on the ballot. We got 42 percent of the vote, a higher percentage than feminists got on the first women's suffrage referendum. In 1988, the law was on the ballot in Bellingham, Washington, in the presidential election; we got 62 percent of the vote. The city had tried to keep us off the ballot; again we had to get a court order to gain ballot access. The City of Bellingham was sued by the ACLU in federal court for having the law, however unwillingly; a federal district judge found the law unconstitutional, simply reiterating the previous appeals court decision in the Indianapolis case – indeed, there was a statement that the harms of pomography were recognized and not in dispute. [. . .]

Women continue speaking out in public forums, even though we are formally and purposefully silenced in actual courts of law. Hearings were held by a subcommittee of the Senate Judiciary Committee on the effects of pomography on women and children; the Attorney General's Commission on Pomography listened to the testimony of women hurt by pomography; women are demanding to speak at conferences, debates, on television, radio. This civil rights law is taught in law schools all over the country; it is written about in law journals, often favorably; increasingly, it has academic support; and its passage has been cited as precedent in at least one judicial decision finding that pomography in the workplace can be legally recognized as sexual harassment. The time of silence – at least the time of absolute silence – is over. And the civil rights law developed in Minneapolis has had an impact around the world. It is on the agenda of legislators in England, Ireland, West Germany, New Zealand, Tasmania, and Canada; it is on the agenda of political activists all over the world.

The law itself is civil, not criminal. It allows people who have been hurt by pomography to sue for sex discrimination. Under this law, it is sex discrimination to coerce, intimidate, or fraudulently induce anyone into pomography; it is sex discrimination to force pomography on a person in any place of employment, education, home, or any public place; it is sex discrimination to assault, physically attack, or injure any person in a way that is directly caused by a specific piece of pomography – the pomographers share responsibility for the assault; in the Bellingham version, it is also sex discrimination to defame any person through the unauthorized use in pomography of their name, image, and/or recognizable personal likeness; and it is sex discrimination to produce, sell, exhibit, or distribute pomography – to traffic in the exploitation of women, to traffic in material that provably causes aggression against and lower civil status for women in society.

The law's definition of pornography is concrete, not abstract. Pornography is defined as the graphic, sexually explicit subordination of women in pictures and/or words that also includes women presented dehumanized as sexual objects, things, or commodities; or women presented as sexual objects who enjoy pain or humiliation; or women presented as sexual objects who experience sexual pleasure in being raped; or women presented as sexual objects tied up or cut up or mutilated or bruised or physically hurt; or women presented in postures or positions of sexual submission, servility, or display; or women's body parts – including but not limited to vaginas, breasts, buttocks – exhibited such that women are reduced to those parts; or women presented as whores by nature; or women presented being penetrated by objects or animals; or women presented in scenarios of degradation, injury, torture, shown as filthy or inferior, bleeding, bruised, or hurt in a context that makes these conditions sexual. If men, children, or transsexuals are used in any of the same ways, the material also meets the definition of pornography.

For women hurt by pornography, this law simply describes reality; it is a map of a real world. Because the law allows them to sue those who have imposed this reality on them – especially the makers, sellers, exhibitors, and distributors of pornography – they have a way of redrawing the map. The courts now protect the pornography; they recognize the harm to women in judicial decisions – or they use words that say they recognize the harm – and then tell women that the Constitution protects the harm; profit is real to them and they make sure the pimps stay rich, even as women and their children are this country's poor. The civil rights law is designed to confront both the courts and the pornographers with a demand for substantive, not theoretical, equality. This law says: we have the right to stop them from doing this to us because we are human beings. [. . .]

Initially an amendment to a city ordinance, this law has had a global impact because: (1) it tells the truth about what pornography is and does; (2) it tells the truth about how women are exploited and hurt by the use of pornography; (3) it seeks to expand the speech of women by taking the pornographers' gags out of our mouths; (4) it seeks to expand the speech and enhance the civil status of women by giving us the courts as a forum in which we will have standing and authority; (5) it is a mechanism for redistributing power, taking it from pimps, giving it to those they have been exploiting for profit, injuring for pleasure; (6) it says that women matter, including the women in the pornography. This law and the political vision and experience that inform it are not going to go away. We are going to stop the pornographers. We are going to claim our human dignity under law.

Notes

1. Public Hearings on Ordinance to Add Pornography as Discrimination Against Women, Minneapolis City Council, Government Operations Committee, December 12 and 13, 1983; reprinted as *Pornography and Sexual Violence: Evidence of the Links* (Everywoman, London, 1988), pp. 60–1, 62–3 and 64–5.

2. The phrase is from Terrence Des Pres, *The Survivor: an Anatomy of Life in the Death Camps* (Pocket Books, New York, 1977), p. 39.

Theory into Practice: The Problem of Pornography

Carol Smart

Pornography has become a major issue for the women's movements in North America, Europe and Australia. To some extent the concern over pornography has replaced the nineteenth-century feminist concern with prostitution. It was prostitution that epitomized the problem of the dual standard of morality and the abuse of women (both of which were reflected in law) in the last century. In the late twentieth century pornography has come to fill this role. For many feminists pornography is regarded as the very essence of patriarchy, indeed it is theorized as the mainstay of male power and female subjugation.

This focus on pornography, and violent or sadistic pornography in particular, has promoted a desire for political action and resistance. Regardless of the differences between feminisms, there is common ground that pornography is a problem that should not simply be ignored in the hope that it will wither away. However, there is less consensus over the exact nature of the problem whilst there gathers apace an urgency that 'something' should be done. This urgency for action is heightened by the expanding currency of the idea that while pornography is the theory, rape is the practice. In other words there is a fear that if something is not done soon, sexual assaults on women will escalate further. Action by feminists has taken the form of 'Reclaim the Night' marches, even direct attacks on sex shops, and more recently a turning to law in the hope that it can stem what is regarded as the flow of masculinist propaganda. This desire for political action has resulted in the interesting situation in which some forms of feminism are hopeful that the law can be used to enforce feminist standards.

Elsewhere I have discussed this strategy in detail but it is important to make a few general comments here. The aim of 'fitting' feminist ideas on pornography into a legal framework that might be 'workable' (in narrow legal terms) or politically 'acceptable', means that many of the subtle insights

Extract from *Feminism and the Power of Law*, Routledge, London, 1989, pp. 114–37, abridged.

and complexities of feminist analysis are necessarily lost. The legal framework (whether civil or criminal) requires that we fit pornography, or the harm that pornography does, into existing categories of harms or wrongs. Hence we are left with a focus on degrees of actual violence or the traditional (non-feminist) concern with degrees of explicitness which are the mainstay of obscenity laws. Hence feminist work on pornography becomes increasingly collapsed into traditional discussions of how sex depraves or how representations of violence cause actual violence. These are undeniably matters of concern, but they do not by any means encompass the complexity of the feminist debate, nor do they permit feminism to set its own agenda in relation to pornography. Unfortunately, the resort to law has had another undesirable consequence. It has aggravated the differences between the various feminist approaches to pornography and has made these differences very public. Campaigning for laws against pornography has meant that feminists who see this as retrograde have had to campaign against such measures. In the heat of the argument much has been lost and the insights of different forms of feminisms have been mutually obscured. Cynthia Cockburn refers to an aspect of this problem in the following statement:

> For me, then, the perceptions of feminism concerning male violence and issues of sexuality do not mark a wrong route taken but offer the chance of a strengthening and changing of socialist feminism by the insights of radical feminism. (Cockburn, 1988: 308)

Cockburn is referring to the way in which socialist feminism as a public, political discourse has largely ignored the questions of male violence and male sexuality, while socialist feminists as women have suffered from the consequences of these issues in their personal lives. Unfortunately the disagreement over the resort to law in the area of pornography has further obscured these areas of common ground. This is not only because there is disagreement about the usefulness of law in this field but because using the law requires compromise and collaboration from feminists. The compromise is in terms of limiting a potentially subtle and multi-layered analysis to fit into a legally constituted statute. The collaboration involves alliances with groups and social attitudes often antithetical to feminism's other values and goals. Hence the development of shared platforms with the moral right and the slippage into law and order rhetoric has made this feminist strategy quite unpalatable to the movement as a whole. The radical feminist campaign on pornography risks becoming a latterday moral crusade which is prepared to concede more power to an anti-feminist legal system in order to achieve limited legislative regulation over some forms of pornography. There is, of course, no guarantee that legal regulation would be effective any more than rape law or equal pay legislation is 'effective' in feminist terms. This raises the question of whether, on this topic which involves such a diversity of feminist views on sexuality and the representation of sexual desires and fantasies, it is a wise strategy to appeal to law at all. Here I shall examine this question, focusing on initiatives that have been taken by feminists in North

America. First, however, I shall consider some of the basic areas of disagreement in the pornography debate.

Defining the problem of pornography

The feminist concern with pornography has emerged from long-standing campaigns on issues of sexual exploitation (e.g. prostitution) and from the more recent recognition that (hetero)sexuality is a site of conflict and oppression, rather than merely a reflection of 'natural' difference between women and men. It also developed from work on images of women in advertising, literature, film and the media. This is quite a different 'genesis' and has incorporated into more traditional feminist work on sexual exploitation ideas from semiotics and theories of representation. These diverse 'origins' have been reproduced in the diversity of analysis that typifies contemporary feminist work in this area. It is impossible in this field to identify a simple bipartisan distinction between different feminist approaches. The idea of radical feminism standing in contradistinction to socialist feminism really is not adequate here. These two categories no longer encompass the complexities of the different feminist positions; for example, where would psychoanalytic feminism fit? It is necessary to identify the major differences, however, so I shall use the categories of pornography-as-violence and pornography-as-representation to identify the two main contributions to the debate.[1] In the first group we find authors like Dworkin (1981) and MacKinnon (1987). In the second we find Brown (1981), Kuhn (1985), and Coward (1987).

It would be untrue to imply that these two positions held nothing in common, but they do theorize the position of pornography in the oppression of women quite differently. Before concentrating on these differences it may be useful to identify their similar starting points and to acknowledge the importance of the pornography-as-violence perspective in putting pornography on to the agenda for feminism as a whole. The most crucial point of agreement is the idea that pornography eroticizes domination and power differentiation. In other words feminism argues that pornography makes power sexual, it also turns women's subordination into a 'natural' phenomenon because it becomes equated with (hetero)sex which is also held to be 'natural'. Feminists have pointed out that if both men and women are sexually aroused by sights or accounts of eroticized domination, then it is assumed (wrongly) that domination (by men) and submission (by women) in the field of sex must be natural. However, this common ground is merely a baseline from which the different feminist positions on pornography develop. Differences emerge as soon as the question of whether pornography is a metaphor for a patriarchal society or whether it is the most significant means of subordinating women is raised. Difference also emerges on the question of whether pornography reveals men's 'true' sexual nature, or whether pornography is a specific regime of the sexual which may be powerful, but is not masculine 'nature' writ large. Further differences occur when women's enjoyment of pornography is raised. Is it that these women are falsely conscious or coerced by men, or does this regime of sexual motives have resonances for women for less conspiratorial reasons?

There is yet one further broad area of compatibility between the two main feminist approaches. This concerns violent or sadistic pornography in which women are portrayed as raped, bound, mutilated, chained, gagged, beaten, and so on. Such images produce anger, distaste, incomprehension, fear and many similar emotions for all feminists. As Kuhn has argued, 'The capacity of pornography to provoke gut reactions – of distaste, horror, sexual arousal, fear – makes it peculiarly difficult to deal with analytically' (Kuhn, 1985: 21).

Yet a divergence of views appears even at this point of similarity. For pornography-as-violence feminists this anger *is* the analysis. Basically if feminists (and many women) find these images problematic and distasteful, it is argued that this sufficiently identifies the problem and provides a basis for censorship. The more anger and outrage that is felt, the more justified this course of action becomes. But there is another way to proceed from this point. As Kuhn goes on to state:

> In the first place, the intellectual distance necessary for analysis becomes hard to sustain: and also feminist (and indeed any other) politics around pornography tend to acquire a degree of emotionalism that can make the enterprise quite explosive. (Kuhn, 1985: 21)

To put it simply, the pornography-as-violence position occupies a strong position in the debate on pornography because it is based on portraying pornography as a tool of unbridled and violent male sexual power. This is a clear political statement which leads to the inevitable conclusion that something must be done. The pornography-as-representation approach has been to analyse this anger, to render the issue of pornography more and more complex, and to insist that there are no simple answers. Whilst this is necessary work it has the consequence of leaving the political field open to more direct action because this appears to be an inevitable answer to the problem. In a climate when subtle intellectual work can be dismissed as woolly thinking (usually a criticism mounted by the moral right) the pornography-as-violence position carries the appeal of the possibility of getting something done. The possibility remains, however, that this might be the wrong thing.

Defining pornography

The liberal approach

Trying to define what pornography is remains the most contentious issue of all. Clearly if something is to be done about 'it' in terms of public policy we need to have a workable definition. How it is defined is inevitably closely linked to a political analysis (no matter how implicit) of sexual relations and representations. The Williams Committee on Obscenity and Film Censorship (1979) provides us with an example from within traditional liberal thinking. In terms of sexual politics it adopts the Wolfenden strategy[2] of treating all sexual matters as arising from individual inclination in a political vacuum. In relation to pornography it argues that for material to be pornographic it must have

> a certain function or intention, to arouse its audience sexually, and also a certain content, explicit representations of sexual material (organs, postures, activity, etc). A work has to have both this function and this content to be a piece of pornography. (Williams, 1979: para. 8.2, p. 103)

Williams identifies these as separate elements of pornography so that 'explicitness' alone, for example, is not enough to identify pornography. Yet in this definition 'explicitness' remains the key to pornography for it is only this that can be *objectively* measured. The intention of the author or photographer is always contentious, and the sexual arousal of the consuming public cannot seriously be 'measured'. So intention and actual arousal can only be presumed, whilst degrees of nakedness, or numbers of sexual organs can be empirically assessed. The Williams definition is therefore really based on the old issue of sexual morality, namely how much can be seen. It is in any case undoubtedly assumed that the more 'explicit' a work is, the more arousing it is. Equally the intentions of the author will be read off from the number of explicit scenes in his work. Hence both arousal and intention are 'read off' from explicitness – it becomes the key to discovering pornography.

It is clear that in his definition Williams was attempting to differentiate between, for example, anatomy books which are 'explicit' and yet are not intended to arouse sexually (although they may) and those which are produced solely for the skin trade market. Yet whilst he may succeed in this where medical books are concerned, he does so simply because cultural norms tend to value anatomical knowledge over the risk that medical students might get turned on by what they see. We will not risk medical mismanagement for the sake of this Victorian type of modesty. However, the safeguard for medical books lies in this cultural norm rather than in Williams's definition – it is doubtful whether it could be so readily applied to other works. Arguably the liberal definition that the Williams Report exemplifies relies on cultural norms that will ignore the existence of arousal in certain limited contexts but its main attention is ultimately directed towards degrees of explicitness.

The focus, therefore, of the liberal definition of pornography is not on the feminist problems of objectification, degradation, coercion. Indeed as Brown (1981) has shown, the concerns of the liberal tradition actually silence feminist concern (see also Kappeller, 1986). This is because feminism is less interested in 'the coexistence of a content and arousal' than the form of their connection. It is this connection that has led feminists to see pornography as objectionable because it degrades women, it objectifies them, and it coerces them in representation and in reality. However, it is not entirely clear that the 'explicitness' which is the core of the liberal definition does not appear in some feminist work. It is arguably a central element of the pornography-as-violence position.

Pornography-as-violence

Dworkin (1981) defines pornography as 'the graphic depiction of whores'. By this she means that women and their sexuality are valued in the way that whores are valued in a male supremacist society. The very definition of pornography assumes women to be debased (by nature). So pornography is not a representation of neutral (hetero)sexual practices (assuming for the sake of argument that such neutrality could exist) but a statement about women and a practice of male power over women.

This definition has been reworked to some extent owing to the perceived need to fit it into a legal framework. Hence MacKinnon has defined it thus:

> We define pornography as the graphic sexually explicit subordination of women through pictures or words that also includes women dehumanized as sexual objects, things, or commodities; enjoying pain or humiliation or rape; being tied up, cut up, mutilated, bruised, or physically hurt; in postures of sexual submission or servility or display; reduced to body parts, penetrated by objects or animals, or presented in scenarios of degradation, injury, torture; shown as filthy or inferior; bleeding, bruised, or hurt in a context that makes these conditions sexual. (1987: 176)

In this definition we have two components. The first is sexual explicitness and the second is coercion – whether or not the coercion is portrayed as enjoyable. The problem is that this definition implies that representations of women being degraded in non-sexual ways are less troublesome. It is the sexual content of the degradation which moves pornography to the top of the political agenda, not the degradation itself. This argument is both the strength and the weakness of this position. Its strength lies in the way it challenges the naturalistic and liberal view that if a thing is sexual it cannot be coercive because sex is taken as natural, springing from desire not culture. In the liberal view the sexual meaning 'overrides' the coerciveness which is central to the representation. From this arises the argument that what is important in pornography is the way in which the sexual 'neutralizes' domination. Presumably for these feminists representations of non-sexualized dominance are not a problem because their meaning is (arguably) clear and unobscured. This is an important point, yet it is the transformation of this insight into a legally enforceable definition which raises political problems for feminism and reveals the weakness of this position. Not only does it lead to a narrowing of feminist definitions of pornography, but it also leads to an underestimation of economic forms of dominance (amongst others) which are not sexual. Indeed it goes further, since this perspective has the tendency to reduce all forms of domination to the sexual, seeing this as the mainspring of all forms of power. As MacKinnon argues, 'pornography causes attitudes and behaviors of violence and discrimination that define the treatment and status of half of the population' (1987: 147).

This definition of pornography raises further problems. MacKinnon goes on to argue that, 'Erotica, defined by distinction as not [pornography], might be sexually explicit materials premised on equality' (1987: 176). This statement implies that it would be possible to have 'explicit' representations of sexual practices, desires, etc., if they were 'premised' on equality. However, it is part of MacKinnon's and Dworkin's thesis that there is no equality between men and women in the area of sex. Indeed, (hetero)sex is, in itself, regarded as a form of coercion. MacKinnon, for example, has argued that in a society where women's 'no' is taken as 'yes', that her consent can hardly be regarded as freely given (1987). This surely means that *any* representation of explicit heterosexual activity is a representation of sexual coercion, which would be unacceptable. Because these feminists argue that heterosexuality is, *par excellence*, oppressive of women it is hard to imagine what an erotica based on equality would look like unless it was exclusively lesbian.

It would seem, therefore, that in this definition of pornography the two conditions of sexual explicitness and coercion become reduced to only one condition. It is not a question of how they connect in specific representations, as Brown has argued, because coercion is always already the essence of (hetero)sex. The only solution to this position is to ban all representations of (hetero)sex precisely because the definition of coercion is so all-encompassing that nothing heterosexual could avoid being so defined. In this respect they come uncomfortably close to taking on the mantle of the moral right, which also argues that all representations of sex are degrading – especially for women.

It is the idea of the possibility of an ideologically sound erotica that has led to a great deal of criticism of this form of feminism. This criticism rests on the basis that it appears that sex might be perceived as acceptable as long as it is tender and loving. It is argued by feminists like Valverde (1985) and Eckersley (1987) that what is proposed is not a feminist erotica but a feminine erotica not unlike the variety already available in Mills and Boon or Harlequin romantic fiction.

This kind of image of sex also comes very close to the moral right's version of pro-family, committed, and only-on-very-special-occasions sex. For example, Roger Scruton, the new right philosopher, also maintains that there is a distinction between pornography and erotica. His distinction has a certain resonance with this feminist notion of sex based on equality:

> Obscenity involves a 'depersonalised' perception of human sexuality, in which the body and its sexual function are uppermost in our thoughts and all-obliterating.

> The genuinely erotica work is one which invites the reader to re-create in imagination the first-person point of view of someone party to an erotic encounter. The pornographic work retains as a rule the third-person perspective of the voyeuristic observer. (Scruton, 1986: 138, 139)

The equality implicit in Scruton's work is not equality between the actors in a sexual scenario, but between the consumer of the erotica and at least one of the parties portrayed in the event. This does of course help us to identify a problem in the notion of an erotica premised on equality, namely 'whose equality?' We can imagine lesbian erotica in which the women portrayed are – for the sake of argument – perfectly equal. Their lovemaking might be caring, non-exploitative and so on. Yet the consumer of the erotica may be in a very different position. Indeed, the mere fact of buying the product in order to enjoy in private the observed or described sexual activities of others implies an unequal power relationship. Scruton imagines that this is overcome as long as the consumer can imagine himself to be in the position of one of the parties to the sexual scenario. Yet as Kuhn has so forcefully pointed out, it is the stock in trade of so-called soft porn to allow the consumer to 'read himself into' the scenario and to determine its outcome (Kuhn, 1985). Scruton's definition of erotica is therefore hardly satisfactory, yet, along with the pornography-as-violence feminists, it attempts to reserve some 'acceptable' form of sex for erotic consumption. The problem is that both assume that the problem lies with the image that is represented in pornography. Both rely on a narrow perception of 'objectification'. For Scruton it is a matter of first- or third-person identification. If it is the former there is no objectification and it is erotic, if it is the latter it is voyeuristic and pornographic. For pornography-as-violence feminists objectification occurs when there is coercion, but equality eliminates coercion, so representations cease to objectify. Both of these positions are highly contentious.

This form of feminist definition of pornography is therefore problematic. It alarms us with images of the most violent sexual exploitation, but provides a basic definition of pornography that has the potential to cover all representations of heterosexuality. Its compelling insights about, for example, the sexualization of dominance are lost when we realize that all dominance is seen as springing from (hetero)sex. Ultimately it becomes a position virtually indistinguishable from the moral right in terms of its antithesis to sexuality and its reliance on blunt modes of legal censorship.

Pornography-as-representation

Pornography-as-representation stresses the distinction between sexual relationships and representations of sex, and attempts to shift the emphasis away from concepts of explicitness to the idea of pornography as a way of seeing. Perhaps the clearest exposition of this perspective is provided by Ros Coward (1987) in which she develops the argument that pornography is a regime of representations. She goes on to explain that, 'The [representations] show bodies (usually naked) in a sexualized way, or people involved in the sex act, according to certain conventions which mean they are interpreted as pornographic by society' (1987: 310). The basic point here is that nothing is intrinsically pornographic, no image or word has an intrinsic meaning which is immutable. But, in addition to this, this basic starting point alerts us to the fact that we bring various and different 'interpretations' to images and words. Hence, Roger Scruton's definition of an 'erotic' representation varies considerably from Andrea Dworkin's or Ros Coward's. Notwithstanding this, there are regimes of representation. This means that there are codes of interpretation which we learn and apply when representations comply with certain modes of signification. Hence, as Valverde (1985) has demonstrated, a story of the sexual desires of nuns and ex-nuns in the context of a political feminist limited-edition publication has one meaning. It has a very different meaning when extracts are published in a magazine like *Forum*. Here the stories are read as a form of titillation, alongside the other stories of sex and sexual problems. So the political intention of the original editors is overridden by codes of interpretation which attach to materials published in *Forum*. The stories themselves remain the same.

Coward herself has done a great deal to reveal that there is a pornographic genre or regime of representations which attaches to how women are portrayed. She has concentrated on advertisements to show that the devices used in what is generally defined as the pornographic are also common in representations of women that we find on hoardings and in women's magazines. For example she identifies the pose, the expression, the juxtaposition of bodies, the arrangement of clothes, the vulnerability of the woman represented, and so on. Very often the only difference between the photograph defined as pornography and that defined as an advertisement is the extent to which 'sexual parts' are revealed.

This returns us to the point about explicitness. I argue above that the moral right view is based on a prohibition of explicitness, that the liberal view comes down to a desire to restrict explicitness, and that ultimately the pornography-as-violence position finds explicitness a problem, in spite of assertions to the contrary. The point is that 'explicitness' in the sense of the display of genitals (male and female) signifies that the image or representation should be read in the pornographic mode. The problem is that this has become the dominant mode of interpreting the sight of genitals, and most especially women's bodies. As Coward has argued, women's bodies are increasingly encoded as having a pornographic meaning. The display of women's breasts in the daily newspapers is not a sign that we are liberated from a prudish view of sex that wanted to hide the female body. Rather it signifies the *open* process of encoding representations of women as pornographic.

The concern of this sort of feminist analysis is not that these images cause men to rape, but that the pornographic genre is becoming the dominant form, silencing other voices and representations, and making an alternative erotica impossible because it necessarily collapses into the pornographic. Because it is impossible to ensure that a representation will only be read in one way, most especially when certain images are now so heavily encoded with a specific meaning, it is impossible to differentiate between the 'intrinsically' erotic and pornographic.

Annette Kuhn (1985) has expanded this analysis to introduce the notion of the forbidden. One way in which we know that a material is pornographic is that it is banned or restricted. And what makes pornography exciting is its forbidden nature. This may be expressed in legal censorship or in the fact that consumers of pornography – even pornography bought openly in a newsagent's – may hide it from their wives, children, parents or friends. Keeping pornography out of sight increases its 'dangerousness' and hence its power. As Kuhn argues, 'In order to maintain its attraction, porn demands strictures, controls, censorship. Exposed to the light of day, it risks a loss of power. Pornography invites policing' (1985: 23). Ironically then, the radical feminist demand for censorship increases the allure of pornography. The more it is repressed, the more it assumes the status of a desired object, but also the status of a truth that moral puritans and some feminists wish to repress. Yet it is this very idea that pornography is the truth of sex, its mere reflection in words or pictures, that needs to be challenged.

This notion that pornography is the truth of sex is bound up with two issues. The first is that photographs simply show reality as it is; the second is that the pornographic regime of sexual desire is the natural order of sex. Coward and Kuhn have both pointed to the fallacy of assuming that the photograph captures reality in their examination of the conventions of photography and film-making. The use of lighting, of certain clothes, of poses and so on, show how 'prepared' photographs and films are. Moreover they are prepared with an intention to convey certain meanings. Although the reading of these meanings cannot be guaranteed, the photographer and film-maker are not 'innocent' of intention.

On the second point, it may be that pornography reveals 'the truth of the current regime of sexual relationships' (Brown, 1981). However, these are sexual relationships constructed under conditions of patriarchy, racism and capitalism. They are in no sense simply natural. Yet pornography, inasmuch as it induces sexual arousal, is assumed to tap a natural response. Yet what is hidden are the codes by which pornography achieves this end. These codes or devices are culturally transmitted and, in turn, they create a standard against which sexual activity can be measured. There is in this a reinforcing cycle of definitions: pornography represents the most desirable (to whom?) form of sex which is also natural, yet in spite of reflecting natural desires and activities, consumers cannot practise these activities in their own personal relationships (viz. the refusal of many wives to imitate the pornographic model). The consumer must therefore use pornography (or prostitutes) to resolve the 'natural' sexual frustration.

As Brown (1981) has argued, one of the main problems of pornography is that it eroticizes women. But it is not that women themselves become the pornographic model (ever available, ever insatiable), but that the expectation grows that this is women's potential and destiny. Women may increasingly be viewed in this light, and pornography comes to inform the everyday viewing of women (Eckersley, 1987). It is this extension of the *pornographic genre* (as opposed to the increasing availability of pornographic material) which causes concern. Not only does it eroticize women, sexual difference and various forms of domination, but it also silences alternative discourses and interpretations which might promote feminist, anti-racist or 'egalitarian' values.

This concern is quite different from the pornography-as-violence and the moral right concern that pornography promotes attitudes which cause men to enact sexual assaults. MacKinnon (1987) and Whitehouse (1977) are both sure of the causal link between pornography and violence against women. Yet even if positivistic social science could claim proof of such a cause (which it cannot), we would have to be cautious of accepting such a scientific paradigm which is rejected elsewhere in feminist and critical sociological work just because it apparently serves a political purpose. As Eckersley has argued,

> The . . . problem is that concentration [on] the 'effects' of pornography at the behavioural level tends to deflect feminist analysis away from other types of 'effects' at an ideological level such as the ways in which pornography contributes to the organisation of the everyday viewing of women as a 'desirable commodity' to be enjoyed by men. The search for 'hard' empirical evidence operates to narrow not only the definition of 'the problem' but also the theoretical framework and the range of possible feminist strategies that might be employed. (Eckersley, 1987: 163)

Following on from Eckersley's point about narrowing feminist strategy, the focus on harm, in the form of sexual assaults, fits with the law and order framework of the 1980s, which is an agenda that has been set without reference to, and in opposition to, feminist aims. Hence the pornography-as-violence form of alarm flows into an already strong current, the direction of which is determined by very different interests overall.

The work of feminists like Brown, Coward and Kuhn in any case alerts us to the idea that the pornographic genre is more extensive than the actual material commonly defined as pornographic. It can be found outside the 'girlie' magazines and shelves of the sex shops and so their political agenda takes us far wider than the potential scope of criminal law and censorship. Advertising has already been mentioned, but it is equally important to recognize that romantic novels deploy devices very similar to those of pornography. As Valverde (1985) has shown, these novels, which are distributed on a worldwide basis, include the basic pornographic device of eroticizing power and power difference. The heroine is attracted to the wealthy, macho man. She is ultimately vulnerable, dependent and powerless in relation to him. She relinquishes her autonomy for him, and so on. A similar device is used in the popular glamorous soap operas where men's wealth is idolized and where membership of the *haute bourgeoisie* is synonymous with sexual attractiveness. In these forms of the pornographic genre there is no sexual explicitness, yet both women and power are eroticized and male sexuality and potency is measured as a correlate of the size of a bank balance.

The devices used by pornography, romantic novels, advertising and soap operas contain significantly similar elements, all of which contribute to the extension of a pornographic perspective on women and on sex. There is no doubt that these dominant meanings may be resisted, but they are voraciously consumed, contributing to a circulation of images of women which are profoundly antithetical to feminism. Such a proliferation demands an alternative feminist voice, yet feminists do not have widespread access to popular publishing and television to promote alternative accounts. This inability to gain access to an equally popular voice or medium has, I would suggest, strengthened the appeal of legal reform as a mechanism for both becoming heard and attacking the perceived problem. It is undeniable that it is the *pornography-as-violence* approach which has succeeded in bringing a feminist perspective on pornography into the public domain through this route. I have argued elsewhere (Smart, 1992) that this success is partly premised upon utilization of an emotive space and a language of disgust already mapped out by moral reformists of a conservative orientation. This success is therefore problematic and will become more so if laws of censorship emerge which are based on similar premises. Laws of censorship, whether civil or criminal, hardly seem likely to solve women's sexual oppression if the history and current practice of law provide a basis of evaluation. Arguably we should rely on what we know about how the law operates rather than on an optimism that new laws will somehow operate more effectively in future. The reliance on law as a solution epitomizes the cliché of hope triumphing over experience. We should perhaps look to law more as a site or public domain in which feminist voices can be heard and become influential, rather than as the site of a solution to a problem over which feminists themselves still disagree.

Notes

1. I am grateful to Beverley Brown for this fomulation of the differences between feminist ideas on pornography. These terms are her insight rather than mine and I have used them here because they indicate the main differences of analysis far better than categories of radical and socialist feminism.

2. The Wolfenden strategy arose from the Wolfenden Report on Homosexuality and Prostitution in 1967. In this report it was argued that, in sexual matters, what consenting adults do in private should not be the concern of the criminal law. However 'public' displays of socially disapproved forms of sexuality should be subject to criminal sanction.

References

Brown, B. (1981) 'A feminist interest in pornography – some modest proposals', *m/f*, 5 and 6: 5–18.

Cockburn, C. (1988) 'Masculinity, the left and feminism', in R. Chapman and J. Rutherford (eds), *Male Order: Unwrapping Masculinity*. London.

Coward, R. (1987), 'Sexual violence and sexuality', in *Feminist Review* (ed.), *Sexuality: A Reader*. London: Virago.

Dworkin, A. (1981) *Pornography: Men Possessing Women*. London: Women's Press.

Eckersley, R. (1987) 'Whither the feminist campaign? An evaluation of feminist critiques of pornography', *International Journal of the Sociology of Law*, 15 (2): 149–78.

Kappeller, S. (1986) *The Pornography of Representation*. Cambridge: Polity Press.

Kuhn, A. (1985) *The Power of the Image*. London: Routledge & Kegan Paul.

MacKinnon, C. (1987) *Feminism Unmodified: Discourses on Life and Law*. London: Harvard University Press.

Scruton R. (1986) *Sexual Desire*. London: Weidenfeld & Nicolson.

Smart, C. (1992) 'Unquestionably a moral issue: rhetorical devices and regulatory imperatives', in L. Segal and M. McIntosh (eds), *Sex Exposed*. London: Virago.

Valverde, M. (1985) *Sex, Power and Pleasure*. Toronto: Women's Press.

Whitehouse, M. (1977) *Whatever Happened to Sex?* London: Hodder & Stoughton.

Williams, B. (1979) *Committee on Obscenity and Film Censorship*. London: HMSO. Cmnd 7772.

Women, Rape and Law Reform

Jennifer Temkin

In the late 1960s, the rape debate was launched in the United States of America. It has since spread to every nation in the Western, industrialized world. In each place the law of rape and the handling by the criminal justice system of rape complaints have been subjected to scrutiny. Generally, both have been found wanting. In this article it is proposed first to discuss some of the problems which rape poses for the legal system and then to raise the question why some jurisdictions have proceeded further in resolving them than has been the case in Britain.

Rape and the criminal justice system

There are a number of interconnecting problems which rape currently presents for the criminal justice system. First, there is the victim, doubly traumatized by the event itself and its subsequent handling by police and courts. Secondly, and in part consequentially, there is the low reporting rate. Thirdly, there are the rapists, prosecuted infrequently and convicted rarely. Finally, there is the law of rape and the evidential rules which surround it.

The victim's experience

Individual accounts by victims of physical and mental suffering which they have endured as a result of rape have formed a vital ingredient of the discourse on the subject.[1] Their reports are borne out by studies which confirm the existence of a rape trauma syndrome. According to Burgess and Holstrom, 'This syndrome has two phases: the immediate or acute phase, in which the victim's lifestyle is completely disrupted by the rape crisis, and the long term process, in which the victim must reorganize this disrupted lifestyle.'[2] A recent study from New Zealand concluded: 'Rape is an experience which shakes the foundations of the lives of the victims. For many its effect is a long-term one, impairing their capacity for personal relationships, altering their behaviour and values and generating fear.'[3]

From Sylvana Tomaselli and Roy Porter (eds), *Rape: A Historical and Social Enquiry*, Basil Blackwell, Oxford, 1986, pp. 16–40.

In addition to the trauma of the rape itself, victims have been further mistreated by the legal system. Be it in England,[4] Scotland,[5] Australia,[6] Canada,[7] Scandinavia,[8] or elsewhere,[9] the rough handling of complainants has been much the same. English television viewers may have been shocked at the verbal brutality of Thames Valley police officers who were filmed interrogating a rape victim,[10] but rape crisis centre workers pointed out at the time that such interrogations were run-of-the-mill. That the officers involved were well aware that the cameras were trained on them is itself of some interest. Some British policemen appear to consider that harsh questioning, far from being undesirable, is precisely what is required, as may be gauged from the following advice extended by a detective sergeant to fellow officers in the pages of *Police Review*:

> It should be borne in mind that except in the case of a very young child, the offence of rape is extremely unlikely to have been committed against a woman who does not immediately show signs of extreme violence. If a woman walks into a police station and complains of rape with no such signs of violence she must be closely interrogated. Allow her to make her statement to a policewoman and then drive a horse and cart through it. It is always advisable if there is any doubt of the truthfulness of her allegations to call her an outright liar . . . Watch out for the girl who is pregnant or late getting home one night; such persons are notorious for alleging rape or indecent assault. Do not give her sympathy. If she is not lying, after the interrogator has upset her by accusing her of it, then at least the truth is verified . . . The good interrogator is very rarely loved by his subject.[11]

In a study conducted by the Scottish Office Central Research Unit, 70 Scottish victims of sexual assault were interviewed. Forty were victims of rape, 28 of assault with intent to ravish. The views expressed by complainers on their interactions with CID officers and uniformed women police officers were mainly critical or negative: 'In the main the criticisms were concentrated . . . on the unsympathetic and tactless manner in which interviewing was often conducted'.[12] The researcher concluded that 'there is considerable scope for the development of police interviewing skills in relation to sexual assault complaints'.[13]

It would be wrong, however, to suggest that police are uniformly unpleasant to rape victims. Holmstrom and Burgess in the United States found that victim reactions to their encounters with the police were mainly favourable.[14] Similarly, Kelly, in 1980, interviewed 100 adult female rape victims from four jurisdictions in the Washington metropolitan area. These women for the most part expressed satisfaction with their treatment by the police. Yet Kelly found that the same women also complained, often bitterly, about police behaviour. Her explanation for this paradox is 'that victims rated police and prosecutors highly because they expected to be treated so poorly'. Many had seen the film *Cry Rape*, which had depicted rape victims being humiliated by the police. Thus, their satisfaction arose from receiving better treatment than they had expected.[15]

A major problem confronting the criminal justice system, therefore, is that of changing the attitudes or at least the behaviour of police who deal with sexual assaults.[16] In the United States, police practices in some states have been transformed.[17] In England, too, there have been recent indications that the police are beginning to query their present methods of handling such cases. Indeed, Deputy Assistant Commissioner Wyn Jones of Scotland Yard's Crime Department has publicly stated:

> There may have been shortcomings in the past. But our intention is to improve the lot of victims. We want to kill the myth that rape is sexually motivated – it is usually intended to inflict violence and humiliation. And we want people to report it every time.[18]

It has to be recognized, however, that there are limits to what can justifiably be expected of the police in this context. The victim of rape is often severely traumatized when she arrives at the police station and in need of a large measure of solace and support. Whilst police lose nothing and gain much by showing kindness and sympathy, the role of counsellor and friend should be shared or left entirely for others to perform.[19] In the United States[20] and elsewhere,[21] state-operated schemes to cater for the specific needs of sexual assault victims coexist with rape crisis centres. In England, government support for rape crisis centres and victim support schemes[22] is vitally necessary since other appropriate counselling services do not appear to exist.

The victim in court   If the police have behaved brutishly towards rape victims, it is the courts which may be said to have set the tone. Indeed, it is often claimed that in rape cares the complainant rather than the defendant is on trial.[23] Certainly the focus of the court's attention is frequently upon her and rather less upon him. Yet the complainant generally has no legal assistance. In England, counsel for the prosecution represents the state and will not have met the complainant before the trial.

Much criticism of the treatment of rape victims in court has centred on the use of sexual history evidence to blacken their character. But other strategies commonly employed against them are equally *oppressive* and invidious. Newby identified three distinct tactics utilized by defence counsel in rape trials in Western Australia.[24] They are also in frequent use elsewhere.[25] The first is continual questioning as to details of the rape. The woman is required 'to re-iterate again and again the details of the rape incident . . . The purpose is to test her story for inconsistencies and to attempt to twist her interpretation of events so as to make them consistent with an assumption of consent.'[26] The second strategy relates to cases where the victim and accused were known to each other. In such cases, questioning will be particularly detailed and the most intimate aspects of any pre-existing sexual relationship will commonly be rehearsed in court. Finally, the defence may seek to challenge the general character of the witness. This may include but goes far beyond references to her sexual past. The idea is to suggest to the court 'that this sort of woman, who behaves in this kind of way, in these circumstances is quite reasonably to be taken to be consenting.'[27] Thus, attention will be drawn to behaviour such as hitch-hiking, excessive drinking or smoking, the wearing of 'seductive' clothing or the use of bad language.

The major question in all this is what are the judges doing during these cross-examinations? The law permits only relevant evidence to be included in criminal trials. What notion of relevance is it that permits prolonged questioning on matters of this kind? It is for judges to control the conduct of a trial. In rape cases they appear all too often to have given defence counsel free rein.

But it is not only for their omissions to act that the judges must be castigated. Throughout the years in England, a steady stream of judicial utterances on rape have caused amazement and consternation. In 1982 Judge Wild at the Cambridge Crown Court summed up to the jury thus:

> Women who say no do not always mean no. It is not just a question of saying no, it is a question of how she says it, how she shows and makes it clear. If she doesn't want it she only has to keep her legs shut and she would not get it without force and there would be marks of force being used.

In the same vein, Sir Melford Stevenson has remarked: 'It is the height of imprudence for any girl to hitch-hike at night. That is plain, it isn't really worth stating. She is in the true sense asking for it.'[28]

It is of no surprise that victims have found rape trials a traumatic experience. Complainants interviewed in the New Zealand study found the experience of giving evidence in court 'negative and destructive'.[29] The report states: 'Three said that they considered the ordeal to be even worse than the rape itself, and one likened it to being crucified. Undoubtedly, the court proceedings added to and prolonged the psychological stress they had suffered as a result of the rape itself.'[30]

The conduct of rape trials is thus a second major problem confronting the criminal justice system. Undoubtedly, strict rules limiting the use of sexual history evidence can help to alleviate the victim's plight in court, but these alone are insufficient to protect her from needless distress and humiliation. Legal representation for complainants is one method of protecting their interest, and is currently provided as of right in Denmark and Norway.[31] But it would appear that a radical change in the attitude of defence counsel and judges to sexual assault is also required. Continuing education programmes for judges should include re-education about sexual assault. Changes in the substantive law might also be helpful in producing new ways of thinking about this type of crime.[32]

Reports, prosecutions and convictions

In England, there has been a fairly regular increase in the number of rape offences (i.e., rape and attempted rape) recorded by the police in the years immediately following the Second World War until the present time. A comparison between the years 1947, in which there were 240 cases, and 1954, in which there were 294, reveals a 22.5 per cent increase.[33] In 1976 there were 1,090 cases and in 1980, 1,225. These figures are, respectively, over four and five times that for 1947.[34] In 1983, 1,334 rapes were recorded and this rose to 2,471 rapes in 1987, almost twice the total for 1980.[35] In other countries, too, increases have taken place. In New Zealand, for example, the number of recorded rapes and attempted rapes rose from 268 in 1975 to 396 in 1981.[36] In the United States between 1970 and 1982, reports of forcible rape more than doubled from 37,860 to 77,763.[37]

It is universally recognized, however, that the number of offences recorded by the police is a small proportion of the number of rapes which actually take place. The United States National Crime Survey of 1979 estimated that only 50 per cent of forcible rapes were reported to the police.[38] Some researchers consider that the proportion of unreported rapes is far higher. Amir[39] and Dukes and Mattley[40] suggest respectively that two-thirds and three-quarters of rapes in the United States are unreported. In New Zealand it has been estimated, on the basis of victim studies conducted there and overseas, that four out of five rape offences are not reported.[41]

In Britain, it is only recently that attempts have been made to assess the level of unreported crime. Some 93 per cent of the sexual assaults uncovered in Scotland by the British Crime Survey were not reported to the police.[42] In England and Wales, the survey estimated that only 26 per cent of offences of rape and indecent assault were in fact recorded, although under-reporting was also found to be a feature of many offences.[43] The survey in England and Wales involved an interview in their homes with one person over 16 years of age in each of 11,000 households.[44] Only women were asked about their experience of sexual offences. No rapes and only one attempted rape were revealed.[45] However, it is most unlikely that this is an accurate reflection of the amount of unreported rape which in fact occurs. The rape trauma syndrome involves feelings of extreme degradation, humiliation and fear. A rape victim is likely to feel inhibited about discussing the matter with an interviewer, particularly one who is male. A survey of this kind is better placed to reveal unreported crimes such as burglary and theft which do not carry the same emotional load. Moreover, sexual assault victims are frequently anxious not to reveal the incident to their families, members of which may well have been present or nearby during the interview.

Figures from other English sources suggest a far higher level of unreported rape. Of the women who reported sexual assault to the London Rape Crisis Centre between 1976 and 1980, 75 per cent did not, it seems, go on to report the matter to the police.[46] A recent survey, conducted by Women Against Rape (WAR), revealed an even higher level of unreported offences.[47] Unlike the British Crime Survey, this research was designed specifically to find out about rape and sexual assault. The methodology employed was quite different. A Women's Safety questionnaire was distributed to 2,000 women in London (mostly Inner London) during the summer of 1982. In order to ensure as broad a cross-section as possible, a variety of distribution points were selected, including high streets, bus queues, street markets, hospital wards, pensioners' clubs, colleges, etc. Women were permitted to answer the survey in their own time and on their own. The questionnaire was on women's safety in general – a matter of concern to most women – to ensure that it was not merely women with a specific interest in rape who answered it. A total of 1,236 women (62 per cent) responded. Of these, 214 had been raped (17 per cent), 60 by their husbands. A further 243 (20 per cent) had been the victims of attempted rape. Thus more than one in six of those who responded had been raped and one in five had been the victim of attempted rape.[48] However, out of 145 women who were raped (this figure excludes most but not all of those in the survey who were victims of marital rape), only 12 (8 per cent) reported the matter to the police.[49]

There are many reasons why rape victims do not report. Their perception of police attitudes seems to be a major factor. Thus, out of the afore-mentioned 145 raped women in the WAR study, 55 per cent of those who did not report thought the police might be unsympathetic and 79 per cent thought that the police would be either unhelpful or unsympathetic. Thirty-one per cent felt too traumatized to face the prospect of police interrogation.[50] In two Australian studies, fear of the reaction of family members was also revealed as significant.[51] Snare suggests on the basis of Swedish research that rape by a stranger is far more likely to be reported than rape by someone well known to the victim. Where there has been some initial voluntary contact, such as having a drink with the offender, she suggests that one in ten cases is likely to be reported.[52] The WAR study provides some confirmation of this. Out of the 145 victims, an estimated 60 were raped by a husband, boyfriend, family member or man in authority. None of these cases was reported. A further 50 victims were estimated to have been raped by a friend, acquaintance or workmate; only two of these cases were reported. The remaining 10 reported cases all involved strangers.[53] It may be that some victims believe that unless the assault conforms to the stereotypical idea of rape, i.e., by a stranger, their story is unlikely to be believed. Certainly 37 per cent of those who failed to report in the WAR study gave as a reason that 'they knew the man well or fairly well and did not think the police would take it seriously'.[54]

A second reason why the official statistics of rape tell only part of the story is that many women who do report rape do not have their complaints accepted by the police. Richard Wright, for example, found in his research into rapes and attempted rapes reported to the police between 1972 and 1976 in six English counties that in about 24 per cent of the 384 cases made available to him, the police decided that no crime had taken place. Of these he writes: 'A number of them were clearly false. But it seemed equally clear to me that a significant proportion represented true rape offences.'[55] Similarly, in the Scottish report, in 44 (22 per cent) out of a total of 196 cases of rape and assault with intent to ravish in the study sample, a no-crime classification was given to the crime report, thus ensuring that the incident did not enter into the official statistics of recorded crime.[56] In 24 of the no-crime cases, the complaint was registered as withdrawn. However, the report notes, 'It did not happen very often that complainers of their own accord and without encouragement withdrew their complaints'.[57]

The prosecution rate for rape also tends to be low. This is so even with respect to the proportion of cleared up offences of rape which are prosecuted. Thus, for example, in the Scottish study, the Procurator Fiscal decided not to initiate proceedings in 30 per cent of cases sent to him by the police with a view to prosecution. This was a much higher no-proceedings rate than research reveals for other crimes of violence in Scotland.[58] The study further illustrates the low conviction rate for rape. In all, a conviction was returned in 49 (25 per cent) of the 196 researched cases. In over one-third of these, however, the conviction was for a lesser offence or for one which was not the subject of the original police report.[59]

Wright's study presents a similar picture. Of the 255 rapes and attempted rapes carried out by solitary offenders which were investigated by the police as genuine in six counties of England between 1972 and 1976, 240 men were involved and 204 men were actually arrested. Of these, 39 never appeared before the courts.[60] Only 22 were found guilty of rape and 13 of attempted rape, making a total of 17 per cent of those arrested. Nine of these were not imprisoned. A further 65 were convicted of other offences in connection with the assault, 42 of a lesser offence, such as indecent assault. Out of the 65, 35 did not receive custodial sentences. Wright concludes:

> Given the attrition of rape cases at every stage from the attack onwards, the rapist who receives a stiff fine must consider himself extremely unlucky. And the rapist who goes to gaol must believe that he was doubly unfortunate – the odds weigh heavily against that happening.[61]

Wright claims that his findings should not be regarded as necessarily representative of the national picture, but other studies indicate the high attrition rate in rape cases elsewhere. Thus, the New Zealand report concluded, 'The chances that a rapist will actually be caught and convicted may be as low as 4 per cent, a figure which is probably much lower than that applying to most other serious offences'.[62]

For those who subscribe to the ideal of the rule of law, the reporting, prosecution and conviction rates for rape should be a cause of deep concern. Of course, low reporting in itself is not necessarily a serious matter. Where victims fail to report crime because their experience of it was not particularly disturbing, it might be said to be pedantic to manifest disquiet. In the context of rape, however, non-reporting would appear to be quite unrelated to reactions of this sort. If large numbers of victims, as the studies suggest, refrain from reporting out of fear that they will be treated without humanity or respect, this is indeed a grave indictment of the criminal justice system. Changes in police practices should produce both higher reporting and prosecution rates. The police, however, are unlikely to wish to expend undue time and energy prosecuting cases of this kind if convictions remain disproportionately hard to obtain. Higher conviction rates may demand alterations in court procedures, in rules of evidence and in the substantive law. They will certainly require changes in general attitudes and assumptions about sexual assault, which reforms within the criminal justice system may in themselves help to achieve.

The law

Rape laws have presented a series of problems for the criminal justice system. First, in many respects, their ambit has been too narrow. This has been a factor in low prosecution and conviction rates. In Michigan, for example, to prove rape it was formerly necessary to show that force was used by the defendant and that the victim did not consent. To establish non-consent, the victim was required to have resisted 'to the utmost' from 'the inception to the close' of the attack.[63] In England, as in many other jurisdictions, rape covers only penile penetration of the vagina. The objection here is that other sexual assaults, often considerably worse in character, are relegated to less important offence categories. Moreover, by confining the offence to women who are not married to the perpetrator, rape laws are discriminatory and deny equal protection to a class of persons on account of their status.

Use of the term 'rape' accounts in part for the narrow scope of the offence. Moreover, the word evokes images and associations which are not altogether helpful in a modern context. For rape, as the dictionary states, is a taking or carrying off by force, the ravishment or violation of a woman or of a country. Arguably today, the law should seek to protect the right of every woman to choose whether to have sexual intercourse or not and its language should reflect this objective.

It is, of course, true that the legal definition of rape in England is sexual intercourse without consent,[64] which, on the face of it, seems rather broad. Certainly it is an improvement on the position which prevailed until the nineteenth century when rape constituted an act against a woman's will so that violence or the threat or fear of it was required. However, whilst 'without her consent' may have a broader meaning than 'against her will', precisely what that meaning is remains a legal mystery. The likely result of this is that police and courts return to the word rape and ask themselves whether the deed really amounts to their own notion of it.

One solution to this difficulty would be the enactment of a comprehensive definition of consent; but such a reform begs a major question. It might be said that a crucial problem in the law of rape is precisely that it focuses unswervingly upon the non-consent of the complainant. Did she consent or did she not? That is the question. It is she who is the object of attention. The prosecution must prove beyond all reasonable doubt that she did not consent and the defence will be irresistibly tempted to raise that doubt by suggesting that she is the type of woman who might well have done. In England, moreover, the judge is obliged to administer the corroboration warning. He must warn the jury that it is dangerous to convict on the basis of the complainant's evidence unless it is corroborated. Perhaps the wonder should be that any convictions are returned at all!

There is nothing inevitable in this legal arrangement. Sexual intercourse without consent can be shifted from centre stage towards the wings even if it can never be removed from the set altogether. For other nefarious conduct will generally accompany the act of non-consensual sex. There may, for example, be violence, a variety of threats, the presence or participation of a gang, or the commission of another offence such as burglary immediately beforehand. There is no reason why the spotlight should not, in the first instance, be directed at the defendant and at acts such as these. Moreover, rather than letting the officials of the criminal justice system interpret rape as they choose, there is much to be said for spelling out in precise terms the circumstances in which a sexual offence is committed.

There may also be a case for a scale of penalties for rape rather than a single maximum of life imprisonment. Under the present system, most defendants plead not guilty to rape and indeed, given the high penalty and the low prospects of conviction, they would be foolish to do otherwise. The advantage of a scale is that it permits a defendant to decide where he fits on it and to plead guilty if he so chooses.

Rape law reform is both simple and hard. It is simple to abolish the marital rape exemption and the corroboration warning. Only atavism and sexism stand in the way. To move further is more complicated. The construction of a ladder of offences instead of the one offence of rape is a particularly complex matter. Whilst in England there is a reluctance to embark upon even the simple tasks, elsewhere the hard ones have been tackled and, it seems, with a measure of success.

The rape debate and law reform in the 1970s and 1980s

In most states of the United States, legislation has been passed to amend the legal framework relating to rape. In some states, radical change has been introduced.[65] In Canada[66] and Australia,[67] law reform in this area is advancing apace. In England, whilst certain amendments have been implemented, relatively little has been achieved and little more is on the present legislative agenda.

Why is it that England has proceeded so cautiously whilst elsewhere there has been a genuine willingness to contemplate and implement radical change? The answer to this question will require the research of political scientists and sociologists perhaps more than lawyers. Here it is intended merely to outline certain possible lines of inquiry.

It is proposed first of all to consider how legislation came to be achieved in two other jurisdictions, namely the American state of Michigan and in Canada. The Michigan statute, passed in 1974,[68] is regarded as a turning point in rape law reform and has been used as a model by other jurisdictions.[69] The Canadian provisions were enacted almost a decade later, in 1982,[70] and thus provide an example of more recent law reform in this area.

Michigan

In the early 1970s, the women's movement in the United States succeeded in bringing the issue of rape to the attention of the nation. During the same decade, rape crisis centres sprang up throughout the country and the Federal Government manifested its concern by making available between 1973 and 1981 an estimated $125 million for research into sexual assault.[71] This led, *inter alia*, to a nationwide study of rape conducted by the Law Enforcement Assistance Administration.[72] Other federal initiatives included the setting up of a National Center for the Prevention and Control of Rape within the Department of Health, Education and Welfare and the launching of prevention programmes and projects concerned with the care of victims and community education.[73] It is thus against a background of growing official concern about rape, prompted by both the dramatic rise in the reported incidence of the crime and the agitation of the women's movement, that the achievement of law reform in Michigan may be viewed.

The achievement of law reform in Michigan[74]   The Michigan legislation was not enacted in response to the proposals of an official law reform committee, neither was it introduced by the state government. On the contrary, it was very much the product of a grassroots initiative resulting from the dissatisfaction felt by many women working in rape crisis centres at the criminal justice system's treatment of rape victims. The events leading up to the passage of the legislation may briefly be described as follows. In June 1973, a meeting of women working in some of Michigan's rape crisis projects was held at the home of Jan Ben Dor. Those assembled (with the exception of a few radical feminists) decided to take action to promote law reform. It was thus that the Michigan Women's Task Force on Rape came into being. It proceeded forthwith to commission Virginia Nordby, a lecturer at the University of Michigan Law School, to draft legislation. With the help of student researchers, she eventually produced a bill. Armed with this, the task force arranged meetings with the Michigan House of Representatives Judiciary Committee, and it finally managed to persuade a white Republican Senator and a black Democratic Representative to sponsor the bill. However, setbacks were soon to occur. A Senate Judiciary Committee lawyer produced an alternative draft bill which would have excluded the provisions on sexual history together with those abolishing the marital rape exemption. The task force was compelled to accept a compromise by which the sexual history provisions were retained but marital rape became a crime only in certain circumstances where the couple were living separately.[75] It was in this form that the bill was passed.

The achievement of what was, despite these alterations, radical reforming legislation is attributable to a number of causes. First, the Women's Task Force on Rape proved to be a highly effective organization. Many of its members were veteran campaigners from the battles for abortion law reform. They published a newsletter, they liaised with women working in the media, they lobbied relentlessly – 95 out of 110 House Representatives were lobbied personally – and they made a point of courting conservative as well as radical politicians. Their recruitment of Virginia Nordby was particularly felicitous. She and her student team left no stone unturned in researching every aspect of the proposed legislation. One member of the House Judiciary Committee commented: 'Of all the issues that have come before the Committee recently, rape reform has been the best researched and best presented.'[76] Nordby was also astute enough to include in her team Elaine Milliken, the Governor of Michigan's daughter, and the governor's decision to support the bill was undoubtedly significant. Of further assistance was the showing on television of *Cry Rape*, a film drawing attention to the ordeal of rape victims[77] who report the offence. It was thus that eventually there existed considerable public support for the bill. In an election year, this was a major advantage since politicians felt it was expedient to vote in its favour.

The reform Michigan's Criminal Sexual Conduct Act has four central features. First, instead of rape, it creates a ladder of offences, each of which is described as criminal sexual conduct.[78] The first-degree offence carries a maximum penalty of life imprisonment, with 15 years maximum for the second and third-degree offences, and two years for the fourth-degree offence. Each degree covers a range of sexual assaults, so that, for example, the first-degree offence covers any act of sexual penetration. The four degrees are differentiated according to the amount of coercion used, whether or not penetration has taken place, the extent of physical injury inflicted and the age and incapacitation of the victim. The law describes with great particularity precisely the conduct which is covered by each degree. In this way, it is hoped to encourage prosecutors to prosecute and defendants who are guilty to plead guilty. Moreover, juries saddled with a stereotypical notion of rape and confronted with a case that does not conform to it may well be prepared to convict of a crime called criminal sexual conduct in the third degree where they would balk at the idea of a rape conviction.

The new Act also dispenses with the need for the prosecution to establish the victim's resistance.[79] The offences of criminal sexual conduct focus entirely on the conduct of the defendant and do not specifically include a non-consent requirement. On the other hand, the Act cannot in all circumstances prevent the defence from seeking to allege that the victim consented, particularly where no weapons were used and where little or no injury was sustained.

The third important feature of the Michigan legislation is its strict regulation of sexual history evidence,[80] which is totally prohibited save in two exceptional circumstances. These are where the past sexual conduct was with the defendant himself and where the evidence relates to the source or origin of semen, pregnancy or disease. Thus, for example, where the complainant alleges that the criminal sexual conduct in question led to her pregnancy, the defence could adduce evidence to show that the pregnancy was in fact caused by sexual activity with another on a particular occasion.

Finally, criminal sexual conduct may be committed by one spouse against another provided that they are living apart and one partner has filed for separate maintenance or divorce.[81] It is also gender-neutral, so that women may perpetrate it and men may be its victims.

Whilst the new law has in no sense eradicated all the problems which face the criminal justice system in dealing with sexual assault – it has, for example, had no appreciable effect so far on reporting rates[82] – its most solid achievement is to produce a clear increase in the number of arrests and convictions for conduct of this kind.[83] It has also improved the treatment of victims within the legal process.[84]

Canada

In Michigan, rape law reform appears to have been achieved mainly by the dedicated efforts of an *ad hoc* committee of women who adroitly handled the legislative process. In Canada, the legislation passed in 1982 was federal not provincial, but women, once again, played a powerful role in securing it.

The achievement of rape law reform in Canada   Before outlining the course of events which would appear to have led up to the passage of the legislation, it is necessary briefly to consider certain aspects of the organization of women in Canada.[85]

Paul Rock has drawn attention to women's 'entrenched place in the institutional structure of Ottawa'.[86] This came about largely as a result of the Report of the Royal Commission on the Status of Women published in 1976 which recommended, *inter alia*, that a Status of Women Council should be created to assist in the improvement of the position of women. The government responded by creating what is now referred to as Status of Women Canada. A cabinet minister was also given responsibility for coordinating government policy on women, and in 1972 it was reported that special advisers on the status of women were to be positioned in a number of key government departments. In 1976, after the Canadian government's endorsement of the United Nations' 'Decade for Women', Status of Women Canada was enlarged and became an independent agency. Its brief was, *inter alia*, to advise, encourage and monitor the progress of government legislation, policies and programmes for women and to liaise between women's organizations and government.

At the same time as women were gaining a foothold in the federal institutions of government, developments were taking place at other levels, particularly in relation to the issue of violence against women. Largely influenced by initiatives taken in the United States and England, rape crisis centres began to appear. Whilst these were never to combine into anything resembling a movement or political lobby, their existence, together with the activities they organized, was of considerable influence in drawing attention to the problem of violence against women. Certainly they suggested to the coterie of women in Ottawa that women's issues were not confined to jobs and career opportunities.

Standing between Status of Women Canada and its offshoots in government on the one hand, and feminist activity in the shape of rape crisis centres on the other, are a number of influential women's organizations, including the National Action Committee on the Status of Women (NAC), which is of particular interest in this context. NAC is a very large umbrella organization to which numerous others are affiliated. Their range is noteworthy and includes the YWCA, the Imperial Order of the Daughters of the Empire and church organizations as well as the rape crisis centres. NAC is active and meets regularly: it holds conferences, issues publications and lobbies Parliament.

It was at the end of the 1970s that activity at a number of levels on the issue of violence against women was to coalesce and accelerate. Of particular significance was the publication of a book by Lorenne Clark and Debra Lewis in 1977 which has since gained a worldwide readership. Avowedly feminist in its orientation, *Rape: The Price of Coercive Sexuality* was described as a 'break-through', providing 'the first solid data on rape in Canada'.[87] One Canadian reviewer, Eleanor Pelrine, commented:

> Clark and Lewis in their carefully documented, rational study of 117 rape complaints laid with the Metropolitan Toronto Police Department in 1970 have struck the first blow against the individual and collective misogyny responsible for perpetuating bad law, inadequate enforcement and injustice before the courts in Canada. The rest is up to us.[88]

The book was immediately influential. Moreover, Clark, who was Associate Professor both in the Department of Philosophy and the Centre of Criminology at the University of Toronto, and Lewis, who was a researcher at the Centre, were soon to demonstrate that their talents were not exclusively academic. Both embarked upon a course of entrepreneurial activity in the wake of the book's publication. Clark spoke at conferences; she was commissioned by the Solicitor-General to compile a bibliography of works on rape; and in 1978 she became Vice-President of NAC. It was she who introduced the issue of rape to that influential committee and it was she who drafted its position paper on the subject. Moreover, she was, it seems, 'always talking to one bureaucrat or another.'[89] Lewis, who had earned her feminist stripes in the Toronto rape crisis centre, was equally prepared to lecture throughout Canada on the rape issue.

The strength and tenacity of these two women must surely earn them a place in the history of those who have laboured in the cause of women, but the extent of their influence has been called into question. Rock's research into the evolution of a policy for crime victims within the Department of the Solicitor-General has led him to conclude that in that particular field they had little direct influence on government. He suggests that government policy-makers retroactively 'bestowed luminosity'[90] upon them and upon feminist activity in this area. In other words, once it was decided that steps should be taken to assist the victims of crime, it was considered expedient to invoke the support of the women's movement. He argues: 'A political community of substance and permanence never really evolved around the social problem of violence to women. Neither did the campaign achieve direct effects.'[91] It will be suggested here that whilst this may indeed be true in relation to policies for victims which emerged from the Department of the Solicitor-General, in relation to sexual assault law reform Clark and Lewis, together with women operating in other ways, were directly, although not exclusively, influential in producing it.

In 1978, the Law Reform Commission of Canada published its Working Paper on Sexual Offences.[92] This has only to be compared with that of the English Criminal Law Revision Committee[93] to appreciate how much the thinking behind it, whether consciously or not, was influenced by feminist discourse. Thus, the approach of the working paper to rape victims is unashamedly sympathetic. There are none of the usual warning statements about false complaints of rape,[94] no suggestion that the concern about rape is out of place or indicative of a layman's misunderstanding. It speaks approvingly of the work of rape crisis centres. Moreover, unlike the Criminal Law Revision Committee, the Law Reform Commission recognized that the substantive law of rape is not to be considered in a vacuum but in the context of its operation in the criminal justice system as well as in society at large. Most significant of all, however, is its central proposition that

> rape is actually a form of assault and should therefore perhaps be treated as such under the law. . . .. The concept of sexual assault more appropriately characterizes the actual nature of the offence of rape because the primary focus is on the assault or the violation of the integrity of the person rather than the sexual intercourse.[95]

This statement may be compared with what Clark and Lewis had to say in their book, published the previous year. Under the heading 'The Female Perspective: Rape as an Assault', they state:

> We are saying that our rape laws should reflect the perspective of women – the victims of rape. They experience rape as an *assault*, as an unprovoked attack on their physical person and as a trangression of their assumed right to the exclusive ownership and control of their own bodies . . . This act is experienced by the rape victim as a denial of her physical autonomy . . . This follows from her belief that she is a fully human person and entitled to all the protections given to persons under the law. Since she knows that the right to exclusive control over one's own body and to freedom from unprovoked physical interference by others, are two of the fundamental rights guaranteed to persons under the law, she quite justifiably expects redress when she is raped.[96]

The repetition must have been effective in bringing home the message to the Law Reform Commission. It singled out 'the protection of the integrity of the person' as a central policy issue.[97] It spoke of 'the right to be free from unwanted infringement of one's bodily integrity'[98] and 'the right to be free from physical assault'.[99] It was in this context that its proposal to abolish rape and introduce a new offence of sexual assault was made.

On the matter of the marital rape exemption, however, the commissioners could not achieve a consensus. Some favoured its complete abolition, while others would go no further than to agree that the exemption should be lifted where the couple were living separately. Thus, the Law Reform Commission of Canada, in June 1978, had reached the position at which the English Criminal Law Revision Committee was to arrive in 1984: [100] it was prepared to recommend that non-cohabiting spouses should not be covered by the exemption, but it would go no further.[101]

In May 1978, one month before the official publication of the working paper, Bill C52 was introduced into the Canadian Parliament. It contained, *inter alia*, provisions designed to amend the law of rape. These were clearly influenced by the working paper's proposals. Rape was to be abolished in favour of a newly defined two-tier offence of indecent assault for which a spouse could be liable provided that he was living separately at the material time.[102]

The events that followed the presentation of the bill are noteworthy.[103] The Canadian Advisory Council on the Status of Women, the National Action Committee and the National Association of Women and the Law all publicly condemned the bill's failure to abolish the marital rape exemption. Delegations were sent to lobby the Department of Justice, including one from NAC which was 40 women strong.

It seems clear that one of the reasons why Bill C52 died never to be revived was because of the lobbying by these groups about the marital rape exemption, as well as certain other aspects of the bill. Rock himself states:

> What is significant about the campaign and the reverses of the Department of Justice is that officials of that Ministry were to become so rudely and abruptly acquainted with the sentiment which women felt about rape and sexual assault. Officials had been unprepared for what had happened. They had been discomfited. Ever afterwards, they were to be solicitous about the victimization of women and the political response of women's organizations.[104]

In November 1978 the Law Reform Commission of Canada produced its final Report on Sexual Offences.[105] This too recommended the abolition of the offence of rape and its substitution by two new offences, described as 'sexual interference' and 'sexual aggression'.[106] On the marital rape exemption, the report commented as follows:

> The great majority of those consulted by the Commission on this question favoured total abolition of the spousal immunity. Difficulties of proof do not appear to be insurmountable and the danger of groundless accusations made from motives of revenge or as preliminaries to divorce or separation proceedings may be counter-balanced by stricter exercise of discretion in assessing the appropriateness of prosecutions. Furthermore, as experience has amply demonstrated, groundless or ill-founded prosecutions have little chance of passing through the filtering processes implicit in our legal system and present-day criminal procedure.[107]

The women's organizations had made their point and had won it. The introduction to the report ends with an expression of thanks by the Commission to a number of groups and associations for their cooperation.

First on the list are 'representatives of women's groups and associations and rape crisis centres'.[108]

In March 1979 the Minister of Justice announced that a new bill was on its way 'following representations I have received from women's organisations and various other groups'. In an information paper published later, in December 1980, a subsequent Minister of Justice promised that the marital rape exemption would go: 'This spousal immunity from rape derives from the traditional belief that marriage meant irrevocable consent to sexual intercourse. If the new law is to protect the integrity of the person . . . marriage should no longer mean forced sexual submission.'

Bills C53 and C127, which eventually followed, proceeded through Parliament while women's groups continued to lobby. For, as Rock points out, 'The more eminent women's organisations had acquired a stake in the campaign to change the law on spousal immunity, previous sexual history and consent.'[109] These issues were no longer matters of concern merely to a few radical feminists. In bringing the debate to a different level in the hierarchy of women's organizations, Clark and Lewis had clearly played a central role. The radicals were still active, however, indicating their continuing concern. Rock has described the marches and the 're-claim the night' demonstrations. He also mentions the use of 'charivari', as on one occasion when women stood outside the home of a man accused of rape chanting, 'We know what you did. We know who you are. We're watching you. We're going to fight back.'[110] The newspaper reports which Rock quotes regarding these events all refer to the period between 1977 and 1981 when legal reform was being debated at the highest levels.

Rock also points to the influence of young, feminist lawyers located in and about Ottawa. He quotes a legal adviser to Status of Women Canada:

> Once the Bill was introduced it became clear that the Government was willing to act in this field so women's groups decided that they'd better act on this thing and not something else. We in Women and the Law group formed this Committee, starting in May 1978, as soon as the Bill came out. We met regularly, at least once a week, for an entire evening or a whole day, until October, to hash out a policy.[111]

Whether or not the legislation finally passed in August 1982 met with the approval of all those women who had actively participated in the law reform saga, the fact remains that the shape the law finally took is largely attributable to the argument put forward by women. In this instance, luminosity was not 'retroactively bestowed'. Women had exercised a direct and powerful influence on the legislation.

The reform   The Canadian reform of 1982 bears a certain resemblance to the Michigan legislation looked at previously, although it is weaker in certain respects and stronger in others.

The crime of rape no longer exists in Canada. Instead, a gradation scheme has been introduced which creates three offences of sexual assault covering rape and certain allied crimes. The three grades are distinguished purely in terms of the level of violence involved and no distinction is drawn between penetration and other sexual acts. Simple sexual assault carries a maximum of ten years' imprisonment but may, at the prosecutor's discretion, be tried summarily, in which case the maximum penalty is six months' imprisonment or a fine of not more than $500.[112] Next on the ladder is an offence carrying a maximum of 14 years' imprisonment, which applies where the defendant, in committing a sexual assault, carries, uses or threatens to use a real or imitation weapon or threatens to cause bodily harm to a person other than the complainant or is a party to the offence with any other person.[113] Finally comes aggravated sexual assault, which is the most serious offence of the three and carries a maximum of life imprisonment. This offence is perpetrated where the defendant, in committing a sexual assault, wounds, maims, disfigures or endangers the life of the complainant.[114]

The new law entirely abolishes the marital rape exemption.[115] It also places firm restrictions on the use of sexual history evidence,[116] although the Michigan legislation is stronger in this respect. Thus, for example, under the Canadian provisions sexual incidents involving the defendant are not vetoed at all, neither is evidence of the complainant's sexual reputation where this is relevant to the issue of consent.[117] Exceptions to the rule prohibiting sexual history evidence exist where such evidence would tend to establish the identity of the person who had the alleged sexual contact with the complainant or where it relates to sexual activity on the same occasion as the offence if this is relevant to the defendant's plea of belief in consent, or, finally, to rebut sexual history evidence adduced by the prosecution.[118] As far as corroboration is concerned, the judge is no longer permitted to issue the corroboration warning, although he will still be able to comment on the evidence.[119]

The Canadian legislation is less radical in its approach to consent: assault is defined by s. 244 of the Canadian Criminal Code as an act committed without the victim's consent so that the prosecution will still be required to establish its absence. But a number of situations in which consent will not be deemed to exist are listed. These include circumstances in which the complainant submits 'by reason of' force used or threatened against her or a third party or through fear of the application of such force.[120]

It remains to be seen what effects this reform will have. Whether or not it encourages prosecutions and convictions as it is intended to do, there can be no doubt that its symbolic achievements are considerable. Abolition of the marital rape exemption and the corroboration warning are vitally significant in terms of the status of women in the eyes of the law.

England

When the rape debate reached these shores in the early 1970s, it met with a receptive and sympathetic response in many quarters. In the mid-1980s, however, radical law reform is as remote a prospect as ever. In considering the broad history of the English law of rape over the past decade and contrasting it with the achievement of reform in Michigan and Canada, two factors stand out for consideration. The first is the lack of academic interest in and commitment to rape law reform; the second is the absence of anything resembling a cohesive and powerful women's political lobby which might have taken up the issue, as well as a general absence of women in the 'corridors of power'.

Rape and academic inquiry In both Michigan and Canada academics liaised successfully with women's pressure groups and political organizations to play a major role in bringing about legislative change. In England, however, the law of rape never became an issue of great interest or concern to academic lawyers or criminologists and remains today an area in which there has been relatively little scholarly endeavour. The contrast with the United States in this respect is dramatic. There, a vast legal literature on rape laws has emerged. Moreover, whereas in England there exists scant information about how the law of rape operates within the criminal justice system, in the United States, funds have been made available to produce valuable empirical research.[121] One reason for the dearth of English writing in this field may be that amongst academic lawyers there has been a continuing preoccupation with the mental element in crime, which has consumed much of their energy and creativity. Subjectivity, the idea that a defendant should be judged according to his individual mental state at the time of the crime, has been the watchword of academic thinking.[122] Given the predilections of some English judges, the perceived need to safeguard the interests of defendants is totally understandable; it may at times, however, have resulted in the eclipse of the victim from academic legal discourse.

It is against this background that the first crucial legal decision to be taken in this period may be viewed. *DPP* v. *Morgan*,[123] decided by the House of Lords in 1975, involved an issue of critical significance in the law of rape. The House of Lords was invited to decide whether a man who honestly believes in a woman's consent to sexual intercourse can be guilty of rape if his belief was based on unreasonable grounds. Their Lordships held by a majority that he could not. Academic orthodoxy perceived the case in one light only: it was seen to raise in stark form the issue of subjectivity and criminal liability. The House of Lords' decision was regarded as a triumph, as a turning point in the development of the criminal law. One writer commented that it was particularly remarkable that the House of Lords had responded to the academic call for subjectivity in an area such as rape where 'there might have been a strong temptation to take a line less favourable to the defendant'.[124] The truth of the matter was rather, perhaps, that in rape the judges felt more comfortable in pursuing the subjectivist line than they would have felt in many other areas of the criminal law.

It was left to the press and to diverse women's groups to protest at the decision in *Morgan*. Mr Jack Ashley, MP, a notable defender of women's rights, was given leave by an overwhelming majority of the House of

Commons to introduce a bill to overrule it.[125] The government subsequently intervened and set up a committee under the chairmanship of Mrs Justice Heilbron to look into the matter.

In considering the arguments for and against *Morgan*, the committee was faced on the one hand with academic opinion[126] and that of the National Council for Civil Liberties,[127] which was solidly in support of the decision, and on the other with what must have seemed to be the far less informed voice of the press and the women's groups. The dissenting speeches of Lords Simon[128] and Edmund Davies[129] in *Morgan* did not sufficiently develop the arguments *contra*, and the reasoning of the Court of Appeal,[130] whose decision the House of Lords had overruled, was too technical and convoluted. The case against *Morgan* was never given adequate legal expression.[131] It is hardly surprising, therefore, that Heilbron came out eventually in its favour,[132] that Ashley and others who opposed it were dismissed as laymen who had misunderstood the case and that the decision was eventually ratified by Parliament in the Sexual Offences (Amendment) Act 1976.[133]

Women – an absent force   In England there are certainly women who are prominent in public life or who can be wheeled into prominence when necessary. At a time when there was a public demand for action, Mrs Justice Heilbron was clearly a wise political choice to head a committee on rape. But the fate of the Heilbron Committee's proposals illustrates perhaps that the existence of a few prominent women is not sufficient to bring about effective reforms in areas of law which are crucial to women's status, welfare and progress.

The Heilbron Committee took the view that the popular clamour against *Morgan* was in part due to a general and justified lack of confidence in the way that rape cases were handled by the criminal justice system. It drew up radical proposals which would have severely restricted the use of sexual history evidence in rape trials[134] and would also have afforded anonymity to rape victims.[135] It is noteworthy that as well as being chaired by a woman, two out of four of the remaining members of the committee were female, as was its secretary.

It was once again Jack Ashley, MP, who was the moving force in seeking to implement the Heilbron Committee's recommendations. He persuaded Robin Corbett, MP, to introduce a Private Member's Bill which was closely modelled on the Heilbron Report. From the outset, however, it became apparent that the clauses dealing with sexual history evidence were likely to founder because of poor drafting. It was plain that if Heilbron's radical approach was to be preserved, redrafting was necessary. This did not happen and the clauses moved unamended to the House of Lords where they were duly savaged by the Law Lords. The government returned with a substitute provision which, while excluding sexual history evidence in principle, gave discretion to the judges to admit it where they considered that its exclusion would be unfair to the defendant. This provision proved, unsurprisingly, to be quite acceptable to their Lordships and it was accordingly enacted into law.[136] Thus, the judges were put in charge of regulating the use of sexual history evidence even though it was largely due to their inactivity that its use had become widespread in the first place. The anonymity proposals were also implemented in a different form from that which was intended by Heilbron. An amendment was introduced to the bill which gave anonymity not merely to the victim, but to the defendant as well.[137]

This debacle may be contrasted with the course of events surrounding the introduction of rape law reform in the two jurisdictions previously considered. Particularly noticeable was the apparent absence in England of a well-organized, well-briefed and powerful women's lobby. Had there been one, the law might have taken a different course.

Rape and the Criminal Law Revision Committee   Both the lack of strong academic support for rape law reform and the absence of a powerful women's voice in its favour may be said to have contributed to the negative approach to the matter manifested by the Criminal Law Revision Committee (CLRC) in its final Report on Sexual Offences published in 1984.[138]

Academic writing is not infrequently a powerfully persuasive influence upon the law reform bodies of England. In the absence of much legal scholarship to provide guidance, the CLRC was left to form its own views on the legal aspects of sexual assault. It is not therefore entirely without relevance that 15 out of 17 members of the CLRC at that time were male, as were its secretary and deputy secretary.[139]

In its report the CLRC proposed that the law of rape should continue to cover only penile penetration of the vagina.[140] It was not prepared to recommend abolition of the marital rape exemption, only that it should cease to operate where the couple were living separately.[141] On the issue of consent, the committee's approach was similarly restrictive. It recommended that legislation be introduced to ensure that threats other than of immediate force be precluded from the scope of rape.[142] The effect of this requirement of immediacy would be to place a fresh limitation on the scope of the offence.

The CLRC's recommendations will ensure that rape remains a crime with a narrow ambit. Since the committee considered the law of rape entirely in isolation from its operation within the criminal justice system and within society, its proposals are not entirely surprising. Although it received representations from a considerable number of women's organizations and groups, their views often appear to have been rejected.[143] Thus, for example, in connection with s. 2 of the Sexual Offences (Amendment) Act, which regulates the use of sexual history evidence, the Report states:

It seems that some people, and in particular some women's organisations, think that these statutory provisions are proving ineffective for the protection of complainants because many judges, so it is alleged, grant leave to cross-examine about a complainant's previous experience upon being asked to do so. Critics do not seem to appreciate that a complainant's previous sexual experience may be relevant to the issue of consent.[144]

The committee decided to ask the Recorder of London to ask the judges at the Old Bailey (the central criminal courts) whether, in their view, the criticism of them was justified. The reply came back that it was not.[145] The committee therefore reported that all was well and that the law with respect to sexual history should remain as it stood save for certain minor amendments.[146]

The Criminal Law Revision Committee has thus set its face against radical reform of the law of rape. The Law Commission is most unlikely to take the matter on board. In England, we have, for the time being it seems, reached the end of the road so far as legislative change at the instigation of the law reform bodies is concerned.

Conclusion

In Michigan and Canada women played a major role in the accomplishment of radical rape law reform. In countries as diverse as Australia, Israel, Denmark and Sweden women have actively and successfully campaigned against antiquated rape laws and retrogressive proposals for reform.[147] In England, by contrast, traditional women's organizations and those of the radical fringe have, for the most part, shown a marked disinclination to do battle for legal change.[148] It is no coincidence that little progress in this area has been achieved. Rape, it seems, is a women's issue in every sense: not merely does it vitally affect women, but without their active political intervention it appears that few initiatives to combat it are likely to be pursued.

Acknowledgement

I am indebted to Professor Paul Rock for his assistance.

Notes

Since this chapter was written, a number of legal changes have taken place or been proposed. In England the marital rape exemption was abolished in 1992: see *R* vs. *R* [1991] 4 All ER 481. The Law Commission has proposed the abolition of the corroboration warning: see Law Commission, *Report on Corroboration of Evidence in Criminal Trials* (1991) Law Com. No. 202, CM 1620. Changes have also taken place in police handling of rape cases: see J. Temkin, *Rape and the Legal Process* (London, 1987), pp. 158–62. For evidential changes in Canada, see J. Temkin, 'Sexual history evidence – the ravishment of section 2', *Criminal Law Review* (1993) 3. The marital rape exemption was abolished in Michigan in 1988: see Michigan Compiled Laws Annotated s. 750.5201.

1. See, e.g., 'Rape – coping with the memories', *Spare Rib*, 109 (August 1981), p. 20; *Guardian*, 24 October 1983; B. Toner, *The Facts of Rape* (London, 1982), ch. 10.

2. A.W. Burgess and L.L. Holmstrom, *Rape – Crisis and Recovery* (Maryland, 1979), p. 35.

3. W. Young, *Rape Study – A Discussion of Law and Practice* (Department of Justice and Institute of Criminology, Wellington, NZ, 1983), Vol. 1, p. 34.

4. See generally on this, *Report of the Advisory Group on the Law of Rape*, Cmnd 6352 (London, 1975); Toner, *Facts of Rape*; London Rape Crisis Centre, *Annual Reports 1977* onwards.

5. See, e.g., R. Harper and A. McWhinnie, *The Glasgow Rape Case* (London, 1983); G. Chambers and A. Millar, *Investigating Sexual Assault* (Scottish Office Central Research Unit, 1983).

6. See, e.g., J. Scutt (ed.), *Rape Law Reform* (Canberra, 1980); P. R. Wilson, *The Other Side of Rape* (Queensland, 1978).

7. See, e.g., Lorenne Clark and Debra Lewis, *Rape: The Price of Coercive Sexuality* (Toronto, 1977).

8. See A. Snare, 'Sexual violence against women', in *Sexual Behaviour and Attitudes and their Implications for Criminal Law*, Report of 15th Criminological Research Conference (Council of Europe, Strasbourg, 1983), p. 48.

9. See e.g., Young, *Rape Study*.

10. The film was shown on 18 January 1982 on BBC television in a series called *Police*.

11. A. Firth, 'Interrogation', *Police Review*, 28 November 1975.

12. Chambers and Millar, *Investigating Sexual Assault*, p. 94.

13. Ibid., p. 95.

14. L.L. Holmstrom and A.W. Burgess, *The Victim of Rape: Institutional Reactions* (New York, 1978).

15. D.P. Kelly, 'Victims' reaction to the criminal justice response'. Paper presented at 1982 Meeting of the Law and Society Association held in Toronto, Canada.

16. In England, in March 1983, the Home Office issued guidelines to the police for the investigation of rape cases: Home Office Circular 25/1983, 'Investigation of offences of rape'.

17. See Ian Blair, *Investigating Rape: A New Approach for Police* (London, 1985).

18. *Guardian*, 25 January 1985. On the same occasion it was announced that nine suites with showers and pleasant decorations were being prepared in police stations around London where victims could be interviewed. Officers have orders to allow women to rest and recover, where possible, before detailed questioning. Specially trained detective inspectors will head rape inquiries, backed up by officers who have been instructed about the 'rape trauma syndrome'. On this see J. Temkin, *Rape and the Legal Process* (London, 1987), pp. 160–1.

19. Under the new scheme for dealing with rape victims in London (see n. 18), police officers will act as counsellors to victims, will assist them to move if necessary and will put their welfare first: *The Times*, 25 January 1984. However, they presumably will not be able to provide the long-term assistance which many victims require.

20. See J. Marsh, N. Caplan and A. Geist, *Rape and the Limits of Law Reform* (Boston, 1982), ch. 2.

21. See, for example, M. Carter and R. Harris, 'Women against rape – community care for victims of sexual assault', in Scutt, *Rape Law Reform*, p. 179.

22. According to Blair, *Investigating Rape*, p. 84, by October 1983, 62 victim support schemes registered with the National Association of Victims Support Schemes had either dealt with victims of sexual assault or had agreed a referral policy with the police. However, it is not clear to what extent the volunteers who run these schemes are equipped to deal with sexual assault victims.

23. See, for example, V. Berger, 'Man's trial, woman's tribulation: rape cases in the courtroom', *Columbia Law Review*, 77 (1977), p. 1.

24. L. Newby, 'Rape victims in court – the Western Australian example', in Scutt, *Rape Law Reform*, p. 117.

25. See, for example, Young, *Rape Study*, Vol. I, ch. 7. Out of 64 trials examined in this study, complainants were cross-examined by more than one counsel in 25 per cent of cases because in each there were several defendants who were separately represented.

26. Newby, 'Rape victims in court', p. 119.

27. Ibid., p. 120.

28. See on this P. Pattullo, *Judging Women* (London, 1983).

29. Young, *Rape Study*, Vol. I, p. 124: 50 victims were interviewed.

30. Ibid.

31. In Denmark this provision was introduced by way of an amendment to the Civil and Criminal Code of Procedure in June 1980. In Norway it was introduced by Act No. 66 of 12 June 1981 which amended the Criminal Procedure Act 1887. The Danish scheme is discussed in detail in Temkin, *Rape and the Legal Process*, ch. 4.

32. See below, 'The Law', p. 283.

33. See on this, *Sexual Offences – A Report of the Cambridge Department of Criminal Science* (London, 1957), p. 12 and App. 1.

34. *Criminal Statistics for England and Wales, 1983*, Cmnd 9349 (London, 1984), p. 38.

35. *Criminal Statistics for England and Wales*, 1987, Cm 498 (London, 1988), p. 35. Changes in recording practices between 1947 and 1983 cannot account for increases of this dimension. Between 1973 and 1983, the number of recorded rapes rose by 33.7 per cent (ibid.). During the same period, the number of offences of violence rose by approximately 80 per cent (ibid., p. 32). However, in 1984, the number of recorded offences of violence against the person was 3 per cent greater than in 1983, whereas there was a 7 per cent increase in the number of reported rapes. *Home Office Statistical Bulletin*, 6/85, 12 March 1985. Changes in recording practices in the Metropolitan Police partially account for rises in the figures from 1985 onwards.

36. *Rape Study*, Vol. I, p. 1.

37. Federal Bureau of Investigation, *Uniform Crime Reports* (United States Department of Justice, Washington, DC, 1983). Blair points out that between 1973 and 1982, the *rate* of increase in the occurrence of the offence (assessed on the basis of the official statistics of crime) was greater for the Metropolitan Police District than for the United States as a whole: see, Blair, *Investigating Rape*, p. 15.

38. United States Department of Justice, *Criminal Victimization in the United States, 1979* (Washington, DC, 1981).

39. M. Amir, *Patterns in Forcible Rape* (Chicago, 1971).

40. R.L. Dukes and C.L. Mattley, 'Predicting rape victim reportage', *Sociology and Social Research*, 62 (1977), p. 63.

41. Young, *Rape Study*, Vol. I, p. 10.

42. *The British Crime Survey: Scotland* (Scottish Office Social Research Study, 1984), p. 15.

43. *The British Crime Survey* (Home Office Research Study No. 76, 1983), p. 9.

44. Ibid., p. 4.

45. Ibid., p. 54. The number of sexual assaults revealed in the second British Crime Survey was also extremely low. See *Taking Account of Crime: Key Findings in the 1984 British Crime Survey* (Home Office Research Study 85, 1985).

46. London Rape Crisis Centre, *Annual Report*, 1982, p. 37.

47. R.E. Hall, *Ask Any Woman: A London Inquiry into Rape and Sexual Assault* (Bristol, 1985).

48. Ibid., pp. 32–3.

49. Ibid., p. 106.

50. Ibid., pp. 108–13.

51. See Wilson, *The Other Side of Rape*, ch. 6; Lee Henry, 'Hospital care for victims of sexual assault' in Scutt, *Rape Law Reform*, p. 170.

52. Snare, 'Sexual violence against women', p. 66.

53. Hall, *Ask Any Woman*, p. 127.

54. Ibid., p. 108.

55. R. Wright, 'Rape and physical violence', in *Sex Offenders in the Criminal Justice System* (Cropwood Conference Series No. 12) (Cambridge, 1980), p. 101.

56. Chambers and Millar, *Investigating Sexual Assault*, p. 38.

57. Ibid., p. 43.

58. Ibid., p. 10.

59. Ibid.

60. R. Wright, 'A note on the attrition of rape cases', *British Journal of Criminology*, 24 (1984), p. 399.

61. Ibid., p. 400.

62. Young, *Rape Study*, p. 14.

63. *People* v. *Murphy*, 145 Michigan Supreme Court Reports 524, 528, 108 North Western Reports 1009, 1011 (1906); *People* v. *Geddes*, 301 Michigan Supreme Court Reports 258, 261, 3 North Western Reports 2d 266, 267 (1942). See also K. A. Cobb and N. R. Schauer, 'Legislative note: Michigan's Criminal Sexual Assault Law', *University of Michigan Journal of Law Reform*, 8 (1974), p. 217.

64. Sexual Offences (Amendment) Act 1976, s. 1.

65. In eight states the marital rape exemption has been abolished. In Minnesota, Pennsylvania and Colorado the corroboration warning is prohibited. A complete restructuring of the offence of rape has taken place in 25 states. Most states have firm restrictions on sexual history evidence. For further discussion, see C. Backhouse and L. Schoenroth, 'A comparative survey of Canadian and American rape law', *Canada–United States Law Journal*, 6 (1983), p. 48; D. Russell, *Rape in Marriage* (New York, 1982), App. II; Berger, 'Man's trial', note 23; H. S. Feild and L. B. Bienen, *Jurors and Rape* (Lexington, Mass., 1980).

66. See below, 'Canada', p. 287.

67. See, e.g., The Crimes (Sexual Assault) Amendment Act 1981 (New South Wales); Law Reform Commission of Tasmania, *Report and Recommendations on Rape and Sexual Offences* (Report No. 31, 1982).

68. See Michigan Act No. 266 of 1974, Michigan Compiled Laws Annotated: ss. 520a–k and s. 5201. (Cumulative Supplement 1976–7).

69. At least 25 states in the United States, as well as Canada and New South Wales, Australia, have introduced a ladder of offences instead of rape. This is the hallmark of the Michigan legislation.

70. See An Act to Amend the Criminal Code in relation to Sexual Offences and Other Offences Against the Person, 1980–81–82–83 (Can.), c.125.

71. This figure was quoted to Ian Blair by an official of the US Law Enforcement Assistance Administration, which is part of the Department of Justice: see Blair, *Investigating Rape*, p. 21.

72. See n. 71.

73. See Blair, *Investigating Rape*, pp. 21–2.

74. See on this J. C. Marsh, A. Geist and N. Caplan, *Rape and the Limits of Law Reform* (1982), ch. 2.

75. See n. 81 and accompanying text.

76. Marsh et al., *Rape and the Limits of Law Reform*, p. 18.

77. See also text at n. 15.

78. See n. 68, s. 520b–520e.

79. Ibid., s. 520i.

80. Ibid., s. 520j.

81. Ibid., s. 520l.

82. Marsh et al., *Rape and the Limits of Law Reform*, p. 27. Police attitudes to rape victims do not appear to have changed markedly either: see ibid., ch. 6. This may in part account for the lack of increase in reported offences. It has been suggested that fear of retaliation and a desire to forget about the rape are overriding concerns for many victims. See Dukes and Mattley, 'Predicting rape victim reportage', pp. 63–84.

83. Marsh et al., *Rape and the Limits of Law Reform*, pp. 28–37.

84. Ibid., pp. 67–73.

85. See on this Paul Rock, *A View from the Shadows: The Ministry of the Solicitor General of Canada and the Making of the Justice for Victims of Crime Initiative* (Oxford, 1986).

86. Ibid., p. 210.

87. By the American writer Diana Russell: see n. 65.

88. Taken from the back cover of Clark and Lewis, *Rape*.

89. Rock, *View from the Shadows*, p. 233.

90. Ibid., p. 234.

91. Ibid.

92. Law Reform Commission of Canada, Working Paper 22, *Sexual Offences* (1978).

93. Criminal Law Revision Committee, Working Paper on Sexual Offences (1980). See also, Criminal Law Revision Committee, Fifteenth Report, *Sexual Offences*, Cmnd 9213 (1984).

94. Compare the Criminal Law Revision Committee Fifteenth Report, paras. 2.7 and 2.92.

95. Law Reform Commission of Canada, *Sexual Offences*, p. 16.

96. Clark and Lewis, *Rape*, pp. 166–7.

97. Law Reform Commission of Canada, *Sexual Offences*, p. 5.

98. Ibid., p. 14.

99. Ibid., p. 21.

100. See below 'Rape and the Criminal Law Revision Committee', p. 295.

101. Law Reform Commission of Canada, *Sexual Offences*, p. 17.

102. Under the bill, s. 149 of the Canadian Criminal Code would have read as follows: (1) Every one who indecently assaults another person is guilty of an indictable offence and is liable to imprisonment for fourteen years. (2). An accused who is charged with an offence under subsection (1) or section 149.1 may be convicted if the evidence establishes that the accused did anything to the other person with his or her consent that, but for such consent, would have been an indecent assault or an aggravated indecent assault, if such consent was obtained by personating the spouse of the other person or by false and fraudulent representations as to the nature and quality of the act, or was extorted by threats or fear of bodily harm.

149.1. Every one who indecently assaults another person is, where the indecent assault results in severe physical or psychological damage to that other person, guilty of an indictable offence and liable to imprisonment for life.

149.2. For the purposes of sections 149 and 149.1 and without restricting the generality of the term 'indecent assault', an indecent assault includes sexual penetration of any bodily orifice.

149.3. No prosecution shall be instituted under section 149 or 149.1 in respect of an offence alleged to have been committed by a person against his or her spouse unless the spouse were living separate and apart at the material time.'

103. See on this Rock, *View from the Shadows*, pp. 215–17.

104. Ibid.

105. Law Reform Commission of Canada, Report No. 10, *Sexual Offences*.

106. Ibid., p. 14.

107. Ibid., pp. 16–17.

108. Ibid., p. 2.

109. Rock, *View from the Shadows*. See also L. Snider, 'Legal reform and social control: the dangers of abolishing rape', *International Journal of the Sociology of Law*, 13 (1985), p. 337.

110. Rock, *View from the Shadows*, p. 214.

111. Ibid., p. 217.

112. Canadian Criminal Code, s. 246.1.

113. s. 246.2.

114. s. 246.3.

115. s. 246.8.

116. s. 246.6.

117. s. 246.7.

118. s. 246.6.

119. s. 246.4.

120. s. 244(3). But a defendant may presumably argue that although he used force, the complainant did not consent 'by reason of' it.

121. See above 'Michigan', p. 285.

122. For an exposition of subjectivist doctrine, see, e.g., G. Williams, *Textbook of Criminal Law*, 2nd edn (London, 1983).

123. [1976] Appeal Cases 182.

124. J. Sellars, '*Mens rea* and the judicial approach to "bad excuses" in the criminal law', *Modern Law Review*, 41 (1978), pp. 245, 248.

125. H.C. Deb., Vol. 892, col. 1416 (21 May 1975).

126. See, e.g., [1975] Criminal Law Review 718–20.

127. For a recent statement of this opinion, see M. Benn, A. Coote and T. Gill, *The Rape Controversy* (London, 1983).

128. [1976] Appeal Cases 182, 215.

129. Ibid., p. 221.

130. [1975] 1 All England Law Reports 8.

131. Recently, however, there has been legal criticism of the case. See, e.g., T. Pickard, 'Culpable mistakes and rape: relating *mens rea* to the crime', *University of Toronto Law Journal*, 30 (1980), p. 75; J. Temkin, 'The limits of reckless rape', [1983] *Criminal Law Review*, p. 5.

132. *Report of the Advisory Group on the Law of Rape* (see n. 4 above), paras 25–84.

133. s. 1. In the United States, a mistaken belief in consent is a defence only where it is based on reasonable grounds: see, e.g., *US* v. *Short*, 4 Official Reports – United States Court of Military Appeals 437.

134. *Report of the Advisory Group on the Law of Rape*, paras 85–142.

135. Ibid., p. 37.

136. Sexual Offences (Amendment) Act 1976, ss. 2 and 3. For full discussion of the parliamentary debate, see J. Temkin, 'Regulating sexual history evidence – the limits of discretionary legislation', *International and Comparative Law Quarterly*, 33 (1984), p. 942. For research revealing that the Act has not been particularly successful in controlling the use of sexual history evidence, see Z. Adler, 'Rape – the intention of Parliament and the practice of the courts', *Modern Law Review*, 45 (1982), p. 664.

137. Sexual Offences (Amendment) Act 1976, ss. 4–6. The *Hutchinson* trial, widely reported in the press in September 1984, has been one amongst several cases exposing the weaknesses of the anonymity provisions. For Press Council criticism of media handling of the case, see *Guardian*, 15 November 1984. In February 1986 the government announced its intention to abolish anonymity for defendants in rape trials. See *The Times*, 17 February 1986.

138. CLRC, *Sexual Offences* (see n. 93).

139. See also *Women and Public Appointments: Report of an Investigation into Appointments to Public Bodies* (Equal Opportunities Commission, 1985) which draws attention to the small proportion of women appointed to public office in the United Kingdom. The Policy Advisory Committee on Sexual Offences, consisting mainly of non-lawyers, was appointed to advise the Criminal Law Revision Committee in its work. Eight out of fifteen of its members were female. See CLRC, *Sexual Offences*, App. A. Its advice was not always accepted.

140. CLRC, *Sexual Offences*, para. 2.47.

141. Ibid., para. 2.85.

142. Ibid., para. 2.29.

143. Ibid., paras 2.45, 2.55, 2.87 and 5.12.

144. Ibid., para. 2.87.

145. Ibid., para. 2.88. The Policy Advisory Committee also asked the chairman of the Criminal Bar Association to ask members of the Bar about the operation of s.2. He also reported back that all was well. Adler conducted a rigorous empirical investigation into the operation of s.2. and reached the opposite conclusion: see Adler, 'Rape – the intention of Parliament'.

146. CLRC, *Sexual Offences*, para. 2.90.

147. The same may be said of Australia. See Scutt, *Rape Law Reform*, which contains the recommendations and draft bill of the Women's Electoral Lobby, and the proceedings of the National Conference on Rape Law Reform held in Hobart in 1980. See also L. Sebba, 'The repeal of the requirement of corroboration in sex offences' *Israel Law Review*, 18 (1983), p. 135, in which the efforts of Nitza Shapira-Libai, the Prime Minister's Adviser on the Status of Women in Israel, to obtain the abolition of the corroboration requirement are described. In Denmark, it is due to the efforts of Mrs Jytte Thorbek that rape victims are now legally

represented in court and can generally expect to be awarded compensation by the court where the defendant is convicted. In Sweden, the proposals on rape made by a government-appointed committee in 1976 were powerfully opposed by women's groups. Snare writes: 'For the first time in Swedish history 15 women's organisations representing the whole political spectrum managed to work out a joint resolution to demand an immediate repeal' of some of its recommendations. The report was abandoned as a result and a new committee on sexual offences, consisting mainly of women, was set up by the government: see Snare, 'Sexual violence against women'.

148. For a recent exception, see Women's National Commission, *Violence Against Women – Report of an Ad Hoc Working Group* (1985).

The 'Woman Question' in the Age of Communism's Collapse

Maxine Molyneux

Soviet women! Participate actively in the renewal of Soviet society! Rear a strong, worthy successor generation! (Communist Party of the Soviet Union, May Day Slogans, 1990, no. 13)

The collapse of 'really existing socialism',[1] and its eclipse as an economic and political alternative to liberal capitalism, has many implications for the populations of the affected countries, not all of them positive. For the half that is female, there will be both losses and gains. As the state retreats from its self-designated role as 'emancipator of women', to be replaced by market forces, civil society and new ideological configurations, vulnerable social groups – such as women – are threatened by the abandoning of old commitments, and by a deepening of existing social divisions and political tensions. At the same time, such groups are now able to form their own organizations and challenge the limited conceptions of citizenship that prevailed under the old state structures.

Although it is too early to predict the outcome of these epochal changes – in some Communist countries it is still possible to talk of 'reforms' under Party rule, while elsewhere it appears that a wholesale move to the free market is in train – the implications for women are momentous. Feminists might view these changes with a degree of ambivalence: on the one hand, welcoming fresh opportunities for debate as state control is relaxed and civil society emerges as a new political terrain; but on the other, fearing that the 'transition from socialism' will lead to a worsening of women's social and economic position, at least in the short to medium term.

At this stage any analysis must necessarily be provisional, but it is nevertheless possible to discern some changes in the definition of women's social position within this new context. This article will examine the three most pertinent issues: how those Communist parties that remain in power, or remain competitors for power, have redefined their policies with respect to women; how the socioeconomic and political situation of women is likely

From 'The "woman question" in the age of perestroika', *New Left Review*, 183, 1990, pp. 23–49, amended.

to be affected by the abandoning of part or all of the orthodox Communist policy package; and how far these new conditions favour the emergence of feminist and women's movements. Whilst the main focus of the discussion will be the Soviet Union before its dissolution and China, where the Communist Party has remained in power, some of the problems and possibilities that can be identified there have also emerged in other parts of the bloc of countries which emulated the Soviet economic model, its social policies and political institutions – not only in Eastern Europe but also in the Communist states of the south. Whereas the USSR waited until after Gorbachev's advent to power in 1985 to introduce major economic and social changes, some of the Third World Communist parties had begun these well before – China after 1978, Vietnam after 1981, Mozambique after 1983. (In Eastern Europe, Poland and Hungary had begun to liberalize – and to rethink policy on women – in the 1970s.) But even where these changes did not always explicitly involve changes in state policy towards women, the new orientations did affect women through their impact on the labour force, population policy and the family. With the launching of perestroika in the USSR after 1985, the great majority of the Communist states became involved in one way or another in this process, and it became increasingly evident that formerly prevalent views on 'the woman question' were being revised, sometimes radically.

The implications for women of these various changes have been of two general kinds. On the one hand, there have been changes in economic policy entailing a revision of earlier commitments in favour of new goals. There is, however, another dimension to reform, so far confined to Eastern Europe: namely, the loosening of state control and the emergence or expansion of civil society. It therefore becomes important to look not just at what state and party leadership declare, but also at what emerges from civil society itself, as the power of these leaderships recedes or is challenged. Such an analysis has relevance to more than the phenomenon of perestroika: it poses much broader questions about the previous social role of Communist states, and the nature of socialist transformation itself.

Women and the Communist state: before perestroika

The starting point in any discussion of the Communist states in relation to gender issues is to establish the significance and meaning of their commitment to women's emancipation. In the socialist tradition and in the practice of Communist parties, the process of women's emancipation was seen as part of the overall socialist revolutionary project, combining ideas of social justice and equality with those of modernity and development. In the classical texts of Engels, Lenin and Marx himself there was a recurrent commitment to the emancipation of women from the bonds of traditional society and the inhumanity of capitalism; and this theme subsequently informed the policies of the ruling Communist parties, committed as they were to social transformation. Emancipation in this context came to mean two things: the mobilization of women into the labour force; and the lifting of traditional social constraints and injustices, thereby enabling them to take part in the effort to develop their societies. A number of classic measures (embodied in the resolutions of the 1920 Congress of the Comintern) were adopted to secure women's 'emancipation', first in the Soviet Union, and later in those states that followed in its footsteps. The most important of these were: the encouragement of women to work outside the home; the introduction of legal equality between men and women; the liberalization of laws on the family and marriage; the promotion of equality of opportunity in education; and the prohibition of sexually exploitative images and writing, and of practices such as prostitution. The earliest declarations of women's rights recognized that women would perform two roles: a 'maternal' function and a role in production. The socialist state was to facilitate this dual function by supplying adequate childcare facilities and provisions for paid maternity leave.[2]

Despite their historical significance and positive aspects, these policies had major limitations. Communist Party officials came to assume – or found it convenient to do so – that the oppression of women consisted almost entirely in their exclusion from paid employment. This, however, ignored both the question of women's inferior position in a segregated, hierarchical workforce, and the stringent demands of their new combined duties. Bolshevik policy on the family, while initially taken with the idea of abolishing the traditional model, soon turned to reinforcing it – while placing it under greater strain – in a way that precluded both a critique of gender roles within the domestic sphere, and consideration of alternative forms of family and interpersonal relationships. From the earliest Bolshevik period, the policies of Communist states towards women and the family were kept subservient to broader economic goals, and changed in accordance with them. Within these authoritarian political systems founded upon centralism and the imposition of orthodoxy, no autonomous women's movement, and no feminist critique of socialist theory and policy, were allowed. Official women's organizations mobilized women in the service of the economic and political goals of the state, in accordance with a narrowly defined set of 'questions of everyday life'. They did not challenge state policy, or in any sustained way tackle the deep-rooted gender inequalities which survived the substantial social transformations.

The Communist record on 'women's emancipation' is one of some advances coupled with substantial failure – an apparent paradox best understood in the context of the development strategies pursued by these states, rather than as resulting from inadequacies in socialist theory itself. Command economies and authoritarian states of the Soviet variety attempted to overcome economic backwardness by pursuing policies designed to increase industrial and agricultural output as rapidly as possible. The success of these policies was made dependent on the mass mobilization of the population into various sectors of the economy, changes which had far-reaching consequences both for women and the institution of the family. Women achieved formal legal equality and a limited emancipation from the 'old feudal order'; along with men, they gained access to education, employment, cheap food and heavily subsidized health and housing. Yet the cost of this model was high, and its accumulated failures and distortions fell, as we shall see, especially heavily on the female sex.

This policy orientation prevailed in Communist countries from the 1920s until the mid-1980s, and despite the variations of culture, history and politics, the Communist parties exhibited a remarkable degree of consistency in this regard. They proclaimed their commitment to 'the emancipation of women' and were quick to declare that the woman question, like those of the nationalities and unemployment, had been 'solved'. Official discourses stressed Communism's achievements in the realms of legal equality and educational provision, but above all they were proud of their record on employment. High female employment rates were achieved relatively early on in the centrally planned economies. In 1950 in the USSR the female participation rate was over 60 per cent, compared with 32.6 per cent in the USA.[3] In 1980, half the labour force of Eastern Europe consisted of women, compared with 32 per cent in Western Europe; and even as the capitalist states began to catch up, by mid-decade only Sweden, Denmark and Finland had higher rates than East Germany (77.5 per cent) and the USSR (70 per cent). The less developed regions under Communist rule also showed significant increases over their capitalist counterparts. Figures for 1980 show that in the Muslim Central Asian republics of the USSR 40 per cent of the labour force was female; in Vietnam 45 per cent; and in North Korea 46 per cent. The average for the Middle East was 20 per cent; for Latin America 22 per cent; and for the far East (the second highest average after the CPEs), 35 per cent.[4] Although in some cases these gaps were narrowing, they nevertheless remained significant. It was also true that women had entered the professions in substantial numbers – in some cases crossing gender barriers that in the West prevailed to the disadvantage of women. Engineering was a case in point: in the mid-1980s, one-third of Soviet engineers were female, compared with only 6 per cent in the United States.

Yet despite these advances, it was evident to many outside observers, and to a growing number of people in the Communist states themselves, that women's participation in the economy had brought them neither equality nor emancipation, and that women remained a subordinate social group in both the public and private realms. The realization that women's lot was a harsh one became part of a more general criticism of orthodox Communism, and contributed to the rejection of the Communist model by the reform movements.

Pressures from above and below

From the 1970s onwards, for reasons unconnected with the emancipation of women as such, policy relating to women was seen to require reassessment. The most pressing issues were demographic, and centred on the birth rate: many states became alarmed at its decline, and took measures to make it easier for women to have more children. This was particularly so in Hungary, the GDR, the USSR, and to an extreme degree in Romania where abortion was outlawed and women were coerced into having a minimum of three children per family. In a few cases – notably China and Vietnam – the opposite consideration prevailed, and coercion and incentives were used to bring down the high birth rate. These demographic considerations were directly linked to the growing preoccupation with an economic performance that was sluggish in comparison with the capitalist states; and in the Soviet Union to the additional fear that the population of the Russian republics would be outnumbered by that of Central Asia. In Yugoslavia, ethnic Albanians were seen to present a similar threat to the Serbian authorities, and 'appropriate' measure were taken to reduce the birth rate in Kosovo.

But other fears, common to these states both in the north and in the south, arose from a perceived disintegration of social life, associated with what some sociologists identified as 'alienation' or 'anomie', and what others linked to the shortage of housing, leisure facilities and consumer goods. The rising rates of divorce, alcoholism and crime were seen as evidence that the state had failed in its duty to support the family. Given the harsh conditions of daily life in most households, it was hardly surprising that families suffered under the pressure; but significantly, the 'decay of family life' was attributed by sociologists and public opinion alike to the pressures on women, especially the 'absent' (that is, working) mother. In the USSR in the first half of the 1980s, theories elaborated by psychologists in the maternal deprivation vein contributed to a general rethinking of policies.[5] The proposal to place a renewed social responsibility on the family would ensure that in practice such responsibility devolved once again upon women. During the 1970s and 1980s throughout the Communist bloc, women's social position became an object of official scrutiny, and the ideological importance given to their role in production was now displaced in favour of their role in the home – a shift which represented a radical departure from the slogans, if not the reality, of the past.

A further link between the crisis of orthodox socialism and the position of women was formed by popular attitudes in these countries themselves. In many cases, the history of Communist Party policy with regard to women was one of a reforming state intervening in society to bring about changes in women's position, often against the wishes and views of a majority of the population.[6] If this was true in the initial revolutionary phase, it remained so throughout the following period. In many cases, the result was that the emphasis on 'the woman question' and on the emancipation and promotion of women could too readily be associated with the dead hand of the same distant and bureaucratic centralizing state, to be resisted and rejected along with its other policies. Such rejection was particularly strong when nationalist or religious interests were at stake – for instance, hostility to abortion in Catholic Poland, or the illegal continuation of arranged marriages and of the *kelim*, or betrothal settlement, in Soviet Central Asia.

This resistance to 'emancipation from above' was compounded by conflicts resulting from the policies themselves. In the first place, the very encouragement of women to participate in economic activity generated its own forms of resistance: women were seen as being unfairly forced to take on additional burdens outside the home, and the formal equality such employment bestowed was vitiated by the arduous and sometimes squalid conditions under which they worked at menial jobs in agriculture and industry. Despite a commitment to various forms of protective legislation, such as the exclusion of women from many hundreds of jobs 'to protect their maternal function', this covert paternalism was remarkable for its inconsistency. Women had always performed heavy labour in the countryside, where no laws 'protected' them – even from the hazards of chemical poisoning. In the towns, women performed such work as rubbish collection as a matter of course, and in factories frequently carried far heavier loads than permitted by law, and worked in insanitary, polluted and noisy conditions. In the USSR in the 1980s for example, 98 per cent of janitors and street cleaners were women, as were 26 per cent of highway-construction crews. And, although women were formally banned from nightshifts, over 70 per cent of Soviet nightshift workers were female – a result of a loophole in the law that permitted women to be employed for short-term emergencies only.[7] Moreover, the gap between the average male and female wage stood at around 30 per cent in most northern Communist states (a gap larger in Vietnam and China), with women concentrated in low-paid jobs in 'feminized' occupations, their distribution in the labour force subject to marked horizontal and vertical segregation.[8] It is little wonder that few women in these circumstances could feel wholly positive about their participation in the labour force, or about government policies in general.

In the political realm, women were excluded even more markedly from positions of power and responsibility, despite a substantial measure of participation at lower levels. Most countries' Politburos contained no women, some had a token one, others a few 'candidate members'; and at ministerial level the few women were typically confined to posts in health and education. The policy of establishing quotas for women in political organizations, limited as it was, had its own negative consequences: since women were most frequently promoted in those bodies with little authority, such as legislatures, the very formal representation was contradicted by reality. In many cases, from Bulgaria and Romania to China and Cuba, the most prominent women occupied their posts less by virtue of individual merit than by family ties.[9] The official women's organizations, supposedly acting to further women's collective interests, were in most cases strict adherents of the Party line, and in some were moribund, corrupt entities, a fact which only added to women's disenchantment with political life.

Mounting dissatisfaction

Ultimately, it was the failure of the ruling Communist parties to deliver enough of the promised material progress, that provided the decisive impetus to reform. This was true for the whole range of social policies, but the emphasis on production to the detriment of consumption, and the elimination of the independent service sector, were failures with special implications for women. The continued scarcity and poor quality of labour-saving equipment for the home made a mockery of Lenin's assault on the drudgery of housework. The shortages of consumer goods, and the many hours spent queueing, more than offset any availability of socialized domestic services. The low standards and variable provision of nurseries; the lack of proper contraception and the consequent high abortion rates of many countries; the appalling conditions in maternity hospitals; the prevalence – especially in the Soviet Union – of male alcoholism as a response to the drabness of social life: all these factors created special problems for women. Official claims made for the superiority of the socialist order rang increasingly hollow among populations who had made their sacrifices and were now impatient for results.

It is useful to distinguish between the actual development and intensification of these problems and the growing intolerance of them by their long-suffering peoples. Taken as a whole, the economic situation of these countries had been, from the late 1960s, one in which growth slowed down to the point of stagnation. But in the sphere of political life the crisis consisted in a growing awareness on the part of both leadership and population of the failings of the system, even though compared to earlier periods the situation was easing. This growing dissatisfaction had several causes: an extension of the real economic malaise into other areas of life; a greater impatience with the shortcomings of the system as a result of higher levels of education and the relative relaxation of political controls; a decline in the opportunities for social mobility as economic growth slowed down; and, evident in all matters to do with everyday life and social affairs, an increasing sense that the socialist countries were now lagging behind the West. All these factors had their impact on popular attitudes toward gender issues: the slowing down of the economy and the stagnation of output and productivity levels rendered the idea of emancipation through employment less and less plausible; at the same time, and as demand grew, the failures of social services, provisioning, transport and so forth, became more evident. The sheer difficulty of making ends meet, in terms of both time and money, placed households under acute strain. These material pressures were duly reflected in the rising number of divorces and – in the countries of the north – in low or falling birth rates.

In addition, the greater visibility of the West produced demands for liberalization that had contradictory implications for women. Their forced participation in the economy was itself said to be an oppression not shared by women in capitalist countries, while the stark contrast with the West in terms of the provision of well-made clothes, domestic appliances, child and baby products, and essential items such as tampons and contraceptives, was felt to be increasingly unacceptable. Yet reinforcing this loss of confidence in the Communist record – which came, if not from feminism, then certainly from a general sympathy for women – was a quite different influence from the capitalist world: namely the desire for greater openness in the area of personal life and in the public depiction of women, whether this took the form of egalitarian sexual freedom, prostitution or pornography. The latter became an important (at least an important *male*) source of interest in the West, producing a situation whereby the restrictions prevailing in Communist societies were seen as imposing a dictatorial puritanism that contrasted with the free sensuality of liberal capitalism.[10]

The emergence of a feminist opposition

A further component of the crisis of orthodox Communism in regard to women was that of explicit opposition to, and critique of, the Soviet model by indigenous women's groups. Feminism has always been a beleaguered force in countries ruled by Communist parties. The worldwide upsurge of feminism in the 1970s did not make much impact in the Communist states, where feminist writings and ideas were officially discouraged. The UN Decade for Women (1976–86) can be credited with making some small inroads by bringing Communist representatives into contact with feminists and feminisms from different parts of the world, and focusing attention on the position of women within the Communist states themselves. For all this, feminists remained isolated and ignorant of the debates going on in the movement outside, and many would-be feminists consequently absorbed the Party line that feminism was a trivial Western irrelevance, one especially unsuited to the different conditions of 'really existing socialism'.

Notwithstanding these unpropitious conditions, however, explicit opposition to Communist Party policy has at times been mounted by women's groups. Autonomous feminist forces had survived in some of the Communist countries prior to the imposition of 'democratic centralist' orthodoxy – notably in Russia (Kollontai, Armand, and others) and in China (Ting Ling). From Lenin onwards, feminism was routinely denounced as 'bourgeois', and seen as a challenge to the orthodox line that it was unnecessary because women had achieved their emancipation under socialism. Yet in the mid-1970s, as part of the global upsurge of women's movements, feminist currents began to emerge in the Communist states.[11] In Yugoslavia a feminist group of teachers, journalists and writers began to campaign for changes in the laws which affected women, focusing on issues such as rape. In 1979 the Leningrad group of writers associated with Tatyana Mamonova published *The Almanac: Women and Russia*. Their club, 'Maria', produced a magazine that combined ideas of women's liberation with mysticism and Christianity. This enterprise provoked charges of anti-Soviet propaganda, the group was dissolved, and four members, including Mamonova, were forced into exile over the following two years.[12] In 1982 in the GDR a women's peace movement associated with Christa Wolf opposed the extension, in times of national emergency, of conscription to women; but although their campaign had some success, the leaders were held for questioning, and at the end of 1983 two of them were imprisoned for six weeks before charges were dropped.[13]

During the same period, active feminist currents arose in some of the countries of the south. In Latin America a continent-wide movement developed, and neither of the two post-revolutionary states in the region was immune to its effects. Cuba's hostility to feminism – expressed in Vilma Espin's regular denunciation of its 'bourgeois' and 'imperialist' character – softened under the impact of changes taking place within socialist movements everywhere. As feminism began to appeal to socialists, so the Cuban leadership began to take note. Members of the Federación de Mujeres Cubanas began to attend feminist gatherings in Latin America, and so to enter into dialogue with individuals and organizations from different parts of the world.

Nicaraguan feminists had an important influence on Cuba at this time. In the very different political context of the Nicaraguan revolution there emerged in the 1980s a loyal feminist opposition, one that took an active part in debating and formulating state policy on questions concerning women. These feminists came from a variety of social backgrounds, and most of them were active in the FSLN, the women's organization (AMNLAE), or in other mass organizations. This movement was conspicuous in not confining itself to the Leninist agenda or the Party line on women. In a number of cases campaigns were fought to change Party policy, even over sensitive issues such as abortion.[14] From the start, relations between Cuban and Nicaraguan women's organizations were less than harmonious, the differences in approach becoming evident in 1987 at the Fourth Latin American and Caribbean Feminist *Encuentro* in Mexico, at which around forty Nicaraguan feminists argued with three from Cuba. Nonetheless, some of this exposure to other feminisms that were not 'bourgeois' or 'imperialist' had an effect on Cuban attitudes in the 1980s. Feminist concerns began to be reflected in some of the research carried out by social scientists, sometimes conducted under the supervision of feminist scholars from the West. In the early 1980s the Frente Continental was founded by the FMC, an initiative which aimed to bring Latin American feminism into line with Cuban priorities and – as one participant saw it – to stop it drifting off into less important issues like sexual politics.[15] Limited though these initiatives were, they nonetheless marked a significant and positive advance on earlier views.

But, in contrast to the Eastern European and Russian cases, there appeared no independent feminist groups, at least none which sought to enter the public realm.

It was such groups, along with writers and film-makers, who, prior to perestroika, began to challenge the orthodox line that the woman question had been 'solved', and in some cases sought to define a programme of reform that was aware, but not uncritical, of the situation of women in the West.[16] Given the degree to which the West had won favour with popular opinion in the socialist countries, these feminist currents, unimpressed by both socialist and capitalist records, came to represent an important alternative point of reference.

New and old Soviet thinking

The initial transformations envisaged by ruling Communist Parties, epitomized in the Soviet policy of perestroika, has led to the liberalization of both economy and political system, together with reduced confrontation with the West and a loosening of ties between the Comecon states. Initially conceived as an attempt to revitalize socialism in order the better to compete, as a distinct social system, with the capitalist West, it soon became apparent that the prospects for such competition were remote, and that the Communist states were seeking more and more to integrate themselves with the West. What was evident even before the collapse of Communist Party rule was that these changes involved the sometimes wholesale adoption of certain Western modes of operation, stimulated by reform from above, and in most cases matched by popular pressure from below. One of the hallmarks of the new phase was the abandonment of the old 'international-ist' model, whereby other socialist countries imitated the USSR; but paradoxically it was the changes in the USSR that nonetheless greatly influenced and accelerated what was occurring in other states, notably the 'velvet revolutions' and collapse of Communist power in Eastern Europe. This comprehensive revision had implications for women in three main areas: state policy, political representation, and the economy.

The discussion after 1985 of policies relating to women took place against a background of more than a decade of concern in the USSR about a range of social problems relating to family life. The divorce rate was the second highest in the world after the USA; alcoholism, 'hooliganism' and crime were on the rise; the birth rate was falling, infant mortality was rising, and a high number of abortions (7 million per year) were being carried out.[17] The rubric of 'everyday life', used to summarize these problems, implicitly excluded the issues of gender relations and the sexual division of labour at work. When controls on the press were loosened, and the claim that social problems had been 'solved' was dropped, a greater recognition of the depth of these problems was apparent in press and Party statements.

This concern was reflected in the policies that Gorbachev began to introduce in 1985, and which he enunciated in his address to the Twenty-seventh Party Congress in February 1986. Here he restated the orthodox position: 'Socialism has emancipated women from economic and social oppression, securing for them the opportunity to work, obtain an education, and participate in public life on an equal footing with men. The socialist family is based on the full equality of men and women and their equal responsibility for the family.' Gorbachev then went on to itemize the social problems in the USSR, and to outline the changes designed to enable women to combine their 'maternal duties' with involvement in economic activity:

> in the twelfth five-year period we are planning to extend the practice of letting women work a shorter day or week, or to work at home. Mothers will have paid leave until their babies are eighteen months old. The number of paid days off granted to mothers to care for sick children will be increased. The lower-income families with children of up to twelve years of age will receive child allowances. We intend to satisfy fully the people's need for pre-school children's institutions within the next few years.[18]

Gorbachev's treatment of this issue included, however, a new element: the revival of the women's councils within places of work or in residential areas to 'resolve a wide range of social problems arising in the life of our society'. These women's councils, or *zhensovieti*, mushroomed in the following years, so that by April 1988 there were reported to be 236,000 such councils in existence, involving 2.3 million women. This emphasis on the political involvement of women was developed later to include the promotion of women within political organizations as a whole. Indeed, Gorbachev's treatment of issues relating to women and the family developed, as did so much of his policy, with an increasing radicalization as glasnost revealed the scope of the problems of 'private life'. By the time of the special Party conference in June 1988, Gorbachev was placing particular stress on the importance of women's political activity as such, beyond the restricted realm of the *zhensovieti* and improvements in 'everyday life': 'Women are not duly represented in governing bodies. And the women's movement as a whole, which gained momentum after the October Revolution, has gradually come to a standstill or become formal (that is, bureaucratized).'[19]

Beyond the policies themselves lay the issue of whether perestroika would succeed, bringing the political liberalization necessary for an effective women's movement to emerge, and consolidating the social services, consumer goods and living conditions that would materially benefit women. This issue would, in the long run, be decisive for women; yet it was precisely here that the contradictory character of the Soviet reforms became clearest. In the political sphere, Gorbachev called for a revival of women's soviets and women's movements. Yet as Soviet writers were soon to point out, the work of the *zhensovieti* required a willingness on the part of Party and employment officials to listen to what they said.

Declining state power and the rise of unofficial groups

The call for women to be promoted to positions of authority was immediately compromised by the decreasing power of the state – whatever Gorbachev called for was not necessarily going to occur. In the March 1989 elections to the Congress of People's Deputies the percentage of women elected fell by over half, from 34.5 per cent to 15.6 per cent. (This plummeting representation occurred throughout Eastern Europe. In Poland in January 1988 the number of women holding parliamentary seats fell from 20.2 per cent to 13.3; and after 1989 similar drops were registered in Romania [from one third of all seats to only 3.5 per cent]; in Czechoslovakia [from 29.5 per cent to 6 per cent]; in Hungary [from 20 per cent to 7 per cent].) In the local elections held in the spring of 1990 the percentage of women elected to the RSFSR Congress fell from 35 per cent to just 5 per cent. This was due in large part to the cancelling of previous quota systems which had guaranteed the representation of certain social groups such as workers, peasants and women; under these, women had 33 per cent of the seats in the Supreme Soviet and 50 per cent in local soviets. However, Gorbachev showed that he could and would act in areas under leadership control, such as in the promotion of women to more senior posts. In September 1988, for the first time in twenty-eight years, a woman, Alexandra Biriukova, was appointed a candidate member of the CPSU Politburo, a post she held until the reshuffle of July 1990. But amidst widespread indifference, and hostility to what was seen as traditional authoritarian imposition of quotas from above, it was unlikely that any state-led promotion of women's political presence would be successful. One of the pre-election opinion polls revealed the strength of popular prejudice against women in politics: 'being a man' was the *main* quality favoured in a candidate.

Outside the formal realm of institutionalized politics, glasnost opened up a new context for political action by unofficial groups – a few within the socialist tradition, others liberal, nationalist and religious. The years after 1985 saw a political explosion in the USSR as previously repressed tendencies erupted into public life. No greater limitations were placed on the formation of women's organizations and the expression of their demands than on any other group. All groups still had to ask permission to exist; not all did. Yet it was striking how, amidst this plethora of forces, new and old, feminist groups and gender issues appeared to play such a small role. The religious and nationalist groups paid scant attention to them, beyond routine calls for the end to women's 'involuntary emancipation' and return to the 'home and hearth'.[20] The 'informal' political forces were little better: in the People's Front that emerged in 1989, women's issues were not given any prominence, and women speakers seemed few and far between in the liberalized political atmosphere. Only five out of 1,256 delegates spoke at the June 1988 Party conference, and only one of these raised issues pertaining to women. Ironically, it seemed that Communist Party policy on women, which had not achieved their emancipation, succeeded instead in alienating the population from any support for ideas of women's equality.

The liberalization of the economy had even more contradictory implications for women. Official sources and newspapers were increasingly admitting that the supposed emancipation of women through participation in economic activity had not occurred. The findings of feminists and sociologists documenting the double burden of women's lives appeared in *Pravda, Izvestiya* and *Literaturnya Gazeta*; and the theoretical journal of the CPSU, *Kommunist*, even published the first feminist analysis of women's oppression in the USSR.[21] The unhealthy conditions under which many women worked, the evasions of protective legislation, women's low pay and their absence in positions of responsibility were all given widespread publicity.[22]

The social cost of economic rationalization

The priorities of perestroika, involving at least rationalization without technological restructuring, and at most, severe stabilization measures, will result in unemployment in the USSR for the first time in sixty years. Leonid Abalkin, deputy prime minister, told Parliament in 1989 that 16–19 million redundancies were expected by the year 2000. Women's representatives immediately expressed concern about the effects on women's jobs. Maria Lebedeva, addressing the plenary session of the Soviet Women's Committee, remarked that 'the scholars make no mention of who these people will be. Let's fill in the blanks: at least fifteen million of these will be women.[23] Other observers noted that the increased autonomy and cost-effectiveness required of enterprises would heighten managers' concerns about the social costs of employing women with children, especially after the increased maternity allowances which enterprises were in part responsible for. Zoya Pukhova, while chair of the Women's Committee, argued that 'in trying to exercise their right to have a short working day or a short working week, to have a sliding schedule or additional time off, women involuntarily come into conflict with management and the labour collective of the shop or brigade.'[24]

However, the matter is far from clear cut. The most vulnerable jobs are in the manufacturing sector, and the most vulnerable workers are the manual unskilled and semi-skilled, and auxiliary clerical staff. But while the first category certainly includes women, the axe could fall even more heavily on men's jobs. Moreover, women in their middle years in both unskilled and auxiliary jobs in industry, while vulnerable to redundancy, are expected to find other work more easily than men in the expanding and already feminized service sector.[25] Women could in theory also find employment in some of the newer light industries being planned. Segregated employment patterns, for all their disadvantages, especially in terms of pay, often serve as protected areas resistant to competition from new labour reserves.

Substantial female unemployment will occur (as it has already in Poland), but one certain outcome is an intensification of gender *segregation* in employment. Working women will find themselves assailed by contradictory messages. On the one hand, economists believe that women are still needed in the labour force, especially if the reform process results in the growth of new light industries and a more developed service sector; while on the other, women are being called upon to take greater responsibility in the home, and to have more children. More than one Soviet commentator has suggested that economic restructuring requiring the loss of labour makes it necessary for women to give up their jobs and return to the home to care for their families. A convenient link between increasing the population and raising productivity is thereby established. Predictably, the right-wing group of Russian patriots associated with *Pamyat* welcomes 'modernization' as a 'way to raise production standards and free woman from involuntary emancipation and return her to the family, where she fills the role of mother, keeper of the hearth and bulwark of the nation.'[26] However, this was not exclusively a neo-conservative and nationalist position: Gorbachev, too, referred to the 'purely womanly mission', investing domesticity and motherhood with an aura of the sacred and natural. Articles in the press frequently appeared calling for the restoration of a more 'natural' state of affairs 'where men are men and women are women'. (This has long been a trope in the social science literature, which in the 1970s and 1980s analysed the 'crisis of feminity' as resulting from 'women's emancipation' – that is, overwork.) Henceforth, efforts would be made to restore some balance in women's lives, which meant making it more possible than before for *women* to combine home and work responsibilities, and of course to have more children. A four-day working week for women, and shorter hours for mothers of young children, were seriously considered in 1990 by the USSR Supreme Soviet. But part-time work – the compromise that has evolved in the West, especially in Britain – has not been seen as feasible, because of the rigidities in the system. (There were only 700,000 registered part-time workers in the USSR, the majority of them female.) But one proposal being debated by Gorbachev's advisers in 1989 was the introduction of higher wages for men to enable them to support their dependent wives at home. This startling about-turn in Communist Party thinking was justified in humanitarian terms by one of Gorbachev's chief advisers as the only way that women would be relieved of the pressure of work and be able to stay with their young children.[27]

The reality for most women is that they will need to work, and that they will probably continue to have few children. Surveys reveal that women have taken advantage of the new maternity-leave provisions introduced selectively since 1981, but expressed little interest in giving up work altogether, even if men's wages were to rise significantly.[28] Unless the USSR remains in a major recession, it is likely that there will be jobs for women to do and women ready to do them. These factors may keep many Soviet women in the workforce, but they will only increase the divisions between men and women workers, both materially and ideologically, as motherhood and household tasks increasingly distinguish men from women as workers with different social attributes and different responsibilities.

The effects of economic liberalization in China

The discussion has so far focused on the implications of the disintegration of Communism for women in the former Soviet Union. One of the earliest hallmarks of perestroika was its claim that the Soviet Union no longer acted as the model for other socialist countries, which were now free to pursue different, national, paths of development. In the case of some countries, notably China, this had long been the position. In other countries formerly close to the Soviet model, for instance Cuba, there was great resistance to the new Soviet policy. Whilst in the USSR perestroika involved a simultaneous liberalization of economic and political life, in some of the less developed countries a measure of economic liberalization proceeded without comparable political change. This was so in China where the democracy movement was brutally repressed, and in Vietnam, Mozambique, Angola and – until its acceptance of political pluralism in late 1989 – South Yemen. Cuba, Albania and North Korea, resisting both forms of liberalization, were the exceptions. While recognizing that no single model exists, it is possible to make some observations about the ways in which Communist parties translated the pressure to reform into policies affecting women, focusing on two areas: population policy and economic liberalization.

China and Vietnam are perhaps the clearest instances of how these two policy areas converged. Both states adopted population-control policies in the 1970s as a way of addressing the problem of slow economic growth, and, especially in Britain pursued similar incentive packages to encourage a reduction in the birth rate. Both also introduced measures to relax state control over some sectors of the economy. More is known about the Chinese case, where the economic liberalization began earlier and where it converged in 1978 with the adoption of the one-child-family policy. This campaign, aimed at reducing the Chinese birth rate through a combination of incentives and punishments, was more effective in the urban than in the rural areas where production is household based and the availability of family labour is directly linked to economic success or failure.[29] Thus, paradoxically, the economic reforms, which enhanced the importance of the household as a unit of production have given an unforeseen advantage to those with large families.[30] The tensions generated by the conflict between these state policies have devolved most directly upon the female sex. There has been a rise in female infanticide, and in the abandonment or divorce of women who give birth to daughters; and the toll on the mental and physical health of women who transgress the law is considerable. Many of these problems are exacerbated by the maintenance in China of customary marriage practices which reinforce the preference for sons over daughters. Sons are valued more because they retain responsibility for the natal family when they marry, and this means providing for their parents in their old age. Daughters marry and leave their family of origin and are expected to vest their interests in their husband's kin. The one-child policy, when added to these practices, greatly increases the premium on having a male child: many couples defy the law and suffer the consequences, the women bearing the brunt of social ostracism, late abortion and sometimes involuntary sterilization.

The economic reforms known as the 'four modernizations', which came into effect in 1978, have also affected women directly, with China going further than many other reforming states in liberalizing certain economic activities, and permitting practices previously banned, such as advertising and Western films. China's efforts to modernize and stimulate production have also involved a rationalization of enterprises to put them on a more profitable basis. As in the USSR and Eastern Europe, this has involved tightening up work practices and laying off labour. Evidence suggests that women's work is particularly vulnerable, and it is they who are often called upon to give up their jobs.[31] Discrimination against women at work is also on the increase, and with unemployment high, enterprise managers have no trouble filling vacancies with men. They tend to see women as a more expensive workforce, as a result of paid maternity leave, crèches and earlier retirement; but since it is usually the husband's employer who supplies the couple's accommodation, this should in theory equalize the costs.[32]

Changing patterns of discrimination

Testimony to the changes is an increasingly self-confident discrimination against women in China. Amidst the growing criticisms of earlier policies – especially the extremes of the Cultural Revolution – prejudice against women occurs in the guise of being realistic about 'natural' differences between the sexes. The famous Iron Girls, once cast in the role of the heroines of work, capable of doing men's jobs as well as men, are now openly derided as 'fake men'. There is more talk, even by the Women's Federation, of recognizing sexual difference, and less of denying or minimizing it. Soon after the policy changes of 1978, women began to be transferred out of jobs such as train driving or construction work into lower-paid work as clerks, or into light-industry female ghettos. Others were simply dismissed. Women were openly talked of as being especially suitable for boring, repetitive jobs because they were good at rote learning and were conscientious. Delia Davin has listed the forms of open discrimination typical of the period of reform:

Factories and other enterprises either demand higher examination scores from female secondary school graduates who apply for employment, or turn them down outright. Technical and vocational schools which take secondary school leavers discriminate against females except for recruitment to training courses in traditional female skills such as nursing, office work and kindergarten teaching. Even university graduates suffer from this prejudice against employing women. Only just over a quarter of students in higher education are female, and China is desperately short of graduates, yet the officials in charge of job assignment report not only that many work units prefer male graduates, but that some reject all women or accept only a tiny number. There have been cases where men with poor marks have been preferred over women with excellent ones, and a notorious instance where members of a laser institute made every effort to recruit a student on the strength of a brilliant graduation thesis, only to change their minds when they discovered her sex. The problem of allocating female graduates is now so serious that some universities have considered reducing the number of female students they will accept.[33]

Although discrimination was rife in the pre-1978 period, it has lately grown on the more fertile soil of the new economic and ideological configurations, and acquired a new boldness.

On the other hand, the relaxation after 1981 of controls over small-scale production has given women forms of income-generating activity some of which can be highly profitable, and which, because they are usually home based, can be combined with childcare and domestic responsibilities more easily than most forms of waged work. The Women's Federation of China, deploring the conditions most women face in industrial jobs, has even expressed the view that women should keep out of industry if they can, as it places them under too much pressure. It has called on women instead to make 'commodity production' – that is, 'sideline' activities – their favoured area of work. This kind of small enterprise is found equally in the urban and the rural areas. In the former, women more typically work with other members of the family running small businesses providing goods and services. Though women may benefit from sideline production and from the higher standard of living it could bring, there are longer-term dangers inherent in the deepening sexual division of labour that has attended women's reintegration into family-based production and abdication from the public realm of work. Moreover, as feminist scholars have pointed out, although the old work-point system contained its own inequalities, it had the merit of making women's contributions visible, and conferring status on the earner. In the new family-based production systems, the income generated is more often than not controlled by the male family head, and women's contribution is usually invisible.

The new property laws also have negative consequences for women. Land has become available to households through the contract system, which is usually made out to male heads of household. As Delia Davin notes, 'a peasant woman's access to the means of income generation . . . now depends on her relationship to a man. This contrasts sharply with the collective era when membership of the collective conferred use-rights to the means of production.'[34] This reinscription of women into the household has been compounded in the countryside by the feminization of agriculture, as men have left to take up more profitable work elsewhere. Although this has placed women in key roles as producers, and sometimes placed them at the head of the household, they are performing work that is unpopular, arduous and usually badly paid.

New signs of cultural oppression

In the industrial sector, economic liberalization in China has brought with it enterprise competition and Western investment; it has also introduced cultural phenomena previously banned. One example is advertising, which appeared in the 1980s for the first time in forty years. Before the massacre in Tiananmen Square, advertising expenditure was growing by more than 30 per cent a year, peaking at US \$227 million in 1986, 5–10 per cent of which was accounted for by the multinational corporations. The Women's Federation has protested at the uses being made of images of women models, and has called for government controls. But it is not just imported imagery that has brought about changes in the portrayal of women: by the mid-1980s the familiar images of socialist iconography – the smiling woman worker at her machine – were being taken down from public hoardings and factory walls. In their place stood the proud housewife, the new consumer, pictured beside her washing machine.[35]

At the popular level, as in the northern cases discussed earlier, there has occurred a reaction to the old puritanism and what could be seen as the return of a repressed femininity, as young women attend to the details of hair, clothes and make-up, and grow anxious again about standards of female beauty and shape. In the literature of the past decade, women writers have been free to reflect on the pain of the hard years of work and self-denial, and have returned to the persistent theme of the lost pleasures of motherhood, of the guilt experienced in leaving the children in care, sometimes for months on end, to fulfil the demands of work. Again, some observers have detected an undertow of 'West is best', and the attendant danger that the disillusion with the past becomes a thirst for its antithesis.

In general, it is clear that those able to afford them can now benefit from the wider availability of domestic appliances and consumer goods. In the period before the student protests, greater tolerance of public debate and discussion permitted the expression of views critical of official and more conservative opinion. The Women's Federation, and on occasion independent women, articulated feminist arguments defending women's place in society as the equals of men. But such feminist movements or networks that might have emerged as part of the democracy movement would find it difficult to mobilize in the atmosphere of fear characteristic of the post-Tiananmen period.

Old problems, new struggles

It is evident that the changes under way in the Communist states produced, in a variety of countries, a major shift away from some of the central tenets of Communist Party belief and policy with respect to women. This is as true of official thinking as it is of publicly expressed popular attitudes. If the old policies, based on a combination of some principle and much instrumentalism, had the merit of promoting positive changes in the name of 'women's emancipation', their overall validity, and the legitimacy of their official language, are now in doubt. The 'woman question', a phrase as redolent of old thinking as 'internationalism', may well disappear, and gender issues – if raised at all – will henceforth be formulated in a very different political language.

The paradox of this change is, however, that the underlying problem will endure: the absence in most countries of a strong feminist input into policy – whether from above or below – means that the policies adopted with respect to women will continue to be determined by the overall priorities of the state, whether economic, demographic or social. Questions of social justice, visions of a society in which old privileges and authority patterns have been surpassed, are unlikely to form an integral part of the new direction of economic development, which for the foreseeable future is more likely to be premised on harsh policies of economic stabilization and adjustment.

As in the pre-reform period, the issue is not so much one of how great the commitment of the state is to women's emancipation, but rather of the very conception of gender relations upon which future policies will be based. The particular issue of gendered divisions in employment and in the home was never seriously tackled by government policies. Instead, in most countries, while the material effects of inequality (women's double burden) were deplored, the divisions themselves, far from being seen as socially constructed, were increasingly talked of as natural, even desirable, by planners and populace alike, as a reaction to the extremism of earlier years.

Traditional gender divisions were reinforced through the structural and ideological biases inherent in policy and in the organization of society. Scarcity and financial hardship deepened the division of labour and mutual dependency in the family. For many households living on the edge of economic viability, both men and women performed a 'double shift': men took a second job or worked in the informal economy, while women put their remaining energies after a day out at work into managing the household, bartering scarce goods and services, and caring for children and relatives. The family, despite all its tensions, evident in soaring divorce rates, was often regarded as a refuge or as a site of resistance against the authoritarian state and suffocating public life. Many women expressed longings to have motherhood and feminity restored to them. These factors taken together implied that reforms aimed at reinforcing women's ties to the family would find substantial resonance within the populations of these states, even if their effect was to intensify gender segregation and inequality. Meanwhile, the threatened roll-back of women's reproductive rights, particularly with respect to abortion, gathered pace in a number of countries as a result of religious, demographic or neo-conservative pressures. In the USSR this issue attracted more attention in a period of 'openness' and speaking the truth. The high abortion rate and horrific conditions in clinics (something which Mamonova's group condemned, and were charged with making anti-Soviet propaganda for revealing) have been the subject of wide public discussion since 1985. The fact that the number of abortions exceeds live births is not so much discussed as a failing of the system's provision of birth-control devices, but as a moral failing of the society – and, to be more precise, is seen as another symptom of corrupted femininity. In other states, legislative changes quickly gathered pace. In Poland, for example, a bill to 'defend the unborn child' by criminalizing abortion was introduced in June 1989. It proposed a three-year prison sentence, for those infringing the law. In Germany, unification under Christian Democracy threatened to impose restrictions on abortion in the East, to bring it more into line with the West where it is illegal unless a panel of doctors argues that it is necessary in order to avoid 'physical or social distress'. Efforts to impose restrictions on the East were successfully resisted in 1990 by feminist campaigners who mounted demonstrations in defence of the existing law. However, the resulting compromise is certain to be overturned in the future. Under Communist legislation, abortion on demand was legal in East Germany, and free up to the twelfth week of pregnancy.[36]

In the field of political representation, similar limitations recur. The new commitment – evident at least in the USSR – to a greater political role for women and to the revival of a women's movement was again limited by the continuation of traditional assumptions within government circles. Although these were being challenged by more feminist perspectives, they still had considerable weight. Political liberalization did, however, open up a space for autonomous women's movements and the raising of feminist issues, and it may be that in time these movements could gain strength and emerge as a significant feminist current in the post-Communist countries. That such movements should be free to publish and press their demands is a necessary precondition for any real challenge to prevailing gender in-equalities in the social distribution of power and rewards in these societies. It is also essential that they play a part in debates over welfare provision and the negative effects of marketization, and in challenging the simplified view of 'Western' freedom, with its elisions and indulgences of sexism in its various guises.

The prospects for Soviet feminism

In the early days of perestroika Soviet women, some of them self-proclaimed feminists, began to make their voices heard. Professional women, among them social scientists, lawyers and journalists, added their criticisms of the social order to the general clamour in their different countries. Women's groups and networks expanded, with new organizations appearing and gathering strength. In the RSFSR by the end of the 1980s, women-focused groups and clubs were springing up, predominant among them literary and arts associations like 'Herald', a Moscow club for women writers; 'Women's Creative Effort', organized by Tatyana Ryabikina; and Olga Bessolova's 'Club of Women's Initiatives' – all serving to promote and encourage members' work. Women film-makers and journalists also established their own clubs, and a Council of Women Writers was set up under the auspices of the existing Writers' Union. The first Gender Studies Centre was established in the Moscow Institute for Socio-Economic Problems of the Population. The objectives of these groups varied, as did their perspectives on women's issues; for example, the 'Transfiguration' (*Preobrazheniye*) Women's Club working in the Academy of Sciences aimed to 'enhance women's role and initiative within the sociocultural spheres'. In Leningrad the human-rights activist Olga Lipovskaya, publisher of the only samizdat magazine for women, *Zhenskoye Chteniye* (Women's Reading), expressed the view that women's situation could not be seriously improved without restructuring the entire social system. *Zhenskoye* contained poetry, essays, and even some articles by Western feminists.[37]

Despite a prevailing climate of hostility and ignorance of the women's movement, some women, like Olga Voroninova, Anastasya Posadskaya, Valentina Konstantinova and Natalya Zakharova of the 'Lotos' group, openly identified themselves as 'self-confessed' feminists, and participated in several international forums bringing women from different countries together for debate. 'Lotos' stands for 'Liberation from social stereotypes', and its members shared a commitment to undertaking theoretical work on gender inequalities. Among other things, they gave publicity to the issues of male violence against women, and the rising incidence of rape in some of the Soviet republics. In articles and public meetings, they also discussed the taboo subject of sexuality, condemning the puritanism and ignorance that surrounds it. Collectively, they rejected the dominant view of the family crisis, arguing that it resulted from the as yet incomplete transition from 'patriarchy to egalitarianism', and that Gorbachev's policies aimed simply to shore up a system that did not work. Consequently, the group took a stand against current attempts to redomesticate Russian women, and called for the equal sharing between men and women of household responsibilities.[38] On 24 July 1990 they helped to found the Independent Women's Democratic Initiative and to draft its declaration. Two members of 'Lotos' helped to write the *Kommunist* article (see note 21), and as a result were invited to submit a position paper to the Council of Deputies, which was later accepted. Some of their members were allowed a role in formulating policy as advisers to an executive body of the Supreme Soviet which concerned itself with 'the position of women, protection of maternity and childhood, and strengthening of the family'.

Nina Belyaeva, a feminist campaigner, has spoken in optimistic terms of feminism's prospects in the USSR, but noted that this was not a common view: 'The women's groups . . . I am told, still amount to a drop in the bucket [sic] – and are without clear goals or independence, all of them intellectual clubs.' She added that most women were too exhausted to have the energy for clubs and movements, and speculated that 'perhaps feminism is only for a well-fed society'.[39] If feminism had taken a precarious hold in the Communist states prior to the reforms, on account of state repression, it now addressed equally resistant forces within civil society. More than in any other formerly Communist country, feminism in the Soviet Union faces particularly entrenched opposition. It is derided and caricatured by men and women alike in a social context where anti-feminism draws on motherhood as a powerful cultural symbol to essentialize sexual difference. The writer Tatyana Tolstaya has attacked feminism's 'Western' rationality for misunderstanding Russian womanhood. She counterposes the idea that Russian women are the embodiment of real power in society, a power wielded within the family, 'at times extending to tyranny'. Soviet society, a product of its repressive history and sentimental culture, has, she claims, become almost matriarchal. Soviet women apparently do not need more power than they already have, they do not aspire to equality with men, they do not want to work or participate in politics, they are not oppressed by men (who are poor, weak and broken things, mere 'property' like 'furniture').[40] However problematic and, arguably, unsubstantiated such notions of female 'power' are, Russian feminists have had to take account of such pervasive but confused sentiments in their campaigns, in order to avoid political marginalization.

Feminist currents in Eastern Europe

Feminist currents – even movements – were active during the 1980s in other East and Central European countries. In Hungary, feminists participated in the opposition movements, and sociologists played an important role by focusing attention on women's particular vulnerability to poverty and overwork. Although most of these currents were composed of educated professional women, there were also signs of working-class discontent and mobilization around concrete women's issues. For the first time, women's sections appeared in some trade unions, with the aim of defending and advancing women's working conditions.[41] In early 1990 a Hungarian Women's Association was formed, and after much debate decided to identify itself as feminist. In Yugoslavia, feminists speak of the existence of a women's movement, its activists campaigning on issues such as violence against women, for reproductive and gay and lesbian rights, and for policy changes via family laws and party-political involvement.[42] And even in Catholic Poland, where feminism had very little impact on Solidarity's policies, there were stirrings in 1989 when Polish women demonstrated in their thousands against the proposed bill to criminalize abortion. In October, some of those involved in the campaign for reproductive rights founded the Polish Feminist Association. A feminist newspaper, *Baba Polka*, appeared and campaigned to defend reproductive rights. At government level there were moves to set up a women's group to advise on policy matters.

In East Germany, where feminists initiated the independent peace movement and were sufficiently established to organize demonstrations and meetings, the issues they raised were debated within opposition organizations such as Neues Forum. Feminist discussion circles generated a number of political initiatives, including the Berlin-based association known as 'Sophie'. In 1989 a group of feminists from Leipzig left Neues Forum because the leadership opposed parity of representation for men and women. They joined the newly founded Independent Women's Association, whose manifesto demanded 'genuine equality and emancipation for women', and called for an end to divisions of labour at home and at work, and shorter working hours for both men and women. In a detailed exposition of its premises and demands, the association outlined its social programme, which sought to retain the gains of the past but overcome the 'patriarchal power stuctures' that oppress and exclude women. Although supporting unification, the association favoured 'a mutual process of reform' that respected 'the internal sovereignty of both states'. It argued for a society based on a market economy, but with some planning role for the state to guarantee democracy and progressive, ecologically responsible social policies. The association called for a 'Ministry of Equity' to be established; for a comprehensive revaluation of women's work in the home and economy; and it favoured quotas for women and men in the areas of social life where one sex predominates. It pledged itself to resist the restrictions on abortion threatened by the process of reunification.[43] The association achieved some political influence in the Modrow government, nominating a minister without portfolio, and helped to draft the Social Charter and draw up plans for a women's ministry. In a joint campaign with the Green Party it received 2.7 per cent of the vote.[44]

In most northern states these manifestations of feminism were paralleled by a small but growing representation of feminist ideas and concerns in the press, not only by journalists and writers but also in letters from readers. These may not have represented the dominant views, but they indicated the existence of a range of popular opinion that echoed the concern already articulated by feminists on questions of work, discrimination and the 'double burden'.

The manner in which East European and Soviet feminists formulate their political priorities are necessarily shaped by the particular circumstances and cultural conditions in their own regions, as well as by differences of theoretical approach. Yugoslavian feminists linked women's issues to racial discrimination against the ethnic Albanians, and opposed sterilization programmes in Kosovo. The same is true of Hungarian feminists in relation to the gypsy population. In East Germany, peace issues have always come to the fore, and the Women's Association has campaigned with other groups for disarmament and demilitarization, in addition to preparing itself for the abrupt and drastic changes in social provision which result from unification. Although a broad consensus exists among feminist groups on the question of abortion and contraception on demand, the need to campaign for social equality, and on issues such as violence and sexuality, there are nonetheless significant differences of approach and analysis. In Russia, there exists a stronger current of support for ideas of sexual difference than is the case in Hungary, East Germany or Yugoslavia, with Russian feminists like Larisa Kuznetsova arguing that women and men have innately different psychologies, and that women's embody superior ethical values, reflected in their caring and nurturing roles.[45] As women become mobilized as political actors, it is inevitable that differences of politics and of perspective will increasingly be reflected both within and between women's movements.

The future: emancipation or new forms of domination?

The first five years of perestroika in the USSR delivered little to women in material terms, and in a number of other countries they were considerably worse off than under the old regime. In most states more women than men have been laid off from work, and everywhere the burden of domestic provisioning has increased, as shortages imposed by rationing have been replaced by those created by rising prices. Fears of further unemployment grow along with concern over cuts in public expenditure. Russian feminists pointed out that the deterioration of social life and proliferating violence in the USSR also have gendered effects – as evidenced by the increase in wife battering and in the growing incidence of rape.

Yet were the reforms to succeed, the overall improvement in economic conditions would greatly reduce the everyday pressures to which women are subjected, and thereby in some measure realize the early Bolshevik hope that economic and scientific advance could lessen the burden of household chores on women, principally by altering the sexual division of labour. As long as men are paid higher wages than women, and as long as many men have to perform two jobs in order to gain an adequate income, then gender roles within the family will not be redefined. The preconditions for tackling the sexual division of labour are, on the one hand, a recognition of this goal by the state and organized civic groups, and on the other, greater employment flexibility in place of the current system which locks men into rigid employment patterns. Women should have the same earning power as men, with both sexes allowed more time for parenting and domestic responsibilities. As Zakharova et al. have said, 'emancipation is a two-way process: men must be given opportunities to participate more in housework and child raising . . . We think that men as well as women should be able to combine parenthood and career ... direct and indirect discrimination against women in the workplace and men in the family should be eliminated.'[46] Their call for government measures and a review of existing legislation to help bring this about underlines the importance of women's claims on the institutions of government in a period when their influence and representation remain minimal.

The socialist programme of women's emancipation was always subordinated to a particular economic model – a result of socialist theory and revolutionary state practice alike. Women's emancipation is certainly dependent upon the direction of economic policy: no programme of social change can be divorced from the general economic conditions in which it takes place. Yet in order to succeed, the policies of perestroika would have to be expanded to include a commitment to establishing real gender equality, coupled with a mobilization of civic support for such a programme. That commitment cannot be derived from, nor formulated to meet, the requirements of economic development alone. In the end, the issue in question is whether the changes being implemented within the former planned economies could eventually provide the opportunity to realize a greater degree of emancipation for women, or whether prevailing attitudes will remain unchanged, and women's inequality will be confirmed by the introduction of new forms of discrimination. Either outcome is possible, but the evidence to date provides few grounds for optimism.

Notes

This article is an excerpt from my forthcoming book *Mobilization without Emancipation? Women, the Communist State and Its Demise* (Verso, London). Thanks to the many friends here and abroad for help in gathering materials and for comments on earlier versions of this article, especially to Barbara Einhorn, Alistair McAuley, Hilary Pilkington and Anastasya Posadskya.

1. The qualified use of the term 'socialist' prefixed by 'existing' is now an anachronism. No entirely suitable adjective to describe these former states has yet emerged: 'Soviet-type', 'socialist', 'Communist', 'state-socialist' can all be objected to on various grounds. Where, for the sake of brevity, I refer to 'Communist' states or centrally planned economies (CPEs), this is simply a shorthand for those countries which are or were ruled by Communist parties, and claimed allegiance to Marxist doctrine, placing a substantial proportion of their economies under state control.

2. For critiques and assessments of the Communist project with respect to women, see Barbara Wolf Jancar, *Women Under Communism* (Baltimore, 1978); Gail Lapidus, *Women in Soviet Society* (Los Angeles, 1978); Sonia Kruks et al. (eds), *Promissory Notes* (New York, 1980); Hilda Scott, *Does Socialism Liberate Women?* (Boston, 1984); and my 'Women's emancipation in socialist states: a model for the Third World?', *World Development*, 9/10 (1981). On China, see especially Kay Ann Johnson, *Women, the Family and Peasant Revolution in China* (Chicago, 1983); and Judith Stacey, *Patriarchy and Socialist Revolution in China* (California, 1983).

3. Labour force calculated as percentage of population aged 15–54. Data from the United Nations publication, *World Survey on the Role of Women in Development* (New York, 1986), and *The Economic Role of Women in the ECE Region: Developments 1974–85* (New York,

1985). These figures are lower than those given by national sources, a disparity due to different methods of calculation.

4. *ILO World Labour Report* (Geneva, 1985).

5. Author's interview with A.G. Karchev, then head of the Institute of Sociology, Moscow, and leading specialist on the family. For discussion, see my 'Family reform in socialist states: the hidden agenda', *Feminist Review*, 21 (Winter 1985).

6. For a vivid account of the nature of Bolshevik intervention in Central Asia in the 1920s, see G. Massel, *The Surrogate Proletariat: Moslem Women and Revolutionary Strategies in Soviet Central Asia 1919–20* (Princeton, 1974).

7. Data from the USSR Central Statistical Administration, reported in *Izvestiya*, translated in *Current Digest of the Soviet Press*, XXXIX (1987).

8. On the Soviet Union, see Alistair McAuley, *Women's Work and Wages in the USSR* (London, 1981).

9. Elena Ceausescu, Vilma Espín and Madame Mao illustrate this point.

10. One of the first acts of the newly liberalized Polish and East German Communist youth magazines was the publication of photographs of naked women, as a sign of their new freedom from orthodoxy. Rupert Murdoch, quick to cash in on the current mood, launched a new tabloid in Hungary called *Reform*, which, with its 'full-frontal female nudes', had by 1990 claimed a circulation of over 400,000 and is expected to produce annual profits of one million dollars. Such images were still outlawed in the Soviet press, but cooperatives were able to produce Pirelli-inspired calendars for sale to the general public. Meanwhile, Komsomol, the Communist youth organization, has presented 'beauty contests' which the Russian feminist Olga Voroninova has described as little more than 'porno shows' (*Tageszeitung*, 24 November 1989). (In 1989, in a more domestic vein, Komsomol organized a 'Wife of the Year' competition.) With respect to pornography, in a context where sex and eroticism were hitherto identified as pornographic, and 'perpetrators' were severely dealt with, it is little wonder that notions of sexual freedom are crudely fashioned, and feminist criticisms dismissed as yet another form of authoritarian intrusion.

11. A definition of feminism is in order here; but such attempts run the risk of being either too broad and inclusive, failing to distinguish between female militancy or solidarity and feminist objectives, or too narrow and based on assumptions that may be sectarian and/or ethnocentric. That there are different feminisms as well as different women's movements alerts us to the heterogeneity of women's interests, and to the varying ways in which they are socially constructed. But what most definitions of feminism agree upon is that as a social movement and body of ideas it challenges the structures and power relations that produce female subordination. Where I refer here to specific groups or individuals as 'feminist', this is because (a) they designate themselves as such; and (b) they conform to the above definition.

12. For a full account, see Alix Holt, 'The first Soviet feminists', in B. Holland (ed.), *Soviet Sisterhood* (London, 1986).

13. Barbara Einhorn, 'Sisters across the curtain: women speak out in East and West Europe', *END Journal of European Nuclear Disarmament*, February 1984; and 'Socialist emancipation: the women's movement in the GDR', in Kruks et al., *Promissory Notes* (Monthly Review Press, New York, 1989).

14. For details, see my 'The politics of abortion in Nicaragua', *Feminist Review*, 29 (Spring 1988); and 'Mobilization without emancipation', *Feminist Studies*, 2 (1985).

15. The Frente Continental was established in Cuba after the 1980 UN Decade for Women mid-decade conference in Nairobi.

16. Films and novels by women contributed to the former in no small measure. For the USSR, see especially Natalya Baranskaya, *A Week Like Any Other*, translated and published by Seal Press, 1990.

17. See Hilary Pilkington, 'Abortion, contraception and the future of Mother Russia', mimeograph.

18. *Soviet News*, 26 February 1986.

19. *Soviet News*, 19 June 1988.

20. 'Statement of the Bloc of Russian Public Patriotic Movements', *Current Digest of the Soviet Press*, 42, 1 (7 February 1990).

21. N. Zakharova, A. Posadskaya and N. Rimashevskaya, 'How we are resolving the women's question', *Kommunist*, 4 (March 1989); translated in *Current Digest of the Soviet Press*, 41, 19 (1989), and discussed by Cynthia Cockburn in *Marxism Today*, July 1989. The authors have now founded a Gender Studies Centre in Moscow.

22. According to Zakharova et al., almost 33 per cent of all women earn less than 100 roubles per month, while the corresponding figure for men is 2 per cent. Some 90 per cent of low-paid employees are women, while 7 per cent of women hold positions of authority, compared with 48 per cent of men.

23. See the report by Maria Lebedeva from the plenary session of the Soviet Women's Committee, in *Izvestiya*, 23 October 1988, p. 6, excerpted in *Current Digest of the Soviet Press*, 40 (1988), p. 23.

24. *Pravda*, 2 July 1988.

25. See Alistair McAuley, 'Perestroika: implications for employment', in Martin Macauley (ed.), *Gorbachev and Perestroika* (London, 1990).

26. 'Statement of the Bloc of Russian Public Patriotic Movements'. This discourse is given particular meaning within nationalist movements, where the reintegration of women within the family is seen as part of the move against the oppressive Soviet legacy. This patriarchal chauvinism is clearly visible, for instance, in the Smallholder's Party of Hungary (slogan 'God, Fatherland and Family') which sees sovietization as responsible for 'denaturing women'.

27. Author's conversation with Tatyana Zaslavskaya, author of *The Second Soviet Revolution* (London, 1989).

28. Polls conducted in the RSFSR have so far shown that less than 20 per cent of women would choose to give up work even if their family incomes remained constant. The picture is very different in Poland and Hungary, where women's responses are more varied, with around 45 per cent preferring to give up work. V. Bodrova and R. Anker, *Working Women in Socialist Countries: The Fertility Connection* (Geneva, 1985).

29. Repressive measures are especially prevalent in Tibet. As a national minority, Tibetans are allowed two children, but refugees report mounting pressure (through forced abortions and sterilizations) to have only one. Third children have no claims on welfare provision or employment.

30. E. Croll, D. Davin and P. Kane, *China's One Child Family Policy* (London, 1985); E. Croll, 'The state and the single child policy', in G. White (ed.), *The Chinese State: in the Era of Economic Reform* (London, 1991); and Delia Davin, 'Gender and population in the PRC', in Haleh Afshar (ed.), *Women, State and Ideology: Studies from Africa and Asia* (London, 1987).

31. Marilyn Young, 'Chicken Little in China: women after the Cultural Revolution', in Kruks et al., *Promissory Notes*.

32. See E. Croll, 'New peasant family forms in rural China', *Journal of Peasant Studies*, July 1987; Delia Davin, 'Women, work and property in the Chinese peasant household of the 1980s', in Diane Elson (ed.), *Male Bias in the Development Process* (Manchester, 1990).

33. Delia Davin, 'Chinese models of development and their implications for women', in Haleh Afshar (ed.), *Women, Development and Survival in the Third World* (London, 1991).

34. Delia Davin, 'The new inheritance law and the peasant household', *Journal of Communist Studies*, 3 (December 1987).

35. E. Croll, *China After Mao* (London, 1984).

36. More than one-third of pregnancies ended in abortion in East Germany in 1990; in the West, the International Planned Parenthood Federation estimates that approximately 15–20 per cent of pregnancies end in abortion each year – about 85,000 of which are legal and another 45,000 illegal or performed abroad; *International Herald Tribune*, 15 May 1990.

37. *In These Times*, 21–7 March 1990.

38. From the paper presented to the Fifth Annual Conference of the European Forum of Socialist Feminists held in Sweden in November 1989; and author's interview.

39. *In These Times*, 21–7 March 1990.

40. Tolstaya identifies women as the true soul of the nation – the trope beloved of nationalists and conservatives. See her enthusiastic review of Francine du Plessix Gray, *Soviet Women Walking the Tightrope* (New York, 1990), in *NYRB*, 31 May 1990. For a critical response to Du Plessix Gray's portrait of Russian women, see the review by K. van den Heuvel in *The Nation*, 4 June 1990.

41. This was also happening in the GDR in 1989.

42. Lepa Mladjenovic, 'Summary on Women's Movement in Yugoslavia' [sic]. Paper presented to the workshop on women's movements, Institute of Social Studies, The Hague, May 1990.

43. Programme of the East German Independent Women's Association, translated by Barbara Einhorn and published in *East European Reporter*, 4, 2 (Summer 1990).

44. Irene Dolling, 'Between hope and helplessness – women in the GDR after "The Turning Point" ', mimeograph.

45. Larisa Kuznetsova quoted in *In These Times*, 21–7 March 1990. See also Du Plessix Gray, and C. Hansson and K. Liden, *Moscow Women* (London, 1980), for ample illustration of the strength of such views among Soviet women. Maternalist and essentializing movements have always posed particular difficulties for feminists, and yet they are among the most common forms of female collective action. In Latin America, for example, women, often in the poorer communities, have been involved in struggles for basic needs provision, citizenship rights, and for other goals such as peace and democracy. Movements of this kind are closely identified with particular social constructions of femininity and motherhood, and the women who participate in these actions often see their politics as a natural extension of their roles in the family, and as based on primordial, intrinsically feminine sentiments. The goals of these movements are usually formulated in altruistic terms rather than as ones designed to advance the particular interests of the actors. In most of these cases, women identify their interests with the household, the welfare of its members, and its conditions of existence in the community. However limited in practice, essentializing movements based on motherhood are not by definition incompatible with all forms of feminism – it depends on their goals, and whether, in defending or celebrating motherhood, they challenge the social devaluation and subordination associated with it.

46. N. Zakharova et al., 'The women's question and perestroika'.

SECTION VI

THE POLITICS OF FEMINISM

One of the clichés of the contemporary media is that we live in a 'post-feminist' age. In order to demonstrate this view – which would, of course, be most convenient to patriarchal social interests – commentators cite the disillusion of young women with feminism and the apparently widespread wish of women to return to a traditional role. Feminists would counter this argument by pointing out that women have never actually left their traditional role: it is entirely mythical to suppose that women have stopped beings wives (or partners in heterosexual relationships) and mothers. On the contrary, women now have both their traditional domestic role and the new one, of wage-earner.

However, rational argument has never been over-present amongst men who feel themselves in some way threatened by changes in the social position of women. Whilst many feminist battles have been fought with assistance from sympathetic men, the battles have been against men who have perceived in the emancipation of women an attack on the rights and privileges of men. The success – rather than the failure – of contemporary feminism can be seen in the eagerness with which men such as Neil Lyndon express inarticulate arguments about 'feminism going too far' and the 'evil of feminism'.[1]

These ideas might not be worth rational discussion were they not so liable to become incorporated in the social world as 'fact'. As Susan Faludi has argued, and convincingly demonstrated, in her book *Backlash*,[2] the media are capable of constructing reality according to their own needs, needs which are related to the gendered pattern of the control of information and communication. The notable successes which women in the West have achieved in recent years (for example through campaigns about the judicial treatment of rape victims and women's right to participate in questions related to the medical organization of childbirth) have been vigorously contested, and issues that touch on women's sexuality (such as abortion and access to contraception) remain widely controversial. In the 1992 presidential campaign in the United States, for example, the issue of abortion played a central part in debates between the candidates.

The majority of feminists would now support the principle of women's right to determine whether or not to have an abortion. This position is not, as its opponents suggest, an argument in favour of abortion *per se* but an assertion of women's right to personal autonomy and self-determination.

The debate about abortion, which seems – at least in the United States – to go on and on, is the most recent manifestation of the contest for the control and regulation of women's behaviour. As Carol Smart has argued in *Regulating Womanhood*, the essential issue in debates about women is the question of who should decide what is appropriate behaviour for women.[3] In any society it is the most powerful who define social norms and values and regulate individual behaviour. In the great majority of societies it has been men who have had the greater degree of social power and hence greater scope for implementing the regulation of women. This is far short of arguing that patriarchy rules the world, since although patterns of universal misogyny can be established and documented, the degree of control of these patterns, and the processes through which they are organized, differs widely. Further, blanket arguments about patriarchy obscure the considerable material differences between societies and cultures. A rapid glance around the contemporary world suggests that whilst women can gain from the individualism of the West, there is also a sense, as many feminists outside the West fully recognize, in which women's social position is consistently more precarious in societies which have accepted theoretical equality between the sexes. Indeed, more traditional societies – in which women's childbearing role is accepted as central to their existence – can provide patterns of social relationships which are very much to the advantage of women.

But a respect for the organization of sexual difference in non-Western societies can become a romantic, and romanticized, account of women's lives in these societies. It has to be said emphatically that discourses about choice, emancipation and liberation, which may be appropriate to women in the West, are often singularly inappropriate in societies in which women, and men, spend their lives in a daily struggle for material survival. Without detracting from the considerable differences in material circumstance between women in the West, it must be acknowledged that the overall differences between North and South are so considerable as to make global generalizations about the condition of women impossible.

In this context, and in the face of mounting evidence about the degree of ill-health and deprivation faced by women even in societies – such as the old Soviet Union – once regarded as relatively prosperous, a feminist programme has to address diverse needs. In parts of Asia and much of Africa the basic survival needs of women – adequate food, clean water and basic medical supplies – have yet to be met. Yet in these societies, just as much as in the industrial North, the agenda of feminism must be concern as much with the form of change as with its content. Where feminists can make a global common cause is on the issue of the right of women to control and influence decisions affecting their lives. Although all political decisions in all societies affect all members of those societies, it is vastly to the disadvantage of women if collective decisions are seen as gender neutrality. Asserting gender difference – and its material implications – has to have a central place on any feminist agenda. Without this assertion, the needs and rights of women are all too apt to disappear.

But although the particular needs of women in general need to be established in any public (or indeed private) discussions, so too do the particular needs of particular women. To use the term 'woman' in the West can carry with it coercive understandings which assume that, for example, a 'woman' is necessarily white, and/or heterosexual. For women of colour, and for women who choose to have sexual relationships outside conventional heterosexuality, the arrogant simplicity of the single term 'woman' can carry a deeply discriminatory meaning. The 'woman question' in the 1990s is an issue of both simplicity and complexity: female (and female desire and femininity) have to be established alongside 'male' as a form of human existence at the same time as the diversity of the female condition has to be acknowledged and allowed. Equally, as Mary McIntosh points out in her concluding essay to Sex Exposed: Sexuality and the Pornography Debate, there is now no turning back from the acknowledgement of women as agencies of history.[4] What remains problematic is their relationship to and/or collusion with patriarchy; in the same collection Mandy Merck raises complex issues (in the context of pornography and her own work on desire) about the political issues involved in refusing to acknowledge the context of debates about sexuality. Since a tradition of great intellectual sophistication within feminism exists alongside a set of public discourses about women and femininity which are extremely limited, the appropriate political strategy of feminism presents difficult questions and choices. Concerning the issues facing women, however, there must be an acceptance of a material context to debates and discourses about women. Let me conclude with a quotation from the Croatian writer Slavenka Drakulić:

> It is precisely the Third World people who have every right to demand that the Western European and American white middle class give up *their* standard of living and redistribute wealth so we can all survive.[5]

Notes

1. Neil Lyndon, *No More Sex War* (Sinclair-Stevenson, London, 1992). Another form of attack on feminism has recently come from Camille Paglia, in *Sexual Personae* (Harmondsworth, Penguin, 1991).

2. Susan Faludi, *Backlash: The Undeclared War against Women* (Chatto & Windus, London, 1991).

3. Carol Smart, *Regulating Womanhood* (Routledge, London, 1991). For different accounts of the issue see Lynne Segal and Mary McIntosh (eds), *Sex Exposed: Sexuality and the Pornography Debate* (Virago, London, 1992) and Catherine Itzin (ed.), *Pornography: Women, Violence and Civil Liberties* (Oxford University Press, Oxford, 1992). The issue has also become a part of debates on pornography.

4. Segal and McIntosh, *Sex Exposed*.

5. Slavenka Drakulić, *How We Survived Communism and Even Laughed* (Hutchinson, London, 1992), p. 139.

Transforming Socialist-Feminism: The Challenge of Racism

Kum-Kum Bhavnani and Margaret Coulson

> Feminism is the political theory and practice that struggles to free *all* women: women of colour, working class women, poor women, disabled women, lesbians, old women – as well as white economically privileged, heterosexual women. (Smith, 1982: 49)

This definition of feminism seems to capture what socialist-feminism in the 1980s should be about. Through struggle, in heated arguments and in writings, black women have been trying to move socialist-feminist politics in this direction. In their article 'Ethnocentrism and socialist-feminist theory', in *Feminist Review*, 20, Michèle Barrett and Mary McIntosh have provided one recent response to these initiatives. The two of us are anxious to take seriously this attempt by white feminists to take up the challenge of the charge of racism which has been made against white feminist analysis.

Michèle and Mary promise a re-examination of their own work in the light of criticisms raised by black women, and they do summarize some of the criticisms which have been made (Barrett and McIntosh, 1985: 41–2). They endeavour to identify 'elements of ethnocentrism in our previous work, and [we] have pointed to important issues where the analysis we have presented has been seriously marred by the failure to consider ethnicity and racism' (1985: 44).

Although Michèle and Mary present an important and interesting contribution, it fails to open up the kind of area of discussion which is needed. This is because they lose sight of the central issue in the challenge that has been made – which is racism. By bringing another issue, namely ethnocentrism, into the foreground, they end up with their own previous conceptual categories intact.

Our own contribution arises out of our reactions to and discussion of their article. We also want to take up some of the arguments raised in 'Many voices, one chant', a special issue of *Feminist Review* (17, 1984) produced by black women about black struggles. That issue was itself situated in a recent history, which includes the setting up of the Organization of Women

From *Feminist Review*, 20, 1986, pp. 81–92.

of Asian and African Descent, the struggles around Imperial Typewriters, Trico and Grunwicks, as well as the development of Women Against Racism and Fascism groups, the autumn 1980 socialist-feminist conference on anti-imperialism and anti-racism, and more recent developments. We see the challenge of the charge of racism as having the potential to motivate a different kind of socialist-feminism. But this is not realized in Michèle and Mary's article; instead the challenge is evaded, is taken up in a very limited way, or even in a way which is potentially reactionary.

The risks of entering this debate

In our conversations, both with each other and with others, we have tried to identify some of the problems of entering into these discussions, given the tensions that are involved. This means recognizing that black women and white women have different histories and different relationships to present struggles, in Britain and internationally. White women who enter these debates must acknowledge the material basis of their power in relation to black people, both women and men. It is also necessary to acknowledge the complexities of this power relationship – as between white women and black men, where white women may be privileged, oppressed, or both.

In contributing to these discussions white women cannot avoid the legacy of racism within feminism. This legacy has a long history which includes the dominance of eugenicism in both the early and more recent birth control movements, the eager acceptance by the majority of the suffragettes of imperialistic nationalism, and at best, the failure of anti-rape campaigns to challenge racist stereotypes of the sexuality of black men. Not only have these generally not taken up racism as an issue, nor seen how their campaigns against male violence are complicated in the context of racism, but by their actions they have reaffirmed racist ideas by marching through black areas and calling for greater policing.

However, we do not subscribe to a politics based on essentialism. We also feel that there are times when black and white political activists have to work together, and in this article we are attempting to do that. Whilst we may sound too critical at some points, not critical enough at others, and sometimes may seem to be stating the obvious, we write this as a political and theoretical piece. We hope that the discussions and actions that may result will contribute to a process which will shift socialist-feminism out of its present rut (sometimes known as its crisis!).

There have been important moments in contemporary socialist-feminism: in the development of analyses of women's work, waged and unwaged, in women's relation to men, to the working class and to capital, and in debates with radical feminists about sexuality. One important commitment of recent socialist-feminism has been to confront the 'masculinist' assumptions that have distorted socialist theory and practice and to transform socialism into something which can more fully represent the struggles and aspirations of women. The *Beyond the Fragments* discussions, initiated by the book written by Sheila Rowbotham, Lynne Segal and Hilary Wainwright (1979), represent one such attempt in the last decade. In saying this, we are horribly conscious of the racism by omission in both the national conference and local discussions which participants of *Beyond the Fragments* rarely challenged. However, the book did represent an attempt to transform socialist-feminist theory. This commitment has been an important project, but only if it is seen as part of a larger process. This socialist-feminism must, itself, be open to being transformed under the impetus of black struggles. But it is still hard to find instances where this has happened.

One femininity or many?

In a women's rights convention in Ohio in 1852, Sojourner Truth claimed the place of black women in the struggle for women's rights and at the same time asserted that the experience of womanhood is not the same for all women:

> That man over there says that women need to be helped into carriages, and lifted over ditches, and to have the best places . . . and ain't I a woman? Look at me! Look at my arm! . . . I have ploughed and planted, and gathered into barns, and no man could heed me – and ain't I a woman? I could work as much as any man (when I could get it) and bear the lash as well – and ain't I a woman? I have borne five children and seen them most sold off into slavery, and when I cried out with grief, none but Jesus heard – and ain't I a woman? (quoted in Carby, 1982: 214)

These words have been widely quoted in the women's movement. But what sense has been made of them? Apart from intended racialism, lack of information has been used as an excuse for leaving black women out of analyses, or black women have been defined as problems, or black women have been exoticized. While Michèle and Mary present some sociological material about the situation of black women in Britain they do not make black women *central* to their political analysis. It seems to us that black women are merely being added on, and the need to transform the whole analysis is not realized. Also, where they present examples to 'emphasize the complex interrelations of class, race and gender power structures' (Barrett and McIntosh, 1985: 38), they use one example from Papua New Guinea under colonialism and the Scottsboro case of 1930s Alabama, USA. Whilst these examples are important in order to gain insight into the operation of British colonialism, and to understand how white women have used their racism in relation to black men, it is a pity that no examples are taken from the contemporary white-dominated women's movement also to illustrate these power relations.

The racism of the women's movement in Britain can be seen clearly from the following example. Reclaim the Night marches, held in the mid- to late 1970s, often went through black areas whilst demanding that the streets be made safe for women, sometimes with an accompanying slogan for 'better' policing. Despite the arguments and protests of black women then, and since, Reclaim the Night marches (for example, one held in Cambridge in 1984) often still carry slogans for 'better' policing. Not only is it racist to march through black areas with demands for safer streets for women (which women?), but also, to understate it, we don't know of many black women who see police protection as any way of doing this. Racism operates in a way which places different women in different relationships to structures of power and authority in society. Certainly Cherry Groce and the family of Cynthia Jarrett are unlikely to have any illusions about 'better' policing. Whilst some white socialist-feminists would have no illusions about 'better' policing, their challenge to that demand has been weak.

There is an important analysis to be made about black women in the role of mother which we can only point to in this contribution. The shooting of Cherry Groce in south London in September 1985 and the death of Cynthia Jarrett in north London in October 1985 in the course of police raids on their homes indicate that many black mothers are in a different set of relationships to the police from white mothers. Black women, as mothers, encounter other state agencies such as the DHSS, schools and so on in a very particular way; they may be asked to produce their passports before being considered eligible for benefit, or before their children are allowed to be enrolled in schools. Clearly they experience these agencies in a way that white mothers would not. At this stage, we are merely trying to indicate that there is a need for further analysis on this issue.

The problem with the concept of gender is that it is rooted in an apparently simple and 'real' material base of biological difference between women and men. But what is constructed on that base is not one femininity in relation to one masculinity, but several. It is not only that there are differences between different groups of women but that these differences are often also conflicts of interest. Whilst it can be difficult, socialist-feminism has to recognize these conflicts and tackle them politically.

The state deals with different women differently

For socialist-feminists, one way into these issues is through an examination of the state and the ways in which it deals differently with different groups of women. Struggles, campaigns, analyses by black people, especially women, against the immigration laws have focused political attention on the significance of these laws in revealing the state's projects in relation to black people. Since the 1940s, immigration and nationality legislation have become central instruments of state racism, irrespective of the political party in government. The state has become obsessively concerned with the entry of black labour into the UK and, in consequence, with the control of black people already here.[1] The main assumption has been that black men enter the labour market, or threaten it, while the extraction of surplus value from black women through their participation in that labour market has often been ignored. This is in spite of the extensive involvement of black women in paid employment.[2] This assumption has been expressed in the sexism of immigration controls. For example, until recently there was some provision for black men to be joined by their fiancées but much tighter controls on women wanting to bring their fiancés into the UK. Appeals against this inequality were upheld in 1985 by the European Court of Human Rights on the grounds of sex discrimination. The British government responded by amending regulations further to tighten the controls on entry of all fiancé(e)s. This contrasts with an earlier decision, included in the 1981 Nationality Act, which allowed some (mainly white) women for the first time to pass on citizenship to their children born abroad. In the first case, the state abandoned its sexism in the negative sense that it reduced the rights of women and men to the same and worse level, and simultaneously consolidated its racism. In the second case, it also proclaimed commitment to sex equality and improved the rights of mainly white women, but further consolidated its racism.[3] Thus under the rhetoric of creating 'equality' between women and men, the state develops further racist practices. While the two of us would not claim to have any easy answers, it is this type of conflict of interests which all of us as socialist-feminists need to confront.

Racism or ethnocentrism?

The challenge of racism can often be avoided, particularly in quasi-academic discussions. In calling their article 'Ethnocentrism and socialist-feminist theory', Michèle and Mary suggest that ethnocentrism is the central problem for socialist-feminism. To us, the central problem for socialist-feminist theory is racism, of which ethnocentrism may be a consequence. As far as we can see, the role of the state and international capital in creating and perpetuating inequalities between black people and white people is lost through the use of a term such as ethnocentrism. Further, the word and indeed the concept seem to imply that the problem is one of cultural bias, supported by ignorance. It then follows that, if more sociological information is presented, the problem can be overcome. We are arguing, however, that to consider racism as the central issue involves a fundamental and radical *transformation* of socialist-feminism.

Despite their intentions, Michèle and Mary's method of re-examination denies the possibility of a radical transformation of their own previous analysis. The conceptual framework of *The Anti-Social Family* (Barrett and McIntosh, 1982) provides the fixed reference point against which modifications and additions are considered in the light of more information about black women. 'Woman' continues to be defined as a universal category and the oppressive and anti-social character of 'the family' is reasserted. Many feminists have been justifiably angered when (male) socialists have used this method in response to feminist critiques of socialist theories and practices. We do not dismiss the significance of the analysis of family/household forms and ideologies. However, we think that if we are to change the conceptual framework we have to begin by asking different questions. When we try to understand the condition of women we ask, what is it that oppresses women? What shapes the lives and identities of women? What shapes the lives and identities of black women? One way into the last question is through an examination of the political dynamic. If we consider what issues black people have been struggling with over during the past five or ten years in Britain, we see that these struggles have revolved around challenging racism, specifically in relation to the state: over deportation and anti-deportation campaigns, and the police. From asking these questions and reviewing these struggles we are drawn to the need for fresh analysis of the relationship between the state and 'the family' and of how this differs for black and white people. This may lead us to an analysis, and some understanding, that the state may have different strategies for each group.

In resisting the pressure to review their conceptual framework/categories, Michèle and Mary let go of the possibility of developing a new and challenging discursive space. In reinstating 'the family' as a key concept and as a key site for the oppression of women, the only concession they appear to make to the charge of racism is in acknowledging culturally different household forms. Because they recast this charge of racism as ethnocentrism, they only identify cultural differences; 'race' drops out of focus and ethnicity comes to the fore and this is reflected in the title of their article. By treating racism as almost synonymous with ethnocentrism, they obscure, and thus avoid examining, how *racism* relates to black families. We shall try to demonstrate how we would approach the relationship between racism, the state and black households.

Racism, the state and black households

We begin from a recognition that not all family/household forms and ideologies are equal within Britain, nor are they dealt with as equally valid by the state. For example, the state's practices in terms of the ideology of family unity are pretty contradictory in relation to black people. As a consequence of immigration controls and practices, many black families are split up, either permanently or for a large number of years. The state shows no respect for the principles of family unity in these cases. For Michèle and Mary to equate this coercive action of the state in splitting up black families with the consequences of the political involvement of mainly white women in peace camps in Britain (1985: 42) is not naive, but an insult to the struggles of black people. But the state claims to desire 'family unity' for black families in other circumstances. For example, if a marriage of black people born overseas comes to an end, with one partner perhaps moving to their country of origin, the state attempts to remove/deport the rest of the family/household, using the argument that family unity must be upheld. For black people the British state's commitment to 'family unity' is strongest where such unity is outside the United Kingdom.[4]

To look at this more analytically we can examine the state's relation to black people through the notion of black labour as surplus labour. We are referring to the argument that capital has an interest in maintaining black labour as surplus labour. By this we mean that such labour is seen as temporary, easily expendable, easily replaceable and in excess of demand. Because of Britain's colonial relationship with the continent of Africa, the Indian sub-continent and the Caribbean, in the 1940s and early 1950s there was *some* rhetoric about colonial subjects coming to work in the 'mother country'. In this limited sense black people were initially viewed as potential settlers, although no social provision was made for such settlers in terms of housing or other human needs. Thus black workers appeared to add to existing pressure on already scarce social resources in poor urban areas. In Sivanandan's analysis (1976), while the economic gain from black workers went to capital, the social costs were borne by labour, but capital and labour were united by racism. Internal and external political pressures including the influence of EEC policy on immigration control led to the rapid development of Britain's racist immigration controls through the 1960s and 1970s, through which black settlers effectively became redefined as migrant labour. Thus, employed black labour in the countries of the white capitalist world retains a temporary status. In Britain, the obsession of the state with the entry of black people into the country has kept alive the idea that all black people in Britain are immigrants – and that all immigrants are black. The use of the term 'second generation immigrant' (Barrett and McIntosh, 1985: 42) reflects these assumptions, though the words themselves are nonsensical. Use of the term implies participation in the racist discourse within which it is located. How long might it take to recognize that black people have been born in Britain? Centuries have clearly not been long enough.

In the contemporary situation of high and increasing unemployment in Britain, and the changing international division of labour, immigration controls were and are constantly being tightened against black people, and particularly against black men. The patriarchal assumptions of the British state as built into immigration laws must be situated in this dynamic of state racism. Thus Michèle and Mary's judgement that the 'opposition [to the immigration laws] should not collude in a reactive way' (1985: 43) is again telling. There is a certain insensitivity in informing those of us who try to challenge immigration laws and regulations that our methods of challenge are such that 'we accept the underlying logic behind the immigration laws of this country' (1985: 43). Many of us do *not* accept the underlying logic, but our solidarity with black people means that we want to challenge the racism of the state. The importance, the problems and the contradictions of trying to win immigration campaigns organized around individual cases, and the political significance of the development of collective campaigns, have been clearly discussed by many of the participants in these campaigns.[5]

The state's relationship to black people is also marked out by ideas and practices which associate black people with crime, deviance and disorder. These ideas and practices are then used to 'justify' particularly heavy and coercive policing. We are not able to present the range of arguments about this here, but we want to signal that policing and 'law and order' are also major means by which the state perpetuates and legitimizes its violence against black people. Stuart Hall et al. (1978), Paul Gilroy (1982) and Errol Lawrence (1982) are examples of writers who have presented analyses on these issues.

That many white socialist-feminists ignore racialist attacks on black households is not new. However, in doing so, they also ignore the fact that harassment and racialist attacks from white women and white men, and sometimes white families, can impel a solidarity within black households. Whatever inequalities exist in such households, they are clearly also sites of support for their members. In saying this we are recognizing that black women may have significant issues to face within black households. Struggles over sexuality and against domestic violence, for example, have been important issues for all feminists, including black feminists, and have involved confronting assumptions about domestic relationships. But at the same time the black family is a source of support in the context of harassment and attacks from white people.

The social potential of this base of solidarity against racialist and racist attacks has been demonstrated in other situations of struggle. In the Imperial Typewriters strike in Leicester in 1974, when the white union leadership allied with the management, the strikers mobilized material, organizational and political support from family and community. Racism and economic exploitation were inextricable both in the causes of the strike and in the political issues which it raised. It is possible to compare this to the Grunwick strike where for a considerable period the trade union movement rallied in defence of the right of workers to organize, and although family and community networks gave support the political significance of racism and of support from the black community was overshadowed.[6] It is such issues which produce contradictory sets of relationships between black women, white women, black households, the state, and the predominantly white women's movement.

The instances which we have discussed above suggest to us that the analysis of *The Anti-Social Family* cannot be stretched to cover the situation of black women in Britain. In many circumstances 'the family' is not socially privileged and protected in respect of black people; indeed, it is often under attack from the state and from individual racialists. In the context of racist oppression, black families are often not 'anti-social' in the sense used by Michèle and Mary but can become a base not only for solidarity but also for struggle against racism. Not only is there a basis for solidarity within black households, but that can also lead to very real material distinctions between black women and white women. For instance, as we have noted elsewhere, black and white mothers may have completely different experiences and perceptions of the oppressive nature of the state. The worries black mothers may have about children being late home from school can be as much to do with fears of police harassment as with fears of sexual assault. To carry this discussion further requires a fuller analysis of the relationship between 'the family' upheld by the state, in dominant ideology and social practice, and black families, within the overall context of a racist society.

In conclusion

We do not wish to summarize our article here – rather we want to tease out some implications of our arguments and to raise further questions. The first point we wish to make is that through arguing that an analysis of racism must be central to socialist-feminism, we do not claim to be presenting 'an answer'. We do, however, see that an analysis which we all, as socialist-feminists, need to develop is based on the idea of a racially structured, patriarchal capitalism (excuse the mouthful!). This leads us to examine how 'race', class and gender are structured in relation to one another. How do they combine with and/or cut across one another? How does racism divide gender identity and experience? How is gender experienced through racism? How is class shaped by gender and 'race'? To take these questions on does require a fundamental redrawing of the conceptual categories of socialist-feminism, and it may help us to develop a more adequate politics.

To have placed 'ethnic difference [as] necessarily . . . as important a consideration as racism itself' (Barrett and McIntosh, 1985: 28) is, at best, to forget the substantial critiques of the concepts of 'multiculturalism' and 'ethnicity' and the ways in which these can be used to bolster and legitimize racism (e.g. Carby, 1979). Thus, Michèle and Mary's conclusion (1985: 44) can appear rather dishonest. They summarize their article but do not explicitly state that they have, in effect, *rejected* the criticisms of Hazel Carby, 'Many voices, one chant' (Amos et al., 1984), and so on. These critiques, amongst many others, have jettisoned ethnicity and ethnic disadvantage as analytical concepts, but Michèle and Mary do not take up and challenge these arguments; they reject them by ignoring them. As we have tried to show, one consequence of not understanding the centrality of racism and its challenge is that socialist-feminism becomes distanced from the political dynamic. The danger of this distancing can be seen in the language used: Michèle and Mary's use of 'disabling' ('[we have] to recognize this disability in ourselves' (1985: 24)) is inappropriate and offensive. Offensive because it ignores the movement of women with disabilities and the criticisms they have made about disablist assumptions. Inappropriate because when feminists have ignored and refused to see or hear black women, this has not been due to a 'disability'. White academic women, especially, are not so powerless; they have some responsibility for the political and academic choices they have made. In the instance of Michèle and Mary's piece, they have *chosen* to highlight ethnicity as an analytic concept rather than racism. Thus, they are not 'disabled', they are mistaken.

The importance of this is in relation to political action. Many feminists employed as academics and teachers have been struggling within their educational institutions for greater equality of opportunities for women through challenging conditions of service, employment practices, gendered segregation in jobs and education, and so on. Rarely do these same women, if white, challenge the racism of such institutions with the same clarity and energy. Indeed, sometimes they see anti-racism as competing with anti-sexism for resources and support – for example, in recruitment of staff or students – thus operating on an assumption that anti-sexism concerns white women and anti-racism concerns black people.

The final point of our conclusion is to repeat that an assumption of automatic sisterhood from white women towards black women is ill-founded. Sisterhood can only be nurtured and developed when white women acknowledge the complex power relationships between white women and white men in relation to black women and black men. This needs to be done not only through acknowledgement, but also through re-examining feminist practices, for example the practices of Women Against Violence Against Women (WAVAW) groups. Even if socialist-feminists have tended not to get involved in WAVAW activities, they still have a responsibility to challenge the politics of other feminists. This re-examination might lead to some insight, and therefore more appropriate political action, in relation to violence against black people – a violence sometimes perpetrated by white racialist women. Another example of an area where black women have had to criticize demands made by white women has been around abortion rights. Yet Michèle and Mary state that 'the right to abortion can unite women across race and class lines' (1985: 40). The demand for 'The Right to Choose' and to assert control over our own bodies *can* unite women – including those who may be defined as infertile. 'The Right to Abortion' has often succeeded in dividing women – rights for white women have meant the abuse of black women.

The attempt to try and transform socialist-feminism is not a worthy cause but a political necessity. As Barbara Smith says:

> White women don't work on racism to do a favour for someone else, solely to benefit Third World women. You have to comprehend how racism distorts and lessens your own lives as white women – that racism affects your chances for survival, too, and that it is very definitely your issue. Until you understand this, no fundamental change will come about. (Smith, 1982)

Notes

One of the reasons we wrote this piece together was to affirm our political commitments to recognizing and working across individual 'difference'. While we both share very similar politics, our experiences and personal histories are very different. For example, one of us is a lesbian and one a heterosexual, one is white and one is black, one was born in the 1930s in England and one in the 1950s in India, and neither of us is married. We both taught at Preston Polytechnic, Lancashire, UK, where we overlapped for three years from 1980 to 1983.

We'd like to thank all those with whom we've discussed these ideas and especially Ruth Frankenberg, Margo Gorman, Lata Mani, Sarah Pyett, Esther Saraga, Andy Shallice and Claudette Williams.

1. The internal controls and checks on black people have been written about in a number of pamphlets and books. For example, Manchester Law Centre (1982) and Paul Gordon (1981).

2. The participation of black women in paid employment has been noted and commented on by a number of people such as Parmar (1982).

3. For a detailed discussion of these issues, see Bhabha et al. (1985).

4. This is commented on by the writers and editors of *Worlds Apart* (Bhabha et al., 1985: 100–1).

5. See, for example, the conclusions drawn in Bhabha et al. (1985) and the discussion by Hansa and Rahila (1984).

6. This has been noted by a number of the strikers as well as, for example, Bhavnani (1982) and Parmar (1982).

References

Amos, V., Lewis, G., Mama, A. and Parmar, P. (eds) (1984) 'Many voices, one chant: black feminist perspectives', *Feminist Review*, 17.

Barrett, M. and McIntosh, M. (1982) *The Anti-Social Family*. London: Verso.

Barrett, M. and McIntosh, M. (1985) 'Ethnocentrism and socialist-feminist theory', *Feminist Review*, 20.

Bhabha, J., Klug, F. and Shutter, S. (eds) (1985) *Worlds Apart: Women Under Immigration Law*. London: Women, Immigration and Nationality Group London/Pluto Press.

Bhavnani, K.K. (1982) 'Racist acts' (three-part article), *Spare Rib*, 115, 116, 117.

Carby, H. (1979) *Multicultural Fictions* (Stencilled paper series) Birmingham: Centre for Contemporary Cultural Studies, University of Birmingham.

Carby, H. (1982) 'White women listen! Black feminism and the boundaries of sisterhood', in Centre for Contemporary Cultural Studies, *The Empire Strikes Back: Race and Racism in 70s Britain*. London: Hutchinson.

Davis, A. (1981) *Women, Race and Class*. London: Women's Press.

Gilroy, P. (1982) 'The myth of black criminality', in M. Eve and D. Musson (eds), *Socialist Register 1982*. London: Merlin Press.

Gordon, P. (1981) *Passport Raids and Checks: Internal Immigration Controls*. London: Runnymede Trust.

Hall, S. et al. (1978) *Policing the Crisis*. London: Hutchinson.

Hansa and Rahila (1984) 'Campaigning against deportations for black women's rights', *Outwrite*, 29 (September/October).

Hull, G.T., Scott, P.B. and Smith, B. (eds) (1982) *All the Women Are White, All the Blacks Are Men, But Some of Us Are Brave*. New York: Feminist Press.

Lawrence, E. (1982) 'Just plain common sense: the "roots" of racism', in Centre for Contemporary Cultural Studies, *The Empire Strikes Back*. London: Hutchinson.

Manchester Law Centre (1982) *From Ill Treatment to No Treatment: The New Health Regulations: Black People and Internal Controls*. Manchester: Manchester Law Centre.

Parmar, P. (1982) 'Gender, race and class: Asian women in resistance', in Centre for Contemporary Cultural Studies, *The Empire Strikes Back*. London: Hutchinson.

Rowbotham, S., Segal, L. and Wainwright, H. (1979) *Beyond the Fragments: Feminism and the Making of Socialism*. London: Pluto Press.

Sivanandan, A. (1976) 'Race, class and the state: the black experience in Britain', *Race and Class*, 17 (4).

Smith, B. (1982) 'Racism and women's studies', in Hull et al. (1982).

There's No Place Like Home: On the Place of Identity in Feminist Politics

Mary Louise Adams

Personalizing politics

> We realize that the only people who care enough about us to work consistently for our liberation is us . . . . This focusing on our own oppression is embodied in the concept of identity politics. We believe that the most profound and potentially the most radical politics come out of our own identity, as opposed to working to end somebody else's oppression. (Combahee River Collective, 1981: 212)

Identity politics: 1851, Sojourner Truth takes the floor at a women's convention in Akron, Ohio (Davis, 1981: 60). 'Ain't I a woman?' she asks rhetorically, defining the category, asserting herself – a mother, a worker, a former slave – firmly within it.

Identity politics: 1928, Radclyffe Hall's polemical fiction brings inversion (homosexuality) to public awareness. She ends her melancholic novel, *The Well of Loneliness*, with a collective demand: 'Acknowledge us oh God, before the whole world. Give us also the right to our existence' (Hall, 1951: 437).

Identity politics: 1983, Bernice Johnson Reagon, political activist and founder of the musical group Sweet Honey in the Rock, addresses a crowd at an American women's music festival:

> Now every once in a while there is a need for people to try to clear out corners and bar the doors and check everybody who comes in the door, and check what they carry in and say, 'Humph, inside this place the only thing we are going to deal with is X or Y or Z'. And so only Xs or Ys or Zs get to come in. Most of the time when people do that, they do it because of the heat of trying to live in this society where being an X or Y or Z is very difficult to say the least. (Reagon, 1983: 367)

A politics steeped in identity and personal experience is very much at the root of present-day women's liberation (see O'Sullivan, 1987), particularly

From *Feminist Review*, 31, 1989, pp. 23–33, abridged.

as it was nurtured in the American black civil rights and other earlier liberation struggles:

> Long before the WM [women's movement], the protagonists of the black movement (and the Chinese and Cuban revolutionaries before them) had insisted that there could be no dichotomy between one's personal lifestyle, behaviour, beliefs and the pursuit of liberationist politics, that who you are and what you do belong to the same continuum. (Bourne, 1983: 12)

Feminists adopted and refined this emphasis on the political ramifications of personal life.

> We weren't going to wait for a revolution before we tried to change our lives . . . the more we could transform ourselves, our relationships, our consciousness, the more we would move towards a possibility for fundamental change. (O'Sullivan, 1987: 51)

'The personal is political' remains a frequently brandished tenet of women's liberation. Unlike traditional forms of organizing on the left, 'feminist (and black) struggle cannot be undertaken without questioning both the values, ideas, and images imposed on women and black people and the relationship these have to the overall exploitative system' (Bourne, 1983: 2).

Coalition politics: from the inside out

> Any kind of separatism is a dead end. It's good for forging identity and gathering strength but I do feel that the strongest politics are coalition politics that cover a broad base of issues. There is no way that one oppressed group is going to topple a system by itself. Forming principled coalitions around specific issues is very important. (Smith and Smith, 1981: 126)

Although current practice may suggest the contrary, political strategies which focus on identity and those which focus on coalition are not mutually exclusive. Successful coalitions rely, in part, on the strength of their members, individuals who hopefully have somewhere beyond the coalition to draw sustenance from – 'homes' as Bernice Johnson Reagon calls them (Reagon, 1983: 359). These homes are the smaller groups we turn to when the coalescing becomes difficult and seems likely to obscure our own sense of priority. Thus small autonomous groups are the building blocks of larger-scale coalitions, like the women's movement, though a number of assumptions make it difficult for us to see that the movement is, in fact, a coalition. The most salient of these is the questionable, but still pervasive, idea of sisterhood. As women, much of the movement has expected us to have similar needs. But obviously the differing contexts of our lives forestall the development of any singular purpose among us. It's the impossibility of meeting everyone's needs in the broadbased, and unacknowledged, coalition of the women's movement that has led to a flurry of identity-based organizing, especially among those groups whose needs topple by the wayside most often.

This search for commonality is not itself a bad thing. However, the women's movement now seems to exist as a cluster of smaller groups constantly negotiating the tension between respectful diversity and fragmentation and rarely pooling their strengths. A. Sivanandan writes about similar problems in antiracist organizing in Britain: 'Alliances do not mean the subservience of one group to another. But at the same time, we must beware the opposing tendency . . . of too much autonomy' (Sivanandan, 1983: 10). Certainly autonomy has enabled groups to pursue their own goals and to fulfil their own needs. But, says Bonnie Zimmerman, 'The distinction between autonomy and separatism is a delicate one . . . As personal politics creates more and more specialized groups, the tendency toward fragmentation grows' (Zimmerman, 1985: 266).

Autonomy-hungry feminists symbolize the movement's continuing failure to account for diversity – a first principle of coalition. The predominance of white women means that the concerns of black and other women of colour are often neglected or poorly handled. Middle-class women tend to rely on methods of organizing that preclude the participation of many working-class women. Heterosexual women can express homophobia while working with lesbians. In a sense the women's movement has not been organized as a multi-voiced coalition but rather as a large, if incohesive, identity-group (the sisterhood), reflecting the identity of the majority (straight, white, middle class). According to bell hooks, 'slogans like "organize around your own oppression" provided the excuse many privileged women needed to ignore the differences between their social status and the status of masses of women' (hooks, 1984: 6). Understandably, particular groups of women leave the sororal fold in frustration hoping that on their own they'll be able to concentrate on their interests, in a manner consistent with their experience, without having to spend valuable time educating about or struggling over their oppression in the course of their organizing. Inevitably, however, the smaller groups that split off still have to confront diversity on some level. A group of black women may break off from a socialist-feminist group to work on, for instance, labour issues affecting black women. After a few meetings the lesbians in this new group may start to feel the weight of heterosexism influencing the agenda. Will they in turn decide to split? 'There is a price to pay,' says Bonnie Zimmerman, 'for a politics rooted so strongly in consciousness and identity. The power of diversity has as its mirror image and companion, the powerlessness of fragmentation. Small autonomous groups can also be ineffectual groups' (Zimmerman, 1985: 268).

If you can't be sure that the other Xs, Ys or Zs are going to be sympathetic to your additional identity as a V or a W, with whom will you organize? June Jordan is an American poet and political commentator:

> It occurs to me that much organizational grief could be avoided if people understood that partnership in misery does not necessarily provide for partnership for change: when we get the monsters off our backs all of us may want to run in very different directions. (quoted in Parmar, 1987: 13)

A shared identity does not guarantee a commitment to the same principles or goals. We have to 'accept or reject allies on the basis of politics' (Clarke,

1981: 135) though identity-organizing as an end in itself can make it seem like a woman's 'identity' is synonymous with her politics. Thus June Jordan asks:

> What is the purpose of your identity? What do you want to do on the basis of that? . . . People have to begin to understand that just because somebody is a woman or somebody is black does not mean that he or she and I should have the same politics. We should try to measure each other on the basis of what we do for each other rather than on the basis of who we are. (quoted in Parmar, 1987: 13–14)

What shall we make of oppression?

> We plead to each other
> we all come from the same rock
> we all come from the same rock
> ignoring the fact that we bend
> at different temperatures
> that each of us is malleable
> up to a point
> ('The Welder', Moraga, 1981b: 219)

Jordan's comment notwithstanding, who we are usually has some bearing on what we do and for whom. There aren't too many white women, for instance, at the forefront of antiracist struggle, a fact which reflects our identity-motivated politics. It's important that an analysis of identity politics doesn't put responsibility for the problems it has generated in feminism on the women who find it necessary to form their own smaller groups. What's at issue is not the 'splitting' but the conditions which seem to make it the only option, particularly the movement's inability to accommodate diversity. Part of this penchant for homogeneity stems from a reluctance by women of privilege to come to terms with the whole of their identities – oppressor as well as oppressed. How much easier it is to examine the ways in which we are denied our full potential than to see how we benefit when others are denied theirs. For white women to recognize black women's concerns about racism we have to acknowledge our own complicity in it and this may threaten our conception of ourselves as oppressed (Carby, 1982: 221), as if it were impossible to acknowledge our privilege in one sphere and, at the same time, our lack of it in another. This tendency to cling to oppression is perhaps a consequence of the woman-as-victim school of feminism which has, for example, overemphasized danger in the pleasure/danger debate about women's sexuality (see Vance, 1984). This kind of thinking divorces us from our own agency and makes it difficult for us to comprehend the ways, subtle or not, we manipulate privilege. bell hooks says white women rely on stereotypes of the strong black woman to support this

> false image of themselves as powerless, passive victims and [it] deflects attention away from their aggressiveness, their power (however limited in a white supremacist, male-dominated state), their willingness to dominate and control others. These unacknowledged aspects of the social status of many white women prevent them from transcending racism and limit the scope of their understanding of women's overall social status. (hooks, 1984: 14)

Suppressing qualms of conscience, we don't take our explorations of identity far enough, content to rest in the muck of frustration and struggle that defines the part of us that is oppressed. But, ironically, that is precisely the place to begin to appreciate the oppression of others and our relationship to it. According to Cherrie Moraga, 'the only reason women of a privileged class will dare to look at *how* it is *they* oppress, is when they've come to know the meaning of their own oppression. And understand that the oppression of others hurts them personally' (Moraga, 1981a: 33; emphasis in original). Minnie Bruce Pratt, a white woman from the American South, tells how in coming to grips with her own lesbianism she broke 'through the bubble of skin and class privilege around [her]' to see that she is 'connected to the struggle of other women and people different from [her]self (Pratt, 1984: 20). But typical expressions of female insecurity obstruct an understanding of the complexities and connections of oppressions. Oppression has become a yardstick of our value to feminism and some women feel like they never measure up. Privileged women worry that their white skin or middle-class upbringings mean they aren't oppressed enough; they can go to great lengths to prove otherwise. Similarly, white Jewish women or white lesbians can sometimes feel they have to draw parallels between anti-Semitism or heterosexism and racism to validate the oppression they feel (see Bulkin et al., 1984; Carby, 1982, discusses the inappropriateness of paralleling any two oppressions). Feminists have devised a closed economy of oppression within which we determine our worthiness to the movement as if various oppressions, like various types of coin, were simply different values of the same single unit. To get our spot on the balance sheet, we spend more time trying to demonstrate our oppression than we do dismantling it. In *Yours in Struggle*, Barbara Smith discourages this type of no-win competitiveness:

> How we are oppressed does not have to be the same in order to qualify as real. One of the gifts of the feminist movement has been to examine the subtleties of what comprises various oppressions without needing to pretend that they are all alike . . . Trying to convince others that one is legitimately oppressed by making comparisons can either result from or lead to the ranking of oppressions, which is a dangerous pitfall in and of itself. (Smith, 1984: 75)

The 'ranking' Smith refers to is surely one of the glaring ironies of a supposedly non-hierarchical movement. While the hierarchy itself is problematic, the constellation of political tactics that maintain it obstructs feminist movement in an example of identity politics at its worst. As long as points are awarded in proportion to the weight of women's oppressions, identity-based organizing will predominate and experience will continue to be manipulated as the lone tailor of feminist politics. The hierarchy is a means of determining whose experience is the most 'authentic'. 'If there are divisions in the same "rank" or group, suppression becomes necessary so as to protect the "official" version's claim to define and describe the oppression' (Ardill and O'Sullivan, 1987: 281). Censuring internal difference ensures that groups are seen to be associated with a specific political position which, depending on their claim to authenticity (via the hierarchy), is given a specific moral weight. Thus a criticism of that position can easily be read as a criticism of the group itself. 'Within these politics there's little room for distinguishing between politics and those who speak them, little space for such things as evaluation of strategies or criticism, or making mistakes' (Ardill and O'Sullivan, 1987: 281). Since the early 1980s, for example, Bonnie Zimmerman has noted an increasingly 'personal tone' in letters written to the American feminist newspaper *off our backs*:

> The raging battles of the past year or two, in particular, have focused around issues of personal identity . . . To adopt a politically incorrect line on any of these issues is to bring down on oneself an accusation of personal invalidation . . . What is at stake in so many of these exchanges are not issues and ideas but identity. The typical tone taken by the writers is one of outrage and indignation, with advocates defending their respective territories in ways that preclude the initiation of meaningful dialogue. (Zimmerman, 1985: 268, n. 32)

When identity can be worn as a 'mantle of virtue' (Bulkin, 1984: 99) there is a danger of 'hunkering down in one's oppression', to use a phrase of Jan Clausen's (cited in ibid.). Suffice it to say that all the vitriolic letters in the world will do little to change the actual conditions of women's lives.

Feeding our principles

Somewhere along the way, the focus on personal experience and personal identity has cut off portions of the women's movement from larger struggles for social change. Oppression is uncovered and fought, not in the wider society around us, but locally in our own groups and organizations. These two approaches should, and can, occur simultaneously but too often they do not, which, given the intensely personal flavour of our politics, is not surprising. For instance, it is important that white women deal with our racism on an individual level so that we can engage in the interpersonal relationships that further political work requires. To this end consciousness raising (CR) and awareness training are precursors to further political action (see Cross et al., 1982); they are not ends in themselves, as is frequently the case. Because we stall in the CR (personal) phase of our antiracism, racism is rarely addressed as an institutionalized tool of the state; it is instead reduced to a problem of feminist organizing, 'a moral problem, a defect of sisterhood' (Bourne, 1983: 15). Severed from its roots in this way, racism seems to be a singular system. The same could be said of anti-Semitism, heterosexism or any other oppression that we choose to confront merely as a series of problems between individuals. We effectively obscure the interconnectedness of oppressions when we see their solutions as atomized personal efforts. Which is probably why so many of us find it important to funnel our energies into our very own oppression. We're unable to see that 'opposition to any oppression "lightens the load on all of us"' (Alice Walker cited by Bulkin, 1984: 143). This is the awareness that feeds the principles of coalition. A conscious reliance on these principles could reconcile the goals of current feminism, permitting the identity-based organizing that empowers and motivates us, while furnishing the diversity necessary for a strong and effective movement. To pursue coalition politics, feminists have to learn that our allies are best chosen on the basis of their political commitments, not their identities. We could apply a similar criterion to strategy, perhaps while remembering that personal experience was first recruited to the feminist cause not as a measure of personal moral worth or as a way to determine political safety but as a means to our liberation.

Notes

Mary Louise Adams lives in Toronto, Canada, where she is completing a PhD on the history of heterosexuality in postwar Canada.

References

Ardill, Susan and O'Sullivan, Sue (1987) 'Upsetting an applecart: difference, desire and lesbian sadomasochism', in *Feminist Review, Sexuality: A Reader*. London: Virago.

Bourne, Jenny (1983) 'Towards an anti-racist feminism', *Race and Class*, 25 (1): 1–22.

Bourne, Jenny (1987) 'Homelands of the mind: Jewish feminism and identity politics', *Race and Class*, 29 (1): 1–24.

Bulkin, Elly (1984) 'Hard ground: Jewish identity, racism, and anti-Semitism', in Bulkin et al. (1984).

Bulkin, Elly, Pratt, Minnie Bruce and Smith, Barbara (1984) *Yours in Struggle*. Brooklyn, NY: Long Haul Press.

Carby, Hazel (1982) 'White women listen! Black feminism and the boundaries of sisterhood', in Centre for Contemporary Cultural Studies (1982).

Centre for Contemporary Cultural Studies (1982) *The Empire Strikes Back*. London: Hutchinson.

Clarke, Cheryl (1981) 'Lesbianism: an act of resistance', in Moraga and Anzaldua (1981).

Combahee River Collective (1981) 'A black feminist statement', in Moraga and Anzaldua (1981).

Cross, Tina, Klein, Freada, Smith, Barbara and Smith, Beverly (1982) 'Face-to-face, day-to-day – racism CR', in Hull et al. (1982).

Davis, Angela (1981) *Women, Race and Class*. London: Women's Press.

Feminist Review (eds) (1987) *Sexuality: A Reader*. London: Virago.

Freedman, Estelle B. et al. (eds) (1985) *The Lesbian Issue: Essays from Signs*. Chicago: University of Chicago Press.

Hall, Radclyffe (1951) *The Well of Loneliness*. New York: Perma Books.

Held, David and Pollitt, Christopher (eds) (1986) *New Forms of Democracy*. London: Sage.

hooks, bell (1984) *Feminist Theory: From Margin to Center*. Boston: South End Press.

Hull, Gloria T., Scott, Patricia Bell and Smith, Barbara (eds) (1982) *All the Women are White, All the Men are Black, But Some of Us Are Brave*. Old Westbury, NY: Feminist Press.

Lewis, Gail and Parmar, Pratibha (1983) 'Review of *Ain't I a Woman? Black Women and Feminism* by bell hooks, *This Bridge Called my Back* edited by Cherrie Moraga and Gloria Anzaldua, *But Some of Us Are Brave* edited by Gloria T. Hull et al., *Women, Race and Class* by Angela Davis', *Race and Class*, 25 (2), 85–91.

Moraga, Cherrie (1981a) 'La Guerra', in Moraga and Anzaldua (1981).

Moraga, Cherrie (1981b) 'The welder', in Moraga and Anzaldua (1981).

Moraga, Cherrie and Anzaldua, Gloria (eds) (1981) *This Bridge Called My Back: Writings by Radical Women of Color*. New York: Kitchen Table Press.

O'Sullivan, Sue (1987) 'Passionate beginnings: ideological politics 1969–1972', in *Feminist Review, Sexuality: A Reader*. London: Virago.

Parmar, Pratibha (1987) 'Other kinds of dreams: an interview with June Jordan', *Spare Rib*, 184: 12–15.

Pratt, Minnie Bruce (1984) 'Identity: skin blood heart', in Bulkin et al. (1984).

Reagon, Bernice Johnson (1983) 'Coalition politics: turning the century', in B. Smith (ed.), *Home Girls*. New York: Kitchen Table Press.

Rowbotham, Sheila (1986) 'Feminism and democracy', in Held and Pollitt (1986).

Sivanandan, A. (1983) 'Challenging racism: strategies for the '80s', *Race and Class*, 25 (2): 1–11.

Smith, Barbara (1984) 'Between a rock and a hard place: relationships between black and Jewish women', in Bulkin et al. (1984).

Smith, Barbara and Smith, Beverly (1981) 'Across the kitchen table: a sister to sister dialogue', in Moraga and Anzaldua (1981).

Vance, Carol (ed.) (1984) *Pleasure and Danger*. London: Routledge & Kegan Paul.

Zimmerman, Bonnie (1985) 'The politics of transliteration: lesbian personal narratives', in Freedman et al. (1985).

False Promises — Anti-Pornography Feminism

Lynne Segal

Few political movements sprang into life with more confidence and optimism than the Western women's liberation movements of the late 1960s and early 1970s. 'Sisterhood', as Sheila Rowbotham enthusiastically declared back in 1973, 'demands a new woman, a new culture, and a new way of living.'[1] Men, perhaps reluctantly, would be swept along as well, she continued: 'We must not be discouraged by them. We must go our own way but remember we are going to have to take them with us. They learn slowly. They are like creatures who have just crawled out of their shells after millennia of protection. They are sore, tender and afraid.'[2] But today many people, women and men alike, are urging all of us to crawl right back into our shells — it's safer, we are told, to stay put, to seek protection, because there is no change in men's eternal and ubiquitous oppression of women. 'Our status as a group relative to men has almost never, if ever, been changed from what it is,'[3] Catharine MacKinnon tells us, in 1992. After all these years, what has feminism achieved? Nothing.

The end of optimism

Yet women's liberation unquestionably *did* expand everybody's horizons, forcing a redefinition of what is personal and what is political. And of course most things have changed for women, much of it due to the persistent pressure of organized feminism. As I argued in *Is the Future Female?*, however uneven and complicated the general achievement of feminist goals seeking women's autonomy and equality with men, they are now widely supported and respectable. A mere twenty years ago women lacked even the words to speak in our own interests, and when attempting to do so invariably met with ridicule.[4] Campaigns against sexual harassment and violence against women, for childcare provision, abortion rights and women's equality generally are all now familiar on trade union and council

From Ralph Miliband and Leo Penitch (eds), *Socialist Register*, 1993, Merlin Press, London, pp. 92–105.

agendas, however much recession and cutbacks in welfare have further entrenched working-class and ethnic minority women in increasing impoverishment. Women today are more aware of their rights, less ready to be exploited and more aggressive.

Despite its own success, however, despair is the theme of much contemporary feminist writing. Once optimism starts to wane, former ways of seeing can quickly become obscured, even disappear altogether. Victories are no longer visible. With confidence in decline, new theoretical frameworks start replacing the old, frameworks which transform memory itself, the stories we tell of our own past, our ideas for the future. We have seen it happen in one radical movement after another since the close of the 1970s. Within feminism, nowhere is this more apparent than in the area of sexual politics.

Only two decades ago, although it feels more like two lifetimes, it was common for women who were politically aware and active to declare themselves both sexual liberationists and feminists. In the early years of the women's liberation movement, women's rights to sexual pleasure and fulfilment, on their own terms, symbolized women's rights to autonomy and selfhood. Despite all its sexism, all its unexamined (pre-Foucauldian) acceptance of drives and their repression, all its complications for women at the time, it was the liberation rhetoric of the New Left of the 1960s, around notions of emancipation and participatory democracy, which provided the inspiration for the emergence of second-wave feminism. Today, however, there has been a shift away from any type of sexual radicalism towards a bleaker sexual conservatism. The same notions of autonomy and selfhood are turned around, used against the very idea of sexual pleasure, at least in its heterosexual varieties, as being incompatible with women's interests. Sexual discourses and iconography are seen as ineluctably linking female sexuality (and hence identity) with female submission.

It is true that there has been some powerful yet positive women's writing on female sexuality, but it comes from and addresses lesbian desire and practice – in terms of its specific challenge to the 'heterosexual matrix' linking sex and gender. Lesbian and gay studies and writing are beginning to blossom in academic institutions and popular publishing outlets. In scholarly texts they introduce a heterogeneous range of discourses, debates, research and analyses which constitute a rich and exciting new field of cross-disciplinary theoretical work on sexuality. This development comes out of the still confident and campaigning sexual politics created by the last twenty years of lesbian and gay struggles and self-reflection. Once merely the object of a medical gaze and elaborate scientific classification, lesbian and gay people increasingly set the agenda for a reversal in which the interrogators are interrogated, and compulsory heterosexuality, heterosexism and the roping of sexuality to gender themselves become the problem.[5]

Two decades of campaigning feminism, however, have yet to produce the same level of confident and diverse reversals which might begin to turn around the traditional male gaze and phallic construction of the heterosexual woman. Instead, contemporary feminist debate and discourses around heterosexuality remain engulfed by the anti-pornography campaigns and politics of the 1980s. The rhetoric of sexual liberation which featured so prominently in the idealistic politics of the 1960s, inspired many women as well as men to dream of a different world of love and freedom. The early women's liberation movement of the 1970s emerged out of that era, both using and contesting its notions of 'sexual liberation' and 'freedom', while organizing around abortion, childcare and men's domestic responsibilities, to build the power of women. All too soon, however, feminist awareness of both the extent of men's violence against women (much of it sexual) and the cultural ubiquity of discourses linking sexuality and female submission produced new depths of pessimism over the possibilities for any sexual liberation on women's terms.

With denunciation rather than celebration the growing mood of the moment, a type of political lesbianism became the sexual ideal for one influential strand of feminism: 'Women who make love to women are more likely to express their sexuality in a more equal way.' Most feminists simply stopped writing about sex altogether, refocusing on the problem of men's violence. Not to focus thus, in Britain, was to court aggressive attack from the 'revolutionary feminist' faction, increasingly active from 1978. Coincidentally, in the United States, Women Against Pornography groups grew rapidly from 1978. Not coincidentally, as Ann Snitow was later to write, this was the time when the mood of the women's movement changed – especially in the US where the feminist anti-pornography campaigns first flourished, and which has always had a profound influence on feminism in Britain.[6] Having just witnessed the defeat of women's rights to state-funded abortion, won only four years earlier, the Equal Rights Amendment (ERA) was coming under serious attack from the growing strength of the New Right, soon to sweep Reagan to power and to derail the ERA. With poorer women facing greater hardship, welfare services being removed, and the conservative backlash against radical politics in the ascendancy everywhere, 'pornography' came to serve as the symbol of women's defeat in the US. From then on, feminists were less confidently on the offensive, less able to celebrate women's potential strength, and many were now retreating into a more defensive politics, isolating sexuality and men's violence from other issues of women's inequality. Today many feminist writers, in tune with the age-old voices of conservatism, insist like Susanne Kappeler that 'sexual liberation' merely reinforces women's oppression.[7]

There certainly are formidable obstacles which continue to block women's moves towards empowering political perspectives, sexual, social and economic, but anti-pornography feminism is, in my view, increasingly one of them. It accompanies, and resonates with, the rise of pre- and post-feminist traditionalisms found, for example, in the assertion of Islamic fundamentalism or the recent Western 'pro-family' backlash against feminism. Because of the place of sex in our culture and our lives, however, it has always been tempting to displace personal and social crises and discontent on to sexuality. It's not so much that sex can drive us crazy, as Victorians once thought, fearing masturbation as the source of all vice and degeneracy, but the reverse. Sex has been given such a central place in our culture and narratives of personal identity that all our craziness – our wildest dreams and worst fears – are projected on to it.

The focus on pornography

To the bewilderment of many of second-wave feminism's founding members (who were often ridiculed for their concern with their own orgasms in seeking to liberate 'the suppressed power of female sexuality' from centuries of male-centred discourses and practices), pornography seemed to become *the* feminist issue of the 1980s. The critique of the sexism and the exploitation of women in the media made by women's liberation in the 1970s had indeed always been loud and prominent. After picketing the Miss World beauty contest as the decade kicked off, pin-ups, pornography, advertising, textbooks and religious beliefs and imagery, all – with spray gun and paint – were declared 'offensive to women'. In the 1970s feminists had not, however, sought legal restrictions on pornography, nor seen it as in any way uniquely symbolic of male dominance – the virgin bride, the happy housewife, the sexy secretary, were all equally abhorrent. With the state and judiciary so comprehensively controlled by men, obscenity laws were known in any case to have always served to suppress the work, if not jail the organizers, of those fighting for women's own control of their fertility and sexuality. Objecting to all forms of sexist representations, feminists then set out to subvert a whole cultural landscape which, whether selling carpet-sweepers, collecting census information or uncovering women's crotches, placed women as the subordinate sex.

Representatively, Ruth Wallsgrove, writing for *Spare Rib*, declared in 1977: 'I believe we should not agitate for more laws against pornography, but should rather stand up together and say what we feel about it, and what we feel about our own sexuality, and force men to re-examine their own attitudes to sex and women implicit in their consumption of porn.[8] This type of feminist emphasis on women's need to assert their own sexual needs and desires, however, and force men to discuss theirs, came to be overshadowed by, and entangled with, feminist concern with the issue of male violence by the close of the 1970s. As I have described elsewhere, it was the popular writing of Robin Morgan and Susan Brownmiller in the USA in the mid-1970s which first made a definitive connection between pornography and male violence.[9] It was in their writing that men's sexuality was made synonymous with male violence, and male violence was presented as, in itself, the key to male dominance. With pornography portrayed as the symbolic proof of the connection between male sexuality and male violence, anti-pornography campaigning was soon to become emblematic of this strand of feminism. It redefined 'pornography' as material which depicts violence against women, and which is, in itself, violence against women.

Andrea Dworkin's *Pornography: Men Possessing Women* is still the single most influential text proclaiming this particular feminist view of pornography, in which 'pornography' lies not only behind all forms of female oppression, but behind exploitation, murder and brutality throughout human history.[10] Following through such logic to draft model feminist anti-pornography legislation – the Minneapolis Ordinance – Andrea Dworkin and Catharine MacKinnon define pornography as 'the graphic sexually explicit subordination of women through pictures or words'.[11] Armed with this definition, they propose that any individual should be able to use the courts to seek financial redress against the producers or distributors of sexually explicit material if they can show it has caused them 'harm'.

And yet, despite the growth and strength of the feminist anti-pornography movement during the 1980s, particularly in the United States and in Britain (where we have seen the emergence of the Campaign against Pornography and a similar Campaign against Pornography and Censorship), some feminists, and I am one of them (represented in Britain by the Feminists Against Censorship) passionately reject its analysis and its related practice. We see it as a mistake to reduce the dominance of sexism and misogyny in our culture to explicit representations of sexuality, whatever their nature. Men's cultural contempt for and sexualization of women long pre-dated the growth of commercial pornography, both stemming from rather than uniquely determining the relative powerlessness of women as a sex. (Other subordinated groups are somewhat similarly sexualized and exploited, whether as Black Stud, Saphire, 'effeminate' male, or working-class wanton.) Narrowing the focus on women's subordination to the explicitly sexual downplays the sexism and misogyny at work within all our most respectable social institutions and practices, whether judicial, legal, familial, occupational, religious, scientific or cultural.

More dangerously (in today's conservative political climate) we risk terminating women's evolving exploration of our own sexuality and pleasure if we form alliances with, instead of entering the battle against, the conservative anti-pornography crusade. These are alliances which Dworkin and MacKinnon have unhesitatingly pursued in the USA, collaborating almost exclusively with the extreme Right: Presbyterian minister Mayor Hudnut III in Indianapolis, anti-ERA, anti-feminist, Republican conservative Bealah Coughenour in Minneapolis, far Right preacher Greg Dixon and, of course, pro-family, anti-feminist Reagan appointee responsible for removing funds from women's refuges, Edwin Meese.[12] Certainly, the most effective opponents of pornography have traditionally been, and remain, men. The men of the Moral Right (like Jesse Helms in the USA) are as deeply horrified by the feminist idea of women as sexually assertive, autonomous and entitled to sex on their own terms, as they are by gay sex or indeed any display of the male body as the object of desire rather than the subject of authority.

Any type of blanket condemnation of pornography will discourage us all from facing up to women's own sexual fears and fantasies, which are by no means free from the guilt, anxiety, shame, contradiction and eroticization of power on display in men's pornographic productions. And even here, those few scholars, like Linda Williams in *Hard Core*, who have chosen to study rather than make their stand over pornography, point to changes in its content which are worth studying, rather than simply dismissing. There is, to be sure, little change in the monotonous sexism of soft-core pornography. But this is increasingly *identical* with the come-on, passive and provocative portrayal of women in advertising, or many other clearly non-pornographic genres – except for the explicit crotch shot. Williams's research suggests that the most significant change in hard-core pornography (one of the few genres where women are not punished for acting out their sexual desires) is its increasing recognition of the problematic nature of sex, with clearer distinctions being made between good (consensual and safe) and bad (coercive and unsafe) sex. She attributes this shift to more women now seeing, discussing, buying, and – just occasionally – producing pornography.[13] The changes in contemporary pornographic production mean that more women are beginning to use it. In the USA, 40 per cent of 'adult videos' are said to be purchased by women. Nevertheless, it is men who predominantly still produce and consume pornography, which means that it is *men's* fears and fantasies which pornography primarily addresses (even though more women are now hoping to enter that restricted country – if they can find the right backing and the images which turn women on).

Uninterested in the particulars of any such shifts, the basic feminist anti-pornography argument sees all pornography as very much of a piece, and its very existence as central to the way in which men subordinate women. Pornography, on this view, both depicts and causes violence against women. Fundamental to anti-pornography feminism, most recently and comprehensively presented in Britain in Catherine Itzin's collection, *Pornography: Women, Violence and Civil Liberties*, is thus the connection made between pornography, violence and discrimination against women. Itzin opens her collection, for example, with the claim that the US Attorney-General's Commission on Pornography (carefully selected by Edwin Meese III in 1985 to seek stronger law enforcement against sexually explicit images) was 'unanimous in its finding of a causal link between pornography and sexual violence'. In fact, as Itzin must know, there were only two feminists on the Commission, Ellen Levine and Judith Becker, both of whom rejected the Commission's findings and published their own dissenting report, claiming: 'To say that exposure to pornography in and of itself causes an individual to commit a sexual crime is simplistic, not supported by the social science data, and overlooks many of the other variables that may be contributing causes.'[14]

Itzin's own collection, despite its numerous essays claiming to provide consistent and conclusive proof of links between pornography and violence, itself unwittingly undermines any such claim. For here, the psychologist

James Weaver overturns what little consistency there was in the previous experimental data which had suggested that it was *only* sexually explicit *violent* material which could, for certain individuals, in specific laboratory conditions, be correlated with more callous responses from men towards women. Weaver's data, however, 'proves' that it is exposure to any sexually explicit images, but in particular to 'consensual and female instigated sex', which produces the most callous responses from men to women.[15] It is not hard to imagine just what the conservative Right might conclude using this data – from banning sex education to banning any feminist representation of sex.

What we might more reasonably conclude from the existing experimental muddle, which provides anything but clear and consistent proof of anything at all, is not really so hard to see. It is never possible, whatever the image, to isolate sexuality, fix its meaning and predict some inevitable pattern of response, independently from assessing its wider representational context and the particular recreational, educational or social context in which it is being received. Men together can, and regularly do, pornographize any image at all – from the Arab woman in her chador to any coding of anything as female (nuts and bolts, for example) – while the most apparently 'violent' images of S & M pornography may be used in only the most consensual and caring encounters between two people. Context really does matter. This might help to explain why inconsistency is the only consistency to emerge from empirical research which ignores both the semiotic and the social context of images of sexual explicitness. As the most recent Home Office report on pornography commissioned in the UK concluded: 'inconsistencies emerge between very similar studies and many interpretations of these have reached almost opposite conclusions'.[16]

Women's experience of harm

Some anti-pornography feminists who are more aware of both the inconsistency and possible irrelevance of the experimental proof of pornography's harm have preferred to call upon the testimony of women's own experience of the harm they feel pornography has caused them. A typical example is the evidence provided by one woman at the Minneapolis public hearings. There she described how, after reading *Playboy*, *Penthouse* and *Forum*, her husband developed an interest in group sex, took her to various pornographic institutions and even invited a friend into their marital bed. To prevent any further group situations occurring, which she found very painful, this woman had agreed to act out in private scenarios depicting bondage and the different sex acts which her husband wanted her to perform, even though she found them all very humiliating.[17] It was only after learning karate and beginning to travel on her own that this woman could feel strong enough to leave her husband. This is indeed moving testimony, but surely all along there was only one suitable solution to any such woman's distress: having the power and confidence to leave a man, or any person, who forced her into actions she wished to avoid, and who showed no concern for her own wishes. Pornography is not the problem here, nor is its elimination the solution.

Another type of gruesome evidence frequently used by anti-pornography feminists to establish links between pornography and violence draws upon the myth of the 'snuff movie', first circulated in New York in 1975 about underground films supposedly coming from South America in which women were murdered on camera apparently reaching a sexual climax. On investigation such movies, like the classic film *Snuff* itself, released in the US in 1976, have always turned out to be a variant of the slasher film, using the special effects of the horror genre, and thus distinct from what is seen as the genre of pornography.[18] There is, however, also the personal testimony of some former sex workers, exemplified by that of 'Linda Lovelace'/ Marchiano. Linda Marchiano in her book *Ordeal* has described how she was coerced, bullied and beaten by her husband, Chuck Traynor, into working as a porn actress. (Interestingly, however, although coerced into sex work by a violent husband, the book actually describes how it was her success as a porn actress in *Deep Throat* which gave Linda Traynor the confidence to leave her husband, remarry and start campaigning for 'respectable family life' and against pornography.)[19]

The more general problem here is that other sex workers complain bitterly about what they see as the false and hypocritical victimization of them by anti-pornography feminists, whose campaigns they believe, if successful, would serve only to worsen their pay and working conditions, and increase the stigmatization of their work.[20] (I am not referring here, of course, to the production of child pornography, which is illegal, along with other forms of exploitation of children.) Some sex workers declare that they choose and like the work they do, and the type of control they believe it gives them over their lives. Indeed, it has been suggested that the feminist anti-pornography campaign itself primarily reflects the privileges of largely white and middle-class women who, not being as exploited as many other women, can self-servingly present the issue of women's sexual objectification by men as the source of oppression of all women.[21]

Whether it is from abused women or abused sex workers, however, what we hear when we do hear, or read, women's testimony against pornography or the pornography industry, are stories of women coercively pressurized into sex, or sexual display, which they do not want – varying from straight, to oral, anal, bondage and group sex. But we would be more than foolish if we saw the harm we were hearing about as residing in the pornographic images themselves, or in the possibility of enacting them (all, without any doubt, practices which certain women as well as men, at certain times, freely choose), and not in the men's (or possibly, although very rarely in heterosexual encounters, women's) abuse of power. The harm, it is important we should be clear, is contained not in the explicitly sexual material, but in the social context which deprives a woman (or sometimes a man) of her (or his) ability to reject any unwanted sexual activity – whether with husband, lover, parent, relative, friend, acquaintance or stranger. And this is one fundamental reason feminists opposed to anti-pornography campaigning are so distressed at each attempt to bring in some new version of the Minneapolis Ordinance, like the so-called Pornography Victims' Compensation Act first introduced into the US Senate in 1989, and cropping up against in New York, in 1992, or Itzin's own proposals taken up by MPs like Dawn Primarolo and Clare Short in Britain.

It is not just that these bills, quite contrary to the self-deceiving rhetoric of their advocates (Itzin and Dworkin claim to be 'absolutely opposed to censorship in every form'), would suppress sexual and erotic materials by opening up the threat of quite unprecedented levels of censorship through harassing lawsuits and financial penalties against producers, distributors, booksellers, writers, photographers and movie-makers. It is also that, again quite contrary to the stated goals of their supporters, such legislative proposals cost nothing and do nothing to provide real remedies against men's violence. State funding for women's refuges, anti-sexist, anti-violence educational initiatives, and above all empowering women more fundamentally through improved job prospects, housing and welfare facilities, would seem to be the only effective ways of enabling women to avoid violence.

Instead, however, the idea that pornographic material causes men's violence tends to excuse the behaviour of the men who are sexually coercive and violent, by moving the blame on to pornography. Men who rape, murder and commit other violent sex crimes against women, children or other men may (or may not) have an interest in violent pornography. However, as overviews of all the available empirical data suggest, the evidence does not point to pornography as a cause of their behaviour.[22] When Itzin, along with so many of the authors in her collection, weirdly but repeatedly cite as 'evidence' for pornography's harm the final testimony of serial killer Ted Bundy before his execution, they surely do more to expose rather than to support their argument. Today both the rapist and, even more hypocritically, tabloid wisdom, has learnt to lay the blame for sex crimes on 'pornography' (whereas once, with the same sort of certainty, they would lay the blame on 'mothers').

Meanwhile, although Dworkin, MacKinnon, Itzin and their supporters continue to argue that it is pornography which violates women's civil rights by increasing discrimination against them, studies in the USA and Europe have tended to reverse the picture. In the US it is in states with a preponderance of Southern Baptists (followers of leading anti-pornography campaigner Jerry Falwell) that the highest levels of social, political and economic inequality between women and men can be found – despite the lowest circulation of pornography.[23] Indeed Larry Baron discovered a positive correlation between equal opportunities for women in employment, education and politics and higher rates of pornography which he attributed to the greater social tolerance generally in these states. Such findings are consistent with those from Europe, where we find far higher levels of overall economic, political and other indices of gender equality in Sweden and Denmark compared to either the USA or Britain, and lower levels of violence against women – coupled with more liberal attitudes towards pornography.[24] Baron's survey, interestingly, also found that gender inequality correlated with the presence and extent of legitimate use of violence in a state (as measured by the numbers of people trained to work in the military, the use of corporal punishment in schools, government use of violence – as in the death penalty), as well as with mass-media preferences for violence (as in circulation rates of *Guns and Ammo*).

Beyond pornography

It is time for feminists, and their supporters, who want to act against men's greater use of violence and sexual coercion, and against men's continuing social dominance, to abandon anti-pornography feminism. It was, after all, a type of feminist anti-pornography rhetoric which facilitated Jesse Helms's successful attack on state funding for exhibitions of gay artists like Robert Mapplethorpe in the US, on the grounds that it 'denigrates, debases or reviles a person, group or class of citizens', in this case straight men. And the frightening truth is that the type of legislation anti-pornography feminism has proposed encourages new and far wider forms of censorship than anyone has yet admitted. Feminists are surely well aware that censorship does not operate simply through any single legal act or institution. Feminist anti-pornography legislation, if passed, would enable women and men to seek financial redress, through the courts, against publishers or distributors of sexually explicit material if they felt they had been 'harmed' by it. Given the current encouragement of rapists today (and certain 'experts') to point the finger of blame at 'pornography' for sexual and violent crimes, such legislation could entail all kinds of self-imposed censorship on anyone trying to market sexually explicit material – particularly material transgressing prevailing heterosexual sexist norms. (Using similar legislation in Canada, the lesbian sex magazine *Bad Attitudes* was recently condemned and fined.)

One fundamental theoretical disagreement in the debate between anti-pornography feminists and their opponents is over the question of fantasy. In defining pornography as 'sexually explicit subordination', anti-pornography feminists want to condemn all representations which in any way eroticize power. Within any erotic power relation, they assume that men always line up as the subjugator, women as the subjected. But, whether looking at the pleasures some men find in the pornography they consume, or the enjoyment women gain from romance novels (*both* characteristically portraying the eroticization of power), it is far from clear where precisely women and men do line up. (In S & M or bondage pornography there are more portrayals of men as submissive and women as dominant than the other way round.)

Even were it possible to detect some fixed positioning of identification in a person's enjoyment of fantasy, we could never generalize from that to predict that person's public status or behaviour in everyday encounters. The indulgence of heterosexual masochistic fantasies of spanking and subordination, for example, once a favourite pastime of the Victorian gentleman, neither undermined his accompanying social and sexual domination of women nor dented his sense of superiority to any other type of person, black or white. There is an autonomy to fantasy life which, if consuming pornography, may provide the setting for us to take up any number of volatile and impossible positions: active and passive, strong and weak, male and female, desired and repulsive, sacred and contemptible, pleasure-filled and suffering, and anything else as well and its opposite, all at one and the same time.

It is the social *context* of pornographic consumption which is all important. Men may use pornography as a form of male bonding, in the boys' night out to the sex arcades. The very same pornographic stimulation, however, may serve quite different functions when consumed in, perhaps guilty, isolation. And boys, of course, have countless other ways of male bonding. A man may also force a woman against her will to enact some sexual act he has seen in pornographic material. This is a situation, however, quite distinct from one where such material is used as a stimulus to some freely chosen sexual encounter – whether heterosexual, gay or lesbian. And of course a man, or occasionally a woman, can easily force a person to do their bidding without pornography, if that person lacks the power to refuse.

Before we start to proscribe any type of representation as in itself unquestionably harmful, we do need to raise all manner of questions about fantasy, what it means and how it works. Just as we do need to raise all sorts of questions about men and women's actual freedom to lead sexual lives of their own choosing, and seek ways of empowering women both socially and sexually. Without a more measured view on pornography, we are in danger of forfeiting the setting of sexual agendas to the Right, with its traditionally repressive attitudes towards women, and towards sexuality generally.

Some men are, as they always have been, quite capable of using violence without the assistance of pornography. We are, it is true, ubiquitously surrounded by images and discourses which represent women as passive, fetishized objects; men as active, controlling agents, devoid of weakness, passivity or any type of 'femininity'. They saturate all scientific and cultural discourses of the last hundred years – from sexology, embryology and psychoanalysis to literary and visual genres, high and low – and they construct the dominant images of masculinity to which so many men, inevitably, fail, in any way, to match up. Women provide the most available scapegoats for the shame and anxiety this failure causes them.

Men don't need pornography to encounter these 'facts' of crude and coercive, promiscuous male sexualities; helpless and yielding, nurturing female sensitivities. The anxious mirrorings of these narratives of male transcendence and female passivity (as well as occasional challenges to them) are, it is true, on offer in the culturally marginal and generally disparaged genre of 'pornography'. Women (or men) may well choose to pull down or deface the sexist pin-ups or pornography which men together may use to create their own exclusionary space or with which they may try to taunt the women around them. (Some women have preferred to paste up their own images of penile display, which usually bring down the pin-ups.) From the Bible and Desmond Morris to Roger Scruton and the *Sun* newspaper, we see messages of male transcendence which we can and should attack. There is a variety of tactics which we can use to discredit, mock or remove images we find offensive from the personal and public spaces of our lives. It is a battle which has only just begun. But there is no compelling reason to focus upon sexually explicit material alone, unless as feminists we do wish to throw in our lot with the initiatives and goals of the Moral Right.

In the end, anti-pornography campaigns, feminist or not, can only enlist today, as they invariably enlisted before, centuries of guilt and anxiety around sex, as well as lifetimes of confusion and complexity in our personal experiences of sexual arousal and activity. In contrast, campaigns which get to the heart of men's violence and sadism towards women must enlist the widest possible resources to empower women socially to seek only the types of sexual encounters they choose, and to empower women sexually to explore openly their own interests and pleasures. We do need the space to produce our own sexually explicit narratives and images of female desire and sensuous engagement if we are even to begin to embark upon that journey. And there are certain to be people who will feel harmed and provoked by our attempts.

There are lessons to be learnt from the current flowering of lesbian and gay studies and politics. They are that it is time for feminists everywhere to expand our horizons and rebuild our hopes. Even in these economically depressed and politically conservative times, we can still recognize our victories and attempt to surmount the real obstacles which stand in the way of building upon them. This will return us to some of the former insights and strategies of socialist feminism, now, however, enriched by the perspectives which black and other more specific feminist priorities can add to them. It will return us, as well to the need to forge alliances with any progressive – not reactionary – forces, working against all forms of political, economic and cultural domination.

Notes

1. Sheila Rowbotham, *Women's Consciousness, Men's World* (Penguin, Harmondsworth, 1973), p. xi.

2. Ibid, p. 38.

3. Catharine MacKinnon, 'Pornography, civil rights and speech', in Catherine Itzin (ed.), *Pornography: Women, Violence and Civil Liberties* (Oxford University Press, Oxford, 1992), p. 456.

4. Lynne Segal, *Is the Future Female? Troubled Thoughts on Contemporary Feminism* (Virago, London, 1987).

5. Diana Fuss, *inside/out: Lesbian Theories, Gay Theories* (Routledge, London, 1992); Jonathan Dollimore, *Sexual Dissidence* (Oxford University Press, Oxford, 1992).

6. Ann Snitow, 'Retrenchment vs. transformation; the politics of the anti-pornography movement', in *Caught Looking* (Caught Looking Inc., 1986).

7. Susanne Kappeler, *The Pornography of Representation* (Polity Press, Cambridge, 1986), p. 160.

8. Ruth Wallsgrove, 'Pornography: between the devil and the true blue Whitehouse', *Spare Rib*, 65 (1977), p. 15.

9. Lynne Segal, *Slow Motion: Changing Masculinities, Changing Men* (Virago London, 1992), ch. 8; and Lynne Segal and Mary McIntosh (eds), *Sex Exposed: Sexuality and the Pornography Debate* (Virago, London, 1992), introduction.

10. Andrea Dworkin, *Pornography: Men Possessing Women* (Women's Press, London, 1981).

11. Catharine MacKinnon, *Feminism Unmodified: Discourses on Life and Law* (Harvard University Press, Cambridge, Mass., 1987), p. 176.

12. Lisa Duggan 'Censorship in the name of feminism', in *Caught Looking* (Caught Looking Inc., 1986), p. 63.

13. Linda Williams, *Hard Core: Power, Pleasure and the 'Frenzy of the Visible'* (Pandora, London, 1990).

14. In Philip Noble and Eric Nadler, *United States of America vs. Sex* (Minnesota University Press, Minneapolis, 1986), p. 311.

15. James Weaver, 'The social science and psychological research evidence: perceptual and behavioral consequences of exposure to pornography', in Itzin, *Pornography*.

16. Dennis Howitt and Guy Cumberbatch, *Pornography: Impacts and Influences* (Home Office Research and Planning Unit, London, 1990), p. 94.

17. *Everywoman*, 'Pornography and Sexual Violence: Evidence of Links', *Everywoman*, 1988, p. 68.

18. See Williams, *Hard Core*, pp. 189–95.

19. See Anne McClintock. 'Gonad the Barbarian and the Venus flytrap; portraying the female and male orgasm', in Segal and McIntosh, *Sex Exposed*, p. 129.

20. See F. Delacoste and P. Alexander (eds), *Sex Work: Writings by Women in the Sex Industry* (Virago, London, 1988).

21. Clarla Freccero, 'Notes of a post-sex war theorizer', in M. Hirsch and E. Fox Keller (eds), *Conflicts in Feminism* (Routledge, London, 1991), p. 316.

22. See Howitt and Cumberbatch, *Pornography*, p. 94.

23. Larry Baron, 'Pornography and gender equality: an empirical analysis', *Journal of Sex Research*, 27, 3 (1990).

24. B. Kutchinsky. 'Pornography and rape: theory and practice: evidence from crime data in four countries where pornography is easily available', *International Journal of Law and Psychiatry*, 13, 4 (1990).

The Master's Tools will Never Dismantle the Master's House

Audre Lorde

I agreed to take part in a New York University Institute for the Humanities conference a year ago, with the understanding that I would be commenting upon papers dealing with the role of difference within the lives of American women: difference of race, sexuality, class and age. The absence of these considerations weakens any feminist discussion of the personal and the political.

It is a particular academic arrogance to assume any discussion of feminist theory without examining our many differences, and without a significant input from poor women, Black and Third World women, and lesbians. And yet, I stand here as a Black lesbian feminist, having been invited to comment within the only panel at this conference where the input of Black feminists and lesbians is represented. What this says about the vision of this conference is sad, in a country where racism, sexism and homophobia are inseparable. To read this program is to assume that lesbian and Black women have nothing to say about existentialism, the erotic, women's culture and silence, developing feminist theory, or heterosexuality and power. And what does it mean in personal and political terms when even the two Black women who did present here were literally found at the last hour? What does it mean when the tools of a racist patriarchy are used to examine the fruits of that same patriarchy? It means that only the most narrow perimeters of change are possible and allowable.

The absence of any consideration of lesbian consciousness or the consciousness of Third World women leaves a serious gap within this conference and within the papers presented here. For example, in a paper on material relationships between women, I was conscious of an either/or model of nurturing which totally dismissed my knowledge as a Black lesbian. In this paper there was no examination of mutuality between women, no systems of shared support, no interdependence as exists between lesbians and women-identified women. Yet it is only in the patriarchal model of

Extract from *Sister Outsider*, Crossing Press, Trumansburg, 1984, pp. 110–13.

nurturance that women 'who attempt to emancipate themselves pay perhaps too high a price for the results', as this paper states.

For women, the need and desire to nurture each other is not pathological but redemptive, and it is within that knowledge that our real power is rediscovered. It is this real connection which is so feared by a patriarchal world. Only within a patriarchal structure is maternity the only social power open to women.

Interdependency between women is the way to a freedom which allows the *I* to *be*, not in order to be used, but in order to be creative. This is a difference between the passive *be* and the active *being*.

Advocating the mere tolerance of difference between women is the grossest reformism. It is a total denial of the creative function of difference in our lives. Difference must be not merely tolerated, but seen as a fund of necessary polarities between which our creativity can spark like a dialectic. Only then does the necessity for interdependency become unthreatening. Only within that interdependency of different strengths, acknowledged and equal, can the power to seek new ways of being in the world generate, as well as the courage and sustenance to act where there are no charters.

Within the interdependence of mutual (nondominant) differences lies that security which enables us to descend into the chaos of knowledge and return with true visions of our future, along with the concomitant power to effect those changes which can bring that future into being. Difference is that raw and powerful connection from which our personal power is forged.

As women, we have been taught either to ignore our differences, or to view them as causes for separation and suspicion rather than as forces for change. Without community there is no liberation, only the most vulnerable and temporary armistice between an individual and her oppression. But community must not mean a shedding of our differences, nor the pathetic pretense that these differences do not exist.

Those of us who stand outside the circle of this society's definition of acceptable women; those of us who have been forged in the crucibles of difference – those of us who are poor, who are lesbians, who are Black, who are older – know that *survival is not an academic skill*. It is learning how to stand alone, unpopular and sometimes reviled, and how to make common cause with those others identified as outside the structures in order to define and seek a world in which we can all flourish. It is learning how to take our differences and make them strengths. *For the master's tools will never dismantle the master's house.* They may allow us temporarily to beat him at his own game, but they will never enable us to bring about genuine change. And this fact is only threatening to those women who still define the master's house as their only source of support.

Poor women and women of Color know there is a difference between the daily manifestations of marital slavery and prostitution because it is our daughters who line 42nd Street. If white American feminist theory need not deal with the differences between us, and the resulting difference in our oppressions, then how do you deal with the fact that the women who clean your houses and tend your children while you attend conferences on feminist theory are, for the most part, poor women and women of Color? What is the theory behind racist feminism?

In a world of possibility for us all, our personal visions help lay the groundwork for political action. The failure of academic feminists to recognize difference as a crucial strength is a failure to reach beyond the first patriarchal lesson. In our world, divide and conquer must become define and empower.

Why weren't other women of Color found to participate in this conference? Why were two phone calls to me considered a consultation? Am I the only possible source of names of Black feminists? And although the Black panelist's paper ends on an important and powerful connection of love between women, what about interracial cooperation between feminists who don't love each other?

In academic feminist circles, the answer to these questions is often, 'We did not know who to ask.' But that is the same evasion of responsibility, the same cop-out, that keeps Black women's art out of women's exhibitions, Black women's work out of most feminist publications except for the occasional 'Special Third World Women's Issue', and Black women's texts off your reading lists. But as Adrienne Rich pointed out in a recent talk, white feminists have educated themselves about such an enormous amount over the past ten years, how come you haven't also educated yourselves about Black women and the differences between us – white and Black – when it is key to our survival as a movement?

Women of today are still being called upon to stretch across the gap of male ignorance and to educate men as to our existence and our needs. This is an old and primary tool of all oppressors to keep the oppressed occupied with the master's concerns. Now we hear that it is the task of women of Color to educate white women – in the face of tremendous resistance – as to our existence, our differences, our relative roles in our joint survival. This is a diversion of energies and a tragic repetition of racist patriarchal thought.

Simone de Beauvoir once said: 'It is in the knowledge of the genuine conditions of our lives that we must draw our strength to live and our reasons for acting.'

Racism and homophobia are real conditions of all our lives in this place and time. *I urge each one of us here to reach down into that deep place of knowledge inside herself and touch that terror and loathing of any difference that lives there. See whose face it wears.* Then the personal as the political can begin to illuminate all our choices.

Notes

Comments at 'The Personal and the Political Panel', Second Sex Conference, New York, 29 September 1979.

Further Reading

In the previous edition of *The Woman Question* it was possible to include a short bibliography, citing further references and suggestions for reading. Such a brief exercise would now be woefully inadequate, and so what follows is an attempt to introduce readers to some of the sources where they might find some further reading. There is a deliberately tentative tone to this comment, in that literature in women's studies, in gender studies and simply on women has dramatically increased in the last decade, and any suggestion of an inclusive or comprehensive list would be misleading.

Perhaps the most important development in bibliographical work on women in the last ten years has been the publication of a number of guides to research in women's studies, of which the most important is S. Carter and M. Ritchie's *Women's Studies: A Guide to Information Sources* (Mansell, London, 1990). The main indexing and abstracting journals are *Women's Studies Abstracts* (by far the most useful and comprehensive, and published in the United States), *Studies on Women Abstracts* (published in Britain from 1983) and *Women in British Humanities Index* (published in Britain from 1989). Other major bibliographical resources include *Bibliofem Feminist Collection, Feminist Periodicals, New Books on Women and Feminism* and *RFR: Resources for Feminist Research*. In Britain the Fawcett Library and the Feminist Library in London and the library of the Equal Opportunities Commission in Manchester also have excellent specialist expertise and resources. These now give readers immediate access to publications in women's studies throughout the world and provide an essential basis for research. A comprehensive guide to women's studies is *The International Handbook of Women's Studies*, edited by L. Brown, H. Collins, P. Green, M. Humm and M. Landells (Harvester Wheatsheaf, Hemel Hempstead, 1993).

Access to information about what has been published has been much improved. At the same time, there has been a growth in periodicals and journals about women, with an increasing development of specialist journals on particular aspects of women's experience. The major feminist journals listed below all regularly review books and act as noticeboards for conferences and meetings. In the main, these journals are published three or four times a year, and represent a diversity of politics and priorities within the feminist community. What follows here is not (as indicated above) a full bibliography (since I would question the possibility of constructing such a list) but an indication of main areas in women's studies and sources of likely information. I have organized the sections below in the same order as the sections of the reader.

1   The context of contemporary feminism

There are a number of very useful collections here which deal with the issue of feminism and postmodernism, and, more generally, introduce readers to the issue of postmodernism. See:

Agger, Ben, *The Decline of Discourse* (Falmer, London, 1990).
Baudrillard, Jean, 'Modernity', *Canadian Journal of Political and Social Theory*, 11, 3 (1987).
Benhabib, Seyla and Cornell, Drucilla (eds), *Feminism as Critique* (Polity, Cambridge, 1988).
Collins, Patricia, *Black Feminist Thought* (Allen & Unwin, London, 1990).
Crowley, Helen and Himmelweit, Susan (eds), *Knowing Women* (Polity, Cambridge, 1992).
Harvey, David, *The Condition of Postmodernity* (Blackwell, Oxford, 1989).
Nicholson, Linda, *Feminism/Postmodernism* (Routledge, London, 1990).
Ramazanoglu, Caroline, *Feminism and the Contradictions of Oppression* (Routledge, London, 1989).
Scott, Joan, 'Deconstructing equality-versus-difference', *Feminist Studies*, 14 (1988).
Tong, Rosemarie, *Feminist Thought* (Allen & Unwin, London, 1989).

Two edited collections of feminist writing (Terry Lovell's *British Feminist Thought*, Blackwell, Oxford, 1990, and Maggie Humm's *Feminisms*, Harvester, Brighton, 1992) also provide further information about current or recent debates in feminism. Bibliographical references are given in all cases with the individual extracts, and it is striking that certain key names recur frequently. The work of Baudrillard, Foucault, Kristeva, Lyotard and Jameson is referred to widely, and the link constantly made between the changing nature of Western capitalism (in particular the shift in emphasis from production to consumption) and the development of new forms of politics, with obvious implications for women. Donna Haraway's essay in Linda Nicholson's *Feminism/Postmodernism* is especially insightful in the links it makes between new technologies, forms of power and the 'outsiders' of the new society. It is important to notice here that feminism, like any social movement, occurs within a political and economic context – so readers are reminded that works such as Braverman's *Monopoly Capital* (Monthly Review Press, New York, 1976) still have a relevance to the discussion of the global context of capitalism.

2 and 3   The concept of sexual 'difference' and its representation

The major shift in theories of representation that has occurred in feminism (and in cultural studies generally) is that of the integration of psychoanalysis (in its various forms) into debate and discussion. For general, and essential, reading on feminism and psychoanalysis see:

Marks, Elaine and De Courtivron, Isabelle (eds), *New French Feminisms* (Wheatsheaf, Brighton, 1984).
Mitchell, Juliet, *Psychoanalysis and Feminism* (Penguin, Harmondsworth, 1976).

Mitchell, Juliet and Rose, Jacqueline (eds), *Feminine Sexuality: Jacques Lacan and the École Freudienne* (Macmillan, London, 1982).

Moi, Toril, 'Feminism and postmodernism', *Cultural Critique*, 9 (Spring 1988).

Sayers, Janet, *Sexual Contradictions* (Routledge, London, 1988).

Sayers, Janet, *Mothering Psychoanalysis* (Hamish Hamilton, London, 1991).

Psychoanalytic theory is now widely used in literary and cultural analysis, and some of the most powerful examples of this development have been by women. Equally there has been a development in the literature which describes and articulates the diversity of women's experiences. See:

Chester, Gail and Nielsen, Sigrid, *Writing as a Feminist* (Allen & Unwin, London, 1987).

Franklin, Sarah, Lury, Celia and Stacey, Jackie (eds), *Off Centre: Feminism and Cultural Studies* (Routledge, London, 1991).

Moi, Toril, *Sexual/Textual Politics* (Methuen, London, 1985).

Moi, Toril, *French Feminist Thought* (Blackwell, Oxford, 1987).

Rose, Jacqueline, *The Haunting of Sylvia Plath* (Virago, London, 1991).

Showalter, Elaine (ed.), *The New Feminist Criticism* (Virago, London, 1986).

Stanley, Liz, *The Auto/Biographical I* (Manchester University Press, Manchester, 1992).

Steedman, Carolyn, *Landscape for a Good Woman* (Virago, London, 1986).

However, while this development has taken place, another major area of debate has grown up around the key question of sexual difference and gendered thinking. Feminist writers, particularly in the United States, have turned their attention to the central issue of gender and epistemology, with all its radical implications for assumptions about the apparent gender neutrality of terms such as 'rationality' and 'objectivity'. See:

Garry, Ann and Pearsall, Marilyn (eds), *Women, Knowledge and Reality* (Allen & Unwin, London, 1989).

Griffiths, M. and Whitford, Margaret (eds), *Feminist Perspectives in Philosophy* (Macmillan, London, 1988).

Harding, Sandra, *The Science Question in Feminism* (Open University Press, Milton Keynes, 1986).

Kirkup, Gill and Smith Keller, Laurie (eds), *Inventing Women* (Polity, Cambridge, 1992).

4 and 5   Reality and the impact of the state

The impact of the state on everyday life has to be both accepted and contested by feminists. There is a considerable feminist literature on the history of women's struggle against the interventions of the patriarchal state in a number of crucial areas (for example, medicine, education and social welfare). This literature demonstrates that in many ways state policies have had a negative or damaging impact on women's lives. From the middle of the nineteenth century, when the British state legislated against the 'danger' of female prostitutes to male soldiers (see Judith Walkowitz, *Prostitution and Victorian Society*, Cambridge University Press, Cambridge, 1980), the British state has been far from exceptional in its ideological perception of women and their appropriate social role. In the latter part of the twentieth century, women of the South have had to contend with development policies which have prioritized male interests and have had a catastrophic impact on the welfare of women and children. For further reading see:

Braidotti, Rosi, Charkiewicz, Ewa, Hausler, Sabine and Wieringa, Saskia (eds), *Women, the Environment and Sustainable Development* (Zed, London, 1993).

Butler, Judith and Scott, Joan (eds), *Feminists Theorize the Political* (Routledge, London, 1992).

Dworkin, Andrea and MacKinnon, Catharine A., *Pornography and Civil Rights* (Southern Sisters, Durham, NC, 1988).

Glendinning, Caroline and Millar, Jane, *Women and Poverty in Britain* (Harvester, Hemel Hempstead, 1992).

Graham, Hilary, *Hardship and Health in Women's Lives* (Harvester, Hemel Hempstead, 1993).

Hall, Catherine, *White, Male, Middle Class* (Polity, Cambridge, 1992).

Hanmer, Jalna and Maynard, Mary (eds), *Women, Violence and Social Control* (Macmillan, London, 1987).

Itzin, Catherine (ed.), *Pornography: Women, Violence and Civil Liberties* (Oxford University Press, Oxford, 1992).

Kruks, Sonia, Rapp, Rayna and Young, Marilyn, *Promissory Notes: Women in the Transition to Socialism* (Monthly Review Press, New York, 1989).

Land, Hilary, 'Who cares for the family?', *Journal of Social Policy*, 7, 3 (1978), pp. 257–84.

Lewis, Jane, *Women in England 1870–1950* (Wheatsheaf, Brighton, 1984).

McDowell, Linda and Pringle, Rosemary (eds), *Defining Women: Social Institutions and Gender Divisions* (Polity, Cambridge, 1992).

McIntosh, Mary, 'The state and the oppression of women,' in Mary Evans (ed.), *The Woman Question* (Fontana, London, 1982).

Mies, Maria, *Patriarchy and Accumulation on a World Scale: Women in the International Division of Labour* (Zed, London, 1990).

Oakley, Ann, *The Captured Womb* (Blackwell, Oxford, 1986).

Spender, Dale, *Invisible Women: The Schooling Scandal* (Writers & Readers Publishing Co-operative, London, 1982).

Walby, Sylvia, *Theorising Patriarchy* (Blackwell, Oxford, 1990).

6   The politics of feminism

The concluding section deals with some of the various forms of politics current within feminism. What is not reproduced here (and indeed is categorically ruled out) are those works hostile to feminism which have already received massive media coverage. For the record, these include such attacks on feminism (and indeed femininity) as Camille Paglia's *Sexual Personae*. Paglia's thesis is that masculinity is the driving force behind civilization; in her work biological reductionism reaches new heights of fantasy. In the face of such views, feminism remains largely committed to changing social perceptions of gender, in order to allow both women and men to take a fuller part in a social life which is not constructed through the separation of male/female, and public/private. The politics of feminism in the late twentieth century offers to those prepared to think outside rigid divisions of gender a truly liberating (and intellectually fascinating) revolution in thought. See:

Barrett, Michèle and Phillips, Anne (eds), *Destabilizing Theory: Contemporary Feminist Debates* (Polity Press, Cambridge, 1992).

Einhorn, Barbara, *Cinderella Goes to Market: Citizenship, Gender and Women's Movements in East Central Europe* (Verso, London, 1993).

Enloe, C. *Bananas, Beaches and Bases: Making Feminist Sense of International Politics* (University of California Press, Berkeley, 1989).

Faludi, Susan, *Backlash* (Chatto & Windus, London, 1992).

Haraway, Donna, *Simians, Cyborgs and Women* (Free Association Press, London, 1991).

Mitter, S., *Common Fate, Common Bond: Women in the Global Economy* (Pluto, London, 1986).

Phillips, Anne, *Engendering Democracy* (Polity Press, Cambridge, 1991).

Journals and periodicals

Australian Feminist Studies
Berkeley Women's Law Journal
Camera Obscura: A Journal of Feminism and Film Theory
Canadian Journal of Women and the Law
EOC (Manchester) *Annual Report*
EOC (Manchester) *Research Bulletin*
European Journal of Women's Studies
Feminism and Psychology
Feminist Library Newsletter
Feminist Review
Feminist Studies
Feminist Teacher
Gender and Education
Gender and Society
Gossip: A Journal of Lesbian Feminist Ethics
Harvard Women's Law Journal
International Journal of Women's Studies
Journal of Gender Studies
M/F: A Feminist Journal
Off Our Backs
Psychology of Women Quarterly
Signs: A Journal of Women in Culture and Society
Trouble and Strife
Tulsa Studies in Women's Literature
Wisconsin Women's Law Journal
Women
Women and Environments: International Newsletter
Women at Work
Women of Europe
Women's Rights Law Reporter
Women's Studies International Forum
Women's World

Index